SAN FRANCISCO SHIP PASSENGER LISTS

BY

LOUIS J. RASMUSSEN

VOLUME III
November 7, 1851 To June 17, 1852

(A Volume of the SHIPS 'N RAIL Series)

San Francisco Historic Records
1204 Nimitz Drive
Colma, California 94015

Printed In The United States of America
by
Adams Press
Chicago, Illinois

To

BARBARA

ACKNOWLEDGEMENTS

I am indebted to the following persons and agencies for the assistance offered:

The Department of Rare Books & Special Collections. San Francisco Main Public Library.

The California Society of Pioneers.

Mr. Allen Ottley, Librarian, California Section, California State Library.

Mr. Richard Dillon, Librarian, Sutro Library, a department of the California State Library.

The San Francisco Maritime Museum and its entire personnel.

The Library of Congress.

CONTENTS

INTRODUCTION

When the reports of the gold discoveries in California first wakened the spirit of adventure, very few foresaw that on the shores of the Pacific Coast of America there would spring a wealthy and powerful State. Fewer, could have predicted the flow of wealth, and the effects of the discovery of gold in California on the fortunes and destinies of America and the Old World.

The time sequence of this volume, the third in the series of fifteen volumes, marks the period of November 7, 1851 to June 17, 1852. Four years had lapsed since the first finding of gold, and during this term the waves of emigration had steadily washed the coast. For a time a culminating point was attained, then the emigration tide began to ebb, and for two or three months, when civil jars and a social discord shook the land, there was a small excess of passenger departures over the monthly influx of strangers. But, as seen in this volume, there followed a return wave of emigrants of more gigantic proportions than had ever journeyed to the State.

The next volume of this series will exceed in size that of previous volumes. It must, to record the fabulous summer emigration of 1852. From the Atlantic States, from Europe, from Asia and from South America, the emigrants were sweeping with increasing strength to the California shores.

This volume records the initial thrust of the 1852 emigrant surge. Every route to California by sea was taken up by hundreds of eager travelers. The rush of passengers was so great from the east coast of America that steamers were engaged full for more than two months ahead. All the world seemed bent on a trip to the gold region. By the tedious passage of "the Horn", through Nicaragua, and over the Isthmus of Panama, thousands were bound for the West. In China, there was reported considerable excitement existing in the Canton districts, among the working classes, favorable to emigration to California. Great numbers of Chinese were preparing to join their countrymen who had previously made passage to San Francisco.

The immense emigration was waking up the agents of governments, and ship companies, interested in the success of the various routes, called forth active exertions for the increase of facilities and travel to the Pacific Coast. Day by day, the expedition to California was daily losing its character of adventure. Men with vision were beginning to regard the State more properly; and the conviction was gaining ground that industry, energy and well-directed talent were more sure of success in California than in any other portion of the globe.

One must, however, bear in mind that the previously mentioned exertions expended by governments and companies were not always for the benefit of the ship passenger. During the period covered by this volume, steps were just beginning to be taken to prevent the impositions which the ship passenger endured.

There were a number of evils incident to the long sea voyage — a passage through the tropical regions, the overloading of vessels, the failure in many instances to supply a sufficient quantity of wholesome food and sweet water, and finally, the shipping of emigrants in old and unseaworthy vessels which either were wrecked or abandoned because of the utter impossibility of pursuing the voyage upon them. In Churchillian prose, one California journal referred to the emigrant's trials as almost incalcuable, depicting it thusly — "So much suffering, inconvenience and useless and wanton destruction of human life has hardly ever taken place before in so brief a time in the pursuits of peace".

By June 1852, most of the public had made up its mind that it had become important to inquire what proceedings could be adopted in order to prevent the future recurrence of shipboard conditions. A bill was introduced in Congress restricting the number of passengers which a ship could carry according to her size. A law was in existence upon the subject, but whether the new enactment was more stringent than the old one was still an unknown factor.

One faction was discontent with restrictions placed on shipowners and captains. This faction had its origin among Eastern and European shipping circles with lineage ties to California. There should be no measures, they argued, which would necessarily interfere with the natural order of trade. Further, they were against legislative provisions which would, in any sense, restrict California emigration. In short, no placement of barriers in the way of commercial traffic. This group saw little necessity in changing the nature of things and adroitly referred to historical precedence — sad occurrences had always been coupled with a journey by sea.

Employing psychology the shipowners and captains noted that the hardships of passengers were and had been self-imposed. The complaints were quite proper, and always very natural. Persons at sea in passenger vessels, under the most favorable circumstances, would be apt to find the curtailment of their every-day shore pleasures, and commonplace incidents not at all in accordance with the poetical ideas of "life on the ocean wave". Passengers were bound to find the circle of their enjoyments narrowed down to very inconvenient and uncomfortable limits on board ships, and with plenty of time on their hands, the golden hours at sea were naturally spent as their ill humors could be best vented. There was no more fitting sphere for the habitual grumbler and fault-finder than on board a "rank and narrow ship". Or, as the author of the "Ancient Mariner" put it — "Housed on the wild sea with wilder usages".

The opposing force to the foregoing faction were the humanitarians. It was their belief that humanity was of primary importance, with California and commerce following in respective order. The humanitarian efforts were not against retarding the tide of emigration, but alleviating the disabilities endured by the travelers. In time, the battle between the factions was settled, and before long, the bout was but a memory, and then even the memory ceased to exist.

Historians emphasize that California left her initial mark in history with the discovery of gold. They often overlook another important mark — it was the movement of people, the mixture of races that developed California, raised and sustained her and, in the end, gave the State tone and direction. This fact strikes the mind as it contemplates the history of the area. Over a century later this cultivation continues to manifest itself in the classes that combine within its borders, producing in a sense, a race which is oftentimes referred to as the ''Californian''.

That ''race'' — the elements, the heterogeneous germs of which were collecting in the 1850's within the California confines, is the subject of this series of ship passenger lists.

All the ingredients were present in California to assist the early pioneers in their settlement. They only had to bring themselves to bear mentally and physically upon the land for the development of its resources, for the stamping on it of a name. And this they achieved.

There were fertile hills and valleys, vast in breadth and magnificence, the softness of climate and resources that one could see no end to their development. There existed a wealth of productions, planted and developed by nature alone. Settlers would find that the northern climes of the State were acceptable for the growth of the hardier fruits and crops. The southern sections, such as Los Angeles and the rich lands about San Buenaventura, would bring forth the grape, the orange, and the pomegranate.

Games of all kinds, the antelope, the squirrel, the hare, birds and fish of every variety were abundant. Rivers, natural highways, pierced the State in every direction; and water privileges scattered without number among the hills. There was gold and quicksilver, granite and sandstone — not to speak of lumber.

With such a land as this, whose resources were almost entirely underdeveloped, it is little wonder that the State could not consumate a race entirely unique in the world.

Liberty, and an amelioration of condition, summoned to the eastern coast of the United States a remarkable mixture of peoples — French, and Italians, Germans, the Celt and Slavonian, the Anglo-Saxon. What liberty had done on one side of the Sierra mountains, the gold mines were doing on the other, only on a larger scale. From every portion of the globe came representatives in search of their individual form of prosperity.

With the arrival of the newcomers, it sadly marked the end of the days and ways of the old native Californian. He was fast disappearing from the scene and nowhere was it more evident than in clothing attire. The showy and very appropriate costume of the old days was now rarely in evidence; it had given place to the more common and every-day coat and pantaloons of the Anglo-Saxon. The old California suit of calsoneras, botas, and a gay serape were items which had run their course.

As one would suppose, the huge influx of ship arrivals in San Francisco brought accommodation problems for the passengers of the vessels. Every respectable hotel and boarding house was full to overflowing. The up-river boats which carried the new passengers from San Francisco by inland water-ways to areas near the gold fields, took hundreds out of the the city daily. However, the number remaining in San Francisco hardly appeared to diminish due to almost daily arrivals of ships from foreign ports.

In April, 1852, the city of San Francisco was "over capacity". Besides the great numbers of newcomers, there were also many natives of California and old residents from the lower portion of the State, who were in the city upon business connected with the U. S. Land Commission. Hotel and public house owners were accumulating staggering profits easily comparible to those which could be attained in gold-mining.

Those who were fortunate to own a shanty, or even a tent for that matter, could engage in the hotel business and be assured of financial success. It took a minimum amount of industry, one did not have to suffer the privations of mining, it bore no threat of legal persecution, and it was all accomplished with the aid of a unique employee who possessed the title of "hotel runner".

The first contact the newcomer met on his arrival in San Francisco was, in most cases, the "hotel runner". It was a meeting not unlike running the gauntlet of an enemy battalian. Hotel runners were stationed along the wharfs like light infantry in preparation of a skirmish. The runners watched the arrival of vessels with as much eagerness as if the fate of nations depended upon the news they carried. Before the boat touched the wharf, or threw a line to make fast, these hungry solicitors of patronage were all over the vessel, expressing a willingness to ease the passenger of his luggage, all the while descanting largely upon the sumptuous fare, healthy location and splendid accommodations of some eating house, bearing a title that might induce one to flatter himself with the idea that he was about to enjoy the comforts of an oriental palace. Instead, of which, the obliging runner generally conveyed the luggage to some dingy and obscure shanty. There the new arrival found beef and potatoes dished out at exorbitant charges, the vilest ruin dealt out of a dirty decanter, and a greasy bunk in the cock-loft.

Many strangers arriving in the city were forced to content themselves with such accommodations, being ignorant of a possible vacancy in a respectable public house. The runners were only employed by that class of public house or tent-owner that had no regular patronage and were entirely dependent upon stragglers. Since local laws legalized the "calling" and required license to be obtained to pursue it, the traveler had to console himself with the reflection that the hordes of runners materially assisted to defray the expense of San Francisco city government.

There were material changes taking place within the makeup of San Francisco itself, even in the short period of 1850 to 1852. One was a marked decrease in the amount of gambling tables for which the city had obtained such an unenviable notoriety abroad. Many of the gambling places which had resounded with the clinking of money were now in a measure being metaphorsed into dry goods stores. A goodly number of saloons, which were running gambling on the side, changed their gambling tables for billiard tables. Those places hard pressed to locate billiard tables hired violinists and piano players (when they were lucky enough to acquire a piano). But even the incessant thumping of a piano and the eternal sawing of catgut failed to attract the previous crowds. The character of the city was altering. Commercial Street had robbed the Plaza of all its gambling glory, and even the tone of Commercial Street was subdued. To be sure, there was still gambling to be found in the city and there was an inordinate amount of saloons. But the day was not far distant when the public gamgling house in San Francisco would no longer outnumber school houses. The saloons were a different matter — they were "institutions".

— Louis J. Rasmussen

REFERENCE POINTS

ADDENDA — Following the Surname Index and the Subjective and Geographical Index will be found addenda entries.

ARRIVAL DATE — Arrival date is the date vessel officially arrived in the Port of San Francisco.

CITIES — Cities, towns or villages are listed under State or Country in which they are located, e.g., Brazil/Rio de Janeiro.

DEATHS — If a passenger died during the course of the sea voyage it is noted in the resume headed "Passage."

FORECABIN PASSENGERS — See "UNIDENTIFIED."

INITIALS OF GIVEN NAMES — Most of the original source records listed "given names" by initials.

KIN (or RELATIVES) ABOARD — It is advisable to survey the entire passenger list and the Surname Index to determine if additional relatives to party in question might have been aboard the vessel.

"Mc" — A number of the early passenger lists shortened the surnames utilizing the prefix "Mc." For example, "McLee" might have been recorded as "M'Lee." In all cases the surname is reprinted as it appeared in the source material. Surnames having a "c" dropped in the prefix "Mc" are listed at the commencement of the "Mc" section in the Surname Index.

NOTES SECTION — Catalogues variations of passenger surnames, ship passenger lists and expansions on the identity of passengers or events.

PORT (or ORIGINAL PORT) OF DEPARTURE — The port of last sailing is listed under the heading "FROM:" The reader must be cautioned that this heading represents the last stated port of the vessel prior to its arrival in San Francisco. For instance, a vessel arriving in San Francisco "FROM" Acapulco (the last port listed in the original source material) may have departed from New York and arrived in San Francisco via Acapulco. Where the original port of departure is known it is always indicated. If the vessel made intermediate stops enroute to San Francisco it is listed (if stated in original source materials).

SPELLING OF PASSENGER NAMES — In transcribing the passenger lists it was noted that there were some apparent errors in the original source records. However, no steps have been taken by the author to correct the obvious errors other than to list the probable corrected name in brackets followed with a question mark.

STEERAGE PASSENGER — See "UNIDENTIFIED."

SUBJECTIVE AND GEOGRAPHICAL INDEX — The Subjective And Geographical Index contains data relative to cargoes, port names and topical information appearing in the ship "Passage" sections. References in the "Notes" section are included in this index.

SURNAME INDEX — All passengers and vessel captains have been indexed and appear in the Surname Index and Surname Index Addenda.

UNIDENTIFIED — Many of the names of the forecabin and steerage passengers were not listed in the original sources. Where this is the case this fact is stated and, if possible, the total number carried in forecabin or steerage is noted.

KEY TO ABBREVIATIONS AND SYMBOLS

Certain abbreviations, symbols and figures are used in footnotes, passage resumes and in the passenger lists. The below key defines their corresponding meanings:

(?) – A surname or given name followed with a second name and question mark, in brackets, indicates that the passenger name may have been listed incorrectly in the original source record. For example, William Speai (William Spear?). In all cases the first listed spelling represents the name as it appeared in the original source. The secondary spelling, in brackets, denotes that the original listing was obviously incorrect, or translation was impossible, or key letters were obliterated. The bracketed name is the author's translation.

___ – Denotes surname or given name not listed in original source. For example, ___ Smith. Where one or more letters of a passenger's name were missing in the original source this is reflected by a corresponding space. As an example, "John J___nes," or "Jo___n Smith," or "Ro___rt Anderson." This could be interpreted as "John Jones," "John Smith," and "Robert Anderson," respectively.

* – Indicates additional data on subject or individual will be found in the "Passage" section, footnotes, or in the passenger list.

(sic)– Listed as found in source.

(x) – Symbol used in index sections. An "(x)" following page number denotes more than one entry for name or subject on cited page.

bbls	– barrels	Gov	– Governor	Mons	– Monsieur
bdls	– bundles	hf	– half	Prof	– Professor
bro	– brother	hhds	– hogshead	Rev.	– Reverend
Capt	– Captain	Hon	– Honorable	R. N.	– Royal Navy
chld	– child	inf	– infant	Sen	– Senator
chldrn	– children	Jr	– Junior	Sgt	– Sergeant
Col	– Colonel	ldy	– lady	S. I.	– Sandwich Islands
ctns	– cartons	Lt,)	– Lieutenant	sis	– sister
cwt	– a hundred-weight	Lieut)		Sr	– Senior or Senor
		Mad, Ml,)	– Mademoiselle	svt	– servant
dau	– daughter	Madlle,)		USA	– U. S. Army
Dr	– doctor	Mdlle,)		USM	– U. S. Marines
Esq	– Esquire	Mlle)		USN	– U. S. Navy
fam	– family	Maj	– Major	V. I.	– Vancouver Island
Gen	– General	merch	– merchandise	wf	– wife

SHIP: ROCKLAND
TYPE: Ship   FROM: New York
ARRIVED: November 7, 1851   CAPTAIN: ___ Windsor
PASSAGE: 150 days from New York. On July 8, 1851 in latitude
9-33N, longitude 25-57W. On August 13, 1851 in latitude
38-18S saw ship "Hamilton" from Callao bound for Cork.
On August 28, 1851 Thomas Mayberry, of Belfast, Ireland,
fell from fore-yard and died in a few hours. Off Rio
Plata was in a heavy gale, carried away fore and maintopmast trestletrees and received other damages. Damage
caused a delay of 10 days to repair; off the Falkland
Islands carried away maintopmast trestletrees and sprang
the fore ones; same gale next day sprung main trestletrees; off Cape Horn sprung main topmast; repaired the
damages in 56 hours.
CARGO: 1 iron propeller, 10 boxes tacks, 98 10 gallon kegs of
whiskey, 252 bbls of butter, 1000 baskets, 50 bales of gunny
bags, 40 iron sills, 50 iron beams, 223 tons coal, 36 iron
columns, 20 kegs shot, 50 boxes starch, 500 boxes soap, 20
cases of matches, 100 ploughs, 140 bbls brandy, 196 boxes
of axes and assorted merchandise.

Passengers

Mrs. Captain ___ Windsor and son	Miss F.W. Frantzer Miss L. Frantzer and servant	Miss R. Frantzer Mr. ___ Snipkins, wife and son

- - - - - -

SHIP: OELLA
TYPE: Schooner   FROM: Santa Cruz, Calif.
ARRIVED: November 8, 1851   CAPTAIN: Tichnor(Tichenor?)
PASSAGE: 24 hours from Santa Cruz, California.
CARGO: 2435 bags of potatoes, 490 dozen cabbages and 250 bags of
onions.

Passengers

C.S. Tuttle and lady	Mrs. H. Tichenor	Miss L.H. Sampson
Mr. ___ Hollenbeck	Mr. ___ Clements	Mr. ___ Harpool
	Mr. ___ Duyer	Mr. ___ Balcroff

- - - - - -

SHIP: GARDINER
TYPE: Barque (British)   FROM: Valparaiso, Chile
ARRIVED: November 8, 1851   CAPTAIN: Robertson
PASSAGE: 54 days from Valparaiso, Chile.
CARGO: Coal (tonnage not listed).

Passengers

R.W. Sherratt   P. Abadie

- - - - - -

SHIP: SEA GULL
TYPE: Steamer   FROM: Port Orford, O.T.
ARRIVED: November 9, 1851   CAPTAIN: Tichenor *
(Continued next page)
(*) Note similar surname with Captain of the "Oella".

PASSAGE: Four days from Port Orford, Oregon Territory. Brings word that the steamer "Chesapeake" has been condemned and sold in Humboldt Bay for sum of $2300. Called on way ports (south-bound) at Trinidad, California and Humboldt Bay, California. This vessel also brings word that the troops have left for the Coquille River to chastise the Indians that murdered five men belonging to T'Vaults exploring party. Coal mines in the vicinity of Port Orford are attracting considerable attention. The land to the north of Port Orford is said to be very fertile.

CARGO: Not listed.

Passengers

M.H.A. White	Col. A.K. Butler	D. Morgan
M. White	W. Clemans	M. Abel
D. Portis	M. Schloss	W.H. Card
H. Steward	B. Charles	J. Sims
D. Woolf	Isaac Lee	E. Pomers
J. Woolf	J. Legton	H. Gilmore
J. Wood	W. Brewet	A. McKay
Francis Rogers	K.V. Cram	J.L. Quinn
G.M. Mellen	G.W. Staples	Dr.____Kis?am
F. May	M. Anthony	Mrs.____Hopkins

and Captain____Hasty with the crew of the steamer "Chesapeake"

- - - - - -

SHIP: MADURA
TYPE: Barque (British)   FROM: Glasgow, Scotland
ARRIVED: November 9, 1851   CAPTAIN: Douglas
PASSAGE: Departed Glasgow, Scotland on March 30, 1851. Sailed via Valparaiso, Chile, latter port in 63 days.
CARGO: 4 casks pickles, 2 casks wine, 15 boxes glass, 42 hhds of whiskey, 4 crates pottery, 2 casks iron, 3 boxes of confectionery, 5 casks tartar, 326 casks and 33 hhds of malt liquor, 18 trusses, 200 jars tripe, 2 casks varnish, 306 tons coal, 2 boats, 555 casks of wine and assorted goods.

Passengers

D. McCloud	L. Miller	J. Stevens
J.J. McDonald	J. Barker	W. Martin

- - - - - -

SHIP: PERI
TYPE: Schooner (British)   FROM: Canton, China
ARRIVED: November 9, 1851   CAPTAIN: Throughton
PASSAGE: 53 days from Canton, China.
CARGO: 2800 bags of sugar, 2400 bags of rice, 1100 cases and boxes of tea, 200 baskets of garlic, 1 case of lacquered ware, 22 cases of silks, 100 boxes of sweetmeats, 200 jars of molasses, 150 rolls of matting.

Passengers

S. Petulio   E. Reed

- - - - - -

SHIP: ORIENTAL
TYPE: Brig   FROM: Lahaina, S.I.
ARRIVED: November 10, 1851   CAPTAIN: Keller
PASSAGE: Departed Lahaina, Sandwich Islands on October 25, 1851.
         Left about 20 whaleships in the harbor, most of them off
         unsuccessful cruises. This vessel brings news that an
         act has been passed to provide for the erection of a
         light-house on the promontory known as "Diamond Hill"(or
         Leahi), and either the construction of another near the
         mouth of the Channel of Honolulu Harbor, or the mooring
         of a light-boat there.
CARGO: 500 bbls of potatoes, 50 bbls of oil, 8000 oranges, 25
       bunches of bananas and 5 sheep
                           Passengers
Andrew Croswell   Mr.____Irving   Mr.____O'Hara
Mrs.____Blossom   ____Conner

        - - - - - -

SHIP: LYDIA
TYPE: Schooner   FROM: Shanghai, China
ARRIVED: November 10, 1851   CAPTAIN: Potter
PASSAGE: 40 days from Shanghai, a quick passage. On October 4,
         1851, the chief mate, Mr. W. Wickham, of Baltimore,
         Maryland, died on board. All hands sick with scurvy.
         This vessel brings intelligence that Mr. Nicholas Baylies,
         an American, has been appointed to the office of the
         Harbor-Master of Shanghai. A new port regulation has been
         passed in Shanghai which states "No vessel under any
         foreign flag, having gunpowder or other combustibles on
         board, shall be permitted to anchor among the foreign
         vessels or in their near vicinity".
CARGO: 2000 fowls, 440 packages of tea, 384 jars of eggs, two
       Chinese bedsteads, 252 bags rice, 50 wool hats and case of
       silks.
                           Passenger
                 Mr._____Bash
                   - - - - -

SHIP: COLUMBIA
TYPE: Steamer   FROM: Oregon Territory
ARRIVED: November 12, 1851   CAPTAIN: C.V. LeRoy
PASSAGE: 70 hours from Oregon Territory. On board is $11,000 in
         treasure for Newell & Company.
CARGO: Not listed.
                           Passengers
J.P. Jeffers   F.M. Smith   Dr.____Dart
W. Mulkey   V.E. Delevand   J.B. Jones
G.G. Polk   J. Kohn   J. Bloomer
J. Thomas   C.J. Backus   W.D. Grokil
A. Holbrook   C. Brewster   J.R. Robb
Dr.____Morse   Mr.&Mrs.____Sparks   3 Misses____Sparks
                    (Continued next page)

M. St. Amant | Mr.___Goodwin | J.W. Russell
A. Adair | E. Walker | J. Aram
W.A. Grimes | W. Deakin | J. Snowden
J. Woody | J. Ward | H.C. Snowden
D. Kelsey | J.H. Price | C. Nottingham
J. Powell | S. Jackson | G. Martin
R. Moore | Mr.&Mrs.___Rhodes | W. Pearer
J. Dickson | C. Sinlay | J. Mentieth
William McDaniel | W.R.H. Sinlay | W. Bingham
J. Glude | J. McFarland | Mrs.___Bingham
J. Woodward | C. Coffin | J. Nabton
A. Dirro | J.R. Campbell | J. Holt
H. Miller | W.N. Norton | Mr.& Mrs.___Spark*
L. Olds | D. Robinson | W. Spark, lady and
W.J. Lusk | G.B. Franklin and | 4 children*
W.H. Evans | lady | C. Parker

- - - - - - -

(*) Note listings on page 3 for "Mr. & Mrs.___Sparks and 3 Misses
Sparks". The surname "Spark" and "Sparks" appeared as listed.

SHIP: OHIO
TYPE: Steamer   FROM: San Diego, Calif.
ARRIVED: November 12, 1851   CAPTAIN: Haley
PASSAGE: Left San Diego, California on November 6, 1851; encounter-
         ed strong headwinds and sea from Santa Barbara to San
         Francisco; was two days loading at San Pedro.
CARGO: 1000 crates of fruit.

Passengers

E.R. Raymond | Capt.___Barker | M.G. Brumhall
Mrs.___Power and | John Truman | J.H. Roberts
   two children | J. Liver | E. Lazard
M. Brodnitz | A. Sanchez | J.S. Kimball
G. Sermie | Mr.___Dougherty | O.M. Child
Mr. Marting | Jose Orata | J. Perris
M. Lowe | Mrs.___Lathrop and | Mrs.___Cazey/sic/
H. Williams | 5 children | R.M. Fuller
L. Luce | D. Black | Jose Arath
M. Gisola | A. Sepulvida | L. Riggao
T. Reler | S. Salis | W.H. Cheevers
Col.___Caperton | J. Ricard | W. Hance
Mr.___Dutra | J. Hamilton, U.S.A. | Pablo Noriega
Mr. Smith /sic/ | W. Curtis | Judge___Merritt
Bishop___Alemany | W. Benson | S. Osio

- - - - - - -

SHIP: MARY
TYPE: Schooner   FROM: Bodega, Calif.
ARRIVED: November 12, 1851   CAPTAIN: Tibbey
PASSAGE: 24 hours from Bodega, California.
CARGO: 12 tons of potatoes and 8000 feet of lumber.

Passenger
E. Cheeney

SHIP: OCEAN BIRD
TYPE: Barque   FROM: Oregon Territory
ARRIVED: November 13, 1851   CAPTAIN: Roberts
PASSAGE: Eight days from Portland, Oregon Territory.
CARGO: 1000 hogs and 83 M of lumber.

Passengers

Capt. J. Jackson	O. Griswold	J. Pratt
Mr.___Aspear	Mr.___Park	S. Cooper

- - - - - -

SHIP: UNICORN
TYPE: Steamer   FROM: Panama
ARRIVED: November 14, 1851   CAPTAIN: Hartford (Harford?)
PASSAGE: 28 days from Panama, via Acapulco, Mexico, 12 days.
         Nineteen females on board. Anchored off North Beach area
         of San Francisco. Following deaths took place during the
         passage:
             October 31,1851- Mr. M. Berry, of Netherlands, aged 50
                             years; buried in Acapulco, Mexico.
             October 31,1851- Mr. Charles Phillips, of St. Lawrence
                             County, New York, aged 35 years.
             November 3,1851- At sea, Mr. Jesse Babb, of Chester,
                             Maine.
             November 3, 1851-Mr. Ebenezer Pierce, of Michigan
                             County, Illinois.
             November 14,1851-Mr. E. Tollman, of Chester, Maine.
CARGO: Not listed.

Passengers

Mons. Bouginval	Mons.___Duerot	Mons.___Brosser
Mons.___Grandvolnet	Mad.___Pinteaux	Mons.___Fournier
(Grandvoinet?)	(Piuteaux?)	Mrs.___Edwards
Mons.___Wandermassen	Mrs.___Smith	Mrs.___Walker
Miss A. Vion	Mr.&Mrs.___Fostner	Mr.___Flanders
Mr.___Mahony	Mr.___Turner	W.W. Young
Mrs.___Mahony	Mr.___Macouspa	Mr.___Devin 2nd
Mr.___Renche /sic/	(Macousps?)	Mr.___Arnold
Mr.___Tissy	Mr.___Macousps 2nd	Mr.___Thomas
Mr.___Viveroux	Mr.___Brisgrave	Mr.___Colson
Mr.___Eley	Mr.___Armand	Isaac Bostwick
(Eloy?)	Albert Smith	B. Haines
H.A. Joy	D. Millikin	T. Thompson
H.M. Hall	W.S. Pierse /sic/	G. Thompson
B. Hall	H. Cooper	Ira Comstock
C. Selover	J. Smith	B. Bishop
Henry Reinecke	Mrs. E. Wagener and	P. Clark
J. Morrisson	2 children	F. Mackayne
M. Burn	J.L. Backus	L.J. Proctor
P. Dalton	N.A. Reddington	C.C. Montgomery
R.R. Hatch	A. Bingham	C. Whaler
B. Wilson	D. Wilson	J. Ryan
S. Douglas	J. Rand	S.A. Hopkins

(Continued next page)

A. Rebello
J. Lane
D.A. Tichnor and
son
O.H. Torrey
M.S. Torrey
A. Mongu
(Mougu?)
John McBride
E. Miller
C. Jinks
Samuel McBride
Miles Mackay
J. Swindles and
sister
J.W. Swift
S. Forest
James Duer
P. Smith
Cris Andrews /sic/
P. Thompson
D. Parks
I.F. Bailey
George Charles
James Charles
O. Enelsworth
R. Brannan
A. McCreary
J.A. Fish
W. Jansen
G. Lacy

T. Town
E.D. Town
H.A. Austen/sic/
C.M. Oakley
H.J. May
D.P. Bassett
G.W. Talbott
E. Hatton, wife
and child
H. Shepton
L. Voris
A. Voris
H. Voris
George Voris
Thomas Shaw
R.C. Clark
J.A. Clark
L. Froi?sart
George Monk
C. Welch
James Newman
Joseph Baldwin
Ralph Jakes
Jacob Williams
Benjamin Kemphfer
C. Swartswaller
W.P. Lewis
E. Tolman
C. Woodbury
H.H. Tobin

George Sargent
D.M. Black
S. Alexander
John A. Armstrong
H.W. Armstrong
W.B. Curtis
W.S. Pierce
J.W. Hunt
L.B. Sreen /sic/
(Breen?)
Mrs.___ Newman
James Regan
Newton L. Gates
David Housel 2nd
D. Housel 1st /sic/
C. Alexander
Herman Tudor
V. Point
J.J. Winkler
J. McIntyre
F. Woodworth
E.F. Walker
W. Sherman and
wife
Asa Mosure
James Carr
D. Davis
N.M. Hartwell
G.H. Davis
B. Sullivan

- - - - - -

SHIP: TELEGRAPH
TYPE: Clipper   FROM: New York
ARRIVED: November 15, 1851   CAPTAIN: Harlow*
PASSAGE: 125 days from New York. On October 31,1851, in lat. 17-
27N, long. 122, saw ship "Eagle", 112 days from New York,
bound for San Francisco. On November 5th was in lat. 25-
56N, long. 126-32. Had almost constant headwinds; there
two days in which trying speed, when sixteen knots per
hour was obtained. Was 60 days to Cape Horn, and twelve
days off the Cape in heavy weather. Crossed the equator
in long. 110W. This vessel registered at 1066 tons. She
is owned by Phineas Sprague & Company, of Boston,and is
designed for the California and China trade.
CARGO: Cherry cordial, gin, brandy, whiskey, wine, 216 bags of
coffee, 200 hf bbls pork, dried fruits, rice, 117 pipes of
bread, 87 cases of oysters and assorted merchandise.
Passenger
Mr. C. Cushman
- - - - - -

(*)One source states the master was Capt.___ Barlow.

SHIP: NEW WORLD
TYPE: Barque   FROM: Oregon Territory
ARRIVED: November 15, 1851   CAPTAIN: Gill
PASSAGE: 9 days from the Oregon Territory.
CARGO: 4000 feet of piles, 50,000 feet of lumber, 500 hogs, 500
        fowls and 500 cabbages.

Passengers

G.D. Clarke	J.B. Stephen	Peter Dewitt
F.A. Clarke	A. Luther	J. Hooper
J.B.Fairchilds	W.C. Bryant	W. Ramsdail /sic/
J.F. Whighting /sic/	T.A. Smith	

- - - - - -

SHIP: FLAVIUS
TYPE: Ship   FROM: Oahu, S.I.
ARRIVED: November 15, 1851   CAPTAIN: Rogers
PASSAGE: 20 days from Oahu, Sandwich Islands.
CARGO: Not listed.

Passengers

Mrs.___ Bunker and son (wife of American Consul at Lahaina)	Mr.___ Folger	Mr.___ Hoffmire
	Capt.___ Cathcart	Capt.___ Bradley
	Mr.___ Kingsbury	Capt.___ Perry
	Capt. C.S. Holt	

- - - - - -

SHIP: INDEPENDENCE
TYPE: Steamer   FROM: San Juan del Sur
ARRIVED: November 16, 1851   CAPTAIN: Wakeman
PASSAGE: 16 days from San Juan del Sur, Nicaragua. Called at
        Realejo, Nicaragua on October 21, 1851 (on the south-
        bound trip from San Francisco). On the northbound trip
        to San Francisco stopped at Acapulco on November 4, 1851
        and left on November 6, 1851. Word is brought that
        Captain G.D. Bailey, formerly of the vessel "Pacific",
        died on October 7, 1851, at Musgrove's Hotel, at San
        Juan del Sur, after a short illness.
CARGO: Not listed.

Passengers

W. Clark	Mrs.___ Vanhouter, two children & 2 svts	J.B. Andrews
Mrs. S.C. Fopus	Mrs. E. Huff	Mrs. E. Perry
Capt.___ Hugg	J.W. Tilley, wife and boy	Mrs. C.H. Dexter
J.W. Myrick and wife		C.H. Hayford
Miss Mary Myrick	Mrs. ___Goyley (Geyley?)	Mrs. S. Clark and two children
Alex Wells	Joseph Northup	T. Clark
E.W. Atwood, wife and 2 children	G.H. Cassard	Joseph Dennis
R.W. Hudson	J.S. Willis	J.H. Kanduse
John W. McCarty	Cyrus Dickinson	Charles Kincadi/sic/ (Kincaid?)
Peter C. Munn	Gabink Lain	J.F. Treat
John Gilman	F. Averill	
E. Hopkins		

(Continued next page)

G.W. Cole and
   wife
S.B. Crocker
James J. Dougherty
W.C. Fuller

Winslow Crocker
William Patterson
J.W. Belden
Joseph Weinsell
C.H. Comstock

W. Barbari
George Goss
  (Gois?)
J.C. Bartlett
Mrs. E. Comstock

    and 141 unidentified in steerage

- - - - - -

SHIP: OREGON
TYPE: Steamer   FROM: Panama
ARRIVED: November 17, 1851   CAPTAIN: Pearson
PASSAGE: Departed Panama on October 30, 1851. Stopped at Taboga to
take on water. Arrived at Acapulco, Mexico on November 6,
1851, received stores, water and coal. Experienced
continued strong westerly winds, accompanied with almost
incessant rain and heavy head sea, from the time the ship
left Panama until near Acapulco. Was detained outside of
San Francisco harbor in consequence of dense fog. The
following died during passage:
    November 10,1851- At sea, Mr. S.D. Gove, from Manchester,
           New Hampshire
    November 13,1851- Peter Roper, a colored man, from New
           Bedford, Mass.

CARGO: Not listed.

Passengers

Mr.___Chapman and
   lady
Mrs.___Gardner
Mr.& Mrs.___Strattan
P. Day
Mr.___Anthony
Mr.& Mrs.___Sweet
Mr.___Moore
Mr.___Paten
J. McChesney
J.S. Tatlor
  (Taylor?)
A.K. Shirley
S.B. Hadley
S.W. Harrington
M.S. Gale
J.M. Payne
E.S. Crown
G.W. Crown
G.A. Cranover
G. HcAlpin /sic/
  (McAlpin?)
G. Milliken
John Gilkerson
J. Pemberthy
John Pemberthy

Mrs.___Hill and
   child
Mr.& Mrs.___Fish
Mrs.___Taylor
H. Tucker
J. Aitken
Mr.& Mrs.___Whigham
  & 2 children
H. Johnson
D.C. Travers
W.E. McCormick
P. Shisly
D. Hunt
C.M. Fairbanks
J.W. Brulton
A. Jones
C. Davenport
W. Springer
R. Spicer
A. Strichlin
A.B. Mayo
J.L. Woodman
J. Higgins
G.T. Dudley
William Sherman
F.W. Case

Mrs.___Vanderbilt
Mrs.___Cartwright
  and 3 children
Mrs.___Cruthers
Miss___Cruthers
Mr.___Cruthers
Mrs.___Jones
J.S. Ray
G.R. Parburt
J. Davis
J.B. Cartwright
A.B. Cartwright
W. Hoffinger
C.A. Sickols
W. Worrel
D.J. Wheeler
M. Chapman
G. Jansen
P. Bush
T. Falconer
J.G. Briggs
J.N. Briggs
L.P. Winslow
J.S. Dodge
H. Brunker
J. Graves

(Continued next page)

S.D. Gove
Charles Fleming
___ Courman
P. Roper
D. Hall
___ Mallory
___ Crosby
C.L. Dow
A.C. Co?tman
S.K. Burley
J.R. Doyle
O.R. Holly
J.H. Rochester
E.P. Davis
J.F. Cummings
B. Rood
W. Ricker
 (Rucker?)
A. Bayles
T. Bergen
D. Farr
J. Farr
H.F. Lambert
J.H. Latham
L. Lawrence
P. Crawley
D.H. Houston
J. Prarmae
 (Prurman?,Prarman?)
William Hancock
S. Dinsmore
J.W. Gilchrist
J. Hood
A. Fulton
A. Dickey
H. Blum
J. Blum
M.H. Witham
H. Leman
L. Ribourd
J.S. Tower
Charles Smith
H.E. Lindsay
J. Root
J. Burr
J. Mary
Mr.& Mrs.___ Low
 and 2 children
H. Laman
D. Mograge
F. Gay

Edward Nichols
J. Gunn
L. Howard
C. Finn
John Stevens
___ Huse
N. Dunham
E. Bailey
J. Brown
D. Shields
A.B. Harvey
S.A. Smith
M. Barnes
___ Hilton
G.L. Potter
A. Hathaway
M.C. Marshall
D.B. Darling
J. Barker
J.S. Rushton
H.R. Rushton
W. Downs
M.A. Kendall
A.T. Rigley
H.M. Colbath
B. Chester
W.P. Ray
D. Whitney
J. Kelly
G. Tensey
A. Tensey
S. Shelton
J. Ludlow
C. Swartz
J.M. Lycam
John C. White
J.C. Dodge
J. Wagden
 (Wegden?)
H. Grattelot
A.H. Wheeler
J. Wright
J.B.Fort
J. Keefe
W. Hannan
J. Parker
Thomas Smith
J. Perse /sic/
E. Stowers
G.W. Pollard
H.B. Carter
(Continued next page)

John Frank
 Hanselman
C. Gaines
R. Barrill
J.B. Foss
___ Ricard
N. Burton
J. Donalds
R.D. Polsifer
 (Pulsifer?)
E. Sturtevant
A.J. Crawford
W. Hunt
H. Canterbury
W. Watson
P. Meach
G. McEwen
___ Hicks
J.A. Howard
A. Norton
L. Littlefield
J. Turner
P.F. Smith
P. Dustan
J. Andrews
A. Andrews
J. Dunn
M.G. Rice
B. Howard
A.F. Hoadley
 (Headley?)
W.G. Dye
J.A. Truesdale
J. Darling
H. Venier
 (Venler?)
E. Gulliver
G.C. Rice
C. Colby
G. Karcher
G. Long
F. Hathaway
J. Edwards
___ Vanarky
P.B. Wolfe
W.H. Gardner
H. Dennis
David Berry
A. Whitten
D.F. Hunt
C.A. Hunt

E. Wolcott
M. Blanchard
J.L. Palmer
James Currie
W. Sylvester
E.L. Newell
Z. Thing
W.H. Knowles
J.L. Mitchell
A. Howard
T.J. Cotten
G.A. Johnson
S. Hillman
T.S. Keene
M. Gray
J. Taisey
P. Rathbone
T.V.W. Rathbone
R. Colcott
John Pascon
   (Pascoa?)
Thomas Simmons
Robert Harrison
Thomas Bee
William Morris
John Morris
B. Woodworth
J.G. Clifford
O.W. Dealing
J. Walker
D. Young
D. McLean
George Danford
J. Cockrane
J. Dodd
A. Labal
William Saidel (Saldel?)

G.T. Hale
H.C. Harvey
T. Daring
   (Darling?)
E. Brigg
H. Randell
A.S. Alden
A. Crane
A. Chase
R.M. Bunker
S.B. Smart
S. Carr
J. Kirsh
F.W. Stimson
James Ruth
J. Tewksbury
Peter Harvey
C. Trump
P. Gross
Robert Jullen
John Bulsen
T. Birbeck
R. Atkinson
J. Beaty
J. Bennett
George Sty
W. Ayres
T. Roper
B. Kelley
P. Slattery
E. Bower
A. Haskall
T.N. Osmer
N. McDonald
James Farrel /sic/
Thomas R. Martin

T. Herring
T. Brannan
   Hancock
B.H. Bartlett
   (S.H. Bartlett?)
A. Smith
J. Peaby /sic/
A. Small
S. Proctor
A. Gitchell
D.P. Stevens
S. Gile/sic/
St. Gile/sic
W. Cochrane
J. McGeary
Edward Mullen
A. Latourette
J. Bradley
S. Coad
William Bristow
William Waters
Thomas Miller
G. Bradshaw
Edward Roe
L. Green
Henry Davis
A.J. Gunnison
A.R. Gunnison
J. Tuck
C.W. Joslin
N. McCollum
M. Lyndsay /sic/
George Gardner
J. Nicks
A. Moses
*William Periss /sic/

(*)On page 9 will be noted "J.Perse"

— — — — —

SHIP: TYPHON
TYPE: Clipper   FROM: New York
ARRIVED: November 18, 1851   CAPTAIN: Charles H. Salter
PASSAGE: 107 days from New York, departed New York on August 3,
          1851. Off Cape Horn on September 28, 1851. Experienced
          heavy weather off the Cape; lost third officer overboard.
          The "Typhon" is of 2100 tons, 207 feet in length. She is,
          excepting the "Challenge", the largest merchant sailing
          ship ever built in the United States. This vessel was
          built at Portsmouth, N.H., by Fernald & Pettigrew, and is
          owned by D. & A. Kingsland, of New York. Her bow is
                      (continued next page)

ornamented by a figure of a leaping horse of full size.
The lower yards are 80 feet in length, topsail yards 64
feet, and the others in proportion.

CARGO: 1 box whips, 3 rolls leather, 100 bolts cotton duck, 122
cases shoes, 6 boxes coffee mills, varnish, tobacco, lemon
syrup, castings, alcohol, shovels, lampblack, 25 kegs of
rivits /sic/, 3-26 foot copper boats, locks and keys, 26
bbls apples, 5 bbls horse shoes, Russian bale rope, furniture
of various types, 68,000 ft of lumber, shot and assorted
goods.

Passengers

Rev. S.D. Gager, wife   Michael Spencer
and 2 children
(Reverend Gager is a Missionary bound for Oregon Territory)

- - - - - -

SHIP: EAGLE
TYPE: Clipper   FROM: New York
ARRIVED: November 18, 1851   CAPTAIN: Farran
PASSAGE: 128 days from New York. Delayed for three days at the
mouth of San Francisco harbor due to a thick fog. Much
light wind on the passage. The "Eagle" is 1300 tons and
207 feet in length. She was built by Perrine, Patterson
& Stack, at Williamsburg, L.I., New York.

CARGO: Cherry brandy, wine, peach brandy, 9 cases of Scotch whiskey,
cider, brown stout, pickles, hams, almonds, rice, 14 smith's
bellows, tin plates, cheese, oysters, ploughshares, grindstones, Genessee flour, boiler iron, iron columns, chewing
tobacco and assorted goods.

Passengers

D. Bailey and lady   Mr.___Scanlan   Dr.___Lee
Mr.___Bailey
and 6 unidentified in the steerage

- - - - - -

SHIP: SYREN
TYPE: Clipper   FROM: Boston, Mass.
ARRIVED: November 18, 1851   CAPTAIN: Silsbee
PASSAGE: 141 days from Boston, Massachusetts. On August 30, 1851
Antonio Joseph, a seaman, off the Western Islands, fell
from aloft on deck and died in two days. The "Syren" is
of 1060 tons burthen and it was built by I. Taylor at
Medford, Massachusetts. Had 20 days of heavy weather off
the Cape.

CARGO: Not listed.

Passenger
G. Chapman

- - - - - -

SHIP: ALDEBARAN
TYPE: Ship   FROM: Honolulu, S.I.
ARRIVED: November 18, 1851   CAPTAIN: Livermore

PASSAGE: 22 days from Honolulu, Sandwich Islands.
CARGO: Cigars, 8 pipes of raisins, chains, sugar, flour, pepper,
refined sugar, nutmeg, smoked beef, mess beef, tool chests,
5 fanning mills, 200 ox bows and assorted goods.

Passenger
N.L. Williams

- - - - - -

SHIP: MONUMENTAL CITY
TYPE: Propeller   FROM: Panama
ARRIVED: November 18, 1851   CAPTAIN: Norris
PASSAGE: 30 days from Panama, via Acapulco, Mexico and San Diego,
California. Passage was stated as "very long and un-
pleasant voyage".
CARGO: 84 packages of unspecified merchandise.

Passengers

Mrs. F. Foster	Mrs. ___ Green	Joseph Collett
J.Q. Adams	D. Mascucie	Miss ___ Bond
Mrs. ___ Van Dewsen	Mrs. ___ Vale	Mrs ___ Bond
Miss ___ Hughes	H.W. Netting, lady	Mr. E. Bond
Miss ___ Kemp	and child	Mr. J. Bond
F.E. Vander Meden	Mr. & Mrs. ___ Blood	Mrs. ___ Dixon and
Mrs. ___ Clark	Mr. & Mrs. ___ Murphy	2 children
J.E. Smiley	William Exley	T. Van Buskirk
G.W. Smiley	Mr. & Mrs. ___ Stigall	Mr. Sosies
Mr. & Mrs Conckwright.	Mr. & Mrs. ___ Guion	George Henshaw
(sic)	Mrs. ___ Fari	Mr. ___ Threig and
Miss ___ Donovan	Mrs. ___ King	lady
Mrs. ___ Swane	Mrs. ___ Wilkins	W. Wright and lady
J. Dixon	W. Elsan and lady	John Comb
Owen Casey	Mr. ___ Rosenberg	Mr. ___ Tagerfelt
James Casey	S.J. Andrews	J. Wellman and
R.P. Woodman/sic/	C. Bunker	lady
N. Gray	W.G. Easan and	George Ward
W.C. Baring	servant	W. Barnett
C.W. Wilcox	J. Hill	J. Burke
J. Rockwell	E.H. Brewster	Mr. & Mrs. ___ Down
John Butler	H. Dibble	Mrs. ___ Kirchner
Mr. & Mrs. ___ Greely and	Mrs. ___ Hurril	Mrs. ___ Nolte and
2 children	Mr. & Mrs. ___ Kagan	child
Master ___ Greely	Mr. & Mrs. ___ Barrett	P. Smith
Master H. Schroeder	D. Baker	George Wilson
Master A. Schroeder	Miss Ann Kenny	G.R. Kane
Mr. & Mrs. ___ Bodecker	Mr. ___ Long	Mrs. ___ Lynch and
and 2 children	Miss ___ Briggs	2 children
Mr. ___ Snavely	T. Van Busker	N.R. Stevens
Asa Day	H. Farnum	W.H. Johnson
George Hase	J.R. Porter	D. Grant
S.A. Davis	B.F. Kimball/sic/*	M. Scott
T.F. Davis	M. Howe	W. Ward
J. Pelland	I. Pelland	G. Rottange

(Continued to next page)

(*)Note H.W. Kinball, page 13

P. Toddy
J.W. Wheeler
W. Lincoln
G.W. Fellows
F.J. Fellows
J.S. Scott
Mrs. R. Scott
Mr.& Mrs.____ Brayton
O.H.P. Kenny
Joseph Alway
R.P. Woodman/sic/
J.W. Carpenter
D.N. Town
H.P. Wing
G. Gould
W.G. White
P. Farley
A. Hannum
H.F. Clements
J. Smart
W.N. Lincoln
C.H. Edwards
G.W. Uril
M. Rotzel
O. Zsidlow
  (O.Z. Sidlow?)
H. Ripley Jr.
G. Peasley
L.H. Card
W. Lowe
Joseph Dibble
P. Moore
C. Kreiser
A.M. Bennet
R. McCloud
L.R. Bailey
J.H. Madison
J. Cole
Mr.____ Harrington
N. Gray /sic/
W.H. Leighton
T. Scrivner
P. Hannegan
O. Hannegan
A.B. Thompson
G.H. Gardner
C.A. Dilling
A. Bailey
O. Trace
H. Lable
H.C. Gaskell

Mr.____ Raymond
Ed Freeman
L. Smiley
Edward Gray
C. Pilbrock
Mr.&Mrs.____ Rigdon
M.E. Mills/sic/
Mr.& Mrs.____ Hall
  and child
M.E. Mills/sic/
D. Wilburn
E.W. Beauman
  (Beanman?)
C.R. Boyellter
P.B. Richmond
J.M. Bingham
A. Precht
Mrs.____ Wilson
Miss H. Wilson
J. Wilson
W. Wilson
Master____ Wilson
H. Frur
W. Frur
J. Rollin, Jr./sic/
H. Rollins /sic/
B. Hamilton
G. Riley
W. Russell
P. Westerbrook
W. Godfrey
E. Miller
C. Allinger
R. Buchanan
L. Griffin
A. Malone
A.D. Wade
H. Smith
J. Thomas
W. Lawrence
P.H. Dale
S.D. Alert
J. Lincolns /sic/
E. Woodford
M. Zingler
E. Pangborn
H. Pangborn
A. Robbil
J. Lynch
H. Laventhall
F.L. Laventhall
(Continued next page)

S.S. Simons
H.F. Simons
E. Simons
James Wheeler
A. Donovan
A.H. Burk
Mr. & Mrs.____ Nallin
  and child
P.W. Poole
G.W. Pearse (dead)
Joseph Derby
A. Mason
H.F. Johnson
  (H.P. Johnson?)
E.H. Mason
C. Chase
H. Wild
A.H. Robbins
John Carr
G. Smith
J.H. Carland
J.H. Haskell
L.F. Davis
M.H. Davis
S. Randall
H.W. Kinball/sic/*
G.B.M. Cleach
J.L. Councilman
E.W. Councilman
W. Barry
W. Bulling
W. Beals
G.Gayer
H. Chambers
D. To?ry
C. Robenbush
J.N. Hovey
D. Howland
A.F. Rice
W.H. Shaw
R.W. Wetheroff
T. Sweet
T.R. Virgin
J.N. Taylor
James Ray
H.D. Stockman
J. Lewis
A. Booth
M. Healy
J. Hopper
J. Kerr

(*)Note B.F. Kimball,page12

A. Gordon	J.B. McDaniel	S. Eider
W. Gordon	W.N. Durgin	J. Gullifer
J. Peasley	M. Ward	C. Morris
S.D. Johnson	C. Denison	J. Burril
S. Briggs	T. Williams	Mr. Nestor
S. Hartley	J.H. Mead	L. Tibbett
T. White	J. Gilpe	D. Thorn
F.L. Frost	J. Leary	A. Langerfetter
S. Smith	H. Davis	J. Langerfetter
L.F. Noyes	H. Furnsall	J. Bell
S.P. Noyes	B. Pedro	M. Koski /sic/
M. Bijo	J. Bagigalope	W. Kosker /sic/
J. Garvil	J.B. Paranco	J. Gelyard
T.O. Leary	G. Paranco	J. Legermason
T. Moran	M. Julien	Master Gelyard
T. Gaughan		

- - - - - -

SHIP: GOLDEN GATE
TYPE: Steamer   FROM: New York
ARRIVED: November 19, 1851   CAPTAIN: Patterson, U.S.N.
PASSAGE: 64 days, 19 hours from New York. Foregoing figure is
running time. This is the first trip to San Francisco
for this steamer. She is the first of a class of vessels
to constitute a new era in steam navigation upon the
Pacific Ocean. Ventilation arrangements on board are
superior to any vessel then engaged in the California
passenger trade. The vessel was built by W.H. Webb in
the city of New York, for the Pacific Mail Steam Ship
Company. Vessel burthen is 2200 tons, carries three
masts, with a top-sail and two top-gallant sails on her
fore and main, and a spanker on her mizen, which without
the aid of steam, gives her sail enough to make port,
should the machinery break. Vessel is equipped with two
oscillating engines, largest of the class constructed to
date (1851). Following is time, from port to port:

From New York to Bahia - 20 days, 0 hours
Bahia to Rio de Janeiro - 3 days, 0 hours
Rio to Valparaiso - 17 days, 23 hours
Valparaiso to Panama - 10 days, 4 hours
Panama to Acapulco - 5 days, 22 hours
Acapulco to San Diego - 5 days, 13 hours
San Diego to Montery - 1 day, 10 hours
Monterey to San Francisco - 9 hours

Head wind was experienced from Panama to San Francisco.
Following deaths took place during the passage from
Panama to San Francisco:

November 6, 1851 - Daniel McKeenan, of Panama Fever,
of Old Town, Maine.
November 10, 1851 - P. Menaman, of Ireland
November 15, 1851 - John Campbell, of Westerly, R.I.

(Continued next page)

November 15, 1851 - Joseph Turner, of Ellsworth, Maine.

November 15, 1851 - Newel S. Page, of Dexter, Maine.

CARGO: 33 packages segars, 169 packages express matter (not identified), 48 packages merchandise (not identified), 2 packages of pistols and 1 package of olives.

Passengers

S. Quincy	F. Brown	Miss E. Taylor
Mrs.___Mahony and son	Mrs.___Hastings and son	F. Johnson and lady
J.H. Trowbridge	D.L. Hastings	E.J. Smith
D. Brady	A.G. Jones, lady and child	Mrs.___Meyers and sister
Dr.___Downer and lady	N. Johnson	J.C. Sargeant
Henry Smith	M.R. Ward and lady	A. Gilman and lady
A.Y. Smith	J.B. Sykes	J.W. Bissell
Dr.___Herman	P. Middleton	P. Daly and lady
___Duprez and two ladies	J.S. Lemalfra (Lamalfra?)	R. Kensely
S.B. Hall	___Ebinger (Ehinger?)	J. Glenn
R. Bowers	W. Green	A. Lauer
J. Scolfield and son	W.C. Parks	A. Kimbal /sic/
J. Davis	W. Nichols	P. McHugh
W.M. Davis	Charles Cross	Charles Pratt
S. Wheeler	W.M. Coomb	W.L. Hasket
E.R. Lambert	J. Corkey	W. Wagner
R.G. Gray	H.H. Taylor	J.S. Kimbal /sic/
D. McMickle	W. McDonald	A. Lame
P. McMickle	A. Merritt	J. Ross
R. Southerstone	J. McMartin	J. Church
J. Hasseller	T. Cutlew	A. Chisholm
W. Foley	J. King	James Cox
L. Foley	B. King	Owen Nary
T. Phelps	J. Barkin	C. Bonham
J. Phillips	M. O'Donnell	W. Dubois
J. Stevens /sic/	R. Basil	W. Perkins
J. Stevens /sic/	F.W. Crosby	W. Larkin
S. Anderson	W. Watson	P. McCormick
J. Kamen	H. McCurry	A. Gooden
W. Cainer	M. Carle (Carie?)	S. Gooden
E. Sage	O.N. Young	F.M. Hebber
H. Burget	E.W. Ladd	J.B. Foss
C. Collins	H. Conklin	J. Turner
F. Appel	F. Sim????	G. Smith
J. Castlebar	A. McKay	J. Wright
S.M. Cochran	A. Powers /sic/	A. Wier
J. Daizell (Dalzell?)	B.S. Cutter	E. Power /sic/
J.L. Chadwick	J.F. Babcock	J. Jones
C.W. Crary	T. Thomas	C. Machedo
J.H. Pasqual	R. Williams	J.A. Peabody
J. Woods		T.J. Williams
		P. Williams

(Continued next page)

J. Richards
P. Martin
C. Mansel (Manzel?)
J. Carter
S. Lay
C. Greenough
J. Gilley
A.W. Roberts
W. Pischbeck
M. Pischbeck
J. Clark
J. Waters
Joseph Ede
R. Cox
C. Reese
J. Trumbath
J. Mitchell
W. Colby
Mrs.___Mickel
Mrs.___Giraud
Mr.___Jule
W. Sparegrove
J. Trueman (Trusman?)
A. Smith
H. Garner
Mr.___Walfer
R.M. Miner
A. Goodly
R. Clough
P.C. Connely
D. Caswell
D. O'Niel
J.R. Morgan
A.C. Member
P.S. Young /sic/
W. Crudden
J. Eustin (Eustis?)
C. Harrison
___Duprez
H.A. Lonford
___Baughton
W.S. Page
W.G. Theilaker
H. Graham
W. Howard
C. Andrews
S. Davis
G. Muncy (Munoy?)
W. Hatch
D. Cartwright
H. Coon

J. Menkey
J. Webster
E. Webster
F. Stoman
J. Bowden
J. McGarnegon
R. Simmons
R. Illsey
J. McKee
H. Miller
H. Peters
J. Williams
N. Williams
T. Williams
J. Blight
Joseph Smith
E. Landon
W. Gale and lady
Mrs.___LeMoine
   (LeMoins?)
Mr.___Abadie
J. Weir
R. McLane
J. Lock
G. Simpton
J. Barracks
C.W. Pease
G. Edwards
G.F. Schermerhorn
R. Case
J. Van Plat (Van
   Piat?)
E. Groves
J. Hance
D.S. Castro
A.H. Brigg
H. Boorfrey
T. Blake
___Ashman
S.S. Crocker
C. Milnor
J. Milnor
A. de la Pietre
C. White and boy
G. Nickerson
J. Wright
C.C. Bonnel
R. Haine (Hains?)
J.G. Hoyt
A. Brimmer (Brimner?)
J. Ingersoll and boy
(Continued next page)

J. Thomas
E. Osborne
H. Osborne
J. Osborne
B. Osborne
L. Murray
J. Woodward
J. Jess
W. Jess
F. Corliss
H. Meager
J. Stevens
B. Hastings
J. Bartlett
G.W. Miller
A. Breed
J. Leavit /sic/
Mrs.___Trapet
J. Lane (Luse?)
J. Karner
Mr.___Luslin
John Swift
G. Dwyer
C.A. Wolf
H. Hyde
E. Fields
M. Druswick
F. Sweeny
H. Malloy
H. Olden
B. Olden (E.Olden?)
W. Hervey (Harvey?)
W. Forbs
J. Basil
S. Sellard
J. Brown
C. Canfield
M. Castret
J.A. Lucky
J. Barns (Burns?)
J.W. Gordon
T.M. Knox
H. Maunditch
T. Dillon
George Harrison
F. Johnson
J.A. Anderson
D. Fratermoull
F. Fratermoull
H. Crome
S.D. Green

H. Barnes
J.H.R. Brown
M.M. Brien
A. Clovis (Clevis?)
S. Clovis (Clevis?)
P. Wilson
H. Bonds
S.M. Churchill
A. Adams
J. Montano
B. Mendega(?)
   (B. Mendege?)
J.L. Lee
A.J. Davis
A. Gobbie
C. ___'mons
S. Dow
A. Dean/sic/
J. Phillips
A. Phillips
A. Valentine
R. Barclay
J. Brogler
R. Briggs
   Elvenstone (?) and
   lady (Eivenstone?)
   Sharky and lady
C. Platt
Mr.___ Green
P. Skinner
J. Pemberthy /sic/
J. Pemberthy /sic/
W. Rogers
D. Ross
A. Warner
H. Gray
J. Trewotha
J. Brown
W. Frelaire
W.D. Morgan
J.A. Binhill (Sinhill?)
W. Murray
John Date
J.H. Lock
E. Townsend
F. Townsend
J.C. Shaw
T.P. Harding
J. McMullin
G. Greenwood
   Lafranc(Lafrane?)

S.F. York
William Miller
W. Hancock
E.P. Beserve
George Buck
T. Chesley
C. Bolt
C. Campbell
M. Vyse (?)
S. Merwin
   Simas (Simne?,
   Simse?)
C. Stone
C. Baily /sic/
W.F. Buckley
F.R. Ford
W.L. Webster
J. Davenport
M. Salaver
A. Dean/sic/
H.R. Drake
S. Tingly /sic/
   (Tingley?)
O. Drake
   Norris and
   lady
P.S. Young/sic/
J. Nickerson
J. Atkinson
D. Buckerlig
L. Murphy
T. Murphy
J. Peirce
J. Bennet /sic/
P. Plass
J. Johns
J. Tringpasse
J. Smith
W. Antig
T.I. Merritt
C. Bilman
W. Woodward
R. McVane
J. Horn
W. Jones
D. Van Akin
J. Simpson
L. Coleman
L. Cooney
T. Wiggiar (Wigglar?)
D. Hudson
(Continued next page)

George Poultry
   (Poultny,
   Poultney?)
B.M. Paulding /sic/
H. Tuttle
C. Turner
A. Indiredge
W. Hardwick
N. Murray (?)
   (H. Murray?)
M.D. Williams
F. Cooper
J. Kearney
S.Sweet
   Lemmermon
L.F. Drake
E.S. Drake
H. Casey
C.E. Staples
Mrs.___Hyde
J. Andrews
G. Andrews
C. Gallaway
R.W. McLaughlin
R. Jasper
F. Olwill
S. Fellows
H. Cutter
M. Mosely
G. Gill
B. Woodbury
H. Hall
T.H. Femey
B.F. Thurber
J. McFee
P. McFee
J. Skinner
H. Taylor and
   lady
E. Park
B. Andrews
P. Burns
J.C. Howard
A.H. Campbell
J. Miller
G. Miller
J. Moores
R. Engs (Enge?)
M. Duprey
Mr. ___ Duprey
H. Jones

S. Martin and	G. Brigham	J. Fance /sic/
Lady	O. Brigham	J. Fance /sic/
C. Roberts	G. Worth	T.J. Elliot
L.W. Johnson	N. Seaman	A. Ferguson
M. Hyde	J. Bates	A. Brown
C.L. Buckingham	W. Bates	D. Malloy
J. Botford		

- - - - - -

SHIP: METTA
TYPE: Barque (German)   FROM: Hamburg, Germany
ARRIVED: November 19, 1851   CAPTAIN: Mencke
PASSAGE: 200 days from Hamburg, Germany, via Valparaiso, Chile, 54
         days.
CARGO: Merchandise (not identified).

Passengers

Miss Bertha Scheff	J.J. Rambach (or Rembach?)
Gustavus Fischer	Francis Bowers

and 9 unidentified in steerage)

- - - - - -

SHIP: HONOLULU
TYPE: Schooner   FROM: Mazatlan, Mexico
ARRIVED: November 18,1851(correct)   CAPTAIN: Swine (or Swins?)
PASSAGE: 29 days from Mazatlan, Mexico.
CARGO: In ballast.

Passengers
Mrs. Grace Brown*
and 27 unidentified passengers
(*) Died at sea. Mrs. Brown was wife of William Brown. She was
one of the twelve females aboard the "Honolulu". Mrs. Brown was
a native of Whealbury, Cornwall, England, reaching the age of 44
years. Burial was at sea, in lat. 23-41N, long 119-46W.

- - - - - -

SHIP: JACOB GROSSE
TYPE: Brig (German)   FROM: Bremen, Germany
ARRIVED: November 20, 1851   CAPTAIN: Kompff
PASSAGE: 210 days from Bremen, Germany, via Callao, Peru, 50 days.
CARGO: 12 chests ground coffee, 173 boxes blue, 16 boxes sootget
       licen, 34 boxes glass, 32 boxes cigars, 358 bundles steel,
       1205 bars steel, chairs, leather goods, beer, pepper and
       liquor.

Passengers

Amelia Trendt	Agnes Trendt	Arnold Trendt
Catharine Trendt	Charles Schruttmutter	Anseline Larel
Eduart Faust	Maria Ehrhard	Sarah Pamton
Maria Pamton	John Pamton	Sam Pamton
Hermann Michels		

- - - - - -

SHIP: MATTHEW VASSAR*
TYPE: Schooner   FROM: Oregon Territory
ARRIVED: November 20, 1851   CAPTAIN: Bowen/sic/
PASSAGE: 6 days from the Oregon Territory.
CARGO: 130 sacks of onions, 500 sacks of flour, 2400 bushels of
        potatoes, 100 squashes, 400 bushels of oats, 300 bags of
        wheat, 200 fowls and 495 hogs.

Passengers

J.B. Leach	J. Casiman	Robert McCullough
R. Sparks	Hugh Lynch	D.A. Lynch

- - - - - -

SHIP: KOH-I-NOOR
TYPE: Schooner (British)   FROM: Lahaina, S.I.
ARRIVED: November 21, 1851   CAPTAIN: Loian
PASSAGE: 16 days from Lahaina, Sandwich Islands.
CARGO: 20,000 lbs of Hobart Town potatoes, 100,000 lbs of
        Sandwich Island potatoes and 10,000 oranges.

Passengers

Mrs.___Kitchell	Mrs.___Chapman	Mrs.___Blanchatt
Mrs.___Coueleanii	William Summers	and two children
(Oueleanii?)	J. Henderson	William Eustis
J. Loring		

- - - - - -

SHIP: LORD RIVERSDALE
TYPE: Barque (British)   FROM: Liverpool, England
ARRIVED: November 21, 1851   CAPTAIN: Watkins
PASSAGE: 225 days from Liverpool, England, via Port William
        Stanley, Falkland Islands, 120 days.
CARGO: 175 cast iron pipes, 5 crab winches, 25 kegs of tongue,
        2250 bags salt, 39 barrels chemicals, 110 kegs of pork,
        tin-plate and tin-ware, 229 crates of earthenware, 27
        packages of furniture, 29 packages of hardware.

Passengers

John H. Dillon	John A. Hayward	Edward Roach

- - - - -

SHIP: JAMES R. WHITING (listed also as J.R. WHITING)
TYPE: Schooner   FROM: Santa Cruz, Calif.
ARRIVED: November 23, 1851   CAPTAIN: W.W. Baker
PASSAGE: 3 days from Santa Cruz, California.
CARGO: 120 tons of potatoes, 10 tons barley, 5 tons of onions,
        19,400 feet of lumber.

Passengers

H. Speel	J. Newil /sic/	J.J. Weeks
Parrish H. James and	William Thompson	Dr.___Andrews
son	___Longfellow	J.G. Robins
C.A. Lormpa		

- - - - - -

(*)Vessel listed at times as "M.VASSAR" and "M.VASSER"

SHIP: OHIO
TYPE: Barque   FROM: Valparaiso, Chile
ARRIVED: November 21,1851(correct)   CAPTAIN: Johnson
PASSAGE: 56 days from Valparaiso, Chile.
CARGO: Soap, brandy, flour, barley, spun yarn, segars.

Passenger
Mr. E.K. Mooney

- - - - -

SHIP: MARY W.
TYPE: Schooner   FROM: LAHAINA, S.I.
ARRIVED: November 25, 1851   CAPTAIN: Ward
PASSAGE: 18 days from Lahaina, Sandwich Islands. Brings
          intelligence that there is an effort in Honolulu to
          establish an Episcopal church. As no representative of
          the church is in the area,a layman, R.C. Willie, Esq.,
          will read the service of the Church of England. The
          service is to be read regularly every Sunday.
CARGO: 1000 bbls of potatoes, 12 casks sperm oil, 61 casks whale
        oil.

Passengers

Capt. C.W. Rand   Capt. A.J. Shockley   W.M. Jyles
R. Martin   William Mindon   Capt. W. Maxfield*
  (*) Late of the whale ship "Arrabella"

- - - - - -

SHIP: LAWRENCE (U.S. Revenue   FROM: Monterey, Calif.
          Cutter)   CAPTAIN: D.B. Ottinger
ARRIVED: Shipwrecked   TYPE: Brig (Cutter)
PASSAGE: This vessel departed Monterey, California, bound for the
          port of San Francisco. On November 25, 1851, just after
          dark, when about 4 miles below Point Lobos, the southern
          extremity of the entrance of the harbor, a storm blew up.
          The vessel was compelled to anchor in the near area, in
          5 fathoms of water. Wind increased and large sea was
          raised, which broke over the vessel. The cables broke
          and the vessel was driven on shore. Position on shore
          was about two miles north of the wreck of the "Mary
          Stewart". Two passengers landed safely.
CARGO: Unknown.

Passengers
Col.___Russell (Collector,   Mr.___Starkey (of the firm
    Port of Monterey)   of Starkey & Brothers)

- - - - - -

SHIP: NORTH AMERICA
TYPE: Steamer   FROM: San Juan del Sur
ARRIVED: November 28, 1851   CAPTAIN: J.H. Blethen
PASSAGE: 11 days from San Juan del Sur, Nicaragua. On November
          23d and 24th encountered heavy gales from the N.W.
          Made the heads at 10:30PM on the 27th and laid off on
          until daylight of the 28th. On board is Mr. Joseph

Proctor and his wife. Mr. Proctor, an actor, is to be
engaged in one of the San Francisco theatres.
Following passengers died during the passage:
> November 23,1851 - Mrs.___ Connolly, wife of Thomas
> Connolly, of California, aged 60 years.*
> November 21,1851 - E.G. Page, of Orino, Maine, aged
> 21 years.
> November 22,1851 - An infant of Mrs N.P. Simmons./sic/

CARGO: Not listed.

Passengers

John O'Niel
Julia O'Niel
Thomas Connelly*
Mrs. T. Connelly*
Miss M. Connelly*
Mrs. H.P. White
Mrs.___ Wake
Mrs.___ Moody
Emily Moody
Mrs. E.D. Moody and
  child
Mrs. P. Perkins
Miss___ Perkins
Mrs. H.D. Coggleshall
Mrs. C.N. Davis and
  3 children
Mrs. Jane Presscott/sic/
  (Prescott?)
E. King
C.R. Ordway
A. Troop
John Frees
Mrs.___ Hunt
J.H. Gorton
D. Dwyer
J. Page
J. Farker /sic/
E.A. Philbrook
A. Whidden
Capt. C.H. Ogle(U.S.A.)
F.M. Randall
Mrs.___ Holmes and
  2 children
Mrs. C.C. Webb
Mr. J.S. Bacon
Mrs. J.S. Bacon
W.R. Richardson
Mrs.___ Richardson and
  child
N. Chipman

Mrs.___ Brown and
  2 children
Mrs.___ O'Brien
W. Hard
Mrs.___ Van Shaick
J.B. Humphrey
Mrs. J.B. Humphrey
D. M'Lellan
Mrs.___ M'Lellan
A.C. Nichols
W. Fains
F.H. Thompson
C. Stevens
Mrs.___ Thompson
Mrs. J.C. Boorman
  and 3 children
D.C. Mcrue /sic/
W. Ayer
E. Webster Jr.
J.M. Morrill
D. McMellan
Mrs.___ Watley
Mrs. E.G. Freeman
F.H. Kendrick
B.E. Willet
R.W. Green
P. Hawkins
A. Carrick
S.M. Bloomer
Mrs. W.L. Kirby
William F. Story
Mrs.___ Keith and
  child
Mrs. F.B. Lewis
J.S. Tappan
O. Wright
J.R. Cooper
Mrs. S.D. Anderson
Joseph Proctor
Mrs.___ Proctor
(Continued next page)

Mrs. R.J. Weeks
J. Schleghter
J. Williams
G.B. Post
M.S. Brown
T. Searin
S. Myer
A. Packard
Mrs. M.P. Simmons/sic/
Mrs.___ Lohen and
  child (Lohse?,
  Lohec?)
Mrs.___ Patrick and
  3 children
A. Webster
Mrs. J.R. Richards
W. Eastwood
William Armington
John Whitcomb
S.D.H. Robinson
S. Ayer
H.G. Cole
Julia Fage /sic/
  (Page?)
J.C. Jepson
J.W. Lawrence
E.G. Paige
W.H. Read
R.D. Morrill
Mrs. R.D. Morrill
Mrs. F. Williams
  and daughter
Mrs. A.B. Davis
Dr. R.R. Davis
J.C. Bullions
F. Henry /sic/
  (Henrys?)
Mrs. S. Henrys /sic/
  and child (Henry?)
W.C. Sackett

(*)Note death as "Connolly" and passenger listing as "Connelly".

Mrs.____Quereau and
   child
Mrs. S.K. Brown
J.S. Johnson
J.T. Praory
Mrs.____Praory and
   3 children
J. Roberts
W.A. McLoughlin
C. Carlton
N.A. Potter
G. White
Thomas Comly
J.D. Hurley
J. Henry
J. Reynolds
D. Linn
J. Haywood
J.H. Hussey
E.B. Foster
G. Lewis
E. Bibber
C. Giron
N. Phillips
R. Chase
A. Southmage
P. Haywood
G. Roberts
B. Barrett
J. Ingraham
G. Bredea (Breden?)
S. Dryden
H. George
B. Hottle /sic/
A. Bremmer
W. White
W.G. Bunker
R.H. Peck
R.L. Ball
J.H. Bunker
T.P. Whitmore
H.M. Mark
W.F. Shepherd
C.M. Shepherd and
   lady
B.P. Rollins
N.P. Hopkins
A. Briteholl
   (Britchell?)
W. Henderson
R. Isaacs

C. Russell
S. Mayerback
Mrs.____Mayerback
Dr. G.C. Chase
H. Hornite
G.M. Harris
R.W. Gray
J.S. Williams
H. Frink (Frisk?)
H. Mygats
H.A. Marsfield
J.L. Groves
S. Sill
R. Conlet
W. Quayle
S. Sylvester
H. Sylvester
J. Dunning
H. Dunning
B. Potter
L.C. Andrews
L.D. Snow
J. Snow
J. Forthacker
K.H. Bailey
H. Graves
W. Judkins
R. Dryden
J. Dryden
A. Morrow
E. Harkin
H. Tuttle /sic/
A. Gould
J. Carpenter
J.E. Marsh
S. Lord
N.C. Dillater
O.G. Dolliver
A. Starkweather
C. Starkweather
H.D. Spooner
C. Bickford
D.A. Stevens and
   lady
J.A. Gardner
H. Covell
A. Brown
A. Combs Jr.
D.C. Henderson
Q. Curry
(Continued next page)

A.S. Marvin
C. Lombard
M. Storms
T. Bude /sic/
   (Budde?)
Mrs. J. McCrady and
   3 children
J. Green
W. Foy
A.B. Youmans
B.F. Colgrove
William M. Collins
N.P. Hopkins
J. Mannce (Maunce?)
   (above name is
   listed twice)
S. Gunner
G. Morse
E. Mountfort
H. Jones
F. Kolby
H. Booker
G.M. Grover
W. Danly /sic/
A.R.T. Corban
W. Merryman
J.A. Watson
N. Megor
J. Turkle
Joseph Turkle
F. Turkle
A. Barrett
C. Brown
J. Barrett
E. Pickering
J.H. Joy
A. Joy
P.H. Soule
J.S. Cutter
C. Whitmore
W.M. Dain
D. Lord
J. Smart
H.S. Carlton
H. Hodge
A. Croxford
S.B. Washburn
R.L. Chapman
G. Hall
H.C. Henderson
R. White

A. Pennell	A. Dodge	A.D. Levy
R.H. Purrington	J.B. Johnson	W.R. Batchelder
A.R.J. Ladd	M. Danton	J.D. Manning
(R.J. Ladd?)	A.J. Felton	J. Johnson /sic/
D. Blidden	J. Covell	E.A. Young
A.R. Clark	George Gould	G.W. Calton
B. Morris	J.W. Johnson	W.L. Williams
J. Roberts	Thomas Cann	W.L. Barnes
O.T. Brown	D. Hubbard	W. Barton
J.A. Chace	D.R. Wilkerson	F. Loring
W.M. Chace	F. Kelly (Kelty?)	O.H. Williams
W. Duddell	J. Stevens	J. Dubois
V.A. Duddell	A. Wood /sic/	M. Marsh
E.A. Duddell	A. Wood /sic/	J. Johnson/sic/
J.J. Hance	J. Vailing	E. Williams
F.A. Herring	J. Toothacker	J. Donnovan /sic/
W. Richards	D.W. Edwards	W. Young
F. Martin	B.F. Slocumb	J. Allen
W.W. Kemp	C. Walker	J. Noble
W.P. Kemp	J.F.F. Read	B.F. Noble
R. Burrill	J. Flood	J.T. Noble
J. Burrill	J. Osborne	P. Hubbard Jr.
A. King	S.H. Jabobs /sic/	C. Hanson
E.S. Graves	(Jacobs?)	W.A. Stewart
L. Ballest (Bellest?,	Switt	Peirce
Billest?,Bullest?)	Laflin	Sampson
Maynard	Palmer	Moore
Hollenback	Robinson	Elliott
A. Richardson	(Robinsohn?)	D.F. Johnson
C.E. Morrison	H.G. Robinson /sic/	

- - - - - -

SHIP: QUICKSTEP (U.S. Survey Vessel)
TYPE: Propellor   FROM: Mexico
ARRIVED: November 29, 1851   CAPTAIN: Alden
PASSAGE: Returns to San Francisco after conducting coast surveys as far south as the dividing line between Mexico and the United States. Mission was to determine the position of various islands, rocks, shoals, etc, which interfere with the navigation on the Pacific Coast.
CARGO: Not listed

Passengers
None

- - - - - -

SHIP: SARAH LAVINIA
TYPE: Not Listed   FROM: Santa Cruz, Calif.
ARRIVED: November 29, 1851   CAPTAIN: Scott
PASSAGE: 46 hours from Santa Cruz, California.
CARGO: 1300 bags of potatoes.

Passengers

D. Wood   G.W. Inskip   C. Indue(?)

- - - - - -

SHIP: MONTICELLIO
TYPE: Schooner   FROM: Honolulu, S.I.
ARRIVED: November 29, 1851   CAPTAIN: Rogers
PASSAGE: 24 days from Honolulu, Sandwich Islands.
CARGO: 30 tons of potatoes and casts of steel.

Passengers

Capt. A. Taber*   J.P. Colburn   R. Robinson
J. Glaspick
        (*)Late of the whale ship "Globe" which was lost in the
        Artic Ocean)

- - - - - -

SHIP: COLUMBIA
TYPE: Steamer   FROM: Oregon Territory
ARRIVED: November 30, 1851   CAPTAIN: Leroy
PASSAGE: 76 hours from Portland, Oregon Territory, Astoria,
        Oregon Territory and Port Orford, Oregon Territory.
        Among the passenger's boarding at Port Orford were Mr.
        ___ Harrison and Mr. ___ Lawson of the U.S. Coast Survey.
        The survey party is engaged in determining the latitude
        and longitude of the point, and have completed a map of
        the harbor. Some inconvenience had been felt on account
        of the scarcity of provisions. Coal has been found at
        Port Orford in considerable quantities.
CARGO: Not listed.

Passengers

W.B. Risor	A. Cheesbro	J.M. Simonsfield
E.C. Rogers	Rev. A. Coltle	S. Welch(B. Welch?)
Rev. Mr. ___ Fitch	(Cottle?)	J.J. McCarven
Mrs. ___ Richmond	C. Taylor	C.W. Cork
B.R. Mael	C.T. Fay	W.D. Carter
Mrs. ___ Peck and	Mr. ___ Callender	Mr. ___ Beaufort
2 children	Mr. ___ Harrison	Mr. ___ Lawson
Mr. ___ Brush	(see Passage)	(see Passage)
Mr. ___ Stearns	Mr. ___ Wackenruder	Mr. ___ Wiren
Mr. ___ Frusher	Mr. ___ Gilman	Mr. ___ Duchesney
Mr. ___ Peniston	Mr. ___ Collins	Mr. ___ Bellows
Mr. ___ Nichols /sic/	Mr. ___ Thorn	Mr. ___ McIlray
Mr. ___ Wright	Mr. ___ Nichols/sic/	W.T. Lard
Amos Sprugin(Sprugia?)	F. Beardsley	F.J. France
Lewis Ainsworth	James Kitchen	Charles A. Wheeler
J. Pauweil	W. Young	W. McClelland
F. Libuit	J. Bowman	J.H. Sutler
J. Dunlap	R. Dutton	J.C. Palmer
J. Conroy	H. Lockwood	William McAllister
W.D. James	W.S. Fouts	J.S. Kennon
W.M. Swain	J. Branker	S. Plummer
Isaac Thompson, wife and 9 children		

- - - - - -

SHIP: OHIO
TYPE: Steamer   FROM: San Diego, Calif.
ARRIVED: November 30, 1851   CAPT: Haley
PASSAGE: 5 days from San Diego, California, via San Pedro,
         California, Santa Barbara, California and Monterey,
         California. Arrived San Pedro on November 26,1851. Two
         days at San Pedro taking on cargo. Arrived Santa Barbara
         on November 26th and left next day. Arrived at Monterey
         on November 28th.
CARGO: Fruit (unidentified types).

Passengers

Prof.___Nooney	J. Myers	M. Selong
H. Racovelett	F. Bradley	G. East
William Fellows	J. Harding and	T. Paris and lady
Capt.___Trusell	family	G. Weaver
P. Sichell	P.M. Caldwell	Mr.___Lyons
L.T. Barton	(Coldwell?)	J. Steeve
A. Mattence	Martin Furst	Capt.___Dennison
Mr.___Adler	Capt.___Schmidt	C. Brethen
Mr.___Edes	(Schmitt?)	Col.___Cost
B. Hoffman	B. Smith	F. Crouse
J. McErey and lady		

- - - - - -

SHIP: CALIFORNIA
TYPE: Steamer   FROM: Panama
ARRIVED: December 3, 1851   CAPTAIN: R.L. Whiting
PASSAGE: 17 days, 11 hours (running time) from Panama, via
         Acapulco, Mexico, San Diego, California and Monterey,
         California. A total of 31 hours for detention at
         Acapulco, San Diego and Monterey. Following deaths took
         place during the passage:
         November 29,1851 - S.D. Corwin, a grocer, of Jersey
                    City, aged 23 years, buried at San Diego,
                    California, of fever.
         November 29,1851 - Amos Sawtell, a baker, of Boston,
                    Massachusetts, aged 42 years, buried at San
                    Diego, California. Leaves a wife and six
                    children at Boston.
CARGO: Mail.

Passengers

Capt. H.D. Hunter	Mrs. S.A. Pieane	Mrs. H. Sage
Mr.&Mrs. J.A. Eaton	(Picane?)	Henry B. Lafitte
C. Babcock	John A. Malone	B.G. Baldwin
Jules David, lady,	Mr. & Mrs. J. Warner	J. Howard
2 children and	Mr. & Mrs. J. Godfrey	C. Happer
2 servants	G. Welch	M.O. Keefe
Miss___David	A. Lyon	John Jones
N.P. Kingsley	D. Stevens	G.S. Geddes
N.H. Kingsley	J.C. Williams	D. Floyd
G. Gilley	James Davis	T.J. Pool

(Continued next page)

L. Olen	A. McKeeran	J.U. Stewart
J. Runbergher	J. Roberts	S. Bragg
M.H. Pattingill	H. Colby	L. Worthley
C.R. Baldwin	B. Richards	R. Perry
E. Grubble	S. Vine	D. Groom
H. Oliver	H. Schneider	J. Sims
Mrs. M.A. Stackpole	Mrs._____Thorn and	N.D. Fitzgerald
Mr.& Mrs._____Sedgewick	child	Judge_____Hall*
3 Misses Sedgewick	F. Champney	D. Prescott
T. Sedgewick Jr.	Charles Hall	Mrs._____Dean
J. Keilesberger	Mrs._____Bloomenthall	J. Aitken
(Kellesberger?)	F.S. Carter	A. Lockwood
Mrs._____Treall and	C.H. Tellen	Mrs.Rosina Zapf
3 children	R. Brewster	Mrs._____Butler
William Hopper	D. Sayre	R. Tront
J. Denninger	J. Linton	T. Crowley
T.A. Murphy	J. Oldfield	J.F. Hampson
J. Robinett	W. Prideaux	C.H. Woods
J.H. Carniff	Thomas Neal	J. Scobble
G. Butt	B.F. Clark	N. Scobble
A. Patten	F. Walker	A.W. Beal
O.P. Palmer	D.A. Gibbons	E. Tibbetts
J.C. Horne	J. Harvey	J. Friese
A. Vanige (Vanigo?)	William Huff /sic/	H. McFarland
E.P. Gerrothy	(Hupp?)	J.H. Tucker
L. Anderson	J.K. Hupp /sic/	W.S. Dennis
Mr.& Mrs._____Wagner	(Huff?)	Mrs. C. Miller
Mrs. E.M. Brierly	Mrs._____Stephenson and	F. Goodrich
R. French	children	C. Roe
G.B. Stillwell	E. Wheeler	W. Landry
J. Brenan	M. Freeman	P. McGray and son
W. Powderry	P. Freeman	Jones Taylor
C. Huttinger	H. Douglass	C. Norton
B. Fitzgerald	A.C. Austin	C. Cockrane
L. Smith	A. Waldron	H.C. Farwell
J.M. Flanders	D. Heims (Helms?)	C.L. Shephard
C.S. McAllister	S.M. Phelps	A. Koehler
B.P. Reed	C. Farnsham	Jacob White
J.E. Simons	P.G. Davis	P. Carroll
Arthur Boyle	P. Smith	A.B. Reed
N.T. Lowell	J. McCain	L. Davenport
A. Mason	B.S. Nichols	Paul Jones
J. Long Jr.	J. Williams	T.G. Church
Little	H.F. Macey	H.W. Rich
F. Churchill	H. Thomas	Mrs. J.A. Hamilton
Mr.& Mrs.W.H. Hall	H. Johnson	S.B. Ellsworth
J.W. Augustus	W.H. Duren	C. Jewett
W.J. Fullerton	N. Rogers	Mrs._____McKenzie and
S.B. Andrews	R. Rose	2 children
Mr.& Mrs._____Morgan	Mrs.Joseph Baldwin	Mr.& Mrs._____Jenkins
and 2 children	and daughter	and 6 children

(Continued next page)

(*)U.S. Land Commissioner for California. See "Notes" Section.

Mr.& Mrs___Snyder
George Martin
P. Leonard
J. Flack
E.W. Perris
S. Cogswell
F. Zinckard
J. Richardson
J.E. Smith
J. Ives
C.H. McCormick
R. Pascoe
G. Rowe
N.H. Skinner
H. Doane
J. Bentz
M. Piettas
M. Linden
M. Kimberly
J. Perry
I. Page
M. Hagner
J. Poor
J.W. Taylor
J.N. Ball
H. Polly
E. Pierson
J.W. Symes
J.W. Andrews
L. Way
William Brownrigge
J. Parker
H.D. Stewart
J. Pettingill
S. McKewan
J. Kesler (Kester?)
W. Morrison
G. Lumsden
J.W. Avery
H. Schlessinger

H.C. Sterling
William Hobart
J. Aspinwall
C. Freeman
G.B. Steward
G. Vanvalkenberg
A. Goldman
W. Batchelder
H.G. Pool
T. Lewis
H. Thorp
C. Tregent
Andrew Wyatt
James McDoald /sic/
   (McDonald?)
John McDonald /sic/
W. Leser
P. Schiel
J. Alton
J. Lander
I. Fletcher
D.C. Cogner
G.F. Brown/sic/
D.S. Miller
I. Achorn
W.D. Young
A. Condit
A.C. Baker
E.S. Spearin
J. Perkins
J. Smiley
J. Holt
Alex Booth
G. Waterman
S. Dailey
J. Gooch
A. Tyler
W. Buchanan
A. Buchanan
H.C. Carl

C. Adam
M. Norton
T. Saxton
J. Attwood
C. Brown
E.B. Warden
J. Paszet
J.G. Brown
J. Ayre
A. Dennis
J.D. Perkins
J.Z. Johnson
C.H. Simons
E. Lawson
C.D. Stewart
D. Eigenbradt
H. Zapf
C. Ferden
I. Frotsche
H. Townsend
I. Chadwick
I. Gould
C.S. Lindsley
O. Brown
S. Taylor
L. Way Jr.
H.B. Mattison
W. Wallace
J. Warner
J.H. Walron
G.F. Brown/sic/
J. Morse
William Labin
John Smith
E. Brownlee
R. Kennedy
W.R.P. Thomas
H. Brock
H. Eaton

- - - - - -

SHIP: VALPARAISO
TYPE: Ship   FROM: New York
ARRIVED: December 2, 1851   CAPTAIN: Kilham
PASSAGE: 160 days from New York. On June 29,1851 in lat. 33-40N,
         long. 45-13W saw the whaling brig "Ocean" from the
         Sandwich Islands.
CARGO: 133 boxes of pipes and tobacco, 3 boxes saddlery, 260 bales
       of hay, 100 bbls bread, 150 boxes of oysters, 500 bbls of
       cement, 16 cases hats, 369 casks liquor, 200 bbls of pork,
       95 firkins butter, 27 dozen shovels, 25 bellows and

assorted goods.

G.J.H. Ballard

Passengers

- - - - - -

J.V.O. Clark

SHIP: NEW ORLEANS
TYPE: Steamer
ARRIVED: December 2, 1851

FROM: Panama
CAPTAIN: J.W. Hammersly,
U.S.N.

PASSAGE: 18 days from Panama, via Acapulco, Mexico, 10 days.
In San Francisco, tied up at Law's Wharf(Clark's Point).
CARGO: Not listed.

Passengers

Mrs. ___ Porter and svt	Mrs. ___ Turner	W. Brown
D.V. Stoedman	___ Wilson and lady	Charles Chesebro
E.W. Goodrich	J. Norton	W. Fallay
James Arnold	E.A. Macks	George Adams
James W. Woods	W. Lawson	Mrs. ___ Phillips
Mrs. ___ Seal	Mrs. ___ Desmond and	Mrs. ___ Murphy
Hy Davis	4 children	E. Meredith and
Mrs. ___ Gould and child	Charles Adams and lady	lady
B. Roach	J.N. Turpien	B. Leob
David Richardson	G.S. Hubbard	N.G. McCormick
W. Matthews	Francis Chauncey	Charles Allard
Edward Rowe	James Smith	Peter McDonald
T.S. Bowers	T. Thompson	F. McManus
J. Arnold	Patrick Kelly	Henry Warren
W. Arnold	Patrick Keefe	R. Davis
John Arnold	John Connor	Thomas P. Fleming
J.C. Whipple	E. Waterman	A.E. Ubanks
Andrew Schollars	L. Fox	A. Howell
A.F. Goodell	F. Ward	O.C. Coffin
Mrs. ___ Bonligny & 4 children	Thomas Morris	J. Bradford
J.W. Perdue	F. Largness	Ann Zealter and 4 children
Benjamin Clark	L. Hyden /sic/	J. Hurnine
John Clark	Thomas Titus	C. Chapman
W. Jones	Richard Morris	F. Chapman
Thomas Baid	R. Castlebury	Henry Ward
Thomas Reed	J.W. Bowrig	John Wilson
J. Carter	W. Northrop	Frank Gell
John Low	J.G. Rogers	J. Nalis
J.H. Brayden	J.L. Rogers	James McCall
John Hyde /sic/	Robert Nash	W. Little
John Hyden /sic/	John Nash	John Hagans
H.W. Riley	J.W. Rantleti	J. Goal
L.I. Collins	N. Williams	V. Barker
D. Hawns	J.D. Nelson	Albert Guest
J.N. Young	R. McCaman /sic/	S. Rudy
	H. Green	J.P. Fleming
		S.G. Nelson

(Continued next page)

(*)One source lists as J.H. Ballard.

J.S. Now	C. Sargeant	P.P. Fox
Francis Darrell	J. Steward	J.P. Corran
A. Evans	J. Boukise (Bonkise?)	D. Cameron
J. Wilcox	W. Thompson	P. Lilly
D. Ryan	W. Delaney	M. Keenan
J. Ryan	M. Sennot	W. Garvey
James Roach	Thomas Foley	Thomas Hartney
John Donney	J. Img	(Hartsey?)
C. Bush	J. Lesham	Mr.___ Stanton
A.E. Horton	Edward Ward	Nathan Stanlky
Benjamin F. Lowell	Mr.___ Ledgely	(Staulky?)
Mr.___ Webster	E. Meands	J.L. Allen
Francis Hoege	Thomas Flanegan	Thomas Lynch
A. Peabody	George Hover	U. Banks /sic/
Mr.___ Bradbury	J.W. Perdem	J.W. Langley
John Haman	David F. Cotter	G.S. Barber
Thomas B. Belcher	Henry Sebert	C.F. Armstrong
L.S. Loane	H.C. Moiloy	John Dordon
E. Winslow	C.R. Waters	Alex Thompson
W.A. Lackey	A.G. Adams	N. Echub
W. Belgo	P. More and son	Jesse Mount
L. Smith	(Mere?)	J.W. Trebell
John Carr	J. Loveless	R. Lard
D. King	J.N. Fletcher	John Gregory
J. Robinson	A. Hull	J.P. Rogers
W. Stuart	C. Westbrook	B. Yancey
Edwin Roberts	Thomas Kinney	Jesse A. Mills
Perry Cannon	Reuben Boston	Edward Dempsey
John Riardon /sic/	Fred Shusteritch	Lucas Hallard
Francis Cotter	J.R. Huntington	Henry Burton
J. Moles	Allen Newhill	Alpheus Davis
H. Whitcomb	Z.E. Leonard	P.F. Flinn
E.J. Anderson	F. Connor	J.O. Neil /sic/
E. Hegley	P. Brenan /sic/	F. Fetine
H.M. Lawtell	F. Crowell	L.M. Daniels
John Anderson	W. Brown	J.L. Willis
J. Stuard	W. Pierce	W. Nations
M. Nooney	G. Golgomore	Coal Bruce
J. Ward	J. Baron	J. Bruce
C. School	I. Baron	J. Vallence
J. Bane	Joseph Baron	Francis Robertson
R. Cooper	R. Young	A. Tinier
W. Schoekley	J. Deen	M. Reep
R.S. Jenkins	W. Callahan	J. Ritter
W. Curry	M. Callahan	P. Clauson
James Nooman	P. McLaughlin	J. Lasthers
H. Hunter	J. Rice	E.W. Champlin
G. Tommichel	T. Boyce	E. Hughes
A. Tommichel	J. Carene	W. Henry
N.D. Whetman	J.Y. Adams	T. Gallagher
Mr.___ Walker	Lim McNamer	F. Farrell
A. Foode	P. Strafford	T. Hudson

(Continued next page)

H. Berry
Isaac O. Mace
Henry Hay, lady &
    2 children
J.T. Bowers and
    lady
J. Edetrall
Mrs.___Allen
J.L. Isaac, lady
    and servant
R. McCaman/sic/
E. Riley
Daniel Riley
Z. Smith
W. Smith
John Marten
James Pierce
James Mitchell
Richard Southey
H.D. Reed
N. Deane
T. Deane
J.L. Merriman
J.C. Tyler
B.A. Thomas
G. Billings
J. Muler
R. Landerer
___Rupert and lady
Robert Graham
J. Bucklayer
R. Thompson
T.J. Brooks
H.W. McVay
W. Anderson
Mary Nalis
F. Alexander
J.A. Merriman
James Adams
Zalous Miller
N.B. Reed
B.Y. Reed
Jeff Pierce
J.L. Beck
J.L. Fogg
B. Turner
G.W. Downs
E.B. Comstock

E. Berkrandle
Capt.___Havens
Mrs.___Canon /sic/
J. Bowls
Mrs.___Sedgeley
Mrs.___Horton
W.H. Hoage (Hooge?)
Miss___Hooge /sic/
G. Opperheimer
John Baptiste
John J. Nelson
S.D. Nelson
M. Rowe
B.B. Willing
T.M. Cain
J.H. Cain
G.W. Cain
Robert Nichols
Thomas Jeffrey
David Harris
John Hendrins/sic/*
C. Branton
J.B. Newman
G.H. Ide
Rufus Howell
G. Lord
C.A. Lord
Samuel Cash
___Perkins
R.S. Hutchinson
A. Mulliner
J. Stewart
S. Rudicil
F.A. Boring
James Scott
Lucy Carroll
James McKeon
W. Barnes
Edward Dallerson
Jacob Roper
L.A. Patterson
E.L. Patterson
M.B. Patterson
A. Schneider
O.C. Gay
J. Hamley
J. Thurston

E. Derham
Capt.___Beverley
Mrs.___Owens and
    daughter
Mrs.___Salisbee
Samuel Thomas
W.A. Godfrey
J.A. Godfrey
H. Beebe
Michael Conner and
    lady
G.M. Young
A. Custon
J.W. Hendrine/sic/*
T.H. Williams
T.M. Monroe
James Williams
James M. Steel
A.M. Mitchell
J.G. Mitchell
H. Benton
John Harris
P. Tomeipher
C. Williard
R. Arnold
W. Peel
L. Reed
J.W. Franks
C. Raleigh, lady
    & 2 children
J. Guston
P. Barber
Henry Nelson
W.J. Nelson
James Quin /sic/
    (Quinn?)
Jane Quin /sic/
    (Quinn?)
M. Cooper
W.T. Libbey
Thomas Coleman
___Beecher
___Bargess
    (Burgess?)
W. Parks
James Haight
J.C. Colby

- - - - - -

(*)Note similar surnames on John Hendrins and J.W.Hendrine.

SHIP: AMIGA
TYPE: Ship (British)   FROM: Valparaiso, Chile
ARRIVED: December 4, 1851   CAPTAIN: Edington
PASSAGE: 59 days from Valparaiso, Chile.
CARGO: 1000 (100 lb) bags of flour, 1993 (50 lb) bags of flour,
       500 kegs of powder, 2798 bags of barley, 30 casks of ale,
       12 bags cork, 4 cases pipes, 146 bags walnuts, 100 tons of
       coal, 1900 bags of beans.

Passengers

A.W. Lodge	Mrs. Amelia Presto and child	Mr. Munoz
		Miss Munoz and 2 svts

- - - - - -

SHIP: AUGUSTA
TYPE: Barque (British)   FROM: London, England
ARRIVED: December 5, 1851   CAPTAIN: Parsons
PASSAGE: 200 days from London, England, via Falkland Islands, 90
         days.
CARGO: 300 kegs and 1 cask paint colors, 100 jugs oil, 2 cases of
       cigars, 1 case pencils, 250 bricks, 16 circular castings,
       1 driving wheel, 4 iron arms, 1 steam boiler, 4 burch
       wheels, 1 spur wheel, 4 iron crush wheels, 5 iron shafts,
       1 fly wheel, 51 grate bars and bearers, 132 tons coal, beer,
       oats, barley, cordials, wine, corks and assorted goods.

Passengers

W. Raper	J. Samingo	R. Patterson
G. Tichet	F. Tiegen	J. Leabeck
C. Timpkin	S. Dade	W. Sibald
E. Guest	J.C. Dade	J. Stein and wife
J. Cable	T. Moss	J.C. Meech
Thomas Mungan	E. Bow	H. Tietgen
J.G. Davidson	Thomas Brown, wife and 3 children	

- - - - - -

SHIP: SPRAY
TYPE: Schooner   FROM: Bodega, Calif.
ARRIVED: December 5, 1851   CAPTAIN: Fipe
PASSAGE: 9 hours from Bodega, California.
CARGO: Potatoes.

Passengers

E. Crosby	S. Thompson	P. Wilson

- - - - - -

SHIP: LOO CHOO
TYPE: Schooner   FROM: Honolulu, S.I.
ARRIVED: December 6, 1851   CAPTAIN: Mason
PASSAGE: 15 days from Honolulu, Sandwich Islands. This vessel
         brings intelligence that the clipper ship "Flying Cloud"
         passed Honolulu on her way to China, on November 6, 1851.
CARGO: 45 casks of zinc, 1 cask and 1 box of unspecified merchan-

dise and 19 bales of unspecified merchandise.

Passengers

W.F. Allen   E. Hall

- - - - -

SHIP: PACIFIC
TYPE: Steamer   FROM: San Juan del Sur
ARRIVED: December 9, 1851   CAPTAIN: Nathaniel Jarvis
PASSAGE: 13 days from San Juan del Sur, Nicaragua. Stopped at
Acapulco, Mexico on November 30, 1851 (at 7:00PM). On
December 5th and 6th experienced heavy head winds from
the NW. On December 7th arrived at San Diego, California.
Underwent unusual difficulties in securing coal for the
passage to San Francisco. Twenty ladies and thirty
children were aboard. Just prior to departing from
San Diego word came aboard that the Indian chief
Antonio Garro, who was the principal instigator of the
outbreak against the whites in the Agua Caliente area,
had been captured by Juan Antonio, the chief of the
Wiscole, and carried to Los Angeles.
CARGO: Merchandise (unspecified).

Passengers

William S. Willis	Thomas J. Bartlett	Eynard Smith
Dr. F.W. Hatch and	Mrs. C.F. Hutchinson	H. Richardson
2 svts	& 3 children	E. Leach
J. Hall	Mrs. D. Williams	A.O. Garrett and
E. Smith	Thomas O. Dunn	son
Mrs. J.R. Crandall	James Robinson	Mrs.___ Garrett and
and daughter	Mrs. F. Moore (P.	daughter
E. Hamilton, wife	Moore ?) and son	P.A. Haven
and 4 children	Mrs. D. Weston and	John H. Grover
Mrs.___ King, 3	children	Mrs. J.C. Young
chldrn & svt	Mrs. Henry Gratlel	Mrs. W.F. Hyde and
James Pratt	(Gratiel?,Gratlei?)	child
George Hardy, wife	Zerilda Reed	Miss Lucy White
& 3 chldrn	Miss Emily Gobbins	Mrs. Martha F. Gobbins
Dr.___ Hopper	Rebecca Gobbins	Mrs.____ Thing
S. Anderson	Mrs. E. Whally	J. Ash
J.P. Sloan	Mrs. L. Stevenson	Samuel Conding and
J. Serensky	J.M. Jordon	wife (Condruff?)
W.H. Hubbs	James L. Groves,	A.P. Moore
Abraham Emanuel	wife & 2 chldrn	John S. Phillips
Miss Sarah J. Pratt	D. Radly	Miss ___ Swetts
D.A. Arnold	John Irwin	Alex Scott and boy
Emery Hawks	Silas Williams	Henry P. Wingate
P.L. Chansley	B.P. Manly	William F. Hyde
H.R. Marks	James Tenno (Tenso?)	Uriah F. Moulton
E. Thorp	John D. Brown	A. Baker and wife
E.K. Elend and wife	E.T. Keyser and	A.M. Humphreys?
(Elred?)	wife /sic/*	(A.N. Humphreys?)
W.B. West	H. Sholes	Robert Johnson

(Continued next page)

(*)Note R.Keysen, A. Keysen and W.Keysen Jr, page 33.

J. Roan
J. Schroder
M. Nelson
Theodore Hyde
Eugene Hyde
A.B. Mareton
F.A. Worrell
W. Anderson
I.C. Wade
J. Mahoney
William Hi?1
   (Hill?)‾
B.F. Hucsey
B. Mayter
R.W. Wilson
D. Berry
N.M. Berry
Allen Martin
L. Norton
J. Williams Jr.
I.C. Parker
J.M. Hawkins
G.F. Gale
T. Small
Mr.___Bates
J.S. Hawley
T. Lyon
P. Reefer
H. Reefer
P. Johnson
O.C. Garden
A. Foster
A. Morrell
H. Morrell
G.B. Shaw
H. Bohanan
B.W. Lowell
A. Stevens
N.P. Read
W. Carpenter
F.N. Whitney
D.A. Coburn
F. Coyden
H.C. Barnum
G. Gorham
E. Caswell
J. White
D.W. Williams
P. Campbell
D. Hunter
T. Gallagher

E. Ide
H. Wheeler
T.S. McLellan
A.G. Carver
A.S. Carver
N. M? ? reton
A.C. ‾Riel
T. McCally?
   (McCully?)
M. Sullivan
J. McKinney
J. Gillenwater
William Waugh
W.C. Staples
W. French
J.H. Phinney
H. Mix
M. Mix
W.W. Whipple
H.C. Shorey
C.B. Ramsey
E. Clark
W.P. Michner
D.B. Lowell
L. Farren
W. Smith
I.E. Weeks
J.G. Fox
C. Martin
T. McConnell
B. Hilton
S. Davis
R. Davis
L.D. Davis
E.S. Glidden
O. Davis
W. Murch
B. Adams
J.D. Codding
A.L. Clark
M.B. Chauncey
J.B. Knight
J.R. Hale
E.B. Smith
H. McKelvey
C.M. Harris
A. Rigney
M.C. Witzler
J.H. Belding
G. Smith
J.S. Joselyn

J.J. Perkins
I. Limerick
J. Davilbies?
   (Davilbias?)
C. McFalon
N.J. Blackwood
J. Scovera
A. Forsyth
C. Crapp
J. Coursey
I. Bonham
William Lawler
H.B. Follett
E. Jewett
J. Shute
G. Hill
H. Shattuck
F.S. Narr
J. Ryan
J. Edwards
E.E. Edwards
L. Gab
J.B. Clark
W. Joy
E. Piedman
L.C. Perry
C.B. Jackson
E.B. Jackson
C. McDermott
J.F. Hamilton
B. Miller
A.H. Lang
C.C. Brown
G. Dyer
J. Godfrey
E. Godfrey
D.H. Robinson
G.B. Thomas
W. Bryant
B. Mowatt
W. Kerr
F.A. Patterson
W.H. Adams
W. Danby
E. Thompson
R. McClay
R. Keysen/sic/*
A. Keysen/sic/*
W. Keysen Jr./sic/*
H. Taylor
W. Hunter

(Continued next page)
(*)Note E.T. Keyser and wife, page 32.

G.A. Woodman   G.F. Grover   G.A. Neal
Capt. D.S. Docham   C. McLeod   H.O. Conroy

- - - - - -

SHIP: ANNA E. MAINE
TYPE: Brig   FROM: Oregon Territory
ARRIVED: December 9, 1851   CAPTAIN: Bogers /sic/
PASSAGE: 10 days from the Oregon Territory. Experienced a heavy
      gale from the NW in latitude 41, split sails, lost boat
      and sustained other damage.
CARGO: 40 tons of potatoes, 25 M ft of lumber, 20 tons of flour,
      300 fowls and 250 kegs.

Passengers

G.W. Adair   G.W. Bowie   J. Howe
J.M. Fordice   P. Keepart   C. Sieman

- - - - - -

SHIP: COL. FREMONT
TYPE: Brig   FROM: San Pedro, Calif.
ARRIVED: December 11, 1851   CAPTAIN: Nason
PASSAGE: 7 days from San Pedro, California. A passenger on
      board, Colonel ___ Ferrell (Ferrill?), Collector for the
      Port of San Diego, California, is the bearer of dispatches
      to Gov. ___ McDougal from General ___ Bean. Dispatches
      concern an Indian uprising in the Southern portion of the
      State of California. Residents were without guns to
      conduct an effective war upon the hostile tribes that
      were devasting the countryside. Local residents were
      attempting to mount an offensive strike.
CARGO: 400 packages of fruit, 20,000 lbs of onions and a quantity
      of barley (unspecified amount).

Passengers

J. Eaton   Judge ___ Witherby   *Col. ___ Ferrill/sic/
T. Gamblin   J. Burnett   A.G. Maynard
C. Justis   J.D. Gewell   Mr. ___ Roberts
D. Pate   Mr. ___ Roberts Jr.

    (*) One source lists as "Colonel Ferrell"

- - - - - -

SHIP: CAROLINA
TYPE: Steamer   FROM: Panama
ARRIVED: December 12, 1851   CAPTAIN: Dall
PASSAGE: 27 days from Panama. Experienced heavy gales during the
      trip. The Isthmus is quite lively by the presence of
      several hundred Americans, waiting passage to California.
      Left Panama on November 15, 1851 at 11:00PM with passen-
      gers and freight. Arrived Acapulco, Mexico at noon, Novem-
      ber 25th. Departed Acapulco on November 27th. On Novem-
      ber 29th, a passenger, David Jones, died of dysentery.
      Arrived San Blas, Mexico on November 30th. Arrived at
      Mazatlan, Mexico on December 1st and departed on December
      2, 1851. On the night of December 3rd, a passenger,

John Boynes, a native of England, died of Isthmus Fever.
On December 6, 1851, Eugene Barnard Casteron, a native of
France, died of the same fever. Arrived at San Diego,
California on December 9, 1851; left for San Francisco at
8:00AM on December 10, 1851.

CARGO: Freight (unspecified types).

Passengers

H. Laffitte	Mrs.___Robinson and	W.J. Fullerton
Mrs.___Morton	3 boys	M. Rodgers Jr.
Mrs.___Turner	Antonio Darmoino	J.C. May
A.S. Mitchell	Mme___Darmoino	J. Burnham
Mrs.___Mitchell	M. Bride?(McBride?)	___Hathaway
Master___Mitchell	___Marble	___Allen
___Pettia	___Wheaton	___Slate
___Chase	___Dyton	___Greenworth
___Lincoln	___Luther	H. Betty (sic)
J. Frisbee	W. Thompson	(Beatty?)
J.T. Hampton	M. Kennison	J.H. Beatty (sic)
M. Farlin	K. Levenson	E. Ellessen
K. Brynoldson	O. Levenson	P.L. Barry
L. Anderson	O. Alson	A.C. Craddock
J. Sherman	J.J. Barton	B. Triste
E.S. Warner	J.W. Adams	John Buckley
Mrs.___Turner's	Antonio Caramryer/sic/	Miss B. Loux
servant	C. Hall	J.W. Dean/sic/
Miss E. Sheffield	A. Van Ryper	A.C. Hammond
J. Duchest	___Thurston	___Hambly
___Hathaway	___Helving	W.H. Hambly
___Clark	___Davis	___Marble (sic)
___Decardon	___Silver	___Robinson
___Greydon	J.B. Bowers	J.W. Marble
H. Greenfel	S. Boynes	C. Mason
J.A. Gwinn	P. Lowern	J. Fambath
D. Back	J. Wright	J. Hynton
M. Kettudge	J.C. Jordan	D. Jones
W. Williams	J. Richards	J. Thomas
N. Allen	J.W. Farrington	J. Louw??
A.B. Ames	M. Farrington	John Southard
D.H. Odway	A.W. Billings	M. Beach
R.D. Marlett	H. Byem	H. Beach
J. Beach	C. Lickwood	___Longjo
J.M. Williams	J.L. Church	J. Smith
T. Lewis	William Browning	J.H. Walton
C.H. Hollister	___Cogswell	J.F. Ryen (sic)
L.H. Robinson	C.M. Cogswell	(Ryan?)
R. Barker (sic)	R.P. Cogswell	A. Gould
O. Parker (sic)	J.W. Dean/sic/	C. White
J. Broely	E. Perkins	D. Edwards
A. Morgan	R.C. March	A. Little
A.W. Rowenn	A.L. Lyon	A.P. Wilcox
A. Murbin	J. Bombers	A. Dunnsmore

(Continued next page)

A. Goodwin
J. Sargeson
J.C. Sprague
____Van Ryper
____Clark
____Rolle(?)
____(Rollo?)
A.F. Marlin
____Tenckler
____Fish
G. Richards
P. Mix
N. Bishop
P. Smith
____Myers
L.J. Coggswell (sic)
O. Cogswell (sic)
F.M. Mamera
W. Walker
R. Buckingham
E. Whittier
____Shiesta
Jean Batiste
H. Percy
E. Durfee
Samuel Cogswell (sic)
Eben Thomas
M. Brosett
____McGasaworthy
E.E. Wheaton
J.J. Wheaton
Eliza Fox
S. McGill
A. Ellis
H. Elias
Mr.____Dowly
D. Andrews
Joseph Silver
Joseph Roe
John Jones
Peter Lynn
Peter Peterson
B. Doily
J. Armstrong

D. Brunton (sic)
J. Smith
J. Bunton (sic)
Capt.____Reynolds
____Burden
____Reynolds
____Cowey
M. Temple
____Riodd
D. Redner
W.H. Harrington
A. Hussey
M.M. Pheters (sic)
G. Buffam
____Preters (sic)
N. Rutherford
J. Rutherford
S. Rutherford
M. Hunt
T. Tucker
H.M. Paschal and
____lady
N. Garcia
J.T. Marsh
R.W. Bennett
D.D. Farr
Joseph Burton
J.S. Maslett
Thomas Martin
James Fielding
A. Mastereon (sic)
F. Blaney
T. McGrath
W. Mussell
F. Souling
A. Francis
H. Lockford
H. Antone
F. Antone
William Howe
A. Peterson
E. L. Shields
J. Malone

S. Dunnsmore
J. Burrell
____Phelps
Thomas S. Lyons
A. Elie
____Wial
____Wa?ten
____(Warten?)
____Thompson
N.C. Farrington
P. Winall
P.L. Goodwin
G. Hubbard
J.W. Atwell
J. Dunn
John Dunn
H. Maby (?)
____(Mahy?)
J.C. Marsh
C. Weston
W.H. Potter and
____lady
Antonio Pinosa
H. Vegora
Thomas McGuire
Benjamin Boyer
Mr.____Greenar
P.L.A. Stolp
E. Thomas
J. Bryody
C. McLoughlin
W. Boyd, wife and
____5 children
R. Smericker (sic)
Mr.____Dericker (sic)
J. Williams
Benjamin Halsey
C. Smate
F. Goulet
Bryan O'Loughlin
John Hansen
J.B. White
E. Odd

- - - - -

SHIP: COLUMBIA
TYPE: Steamer   FROM: Astoria, O.T.
ARRIVED: December 12, 1851   CAPTAIN: LeRoy
PASSAGE: 70 hours from Astoria, Oregon Territory. This vessel
         brings intelligence that the Indians are quiet, with the
         exception of difficulties at Port Orford, O.T. where

Companies "A" and "E", 1st Dragoons (U.S. Army) (Dismounted) engaged the Indians. The encounter took place a few miles from the Fork of the Coquille River. Lt. George Stoneman led Company "A" and Lt. Thomas Wright was at the head of Company "E". On board this vessel are 119 U.S. troops taken on board at Port Orford.

CARGO: Not listed.

Passengers

Gov.____Ogden	Thomas Wygaut(?)	F.S. Webster
W. Pomeroy	(Wygent?)	M. Simonds
O. Winter	J.B. Smith	William Drury
Thom. Pritchard	Alonzo Leland	E. Reed
James Taylor	John S. Hill	John Jones
M. Clifton	James Mason	Thomas S. Gillihan
J.O. Lufain	J.M. Kirkpatrick	Thaxter True
Lewis Castoff	John O'Brien	E. McQuesteru
J.C. Henderson	James Elliot	John McQuesteru
J.F. Bagden	W.H. Stapleton	H. Spann
W.R. Foster	James M. Lee	W.N. Carle
Nathan Barker	John Franklin	Sam Seabolt
H. Pruit	Joseph Moore	E. Miller
	and 119 U.S. Troops	

- - - - - -

SHIP: QUADRATUS
TYPE: Schooner   FROM: Oregon Territory
ARRIVED: December 13, 1851   CAPTAIN: Means
PASSAGE: 16 days from Oregon Territory. On December 1, 1851, in lat. 44-42N, experienced a severe series of gales of wind. Split mainsail and squaresail.
CARGO: 2620 bags of potatoes, 44 kegs of sourcrout, 40 bushels of beets, 27 M ft lumber, 4 bbls of salmon and 2 bbls of cranberries.

Passengers

Mr.____Murphy	Mr. S. Roberts	Mr. D. Lathrop
Mr. E. Trask		

- - - - - -

SHIP: TENNESSEE
TYPE: Steamer   FROM: Panama
ARRIVED: December 14, 1851   CAPTAIN: G.M. Totten(U.S.N.)
PASSAGE: 15 days from Panama, via intermediate ports. Running time was 13 days, 11 hours. Left Taboga on November 28th, arrived at Acapulco, Mexico on December 5th. Left Acapulco on December 6th and arrived at San Diego, California on December 11th. Left San Diego on December 12th and arrived at Monterey, California on December 13th. Departed Montery on same day, at 2:00PM. Made the heads of San Francisco harbor, but was detained until daylight by fog. Among the passengers are Judge G.C. Cooley, of Boston, the U.S. Attorney to the Land Commissioners, and Samuel W. Comstock, Vice President of the Pacific Mail

Steamship Company. Mr. Comstock was, in some measure,
recovering from a sickness contracted at Panama. A number
of passengers on board the "Tennessee" had been ill during
the passage. A purse of $200 was collected and given to
the ship's Surgeon, Dr. Alex McNaughton, in recognition of
his medical services.

CARGO: Not listed.

Passengers

Samuel W. Comstock	J.C. Olmstead	Mrs.___ Ham and
W.E. Keyes	Mrs.___ Olmstead	child
Mrs.___ Keyes and	Mrs.___ Krah and	Mr.___ Skinner
child	5 daughters	Miss___ Shirley
W. Baker	S. Peck	J.M. Hood
Mrs.___ Bourne/sic/	Mr. J. Bourne/sic/	E.B. Hood
L. Goldsmith	Mr.___ Travis	G. Williams
G. Canfield	Mrs.___ Daniels	H. Russell
Miss___ McVigar	Rosa Teft	T. Seabury
B. Wood	Mrs.___ Carman	G.W. Letter
J. Nesbitt	H. McCormick	J. Hagar
Mrs.___ Nesbitt	Mrs.___ Vanhorn	Mrs.___ Hagar
Dr.___ Parrott	Mrs.___ Crane and	H. Greene
Mrs.___ Neville	3 children	G. Blackwell
Mrs.___ Bigger	Mrs.___ Nation	W. Queen
Mrs.___ Russell	R.D. Thayer	L.C. Flanders
A. Durand	Mrs.___ Olivia	E. Fisher
A. Johnson	Mr.___ Anderson	Ellen Crowly
Mrs.___ Wood	G. Gordon	William Clark
Mrs.___ Chesley	Mrs.___ Reynes	Mrs.___ Clark and
J.F. Stewart	E.R. Clark	child
M. Rossin	L. Johns	Judge G.C. Cooley
J. Sterns	H. Johns	Mrs.___ Mane and
Mrs.___ Flanders	Mr.___ Woodbridge	child
and 4 children	Mrs.___ Woodbridge and	H. Brown
J.A. Brown	3 children	Miss___ Letcher
V. Rice	J. Simpson	Mrs.___ Anderson
Capt.___ Drew	J. Chapin	Mrs.___ Brown
O. Loucks	O. Wheeler	T. Campbell
G.P. Loucks	J.W. Owens	Mrs.___ Campbell
J.A. Woolf /sic/	O. Bowne	L. Carman
(Woolfe?)	J.N. Hagar	S. Carman
E. Woolfe /sic/	W. Hoffman	W. Estabrooks
(Woolf?)	J. Hall	J. Neustadt
A. Henrichs	John Campbell	G. Graster
Mrs.___ Brown	J. Campbell	T. Russell
A. Nelson	J. Doyle	Mr.___ Bigger
A. Rivas	A. Morrison	E.I. Rorve
N. Lamson	D.A. Rice	W. Littlebridge/sic/
H.N. Moore	D.W. Barnes	S.S. Chipman
S. Woodbridge	K.H. Dimmick	I. Martin
T.F. Nade	P.W. Willett	Mrs.___ Martin
J. Maggrow	A.K. Sterne	A. Dennis

(Continued next page)

H. Ruble(?)
(Rubie?)
Mrs.___Nelson
E.M. Ford
A. Ketcham
J. Gurter
M. Kunsey(?)
(Kuasey?)
H. Stone
P. Huntly
A. Coburn
A. Niles
J. Fleckey
T. Lawhaff
S. Strellini
R. Jenkins
J.L. Chase
M. Knight
J. Lord
K.P. Knapp
Thomas Herrick
Antonio Flores
Mrs.___Flores
M. Myers
D. Forbes
S. Smith
J.M. Gleason
F.A. Dexter
F. Lewis
G. Russell
George McGee
A. Skeels
R. Dunn
J. Costello
J. Reed
S. Damon
J. Titcomb
J. Cogswell
B. Hathaway
J. Neville
A. Wilson
J. Doolittle
N. Gurney
A. Denby
J. Banner
J. Alpy
L. Chichester
H. Ulrich
James White
J.B. Nutting
E. Ferguson

Mr.___Clifton
C. Sullivan
J. Pugh
G. Fossett
J. Hobard
J. Deans
O. Jones
J. Leme
D. Whiting
D. Thompson
S. Williams
D. Torey
L. Emory
J. Gallega
J. Russell
W. McQueston
B. Blake
M. Kennett
J. Hathaway
John Hartman
William Rose
L.O. Hurlbut
J.A. Hyde
S. Hall
H. Rownsville
T. Molineaux
H. Falconer
C. Hervey
H. Emory
A. Hastings
C. Tallman
J. O'Neil
C.L. Carey
W. Mason
___Freeland
J. Crowell
W. Clark
P. Ferguson
D. Jones
___Torvus
W. Williams
R. Nordon
C.F. Payne
A. Frey
I. Beach
L. Beach
S.A. Conig
F.S. Roe
J.C. Davis
A. Myers
(Continued next page)

G. Villiers
Mrs.___Campbell
E. Young
D. Morris
J. Haskins
I. Southwick
R. Hughes
R. Evans
M. Houghton
C. Rogers
W. Story
J. Borey
J. Kennedy
L. Antonia
L. Pallezo
J. Taplin
J. Bigelow
D. Barber
W. Richardson
J.H. Hannan
William Masten
John Lafitte
A. Hammond
J.S. Morris
R. Parker
T. Bidwell
R. Johnston
William Styles
J. Knight
J. Stripple
J. Drew
J. Weisendack
W. McCormick
J.F. Birch
T. Wheeler
J. Ireland
M. Miller
J.W. Balis(?)
(Balia?,
Balin?)
___Barber
J. Holbrook
J. Shaw
K. Tirell
J. Frazier
F. Bowen
J. Pottle
A. Garabaldi
H. Hutton
J.C. Priest
G. Pass

J. Pass
H. Hathaway
G. Nichols
W. Divers
B. Butler
A. Joseph
J. Allman
J. Cilley
C.A. Lane
S. Connor
J. Napple
A. Brown
N.J. Winthrop
T. Winthrop
N. Winthrop
C.M. Prescott
A.J. Day
J. Tennent
R. Francis
H. Andrews
T. Daly
J.H. Fuller
A. Johnson
H. Knowles
H.J. Tanner
J. Smart
R. Semault
J. McKew
A. Yokurm
C. Robertail
C. Stewart
D. Leavitt
J. Barton
M. Francis
James George
J.M. Owen
J. Weller
G. Bellamy
J. McDonnell
P. Carris
W. Davis
A. Armstrong
W. Johnsone/sic/
W. Haddock
F. Ashton
N. Whitesell
A. Simpson
C. Lyon
S.G. Blake
S. Brown
J. Brown

J. Durkitt
H. Human
G. Schaffer
D. Ingram
G. Corwin
W. Scurcy(?)
  (Seurcy?)
C. Matthewson
R. Varney
M. Rowsack
Ol. Allen
W. Carvath /sic/
T. Carth /sic/
E. Crocker
R. Phillbuck
J.L. Smith
J. Phillips
J.S. Smith
C. Wells
G.G. Lowell
F.W. Wyck
G. Page
J.C. Green
J. Human
J. Hazard
R. Prince
F. Boucher(?)
  (Boncher?)
A. Dominga
P. Myers
James Cotton
H. Young
William Hunter
H. Manning
D. Bancher
R. Raymond
A. Stanton
J. Pardie
T. Winsloo /sic/
J. Pease
A.J. Smith
W. Newcombe
O.S. Dixon(?)
  (D.S. Dixon?)
R. Ruble(?)
  (Rubie?)
R. Hudson
F. Schultz
A. Stevens
M. Rose
J.M. Bagley
(Continued next page)

J. Priest
A. Bryant
J. Myers
J. Duckett
J.C. Brown
W. Wiley
D. Hart
D. Clough
W. Thompson
D. Thompson
J. Whitley
S. Slavoskey
Mrs._____Slavoskey
T. Walter
H. Ferguson
H.M. Drum
P.J. Drum
H. Johnson
W. Tinkham
S. Davis
B.A. Mosler
Mrs._____Smith and
  child
W. Littlebridge/sic/
H. Booth
R.S. Kane
Native John
D.A. Chesebro
R.D. Chesebro
James Kent
S. Taylor
C. Blethen
J. Bandry
C. Wetherill
C. Wellbrick
J. Nubie
R. Morey
N. Hulbert
W. Carlis
W. Denman
J. Mitchell
J. Lagne (?)
  (Lague?)
S.B. Lock
J. Read
J. McDonogh
E. Backer
A. Maddison /sic/
J.J. White
D.C. Ives
J.W. Downer

W. Saunders	J.C. Palmer	L.A. Davis
S.W. Crockett	J. Palmer	P. Brown
I. Schawe (?)	J.W. Kelly	Sally Brown
(Schawa?)	J. Deming	Sarah Brown
C. Alexander	G. Stevens	W. Rich
M. Corwin	W. Stevens	T. Rich
W.P. Miller	B.F. Baker	C. Rich
W.K. Barne	T. Berford	N. Wofford
W. Pearson	J. Riley	H. Whitner
G. McCloskey (?)	C. Peck	G. Ellis
(McCloakey?)	G. Riley	J.W. Dow
E. Reede	R. Fayle	P. Ryer
J. Tutara	J. Stevenson	M. Mosler
L.G. Lowe	T. Watson	G.R. Edwards
J.D. Bragg	I. Hathaway	J. Spinner
W.C. Dunlapp /sic/	J. Cherry	M. Winsloo /sic/
J. Harvey	M. Higbaum	H. Winsloo /sic/
J. Shaw	A. Roose /sic/	J. Starks
H. Shaw	W. Doughty	M. Crawford
J. Trimby	C. March	W. Farmer
H. Lafevre	C. Hunter	J. Bickford
J. Lafevre	P. Coleman	J. Skinner
E.M. Wood	J. Whitehead	A.L. Crane
W. Palmer	L. Mallen	L. Hathaway
J. Waite	P. Kenyon	J. Ad____
J. Merriman	J. True	M. Fadden
N. Merriman	T. Read	N. Parsons
A. Turner	S. Freeman	F. Flibburn
E. Turner	C. Freeman	J. Bridgman
J. Hurzey	F. Freeman	A. Bridgman
C. Bicknell (?)	W. Williams	L. Lock
(Ricknell?)	J. Dougherty	J. Stevens
H. Cox	J. Bonton /sic/	W. Parmentier
A. Egan	R. Lewis	D. Culver
W. W?ese (Wrese?)	J. Bonton /sic/	R. Banks
J. Crowley	R. Cornell	F. Murphy (?)
Z. Winson	C. White	(P. Murphy?)
S. Jones	J. Tript	C. Hencox /sic/
C. Henderson	A. Cleveland	R. Bastin
J.F. Hess	J. Reede	C.W. Fhigge
J. Kinnson	J. Mack	

- - - - - -

SHIP: SEA BIRD
TYPE: Steamer   FROM: San Diego, Calif.
ARRIVED: December 17, 1851   CAPTAIN: Robert Haley
PASSAGE: 4 days from San Diego, California, via intermediate
         ports, and 8 hours, 20 minutes from Monterey, California.
         Fine weather on trip up the coast. This vessel brings
         intelligence that the Southern California Indian upris-
         ings have been suppressed, but it is feared the peace is
         only temporary. The Indian Chief Antonio Garra(sic) is

to be tried by civil authorities.
CARGO: Not listed.

Passengers

Major___Fitzgerald	T.K. Holt	P. Poneca
A. Delanotte	T. Orchard and	W. Judart
J. Lanfrance	family	H. Bowman
___Lyman	Hon. A.F. Hinchman	Dr. J.B. Shaw
N.A. Den	Col.___Powell	___Reed
E. Ditman	W.J. Tarr	S. Unda
J.M. Brady	F. Gasteri	A. Donzelle
___Levey	___Blackey	J. Myers
___Terehage	J.P. Leese, Esq.	Hon. P.A. Roach
Mrs.___Eagan and	Dr.___Randall	Dr.___Blankman
son		

- - - - - -

SHIP: EMPIRE
TYPE: Schooner   FROM: Santa Cruz, Calif.
ARRIVED: December 17, 1851   CAPTAIN: Brown
PASSAGE: 48 hours from Santa Cruz, California.
CARGO: 40 tons of potatoes.

Passengers

Major___McQuinn	H. Balcroft and	___Cobb
C. Alder	lady	J. Elder
___Olmstead		

- - - - - -

SHIP: JULIETTE*
TYPE: Schooner   FROM: Oregon Territory
ARRIVED: December 17, 1851   CAPTAIN: Collins
PASSAGE: 7 days from the Oregon Territory. Experienced light
         breezes and calms the whole passage.
CARGO: 35 tons potatoes, 5 tons and 153 sacks onions, 624 quarter
       sacks of flour, 65 bbls flour, 30 bags oats, 10 bbls of
       cement, 300 lbs butter, 400 fowls, 65 bbls salmon, 30 boxes
       of tin and 150 hogs.

Passengers

A.C. Hill	R. Van Duzen	L. Mitchell
Capt.___Nye		

- - - - - -

SHIP: TRAVELLER (also listed as "TRAVELER")
TYPE: Schooner   FROM: Bodega, Calif.
ARRIVED: December 17, 1851   CAPTAIN: McIntosh
PASSAGE: 36 hours from Bodega, California.
CARGO: 1500 heads of cabbage, 6 sheep, 5 tons onions and 50 tons
       of potatoes.

Passengers

Mr.& Mrs.___Miller	___Sinclair	___Stevens

- - - - - -

(*)Vessel sometimes listed as the "JULIET".

SHIP: COLUMBUS
TYPE: Steamer   FROM: Panama
ARRIVED: December 18, 1851   CAPTAIN: Isham
PASSAGE: 21 days from Panama, via intermediate ports. Left Panama
on November 26, 1851 and arrived in Acapulco, Mexico on
December 5th. Coaled and watered in Acapulco and left
26 hours after arriving. Arrived in San Diego, California
on December 15th and took on board coal, water and mail,
sailing 10 hours after arrival. There was some fever on
board during the passage.
CARGO: Not listed.

Passengers

Mrs.____Goodale	S. Fletcher	Mrs.____Keterell
W. Reynolds	A. Sink and lady	J.R. Keterell
Mrs.____Loyd and	J. Thompson and	G. Bond
child /sic/	lady	J. Hall, lady and
(Lloyd?)	N. David	2 children
Mrs.____Foreman and	Mrs.____Wilson	John Miller
child	C.M. Prescott	Mrs.____White
O.A. Pierce	William Patrick	William Frey
Stephen Hogg	E.W. Coburn	W. Henderson and
A. Wood	S. McClure	3 boys
C.E. Tiller	J. McNaughton	J. Phips /sic/
Mrs.____Kearn	Mrs.____Carey and	J. Kradee
Dexter A. Davis	child	A.B. Clifford
H. Cunningham	A. Gall	Samuel Adley
D. Foreman	William Gates	Eben Morrell
C. Foreman	R.E. Ludlow	J.L. Lane
A. Cowen	B.G. Ferguson	F. Dacutt
J.R. Gifford	A. Julian	F. Jackson and
F. Sylvester	Mary Ann Graham	son
A. Thompson	J. Stanley	G.H. Whetson
John Peacock	W.H. Harrison	F. Chapiu /sic/
W. Wright	J. Miller	(Chapin?)
Mrs.____Coburn	Mrs.____Henderson	J.W. Cares (?)
N. Torrey	L. Kearn	(Carea?,
Mrs.____Polets and	J.Y. Smith	Caren?)
child	W.R. Kinney	H. Crown
____Ludwick	C.C. Colven	J.J. Tunis
Mrs.____Kinney	S. Trebord	Mrs.____Jerwick (?)
John Dexter	J.D. Bard	(Jarwick?)
William Foreman	R. Edwards	E. Morrell
G.C. Dunn	L. Hallock	J. Dolwell
H. Colby	S. Alphaugh	R. Wilcox
J. McDowell	John Kennedy	Mrs.____Dhontt
Jonas Polets	C. Bolesley	J.F. Fisher
J. Kennedy	J. Millery	W. Cobby
G. Caliorda	B.F. Trotten	D.O. Yate /sic/
D.O. Sullivan	D.M. Rennan (?)	W. Loyd /sic/
J. Foster	W. Midgely	O. Gifford
J. Alota	____Eddy	____Freeman

(Continued next page)

B.F. Mace
P.O. Connor
M. McNeil
G. Oreto
  Tulis
G. Perano/sic/
L. Coleman
  Smith
A.O. Porter
  Saunders
F.Ghere
G. Caninello
  Jackson
A. Farnum
  Thorum/sic/
A. Crownly
G. Calliordo /sic/
  Brown
H. Farnum
D.O. Connor
M. Larkey
J. Hughes
William Fay
G. Perano/sic/
  Hardy
A. Garoni
H.H. Lewis
  Carr
A. Tarre
A. St.John
John Hill
J. Pack
H. Powers
J. Dooley
  Hardy and
  2 children
M. Green
S. Austin
M.H. Fuller
J.B. Ayres
J. Puller /sic/
  (Fuller?)
H. Miller
  Bartlett
R. Baldey
J. Fetterplace
H.D. Rodgers
W.H?pping
H.C. Rose
J.B. Catshaw
F. Hose (?)(Hoss?)

A. Caliorda
  Fisher
B.F. Fenley
C. Cannora
  Rouse/sic/
F.M. Kelley
J. Blade
  Boile and
  lady
  Thompson
  Kenna
M. Hannor
  Batchelder
G. Mortall
S. Pierce
  Hunt
J. Carr
G. Castano
J.W. Newcomb
H. Sherman
G. Garribaldi
  Randall
R.C. Philbrick
G. Nicolini
  Laraid
F. Grinna
H.M. Pike
  Goodwin
G.W. Nurelco (?)
  (Nurelee?,
  Nurelec?)
T. Roach
A. Hance, lady
  & 2 children /sic/
William O. Donnell
J. Lockwood
C. Philips
W.P. Douglas
G. Solaire
A. Garrison
A.H. Wilkie
J. Page
F. Margaratello
  Rouse /sic/
J.N. Davis
J. Massett
A. Harcy
John O'Neil
J. Opps
A. Naitrus, lady
  & 3 children
(Continued next page)

S. Fanning
  Terrell
H. Fenister/sic/*
D. Hellingia
  Kennan
W.M. Modria
J. Goard
P. Perbore
S. Ferguson
S.G. Smith
R. Beach
L. Mussell (?)
  (Munsell?)
S.R. Chandler
G. Harkness
  Withan
P. Hughes
J. Rodgers
G. Larezola
  Onicho
S. Flood
G. Madison
  Getchell
J. Howe
  Tucker
M. McCormick
J. Jackson
Aug. Parron
  Thorum/sic/
  Davis
C.F. Cooke
A.B. Davis
B. Tansey (?)
  (Tansey?,
  Tanrey?)
J. Cormick
J. Flint
A. Sturgis
J. Tate
J. Molinel (?)
  (Mollinel?)
G. Seaton
William Dance /sic/
R. Dance /sic/
J. Carter
P. Joice
M. Whithan
R.N. Gilmore
H. Sucesly (?)
  (Sneesly?)
I. Habbert

(*)Note J. Feniston, page 45.

___Davis	___Emory	L. Mustaph (?)
W.J. Heman	W.A. Loomis	J. Catshaw
J. Thayer	J. Sawyer	J.N. Wilkie
A. Eaton	A. Fox	S.J. Lowo /sic/
M. Hore	E. Williams	O.F. Long
H. Brinch	E. Morton	J. McDermott
J. Feniston/sic/*	J. Pettigrew	W. Pearsons
J.S. Whitmore	M. Mooney	J. French
___Hill	___Oristo	John Donnelson
J. Ingersoll	L.M. Baird	W. Walcott
George Green	J. Brown	W.H. Gansell
J. Ewbanks /sic/	J.N. Davis	J. Nipple
J. Funerg	G. Schaffer	M. Hanks
J. Roberts	J. Robinson	C.H. Taylor
W.Hously	M. Packard	___Seighbohn
W. Hartshorn	R. Burgess	E. Brown
J.C. Catshaw	L. Labadin	R. Bean
T. Ewbanks /sic/	M. Hodges	A. Jones
E.W. Hunt	J. Berryman	J.C. Avery
W. Warnock	G. Sturges	O. Clough
J.B. Read	M. Payne	M. Waterhouse
J. Warren	J.T. Grinnell	

- - - - - -

SHIP: UNDINE
TYPE: Barque   FROM: Panama
ARRIVED: December 20, 1851   CAPTAIN: Haywood
PASSAGE: 76 days from Panama. Experienced light breezes and
         foggy weather. Anchored off "North Beach" area in San
         Francisco. Following deaths took place during the
         passage:
              October 17,1851 - H. Brinkman, a Prussian, aged 22
                   years. Death took place off Tehuantepec.
              October 23,1851 - Peter Bruder, of Bavaria, aged 21
                   years.
              October 24,1851 - Stephen Shenley, of Ireland, late of
                   Wisconsin, aged 25 years.
              October 31,1851 - William Smith, of Scotland, aged 40
                   years.
              October 22,1851 - W.B. Holeman, of Milo, Maine, aged
                   24 years.
              October 10,1851 - J. Silvia, of Madeira, aged 25 years.
              October 10,1851 - ___Graham, late of New York, aged
                   45 years.
              December 9,1851 - D. Dudley, of Ireland, late of
                   Wisconsin, aged 55 years.
CARGO: In ballast.
                         Passengers
J.N. Gillard	A. Squires	L. Brown
J. Eagan	L. Febous	F. Carter
G. Ferrill	N. Nickolls	C. Moult
	(Continued next page)	

(*)Note H. Fenister, page 44.

___ Chisholm	Z. Neal	G. Messeron
L.N. Thompson	G. Backet (?)	R. Boyle
F. Julien	(Backer?)	M. Fre?het
W.F. Lomell	D. O'Brien	M. Tobin
P. McCarty	N. Malyer	A.D. Wallace
S. Taylor	H. Lowell	A. Allen
L.S. Proal	___ Leare	___ Mahoney
W. Holman	J. Owls	J. Sims
S. Silver	H. Taber	A. Baree (?)
E. Zell	A. Ranston	(Barce?)
L. Corwin	___ Mettapee (?)	W. Dennison
___ Lathrap /sic/	(Mettapec?)	___ Smith
D. Davis	C. Sprague	O. Michigan
L. Guilder	L. Boyle	L. Lecompt
J. Carroll	W. Smith	L. Forke (?)
G. Cropper	L. Prune	(Forks?)
G.P. Stickle	N. Mayfield	S. Kidder
D.H. Shing	P. Fribo	G.B. Fly
J.B. Flint	W. Kingsbury	J. Black
___ Anderson	P. Courtney	D. Bird
___ Hudson	L. Paduce	**Z. Tabor
Mrs. ___ Adams	Mrs. ___ Norton and child	Maria Incarnacion

(**)Note passenger listed as H. Taber.

- - - - -

SHIP: CARIB
TYPE: Barque   FROM: Valparaiso, Chile
ARRIVED: December 20, 1851   CAPTAIN: Ripley
PASSAGE: 52 days from Valparaiso, Chile. Had light breezes and
          foggy weather.
CARGO: Merchandise (unspecified).

Passengers

Mr. D. Yates   Mr. G. Cunningham   Mr. D. Hooper
Don Casson

- - - - -

SHIP: CIRCASSIAN
TYPE: Bark (British)   FROM: Havre, France
ARRIVED: December 21, 1851   CAPTAIN: Lewthwaite
PASSAGE: 180 days from Havre, France, via Valparaiso, Chile,
          48 days.
CARGO: 1444 bottles in iron, , wormwood, sugar, tobacco, vinegar,
        37 cases sardines, 300 baskets champagne, 480 cases brandy,
        glass, cutlery, 2 cases muslin, 2 bbls shot, 70 cases of
        vermicelli, 30 cases maccaroni, soap, gin, wine and assorted
        goods.

Passengers

Charles R. de San Martin   Samuel de San Martin
John B.S. de San Martin   Madame Montlezun More
Madame Montlezun Fille*/sic/   Miss Mary Battez
(Continued next page)
(*) See passenger with surname "File" on page 47.

Mr. Esketh	Miss Guvarit	Mr. Ramos Costa
Mr. Desmarios	Mr. Garnot	Mr. Prosper
Mr. Berangeur (?)	Mr. Fostas	Mr. Solar
(Berengeur?)	Mr. Soltere	Mr. Vinas
Mr. Wallois	Mr. Parisse	*Mr. File/sic/
Mr. Faucompre	Mr. Boisnard	Mr. Talbot
Mr. Lyons	Mr. Avignon	Mr. Rinet
Mr. Bournouvelle	Mr. B. Jules	Chevalier Alexander

(*) See "Fille" on p.46.

- - - - - -

SHIP: GEN. PATTERSON*
TYPE: Schooner   FROM: San Diego, Calif.
ARRIVED: December 25, 1851   CAPTAIN: Not Listed
PASSAGE: 18 days from San Diego, California, via San Pedro,
         California. Experienced gales from NW to NE, with thick
         weather.
CARGO: In ballast.
  (*)U.S. Quartermaster   Passenger
     Vessel   Major Miller, U.S.A.

- - - - -

SHIP: AVONDALE
TYPE: Barque (British)   FROM: Montevideo, Uruguay
ARRIVED: December 26, 1851   CAPTAIN: Armstrong
PASSAGE: 104 days from Montevideo, Uruguay, via Honolulu, Sandwich
         Islands, 27 days. The "Avondale" brings the cargo of the
         British ship "Mount Stuart," from London for San Francisco,
         condemned in Montevideo in June, 1851. "Avondale" made
         anchor in San Francisco off the foot of Clark's Point.
CARGO: 28 hdds bulk beer, 1279 packages bottled beer, 20 cans oil,
       boots and shoes, 2 cases scales and weights, 9 cases of
       lamp glass and cotton, 15 packages painter's colors, 2 iron
       grates, cigars, 1 case seeds, 20 casks oilman's stores,
       sugar and unspecified goods.

Passengers

Burtin Brown and	Henry Selby	Smyth Clark
lady	C.A.G. Fouchard	H.J. Heap
Miss Brown	J.E. Townes	Mr. Hancock
Master Brown	Capt. Leighton	Capt. Harwood
Theodore Brown	Mr. Browning	O. Sweet
C. Aikins	J. Paitlips	J. Teazel
W. Brannan	A. Leonard	A. McCleman
O. Nelson	Tentram(?)	C. Heath
T. Lapsley	(Teatram?)	G. Cole
J. Gardner	T. Harris	Hazeman
T. Whitford		

- - - - - -

SHIP: POTOMAC
TYPE: Brig   FROM: Apan, N.I.
ARRIVED: December 26, 1851   CAPTAIN: Smith
                    (Continued next page)

PASSAGE: 60 days from Apan, Navigators Islands, via Honolulu,
Sandwich Islands, 29 days (this vessel bound for Stockton,
California). Laid anchor in the "North Beach" area of
San Francisco.
CARGO: 250 hogs, 150 fowls, 100 turkeys and 15 bbls of cocoanut
oil.

Passengers

Dr.___Vancrauft, lady Gustave Woldow and   *Capt. John Harrison
  & 2 children   lady(for Stockton,   Capt.William Cuthbert
Joseph Patch   California)   Joseph Prime
William Williams

(*) Formerly of the British barque "Novelty", wrecked
on Clarence Islands.

- - - - - -

SHIP: NEW ENGLAND
TYPE: Barque   FROM: Mazatlan, Mexico
ARRIVED: December 26, 1851   CAPTAIN: Hartford
PASSAGE: 28 days from Mazatlan, Mexico. Made the land near San
Francisco harbor on the 17th day out of Mazatlan, since
that time had thick weather and heavy gales of wind.
Dropped anchor off "North Beach" of San Francisco.
CARGO: Merchandise (unspecified).

Passengers

Capt. A.D.B. Stagg   Capt. R.B. Child   J.J. Connolly
J. Anderson   F. St. Our   Dr.___Pifses
G. Mandanato   E. Jordon   L. Contrera
     and 45 unidentified in steerage

- - - - - -

SHIP: MONTESQUIEU
TYPE: Ship (French)   FROM: Bordeaux, France
ARRIVED: December 26, 1851   CAPTAIN: Thevnard
PASSAGE: 180 days from Bordeaux, France, via Valparaiso, Chile,
57 days. Anchored off "North Beach" in San Francisco
harbor.
CARGO: Not listed.

Passengers

Miss___Montrechard   Mrs.___Felginnes(?)   Mr.___Goniie(?)
Mr.___Montrechard   (Falginnes?)   (Gonije?)
Mr.___Espiert   Mr.___Duperains   Mr.___Rochet
Mr.___Eizar(?)(Elzar?)   Mr.___Jeanet

- - - - - -

SHIP: CORNELIA
TYPE: Brig (Mexican)   FROM: Guaymas, Mexico
ARRIVED: December 26, 1851   CAPTAIN: Bostos
PASSAGE: 29 days from Guaymas.
CARGO: In ballast.

Passengers

Mr. D. Campa   Miss F. Carpena   Miss C. Ximenas
(Continued next page)

Miss F. Garcia
and 51 unidentified in steerage
- - - - -

SHIP: MARY WATERMAN
TYPE: Barque   FROM: San Juan del Sur
ARRIVED: November 26, 1851   CAPTAIN: Nevens
PASSAGE: 40 days from San Juan del Sur, Nicaragua. Had a pilot on
board for five days, with thick weather and heavy gales.
Split the maintopsail and mainsail. Dr.___Blanch, a
native of France, died on board at San Juan del Sur.
CARGO: In ballast.
                        Passengers
              Mr.___Atwood   Mr.___Roberts
              and 5 unidentified in steerage
- - - - -

SHIP: JACKIN
TYPE: Brig (Swedish)   FROM: Hongkong
ARRIVED: December 27, 1851   CAPTAIN: *Lindguist /sic/
PASSAGE: 70 days from Hongkong, China. Experienced a constant
succession of gales and heavy weather from NE, East and
SE; hove to for 27 days during the passage; lost 2 jibs,
2 staysails, 2 fore topsails, split 2 main topsails, 2
foresails, 2 mainsails, trysail, lost main topmast and 2
boats. On December 13th, in lat. 44-55N, long. 153;
experienced a hurricane from SE, barometer standing at
28-80. Blew with great violence for 24 hours. A report
brought back by this vessel states that there has been
a conspiracy in the Imperial family to remove the present
Emperor Hien-Fung.
CARGO: 23 pkgs lacquered ware, 9 pkgs Chinaware, 24 pkgs of silks,
12 casks brandy, 1 box Chinese tracts, 18 set camphor wood
trunks, 138 pieces granite, 20 bird cages, 88 bundles of
Swedish iron, 350 cases and 915 boxes of tea and assorted
goods (unspecified).
                        Passengers
              F. Durkheim   ** Mr. R.L. Ogden
              and 100 unidentified Chinese in the steerage
(*) Carried also as "Lindguest".
(**) Identified as "formerly of San Francisco".
- - - - -

SHIP: BALTIMORE
TYPE: Brig (Hawaiian)   FROM: Honolulu, S.I.
ARRIVED: December 27, 1851   CAPTAIN: Penhallow
PASSAGE: 14 days from Honolulu. Experienced severe gales on the
passage; for two days held off the San Francisco harbor
in heavy gales and thick weather. It is noted that Mr.
E.B. Gillam, 1st officer of the "Baltimore", late of
Savannah, Georgia (where he left a family), died on
November 2, 1851. No activity exists in the Sandwich

Islands in exports. The stock of sugar, molasses, syrup and coffee is very large, and accumulating very fast, there does not exist the slightest demand for either article (per a dispatch returned by this vessel).

CARGO: 34 tons of red ash coal, 45 boxes pie fruit, 9000 gallons polar oil, 1 case Britannia ware and 1 package of specie in amount of $1077.90).

Passengers

R.J. Gerard
_____ Asing /sic/
_____ Asang/sic/(from China)
L.B. Harkness
John Chute
M.A. Chute
W. Ensworth
J. Boileau
Peter J. Dillingham

J.A. Rogers
Daniel Bennett
W. Cook
W.G. Aspinwall
Mrs. C. Hammond
Alfred Halsey
Anthony Johnny
J. Wetherly
Manuel Sylom
George Lee

B.H. Daly
W.L. Green
Thomas Boyd
R. Welch and son
Isaac Furgerson
Manuel Small
Andrew Sylver
Manuel Cardos
_____ Alavi
Nora Quade

- - - - - -

SHIP: COLUMBIA
TYPE: Steamer   FROM: Portland, O.T.
ARRIVED: December 28, 1851   CAPTAIN: LeRoy
PASSAGE: Departed Portland,Oregon Territory on December 23, 1851, during a violent snow storm. Touched at Astoria, Oregon Territory and departed Astoria at 8:00AM on December 24, 1851. Encountered a heavy south-east gale on December 25th and 26th, which was accompanied by severe thunder and lightning. This vessel brings news that the Legislative Assembly of Oregon Territory is in session. After considerable discussion it was decided by the Assembly that the only legal place, according to the Location Law of the Territory, for the seat of government, was the town of Salem. Accordingly, the Assembly convened at that place on December 1, 1851.
CARGO: Not listed.

Passengers

Frank Tilford
Robert Lear
Mr._____ Ogburn /sic/
Col. Redick McKee, Indian Agent
J. Young
A.N. Simmons
George N. Long
J. Wait
R. Garritt
A. Beckett
Louis Leggett
C.E. Edwards
E. Treadway

A.W. Jackson
M. Switzer
Mr._____ Leland
Mr._____ Havens
Mr._____ Loring
E.L. Stone
C. Kean
David Kirkpatrick
Daniel Bacon
John Hathaway
H. Coleman
Thomas Topp
Joseph Barnard
D.H. Webber

T.J. Moore
J.S. Douglass
Mr._____ McDonald
Mr._____ Gibbs
Mr._____ Johnson
J.W. Arnott
J. Varnum
Louis Rempis
Charles Rempis
Mr._____ Barnes
Mr._____ Philibert
Jer. Gould
J. Skinner
Mr._____ Rinearson/sic/

(Continued next page)

William Finlay, wife   D.W. Swan   C.E. Scott
    and children   R.P. Johnson   Mr.___Couette
John Thomas   Mr.___Deshan(?)
                              (Deshen?,Deshon?)

- - - - - -

SHIP: LOUISIANA
TYPE: Barque   FROM: Oregon Territory
ARRIVED: December 28, 1851   CAPTAIN: Honsbury
PASSAGE: 16 days from the Oregon Territory.
CARGO: 1200 bushels of potatoes, 14 bbls of cranberries and 100
       dozen eggs.
                           Passengers
A. Jackman   H. Deen   C. Lincoln
L. Baughman   L. Bell

- - - - - -

SHIP: JOHN DUNLAP
TYPE: Schooner   FROM: San Blas, Mexico
ARRIVED: December 28, 1851   CAPTAIN: Sanger
PASSAGE: 38 days from San Blas, Mexico. Experienced severe gales
         of wind on the passage. Spent 15 days off the San
         Francisco harbor with thick weather and heavy gales.
CARGO: 10,000 oranges, 12 dozen fowls, 30 hogs, 400 gallons of
       Muscal wine and 12,000 lbs of onions.
                           Passengers
Don Juan Bouichar   Capt.___Lewis and   Don___Marena
                           lady
              and 14 unidentified in steerage

- - - - - -

SHIP: TARQUINA
TYPE: Brig   FROM: Oregon Territory
ARRIVED: December 28, 1851   CAPTAIN: Reed
PASSAGE: 13 days from the Oregon Territory. On December 27, 1851,
         saw the steamer "Constitution", hence for Honolulu; she
         was standing in for Point Reyes.
CARGO: 1600 bushels of potatoes, 1600 bushels of onions and 400
       hogs.
                           Passengers
William M. Vance   W. Mulkey   J. Atwood
D. Woodson

- - - - - -

SHIP: FAWN
TYPE: Brig   FROM: Gardiner, O.T.
ARRIVED: December 29, 1851   CAPTAIN: Bunker
PASSAGE: 11 days from Gardiner, Umpqua River, Oregon Territory.
         Experienced heavy gales from the SE and S.W.
CARGO: 56 bbls of salmon, 60 cords of wood, 1500 ft square timber.

(Continued next page)

Passengers

Mr.___Frye   Mr.___Loughridge   Mr.___Lyman
Mr.___West

- - - - -

SHIP: ALICE TARLETON
TYPE: Barque   FROM: Talcahuano, Chile
ARRIVED: December 29, 1851   CAPTAIN: Coffin
PASSAGE: 58 days from Talcahuano, Chile, via Callao, Peru.
        Experienced severe weather on the coast. On December
        26,1851, in a heavy gale from the SE, sprung six leaks
        and had to throw part of the cargo overboard. Was within
        500 miles of San Francisco harbor for 18 days.
CARGO: 3000 half sacks of flour, 8000 quarter sacks of flour and
      a quantity of bran.

Passengers
Mr. C. Green   J.W. Hale

- - - - -

SHIP: SAN DIEGO
TYPE: Schooner   FROM: Bodega, Calif.
ARRIVED: December 30, 1851   CAPTAIN: Haynes
PASSAGE: 2 days from Bodega, California.
CARGO: 212,000 shingles, 5 tons of carrots and beets, 2000
      cabbages.

Passengers
H. Meiggs   H. Luther

- - - - -

SHIP: SULTAN
TYPE: Barque (British)   FROM: Bordeaux, France
ARRIVED: January 2, 1852   CAPTAIN: Welsh
PASSAGE: 190 days from Bordeaux, France, via Valparaiso, Chile,
        50 days.
CARGO: Wine,2000 bags flour, 47 bags walnuts, 175 bbls eggs, 137
      bags corn, 493 bags of unspecified goods.

Passengers
Mr.___Manson and lady

- - - - -

SHIP: COLORADO
TYPE: Brig   FROM: Humboldt, Calif.
ARRIVED: January 9, 1852   CAPTAIN: Bell
PASSAGE: 18 days from Humboldt, California. Experienced heavy
        gales from December 21 to January 3rd. After January 3rd
        had light winds from the SSE.
CARGO: 20,000 ft square timber, 60,000 ft assorted lumber.

Passengers

A.P. Kent	C.D. Robinson	P. Johnson
W.L. Stansbury	L. Holmes	D. Pickard
S.A.C. Moore	William Collingwood	M. White

(Continued next page)

F. Maigret   J. Buch   L. Mara
                and 9 unidentifed Chinamen
                    - - - - - -

SHIP: TRAVELER(also listed as the "Traveller")
TYPE: Schooner   FROM: Bodega, Calif.
ARRIVED: January 13, 1852   CAPTAIN: McIntosh
PASSAGE: 24 hours from Bodega, California.
CARGO: 45 tons potatoes, 80 pumpkins and 2 bags of onions.
                    Passengers
            Mr. F. Boudinot   Mr.___Newcomb
                    - - - - - -

SHIP: SPRAY
TYPE: Schooner (3 masted)   FROM: Valparaiso, Chile
ARRIVED: January 14, 1852   CAPTAIN: Hall
PASSAGE: Departed Valparaiso, Chile on November 30, 1851.
CARGO: 6000 half bags of flour & 400 bags barley.
                    Passengers
            Capt. O.H. Crary   G. Berger
            and lady
                    - - - - - -

SHIP: SOPHIE
TYPE: Barque (German)   FROM: Newcastle, N.S.W.
ARRIVED: January 14, 1852   CAPTAIN: Decker
PASSAGE: 108 days from Newcastle, New South Wales. Called at
          Valparaiso, Chile, with a 30 day run from Valparaiso
          to lat. 31N. From the latter position to San Francisco
          experienced calms and light breezes. Was off San
          Francisco harbor for 3 days.
CARGO: 420 tons of coal.
                    Passengers
            E. Gordon   J. Bennett
                    - - - - - -

SHIP: SEA GULL
TYPE: Steamer   FROM: Oregon Territory
ARRIVED: January 15, 1852   CAPTAIN: Tichnor
PASSAGE: 7 days from Oregon Territory, via Port Orford, Oregon
          Territory and Trinidad, California. Experienced heavy
          weather from southeast; lay-to for 3 days, blowing a gale;
          made the run from off Columbia River in 4 days, including
          touching at Port Orford and Trinidad.
CARGO: 1000 bushels oats, 1000 sacks flour, 200 sacks potatoes,
          mail from Port Orford and Trinidad.
                    Passengers
J. Church   S.L. Barry   C. Man
J. Spencer   J.C. McKay   M. May
J. Dange(?)(Dangs?) Capt.___Kane   Mr.___Rockwell
Mr.___Grazier   E. Samson   J. Derka
                (Continued next page)

Mr.____Harper and   W.I. Mere   B. Henderson
    lady   Major____Wendall   E. Fletcher
S.A. Grapler   W.W. Hanks
          and eight soldiers of the U.S. Coast Survey
                    - - - - - -

SHIP: J.K.F. MANSFIELD
TYPE: Schooner   FROM: Oregon Territory
ARRIVED: January 19, 1852   CAPTAIN: Scott
PASSAGE: 8 days from the Oregon Territory. Experienced nothing but
         light winds and calms the passage down.
CARGO: 200 hogs, 600 lbs butter, 90 dozen eggs and 40,000 pieces of
       assorted lumber
                    Passenger
                    H.B. Williams
                    - - - - -

SHIP: LEONESA
TYPE: Brig   FROM: Puget Sound, W.T.
ARRIVED: January 20, 1852   CAPTAIN: Howard
PASSAGE: 10 days from Puget Sound, Washington Territory. Brings
         intelligence that the British brig "Uno", belonging to
         the Hudson Bay Company, while lying at anchor in Neah
         Bay, Cape Flattery, was driven ashore in a heavy gale
         and totally lost. The vessel was plundered and burnt by
         Indians, who also stripped a lady passenger and two
         children on board, and took two boys prisoners, who were
         afterwards recovered.
CARGO: 13,400 feet of piles.
                    Passengers
         Capt. B.H. Hill, U.S.A.   C.T. Fay
                    - - - - - -

SHIP: DAVID CROSS
TYPE: Ship (British)   FROM: Valparaiso, Chile
ARRIVED: January 21, 1852   CAPTAIN: Kerr
PASSAGE: 52 days from Valparaiso, Chile.
CARGO: Flour, cement (50 bbls), barley, beans and 185 tons of
       coal.
                    Passenger
                    Mr. E. Morrison
                    - - - - -

SHIP: ROANOKE
TYPE: Schooner   FROM: Santa Cruz, Calif.
ARRIVED: January 21, 1852   CAPTAIN: McAlmond
PASSAGE: 3 days from Santa Cruz, California. Experienced severe
         gales from SE and was driven to the northward of the
         Farallone Islands.
CARGO: 85 tons of potatoes and 8000 ft of lumber.
                    Passengers
          (Continued next page)

Passengers

Mr.____Hammond   Capt.____Whiting   Mr.____Callahan
Mr.____Hodge   Mr.____DePew   Mr.____Southers
Mr.____Gordon

- - - - - -

SHIP: OHIO
TYPE: Steamer   FROM: San Diego, Calif.
ARRIVED: January 27, 1852   CAPTAIN: Hillard
PASSAGE: 5 days from San Diego, California, via intermediate ports.
         Very rough over the bar coming into San Francisco harbor.
CARGO: Not listed.

Passengers

Mr. J. Judson Ames   E. Jones   C. Neieva
R.M. Hymont   Mr.____Powell and   Mrs.____Stevens
L. Straus /sic/   lady   E. Robb, lady and
Mr.____Flint   H. Mix   child
J.M. White   B. Miller   W. Borland
E. Escott   J. Lynch   Mr.____Flan
T. Beese   A.E. Stevens   L.B. Williams
O. McBride   J. Stevens   H. Russell
L.D. Crandall   T. McClure   B. Bosarth
W. Brown   J. Story   W. Stokes
C. Lee   Mr.____Story   S. Willson /sic/
B. Cunningham   W. Bird   C. Hallock
H. Marlborough   John Smith   J.J. Langdon
A. Thompson   R.H. Gould

- - - - - -

SHIP: SEA BIRD
TYPE: Steamer   FROM: San Diego, Calif.
ARRIVED: January 28, 1852   CAPTAIN: Haley
PASSAGE: 2½days from San Diego, California. From Point Conception
         experienced strong winds and heavy head seas.
CARGO: Not listed.

Passengers

Thomas D. Johns   Charles H. Lowton   George Bonny
Mr.____Packard   E.R. Raymond   Mr.____Lassord
John Foster   S. Morris   J. Rodgers
John Foster, Jr.   Mr.____Parrie   J.H. Haskell
O.W. Childs   Mr.____Bledsow   C. Handcock /sic/
P. Blackman   Mr.____Rarralle   John Blay
B. Marrea   D. Overtown   P. Blay
J. Rugullardo   M. Jeffere /sic/   P. Blaco
C. Rugullardo   D. Renardo

- - - - - -

SHIP: COLUMBIA
TYPE: Steamer   FROM: Oregon Territory
ARRIVED: January 28, 1852   CAPTAIN: LeRoy
PASSAGE: Passage time not listed. This vessel brings intelligence
         that letters had been received at Portland, Oregon Terri-

tory, from one of the Queen Charlotte's Island Expeditions.
A group had landed and found the natives friendly.
CARGO: Not listed.

Passengers

Judge___Nelson	Col.___Allen	Mr.___Agnew and
F. Meek, lady and	Dr.___Davenport and	lady
child	lady	Mr.___Frank
E. Pomeroy	C. Abon	Mr.___Grater
Mr.___Burnett	C.D. Murray	Capt.___Frost
J.B. Meir	Mr.___Babcock	Mr.___Northup/sic/
Dr.___Carpenter	Mr.___Backus	C.A. Smith
James Toney	J.K. Terry	William M. Cherry
Peter Rebold	Paul Peterson	J.F. Angell
Ashby Pierce	B.H. Krill	Jerome Edgar
Mr.___Foster	J.N. Roberts	H.F. Pugh
Mr.___Light, wife	John Dillon	J.C. Guy
and 6 children	Preston Hampton	John McQuery
N. Bishop	J. Webb	J.M. Toole
W.S. Kean	M. Anderson	William H. Hart
G.W. Eggleston	John Willing	William Jolly
R. Backus	R. Atwater	Isaac Wright
William Fraser	Valentine Smith	Alex Hanson
F.S. Garrison	Henry Smith	

- - - - - -

SHIP: J.C. LEGRANGE*

TYPE: Brig   FROM: Panama
ARRIVED: January 28, 1852   CAPTAIN: Gregory
PASSAGE: 61 days from Panama, via Acapulco, Mexico, 33 days.
CARGO: In ballast.

Passengers

Dr. E.H. Huthinger	H.G. Moore	S. Taylor
and lady	L. Searce	H. Taylor
B.B. Brown	N. Favard	W. Whitton
Jonathan Brown	J. Nash	J.W. Close
J.H. Davis	J. Bohen	J. Hughes
J. Horan	F.G. McNulty	J. Labadie
C. Haggert	H.A. Shiel	A. Batterman
E. Taylor	E. Scott	E. Pierce
L.O. Hobert and	J.C. Winter	W. Pinckney
son	W. Brown	F.R. Pinckney
O.F. Cottle	J. Weeks	Mr.___Harney
G. Idel	M. Loper	___Donaldson
A.C. Turner	Mr.___Smith and	Mr.___Caronator
A. Garrala	lady	and lady
___Dana	___Bandy	O. Rice
L.B. Clark	E. Oram	J. Riley
L. Clark	J. Smith	J. Collins
J. Welch	___Machind	Horan Salina
___Pontigillie	___Melrose	___Bernard
J. Buolena	H. Buolena	___Orser

(Continued next page)

(*)Listed as in source. Vessel believed to be the "J.C. Legrand".

J. McKenna	J. Egan	A. Thompson
Thomas Morton	J. Donnelan	J.W. Thompson
M. Mooney	J. Wood	W.O. Donnell (?)
A.B. Vernice	___Springer	(W. O'Donnell?)
___Cober	A. Beam	

- - - - - -

SHIP: MARIETTA
TYPE: Ship (Austrian)   FROM: Valparaiso, Chile
ARRIVED: January 28, 1852   CAPTAIN: Jeuranaovich
PASSAGE: 55 days from Valparaiso, Chile. Anchored below Clark's
Point in San Francisco harbor.
CARGO: 50 sacks walnuts, 160 bags barley, 4040 bags flour, 150
boxes maccaroni, 5 bbls eggs, 1 package garlic, 378 boxes
figs and 42 boxes sweetmeats.
Passengers
Mr. J.R. Laurena   Julio Chapapo   N. Pinto
and 100 unidentified in steerage

- - - - - -

SHIP: WILD PIGEON
TYPE: Clipper   FROM: New York
ARRIVED: January 28, 1852   CAPTAIN: Putnam
PASSAGE: 103 days from New York. Had light winds the whole passage.
Had three skysails set for 75 days; for 24 days had sky-
sails and royal studdingsails set, and never shifted a
rope. On December 17, 1851, in lat. 55-59, long. 82-30,
saw a large clipper ship, and was in company three days,
showed a blue flag and white cross; supposed to be the
"Tradewind", from New York, bound for San Francisco.
(The "Wild Pigeon" was one of the small class clippers.
She was built in Portsmouth, New Hampshire, by Mr.
G. Raines. Her tonnage was 996; length, 189 feet;
breadth of beam, 36 feet; depth of hold, 22 feet.)
CARGO: 1 bale copper, 200 boxes soap, 8 pairs iron doors, 108 tons
coal, 250 bbls flour, 3 bbls butter, 2 kegs emery, 39 wheel
barrows, 4 kegs shot, 1 piano, 6 cases copper, 100 kegs
nails, 10 dozen shovels and 3579 packages of undescribed
merchandise.
Passengers
D. Olyphant Vail   Mr.___Ludlow

- - - - - -

SHIP: PONDICHERI
TYPE: Ship (French)   FROM: Bordeaux, France
ARRIVED: January 28, 1852   CAPTAIN: Prudhomme
PASSAGE: 166 days from Bordeaux, France. Anchored below Clark's
Point in San Francisco harbor.
CARGO: 9 boxes porcelain, 6 cases of coats, 1500 bbls brandy, 29
boxes shirts, 2 boxes cigars, 100 boes oil, 12 boxes hats,
1000 baskets anisette, 25 boxes syrup, 3250 cases red wine,

(Continued next page)

10 cases sweetmeats, 25 boxes syrup.

Passengers
Mr.___Laturek

- - - - - -

SHIP: TRADE WIND
TYPE: Clipper   FROM: New York, N.Y.
ARRIVED: February 1, 1852   CAPTAIN: Osgood
PASSAGE: 121 days from New York, N.Y. Was 60 days to Cape Horn,
16 days off the Cape in heavy gales, and 18 days from the
line to San Francisco. Greatest day's run on the passage
was 293 miles. Had a pilot on board for two days and was
off San Francisco harbor with light weather for four days.
Came to anchor inside of Fort Point.
(This was one of the largest ships to enter this port
up to arrival date. She was registered at 2029 tons
and had on board 2800 tons of measurement goods. Her
dimensions were 244 feet length, 43 feet breadth of
beam, and 23 feet depth of hold. Vessel had a round
stern and billet head.)
CARGO: Not listed.

Passengers
Mr. C.W. Jones

- - - - - -

SHIP: B.L. ALLEN
TYPE: Schooner   FROM: Panama
ARRIVED: February 2, 1852   CAPTAIN: Carter
PASSAGE: 40 days from Panama. Had light winds most of the passage,
and for 14 days did not make 200 miles. There were eight
deaths on board during the passage. The following died:

December 25,1851 - Christian L. Toboy, from Franklin,
Wisconsin, aged 35 years.

December 25,1851 - Richard Faul, from Jefferson,
Wisconsin, aged 43 years.

December 29,1851 - Benjamin Wingham, from Michigan,
aged 43 years.

December 29,1851 - Matthew Keath, from Rhode Island,
aged 20 years.

January 3, 1852 - Frederick Broastor, from Illinois,
aged 27 years.

January 5, 1852 - George Wrangham, from New Diggings,
Wisconsin, aged 40 years.

January 9, 1852 - John Smith, from Washington County,
Ohio, aged 23 years.

January 23, 1852 - George Burgess, from Wisconsin,
aged 32 years.

CARGO: In ballast.

Passengers

W.C. Storer	T. Hooper	E. Thompson
R. Stewart	J. Patrick	J.C. Watson

(Continued next page)

N. Porter and lady
J. Connell
H. Tulley
G. Coit
J.W. Wright
G. Graham
G. Martin
E. Thornton
R. Hillhouse
T. Lackey
W. Watson
H. Dobinson /sic/
Mrs.___Donnough
Mr.___Scorson
W. Johnson
H. Hant?man
T. Horne

J. Woodward and lady
J. Walker
Mrs.___Markley and 3 children
W. Elliott
R. Burrett
J. Wright
J. Ward
J. Richards
E. Woodward
F. Braston
G. Wrongham
T. Smith
Z. Young
C. Thompson
J.N. Hance
M.L. Atkins

D. Winas
H. Brown
D. Brown
Mr.___Crawford and son
J.S. Swan
G. Klink
W. Thompson
G. Beers
W. Burge
E. Rudder
W. Montgomery
T. Knowlan
D. Salmon
T. Bissett
J. Austin
J. Holoday

- - - - - -

SHIP: PANAMA
TYPE: Steamer   FROM: Panama
ARRIVED: February 3, 1852   CAPTAIN: Watkins
PASSAGE: 22 days from Panama, via Acapulco and San Diego,
California. Left Panama on January 12, 1852 and arrived
Acapulco, Mexico on January 19th. Left Acapulco on same
day. On January 26th broke the lever shaft in the centre;
kept under way at about 6 knot speed. Forced to stop in
order that Chief Engineer, Mr. John Graham, could put
bands around the break. Got under way but determined
it would not be safe to proceed on voyage; changed course
for San Diego, California and arrived there on January
27th. Repairs made with obligations to Major J. McKinstry,
Quartermaster at San Diego. Departed San Diego on January
28th, and after having been out 6 hours, put back into San
Diego for purpose of making repairs more secure. Again
departed San Diego on January 31st. The following deaths
took place during the passage up from Panama:
        January 29,1852 - Augustus W. Robinson, aged 55 years,
                          of disease of the heart, of Chicot
                          County, Arkansas.
        January 29,1852 - William Reynolds, aged 34 years, of
                          general debility, of Wales.
        January 29,1852 - John Q. Jones, aged 22 years, of
                          fever, of Scituate, Mass.
        January 30,1852 - Coman Smith, aged 53 years, of
                          general debility caused by fever,
                          of Scituate, Mass.
CARGO: 476 packages unspecified merchandise.
                          Passengers
William G. Stout   D. Chambers, wife   H.B. Chambers
                          and son
                   (Continued next page)

A.L. Richardson
Mrs. J. Reynolds,
child & servant
Miss J. Byron
Mrs. B. Gardner and
son
Mrs. E.R. Colcord
Mrs. C.A. Deau /sic/
J. Mills
Mrs. A. Coleman
Mrs. E.J. Hoyle
Miss M. Craig
A.W. Peabody
J.H. Kent
W.F. Forbes
L.W. Fisher
S. Meadan
J.E. Meadan
O. Cottle
Thomas Evans
L.L. Long
John Barnwall
W.W. Barnwall
V.R. Smith
H.S. Coleman
J. Hollingshead
W.C. Mays
E.C. Barnes
M. Macdonald /sic/
T.A. Williams
T. Havens
David Evans
S. Welsch /sic/
D. Morgan/sic/
O. Knapp
H. Whitcomb
W. Rowell
J.H. Flint
Daniel Jones
F. Cameron
E. Foss
G.H. Hopper
H.S. Noble
W.H. Smith
S. Carter
George L. Lane
C.H. Fitch /sic/
Dan Cronley, wife
and child/sic/
P. Daly
W. Morris

Mrs. C. Hall
Mrs. Lucy Brown,
child & servant
Mrs. Z. McCollum
Mrs. J. Sturges
Mrs. A. Schmidt
Mrs. J. Somers
Miss R. Robinson
Miss Rebecca Robinson
Joseph Dinat, wife
and son
Miss D. Dinat
J.H. Roake
F. Harford
Dr. Alexander Jones
W. Baker Jr.
J.C. Root
E. Fairchild
Charles Janin
Simon Welch
James A. Patterson and
wife
J. Parks
N.D. Hall
Joseph Byers
D. Byers
J. Abercrombie
J.P. Simms
Joseph Lohman (?)
(Lehman?)
John G. Jones
J. Reynolds
J.S. Merrill
Stephen Brown
R. Levy
D.M. Libby
D. Libby
Hy Libby
H. Rourbach
C.H. Fitch/sic/
J.P. Chamberlain Jr.
J.P. Brorha
W. Harford
J. Brander
John Halm /sic/
N. Smith
J. C. Tracy
William Taylor
J. Reisner
D. Morgan/sic/
J. Davis /sic/
(Continued next page)

Mrs. J.M. Page, son
and servant
Miss H. Lawrence
Mrs. S.C. Perkins
Horace Ballou and
wife /sic/
B.G. Lathrop, wife
& 3 children
Stephen Simons and
wife
Mrs. Ellen Horton
Mrs. A.E. Dolsen
P.G. Childs
W. Saddler
J.A. Ganlay
S. Moore
J.F. Schander
G.W. Sutton
Charles Tabacle
John Nuttall
John Gray
T. Dunning
R.W. Patterson
E.R. Patterson
M. Roberts
Samuel Roberts
G.R. Baker
T.H. Whapey
W. Hamilton
E. Lewellyn
J. Davis/sic/
J.F. Henry
H. Quimby
Walter Wood
W.D. Wood
John Cypher
S. Cypher
M. Hildreth
H. Hildreth
J. Hildreth
Henry Hildreth
F.W. Faulkner
J.F.I. Bennett
J. Eversfield
W.W. Delashautt
J. Williams, wife
and son
J. Mattesh
J. Wolmering
D. Evans
J. Benevolo

W. Heister
M. Remter
N. White
S. Bagner
J. Malona
J. McCarty
H. White
C.F. Chuhuck
E. Wellya (?)
 (Wellys?)
J. Coutollena
W. Wolfe/sic/
William Bollitt
J. Smith
E. Morgan
P. Donohue
T. Burns
J. Blackman
R. Levi
D. Williams
David Williams
David Jones
P. Boyle
G. Darron
Thomas Bow
J. Aiken
R. Leggett
S. Frank/sic/
J. Dyer, Jr.
J. Andrews
H.H. Messinger
H.R. Woodruff
G.H. Stebbins
A.D. Heald
M. Sanburn
J. Hammon
T. Nash
William Henry
R. Todd
A.S. Gilmore
S. Patterson
J.P. Howard
W. Pollett
J.M. Hamblet
E. Buck
W. Wolfe/sic/
Job Dixen /sic/
S.M. Reynolds
S. Frank/sic/
H.A. Green
W. Tibbetts

G. Henser
F. Fardiner /sic/
 (Gardiner?)
J. O'Neil
J. Ewan
J. McAnnally
P. Daguahan
J.E. Williams
T.A. Williams
J. Redgeway /sic/
A. Freshman
W. Gillis
James Hogg
W. Cole
R. Hose ?
 (Huse?)
W. Kerwin
S. Saivance
N. Kuber
J. Joseph
W. Berrucks
Job Powers
J. Hare
I.I. Everhard
William Kenyon
George Kenyon
D. Ryan
S. Parsalis
W.W. Hopkins
E.H. Harrington
J.F. Harrington
A.B. Knowlton
William Cole
L. Thayer
D. Donnohoe /sic/
C.H. Filburch
C. Cottenheim
L. Savadge /sic/
 (Savage?)
B. Savage /sic/
A.F. Gilmore
M. Gray
L.C. Fuller
C. Lesler
B.O. Day
Lemuel Wells
C.P. Hunter
D.B. Woodward
J.N. Sanford
J. Roland
T. Simmons
(Continued next page)

J. Richards
H. Mire
T. Jones /sic/
D. Jones
W.M. Shaw
W. Wheeter /sic/
 (Wheeler?)
M. O'Donnell
M. Crudgi
W. Pritchard
C. Shick
P.M. Ginniss
J. Geesh
J. Jackson
P. Crowley
J. Benns ?
 (Benna?)
T. Jones/sic/
T. Reulas
A. Riverras
J. Noble and wife
A. Noble
Miss M. Noble
S. Ford
N. Doe
J. Blackburn
J. Sanford
T. Rossey
S. Cornell
S.D. Pemrock
M. Witherby
C.N. Holder
J.J. Ellis
R.B. Lovejoy
P. Dailey
L.C. Foss
J.H. Croucher ?
 (Crouther?)
H. Little
A. Tate
W.H. McKee
E. Field
C. Cowen
R. Cowen
A. Loyd /sic/
W. Jymmes
R.F. Faulkner
D.W. Keyes
C.H. Rose
J. Doane
J.R. Wilson

O. Hollman
E.R. Carpenter
R.M. Bloomfield
J. Douglass
H. Gilbert
C.L. Morton
P. Smith
A. Tailor
C. Tailor
M. McMaster
C. Tilden
I. Irving
W. Irving
O. Benson
W. Yates
P. Tibbetts
J. Haines
D. Tabor (?)
  (Taber?)
W.A. Briggs
P.P. Davis
Mrs.____Smith
A. Dennen (?)
  (Dennon?)
J. Thomas
J.L. Fletcher
H.B. Heustis
W. Wood Jr.
C.D. Wood
P.T. Southworth
C.G. Sweetland
D. Little
J. Wolfe
Joseph Roper
James Porter
John Porter
C. Porter
L. Aures
W.H. Taylor
John Shaw
R.H. Atwood
L.F. Mott
W. Lilly
C.A. Hopkins
J.R. Cameron
W. Morris
A.H. Washbvn/sic/
  (Washbun?)
H.F. Culver
A. Boyer
C.C. Nye

C. Barker
J.B. Hayt /sic/
T. Case
B.F. Hill
S. Ridgeway /sic/
W. Ridgeway /sic/
J. Ridgeway /sic/
A.L. Elwood
J. Sherman
G. Farnsworth
W. Farnsworth
R. Pratt
C.H. Young
A. Hall
A. Hurst
W. Water
Thomas Gilman
Peter Smith Jr.
J. Hall
G. Miser (?)
F. Walker
W. Greenwood
S.H. Gale
W. Atwill
Charles Atwill
L.L. White
Peter Wicker
W. Thomas
L.F. Oakley
C.A. Fuller
E.M. Holmes
W. Carpenter
W. Moore
R.P. Reynolds
J.W. David
J.M. Mays
A.G. Mays
N. Marsh
E.J. Kidder
M. Wilson
Daniel Williams
J. Joseph
C.D. Brown
George W. Thomas
G.F. Stephens
D. Jones
W. Rider
F. Thompson
Samuel Thompson
E. Smith
C. Hancom
(Continued next page)

J. Messersmith
J. Steele
J. Goodline
G.A. Putnam
C. Kellogg
Job Bragg
E. Wolfe
J. Alexander and
  wife
S. Spaulding
G. Gray
H. Reynolds
J.M. Sykes
W.B. Cowen
Lewis Pardee
E.H. Pardee
A.F. Pardee
G. Geissler
L.M. Atwood
W.R. Atwood
M. Meagebeam(?)
  ____Randall
F.J. Farnham
T.G. Lancy
L.J. Maxim
W.N. Sibley
R. Hughes/sic/
C. Hodgedon
P. Barlin
B. Esmond Jr. (?)
  (Edmond?)
C.L. Wright
John Noral
A.G. Brazie
L. Gaus
W.H. Sawyer
E.W. Hunt
L. Weeks Jr.
Alex Weeks
E. Morgan
R. Hughes/sic/
Thomas Johns
Theodore Jones
W.P. Campbell
J. Delashutt
Joseph Delashutt
John Tompkins
J. Hifferman
A. Parkhurst, Jr.
John Wilson
Job Bennett and wife

J. Barnes	C. Freeman	J. Clark
J. Whittaker	E. Sweet	A. Gray
D.K. Carver	M. Templeton	D.A. Hoyt
G.F. Dansing ?	C.P. Greenly	D.B. Hoyt
(Dancing?,Dunsing?)	C.W. Lane	W.R. Harris
H.A. Goodman	U. Grunebar ?	M. Renloh
D. Wills	(Grubebar?,	Job Chauncey, Jr.
W.L. Uraun	Gruhebar?)	

- - - - - -

SHIP: TRAVELER(also listed as the "Traveller")
TYPE: Schooner   FROM: Bodega, Calif.
ARRIVED: February 3, 1852   CAPTAIN: McIntosh
PASSAGE: 20 hours from Bodega, California.
CARGO: 36 tons potatoes, 3 sacks onions and 67 pumpkins.

Passengers

Mr. L.P. Harrison	Mr. D.P. Thayer	Mr. D.B. Watson
Mr. D.P. Turnbull	Mr. R. Wolland	

- - - - - -

SHIP: GOLDEN GATE
TYPE: Clipper   FROM: New York
ARRIVED: February 5, 1852   CAPTAIN: Truman*
PASSAGE: 113 days from New York, N.Y. Took 56 days from New York
to Cape Horn, 30 days from the Cape to the Line, and 24
days from the line to San Francisco. Greatest day's run
was 290 miles. Much light weather on the passage, was
within 300 miles of San Francisco for last 8 days.
(This vessel was built by Mr. J.W. Westervelt, and
the following are her dimensions: 1450 tons; length,
195 feet; breadth of beam, 42 feet; depth of hold
21½ feet)
CARGO: Butter, glassware, soap, shovels, vices, 38 anvils, shoes
and boots, pipes and tobacco, 53 plates of boiler iron, 2
wagons, 1 keg shot and balls, horseshoes, 203 tons coal,
wine, books and assorted goods.

Passengers

Mr.____Sabatie   Mrs.____Reed, son and three daughters

- - - - - -

SHIP: SURPRISE
TYPE: Barque (French)   FROM: Mazatlan, Mexico
ARRIVED: February 5, 1852   CAPTAIN: Allay
PASSAGE: 22 days from Mazatlan, Mexico.
CARGO: In ballast.

Passengers

O. Espagnot	Mr.____Redding	Mr.____Ferguson
J. Sweeney	S.M. Espagnot	W.A. Chick
Miss Mary Chick	Mrs. E. Chick	R. Chick
W.A. Bagley	J. Moreno	

and 60 unidentified in steerage

- - - - -

(*)One source states Capt.____Freeman was the master.

SHIP: PACIFIC
TYPE: Steamer   FROM: San Juan del Sur
ARRIVED: February 5,1852   CAPTAIN: Nathaniel Jarvis
PASSAGE: 11 days and 20 hours from San Juan del Sur, Nicaragua,
         via Acapulco, Mexico. Left San Juan del Sur on January
         21,1852, at 8:00PM. Arrived at Acapulco on January 26,
         1852, at 8:00AM. Sailed from Acapulco on January 28,
         1852 at 11:00PM. On February 2, 1852 was hailed by the
         brig "Tryvenia" at anchor, the east side of Cerros Island,
         47 days from Panama, for San Francisco, with 120 passengers,
         in distress, out of bread and water, six persons having
         died on board. Took off all the lady passengers and
         children; left her at 7:00PM, taking in water. Among the
         passengers will be found the names of two theatrical
         arrivals, Mrs. Alexina Fisher Baker and her husband, Mr.
         Lewis Baker.
CARGO: Not listed.

Passengers

Mrs. Mary Brown and child	J.L. Baker and wife	Mrs. C. Woodworth
Mrs.___ Mars	Mrs. J. Weil and body	Mrs. M.H. Howard
Miss___ Mars		J.S. Gilbert
Miss J. Mars	Mrs.___ Wolf	Mrs. B. Barnard
R.J. Bromley	George Nixon (?) (Nixen?)	C. Edmond
Miss___ Sylvester		E. Mallow and wife
T.M. Eastman	George W. Meyer(?) (Moyer?)	Mrs.___ Pray, 2 children and
J. Rittenbaumer	L. Meyer /sic/	svt (Prav?)
M. Hill	J. McCormick	C.H. Seaman
C. McCluskey	Abraham Tiffney and wife	H. Scott
S. Conrad		George L. Banney (?) (Bonney?)
Ann Conrad	C. Baig	
D.L. Debyell, wife & 2 children	A. King Jr.	S. Dunning
	F. Crozier	Mrs. L. Preston and child
Mrs. J. White	Joseph Davis	
H.A. Swift	Mrs.___ Jennars and 4 children	F. Lambert
A. Mead		E.B. Perry
W. Mead	W.E. Riddle	George Birdsall, wife and 2 chldrn
M. Boyd	C. Woodman	
E.N. Hill	C. Niles	G. Boyington
P.M. Flanders	H. Niles	G. Simpson
C. Packard	D.S. Moss	A.J. Merriam
H.T. Alden	A. Geyer	A.M. Gray
G. Copeland	B. Stetson	W. Gueyney
A. Toomer	William Thompson	G. Calande
J. Relyras	D.E. Peck	J. Pragory /sic/
H. Reed	S. Stapleton	J.H. Much
W.H. Davis	T.J. Preston	C.T. Bryant
B. Garorance	J. Hill	J.W. Bryant
J. Folsom	John Cole	W.J. Pratt
G.W. Harrison	J. Neish /sic/	C. Cole
R. Nye(?)		B. Cole

(Continued next page)

J. Pomroy
Thomas Rooney and
  2 boys
C.W. Platt
C. Butter
J.R. Richardson
W. Hasford
A. Taggart
O. Dyer
M.F. Lockwood
M. Stephens
C.W. Evans
A. Olmore
E. Winslow
S. Corwin Jr.
J. Simpson
W.F. Dorman
W.O. Sleeper
S.A. Drake
J. Sheakley
J. Newcomb
D. Carrington
S. Berry
Joseph Cook
E.T. Jackson
H. Lamb
David Place
D. McGowan
G.A. Booth
B. Mullen
M.H. Bevan
W. Jamieson
William Ware
A.H. Ware
B. Watts
Henry Ray
Hiram Miller
J.L. Veszey
C.A. Mills
N.T. Blaney/sic/
R. Blany/sic/
R.G. Watkins
Isaac Mead
George Mead
Phillip Clerken
Robert Davy
Joel Brown
John Adams
J.S. Adams
D. Mitchell
J.J.H. Kellor

Thomas W. Rogers
John Murray
M. Marshall
N.O. Mathews
L. Nichols
J. Abbott
S. Lowery
U. Lowery
N.A. Pettygrou /sic/
D. Trollop
J. Parson
William H. Fitch
N.W. Morrill
H. Terbrush
N.G. Reed
W.M. Reed
R. Bufford
W.H. Snell
A.L. Woodruff
W.J. Lammar
T. Nason
W.H. Dodge
A.F. Dillon
Charles Blandford
I. Elliott
W.A. Irwin
J. Woodbury
P. McManus
James Kane
Terrence Kerins
E.W. Clark
M.S. Kiddon
L.A. Young
J.W. Brackett
L. Wood
H. Wood
Lyman Eaton
J.W. Underwood
L.W. Gleason
W. Bird
W.H. Briggs
John Robinson
G. Burlingame
E. Morey
J.H. Ballard
Morris Oram
H.W. Moore
G.B. Day
F.S. Ford
D. Stickney
R. Block
(Continued next page)

Charles J. Helmer
B.F. Curnass
George Jordon /sic/
N. Flint
J.M. Gray
E.J. Perry
J. Mithcell
Benjamin Roe
J.C. Smith
G.O. Briean /sic/
L. Tinkham
J. Farrant
W. Shattuck
J. Richardson
J. Doyle
P. Cosgrove
W.H. Moody
R. Bangs
S.L. Brown
D.W. Grant
B. Dodge
H. Smith
Oliver Carver
Anthony Crosby
W.P. Bond
W.G. Soraery
C.C. Bartlett
I.S. Welton
John Morgan
W. Thorpe
A. Martin
Leonard Martin
D. Boyd
E. McDonald
L.B. Buxton
G.W. Wright
C. Jones
George Ware
T.W.G. Davidson
C.L. Raynor
E.L. Chapman
Joseph Layton
George Butts
Myron Feeder
E.B. Mc_____(?)
Henry Carter
M.T. Ashly
R.S. Barnes
D. Cole
J. Mittzer
W.H. Holbrook

L.O. Preston and
    wife
Mrs.___Lindsey
H.B. Platt and wife
J. Croylin
E.G. Meeks, lady,
    nurse, 1 child
    & 2 infants
E.G. Higgins
J. Thomas
G. Harvey
T. Bean
S. Bean
J. Spear
S. Water
    ___Buswell
M. Buswell
J.Y. Williamson
J. Nye
N. Osgood
T. Pusher
G. Pusher
P. McCann
J. Gilley
A.H. Fogg
J.A. Morgan
    ___Collins
E.F. Niles
William Niles
C.E. Hatch
E.B. Chase
C. Rogers
B.F. Story
Asa Cram
J. Blis /sic/
George A. McIntosh
E. Welt
R.H. Wilson
John Mather
S. Broderick
W. Watson
W. Simpson
F. Taylor
James M. Gulliver
C. Teaffer
A.S. Vankensen
N. Bersh
J. Lawless
John Wilson
W.M. Kennan
O. Mason

F. Pea?ks
E.B. Sammis and
    wife
Samuel Isaac
J. Peel and svt/sic/
J. Peel Jr. /sic/
W.L. Henderson
Miss___McMuston
J.O. Turner
D.T. Russ
M. Wadleigh
J. Pernell
Mr.___Thompson
D. Wooster
F.O. Saunders
R. Craton /sic/
J. Crayton/sic/
G. Tobin
B. Otis
T. Goldthurst
P. Lamb
A.P. McMaster
L. McMaster
W. Kingly
G. Pearks
J.M. Aldon
F. Buckley
R. Buckley
O. Buckley
C.W. Meddock
Mrs. C.W. Meddock and
    daughter
A.W. Brotham
W.M. Graves
J.B. Smith
G. Smith
E. Hubbard
J. McIntosh
R.W. Spalding
M.J. Turner
John Shaffer
A. McCurdy
Seth Flanders
John Eastman
J.W. Vanper
M.H. Haslor
Charles Martin
S. Condon
H. Condon
J. Condon
L. Mason
(Continued next page)

T. Goin and wife
Mrs.___Armstrong
    and 2 children
W.H. Clark and wife
Mary A. Peel /sic/
Mary Peele /sic/
    ___Randall
C.L. Goodwin
F. Castel (?)
    (Castei?)
D.D. Kent
B.S. Kent
S.R. Dennett /sic/
N.G. Dorr
H.P. Dyer
A. Shepherd
J.H. Drake
R. King
F. Morrill
J. Adams
C. Adams
J.W. Reed
P. Cornwell
A. Dunn
W. Gisson
Mrs. T. Rooney
A.H. Berry
J. Mullins
E.L. Smith
Mr.___Monson
M. Brans
W. Brans
John Stretch
John Elliott
R. Wood
A. Hank
H. McWilliams
D. Rugg
U. Rugg
G. Wilson
John Donovan
George Hasford
Charles Smith
J. Strubi (?)
    (Strubl?)
Thomas Barrett
E. Powers
C.H. Plumb
J.B. Plumb
Thomas Shannon
J. Mason

W.M. Markham	James E. Patterson	M. Jennings
J.H. Vansickle /sic/	W.L. Knapp	J.H. Holman
J.F. Hoyt	J.P. Burton	L.W. Stevans /sic/
Mrs. Alexina F. Baker (added)	Lewis Baker (added)	

- - - - -

SHIP: REPUBLIC
TYPE: Steamer   FROM: Panama
ARRIVED: February 6, 1852   CAPTAIN: Hudson
PASSAGE: 21 days from Panama, via intermediate ports. Sailed from
Taboga Bay at an early hour on January 16, 1852. Experienced unusually strong northerly winds in the Gulf of
Tehuantepec; stove pilot-house during the blow. Arrived
off Acapulco, Mexico on evening of January 23rd, but owing
to a thick haze did not run in until daylight. On January
28, 1852, at 7:30AM, a passenger, James O'Neal, died of
typhoid fever. He was from Lowell, Massachusetts and was
aged 24 years. Touched at San Blas, Mexico and carried
the body on shore for burial, Rev. S. Reynolds reading
the funeral service. On January 29th arrived at Mazatlan,
Mexico, in the morning and sailed the same evening. On
February 1, 1852, a passenger, William Mathews, from
Pennsylvania, died. He was aged 29 years and during his
illness, from choice, he was attended solely by his
friends. On February 3rd entered San Diego harbor at
11:00PM. Found the steamer "McKim" still laid there; many
of her passengers had gone overland to San Francisco,
after having received provisions for the trip from the
military supplies at San Diego, California. Touched at
Monterey, California on February 6th.
CARGO: Not listed.

Passengers

Madame___Greyer	L. Levy and lady	Mr.___Beatty
B.F. Eaton	Rev. J. Reynolds	Miss N. Clayton
E. Atkinson	Mrs.___Naglee and	Miss M. Keefe
Mrs.___Atkinson	2 children	Mrs.___Harris
& 2 children	C. Brainard	G.S. Leet
F.A. Stenson	A. Brackets	Mrs. E.C. Glover
E. Goodman	J. Carbin	H.D. Hanscome /sic/
E. Hosmer	E. Wheeler	C. Sweet
A. Hayward	George H. Meyer	Charles Maurice
W. Thompson	J.N. Hillbrant	Maurice Martin
John Delaney	J. McKane, lady and	W.J. Hawkins
E. Hall	2 children	Pat Kinney
F. Hall	Thomas Crowell and	Mrs.___Smith
L. Decker and	lady	H. Cake
lady	N.J. Parker	J. Castrell and
J. Cohen	Maurice Sanders	lady
D. Wheeler	W. Altree	R. Thompson
George Bates	H.W. Newton	J. Monroe

(Continued next page)

A. Smith
Smith
William Keggie
A. Gaelch (?)
(Gaelcb?)
Marcus Torrey
O. Flequen
J. Westwood
W. Ryan
A.C. McCoy
R. Korkman
William Van Metter
J. Bingham
J. Tole
Wesley Carlisle
W. Hyle
Daniel McCoy
J.W. Neal
T. Jefferson
G.A. Hall
T. Sexton
L. Houghton
J. Northup
J. Somers
Miss___Heiser and
sister
J.M.M. Metyle
B.F. Rose
J. Sigman
William Steward
D. Richardson
O. Bayley
Boston
F. Lovell
C. Cotter (?)
(Cotten?)
J.F. Kelley
E. Wagner
T. Parker
D. Campbell
J.V. Hathaway
James Dewey
J. Jordan
S. Williams
John Lebar
A.I. Peirse /sic/
Dodge
I. Head
J.B. Haines
H.T. Livingston
J.F. Silver

D. Fuller
W. Eveleth(?)
(Evelath?)
S. Caby
P. Mattheso /sic/
C. Melin
James Franconi
W. Clark
W. Runyon
S. Kenworthy
J. O'Neil /sic/
William Bates
William Rich
Robert Davidson
J. Lane
S. Benton
William Coste
W.P. Rice
W.T. McLellen
J. Hughes
W.D. Kierse(?)
(Bierse?,
Rierse?)
P. Hawke
J. Trouilette
S. Harmon
A.S. Hall
James Creighton
R. Macdonald /sic/
M. Westerville
G. Russell
H. Daniels
M. Fitch
C. Clark
A.C. Coats
Coats 2nd
W. O'Hara
J. Close
F. Luther, lady and
2 children
H. Squares
W.W. Alley
H.E. Maddox
W. Warren
N. Withey
James Brewster
A. Boardman
J.H. Abercrombie
Vhich /sic/
D.M. McCutcheon
Joseph Morante
(Continued next page)

Sandford
James Rorlies
W. Brylon
W.C. Wooden
P.R. Wooden
H. Dean
James Stephenson
Samuel Stepenson
George Smith
J. Roberts
J.S. Odgers
Samuel Glover
J. Nicholson
N. Stotts
Ira Ball
George Chambers
A. McFree
W.B. Ford
J.S. Ford
Edward Smith
J.R. Williams
Hiram Russel /sic/
P. Kipper and wife
B. Kipper
Bernard Martin
M. Stinson
J. Cristman /sic/
W. Payne
S. Creason
J. Anderson
J. Richards
J. Todd
W. Bridge
H.S. Bonney
A. Lyon
J. Badts
J.T. Dunstan
J. Welsh
P. Bush
H. West
C. Houghtalang /sic/
Dunlap
M.J. Bowers
B.J. Barker
Mrs.___King
W. Hedges (?)
(Hodges?)
Mr. Quien Sabe
M. Rodgers
R. Talent
M. Silver

J. Brown
Joseph Wythe
___ Hitchcock
Stephen Norris, wife
& daughter
W. Helen
W.P. Alley 2nd
Thomas Coffin
William Langley
H. Nye
J. Thayer
___ Leffer
T.S. Lyhart
S.A. Pennock
M. Decker
W. Carroll
J.J. Cowan
L.B. Treat
J.H. Brumegem
___ Danforth
M. Casat
C. Gougat
D. Dunningham
W.A. Reeves
J. Reeves
J. Peiley (?)
(Pelley?)
J.D. Ware
A. Barsaille
W.T. Johnston
S. Parshall /sic/
J. Bucklao (?)
(Buckleo?,
Buckloo?)
L. Truss
M. Kinsmyer (?)
(Kinamyer?)
W. Hanford
L. Jones
W. Davis
J. Evans /sic/
J. Edwards
W.B. Cowan
M. Callohan
M. Nagle /sic/
P.R. Livingston
R. Clark
S. Frisancho
W. Bryant
Senor___ Fenander
Senora___ Espinola

J. Williams/sic/
M. Hiness (?)
R. Tarball
T. McMurray
E. Bellows
G. Stowell
J.C. Wood
W. Merritt
M. Roberts
A. Hall /sic/
N. Halt /sic/
S. Allen
L.E. King
E.C. Lovering
A.C. Shotwell (?)
(A.G. Shotwell?)
J. Lyon
___ Hayden
Rev.Mr.___ Bird
A. Lenox
___ Jones
G.B. Fayette
B.P. Christopher
N. Marshall
J. O'Hara
W.H. Graham
W. Taggett
A. Van Buren
G. Kenny
J. Kenny
E. Kenar /sic/
S.R. Kelly
___ Langdale
J. Hoffman
S.M. Robertson
G. Whiting
M. Chamberlain
L.H. Cleaver
W. Mathews
Thomas Williams
J. Williams/sic/
D. Thomas
M. Thomas
E. Curran
Mr.___ Brenan
Capt. O. Daggett
L. Schwarz
R. Maul (?)(Maui?)
S. Bloomfield
Senor___ Sancho
Senor___ Sanchez
(Continued next page)

John Sylvester
T.E. Tucker
M. Schenck
John H. Todd
W.W. Brainwall
J. Wilson
James Hitchings
G. Brown/sic/
T. Falkner
O. Hanscomb /sic/
___ Washburn
J. Henderson
M. Zurman
Thomas Anderson
R. McKintley (?)
(McKittley?)
J. Norris
___ Knapp
E. Duncke
B. Galliard /sic/
P. Galliardet /sic/
___ Yates
O. Wells
A.L. Milliet
J.C. Wigginton
E.W. Moss
C. Pugh
D. Stewart
J. Thomas
P. Courey
G. Brown/sic/
J. Penn?
J. Lafkin /sic/
Mrs.___ Lufkin /sic/
L. Lahman
A.J. Somers
J.D. Vaughn
D. Lewis
J. Lewis
E. Ellis
E. Reese
S. Giarrun
A. Hall/sic/
W. Lesher
Madame___ Goux
J. Evans/sic/
J. Gavin
J. Sirey and lady
M. Sherman
M. Culbert
___ Espinola

Senor___Lopez, lady & 2 children	Mr.___Parsons	Senor___Louis Senor___Roderiquez

- - - - -

SHIP: SEA BIRD
TYPE: Steamer   FROM: San Diego, Calif.
ARRIVED: February 7, 1852   CAPTAIN: Haley
PASSAGE: 61 hours from San Diego, California, via intermediate
         port of San Pedro, California.
CARGO: Not listed.

Passengers

Mr. W. Riley	Mr.___Hunter	Mr.___Taylor
Mr.___Forbes	J.C. Williams	___Estudillo
E. Crawford	John Wright	H. Carpenter
E. Sweet	James Kelley	L.D. Holcomb
Larco Garcia	J.F. Simmons	Mrs.___Roer
John Clawson	W.T.B. Sanford	G. Bower
J. Rodgers	V.C. Percival	Mr.___Martin
P. Francisco	A.S. Reed	L. Couch
S. Watkins	Henry Palmer	J. Harris
J.B. Lease /sic/	David Spence	C.H. Johnson/sic/
(J.P. Leese?)	C.H. Johnson/sic/	Capt.___Cooper
W. Munras	M. Tabois	M. Pacheco
J. Royle	J.R. Macey	John Comfort
E. Brown	John Gonman Sen.	J.H. Swain
J. Ferguson	John Gonman Jr.	F. Manuel
W.P. Allen	W.P. Smith	C. Manuel
John Bartlett	L. Bo?ke	A. Ferguson
F. Giddy	(Booke?)	P. Garcia
Henry Patterson	Dr.___Fitch	___Curtis
J. Conway	C. Paulison and lady	Miss___Furnish

- - - - -

SHIP: MARY A. JONES
TYPE: Brig   FROM: Valparaiso, Chile
ARRIVED: February 7, 1852   CAPTAIN: Thomas
PASSAGE: 45 days from Valparaiso, Chile.
CARGO: In ballast.

Passengers

S.R. Nurse	Capt. D. McCarty	Capt. F. Smith
Capt. S. Cushman	W. Watson	W. Nelson
P. DeKock	E. Fletcher	C. Cormiel
Miss Juana Ramirez	Miss Cista Palma	

and 60 unidentified in steerage

- - - - -

SHIP: GRECIAN
TYPE: Brig   FROM: Oregon Territory
ARRIVED: February 7, 1852   CAPTAIN: Elliott
PASSAGE: 7 days from the Oregon Territory.
         (Continued next page)

CARGO: 120,000 feet of unspecified lumber.

Passengers

M. Marvin   V. Anderson   C. Goodrich
W. Berry

- - - - - -

SHIP: VESUVIUS
TYPE: Barque   FROM: Oregon Territory
ARRIVED: February 7, 1852   CAPTAIN: Woodburn
PASSAGE: 9 days from the Oregon Territory.
CARGO: 50 ploughs, 110 bags wheat and 112,000 feet of unspecified
        lumber.

Passenger
Mr. S.J. Oakley

- - - - -

SHIP: OHIO
TYPE: Steamer   FROM: San Diego, Calif.
ARRIVED: February 8, 1852   CAPTAIN: Hilliard
PASSAGE: 4 days from San Diego, via intermediate ports. Left at
San Diego the steamer "McKim", uncertain when she would
leave, being in distress. Brought up a number of her
passengers. On February 6, 1852 arrived at the embarcadero
on the coast near San Luis Obispo, California, and sent
off a boat containing the second mate, Thomas McCullen,
Purser E.S. Deane, Hon. H.A. Tefft and three seaman,
William T. Parsons, William Jeston and William Stevens.
When about 100 yards of the shore, the boat capsized, and
all in her except Purser Deane and Seaman Stevens were
drowned. Mr. Tefft (Henry A. Tefft) was a Judge of San
Luis Obispo, California and a native of Washington
County, New York. He had come on board at Santa Barbara,
expecting to land at San Luis Obispo, meet his family, and
proceed on the "Ohio" to San Francisco.
CARGO: Not listed.

Passengers

Mr. Goodman	T. Dowels	Mr. Agull
W. Green	G. Dowels	T. Carter
G.V. Bond	W.W. Church	G. Carter
Bond	D. Melarkey	W.T. Kelley
W.B. White	W. Adair	R.S. Stricklin
A.A. Johnson	J. Holcomb	S. Richison
J. Minard	A. Thompson	A. Cleaveland
J. Brown	G. Goodlet	J. Dunell
James Brown	L. Sanford	M. Montgomery
C.H. Townsend	C. Dunbar	J. Poor
Mr. Oldershaw	D.M. Lawrence	W. Brown
T. Armour	J.B. Davis	R. Engenhart
P.E. Jeffries	A. Crowell	L. Richison
F. Carl	O.F. Tay	G. Blackburn
P. Carl	J.W. Oldham	J. Kyle

(Continued next page)

F. Symester	R. Braston	J. Hird
Mrs.___Obushine	E.M. Tuttle	W.P. Fivits
B. Cox and lady	J. Harriman	G.E. Harris and wife
W. Roberts	E. Church /sic/	D. Douglass
H. Derby	E. Church /sic/	T. Harvey
S. Derby	A. Church	J. Norton
J. Willis	B.F. Joy	S.D. Randal /sic/
H. Dousman and wife	J.M. Jeffs	J. Salar
M. Roche	J. Manferas	Mr.___Cohen
Mrs.___Martin		

- - - - -

SHIP: FAYAWAY
TYPE: Schooner   FROM: Bodega, Calif.
ARRIVED: February 8, 1852   CAPTAIN: Kissam
PASSAGE: 20 hours from Bodega, California.
CARGO: 1 ton turnips, 65 tons of potatoes and 16,000 ft lumber.

Passenger
Mr. J.O. Farrell

- - - - -

SHIP: OREGON
TYPE: Steamer   FROM: Panama
ARRIVED: February 11,1852   CAPTAIN: Pearson
PASSAGE: 14 days and 7 hours from Panama, via Acapulco, Mexico and
San Diego, California. Left Panama on Monday, January 26,
1852. Stopped at the Island of Taboga to take in water
and other stores, and at 10:00PM, proceeded to sea. On
Tuesday, January 27th, at 6:00AM passed Point Mala. At
12 midnight, arrived at Acapulco, Mexico. On Monday,
February 2nd, having received on board coal and stores at
5:00PM, proceeded to sea. On February 5th made Cape St.
Lucas. On February 6th, at 1:00AM, Mr. Lal Richards, a
steerage passenger, died from the effect of a heavy fall
that he received while in a fit. At 7:30AM his remains
were committed to the deep. He was from Cornwall, England.
At 11:00AM was boarded by Capt.___Hull, of the whale
ship "Catherine", of New London, 2 months from the Sand-
wich Islands, and 16 months from home. Had on board 150
barrels of oil and had sent home 1500 barrels. On
February 9th, arrived at San Diego, California at 1:00AM,
found there the propeller vessel "McKim", 72 days from
Panama. Left San Diego at 10:00AM, and continued voyage.
Arrived San Francisco, in a dense fog, on Wednesday,
February 11th at 8:00AM. Running time from Panama to
San Francisco was 14 days and 7 hours.
CARGO: Not listed.

Passengers

Mr.___Foss and lady	H. Jacks, lady and 3 children	Miss___Jacks
Mrs.___Woods & infant	Mrs.___Jacks	Miss___Miller
	(Continued to next page)	Mrs.___Hayes

Mr.& Mrs.___ Bailey
 & 3 children
T.L. Smith
J.M. Robinson
C.K. Smith
Mr.& Mrs.___ Palmer
 & 3 children
A. Reddington /sic/
Mr.___ Folinsbee
 (U.S.N.)
Mr.& Mrs.___ Bowne
 and child
J.L. Hooper
D. Collins
W. Damon
L. Howard
B. Hill
O. Allen
J. Batchelder
W. Davis
W. Ingram
I. McGinnis
G.B. Mauser/sic/
Mrs. E. Mason
Mr.& Mrs.___ Philips
 & 3 children
Mrs.___ Norwood
Miss J.W. Lougee
Miss S.L. Lougee
Mrs. E. French
Mrs.___ Vincent
Capt.___ Hunter
 (U.S.M.)
D.L. Fish
G.B. Harger
M. Webster
K. Reiser
J.E. Herring
B.F. Reynolds
Joseph Bickford
James Laney
M.M. Woodward
C.C. Drew
J. Bryant
B. Bryant
E. Marsh
R. Waymouth
J.A. Nourse
J. Kelly
M.J. Fuller
R.M. Bridger

Mr.& Mrs.___ Totman
V.C. Healey
W.L. Healey
Mrs.___ Turner
C.A. Thackston
Mrs.___ Hoffmeyer
Mrs.___ Jones
C.H. Jones
J.C. Baldwin
Mr.___ Rattle
Mr.& Mrs.___ Fellows
 & 4 children
Miss___ Fellows
S. Hartnett
P. Dismond (?)
 (Diamond?)
C. Sprague
C. Swift
L.P. Jones
F. Haulthaus
F.C. Fletcher
S. Stetinins
D. Childs
Miss___ Jenkins
Mrs.___ Loveland,
 infant & svt
Mrs.___ Parker and
 infant
Mrs. J.E. Hollow
Mrs.___ Davenport
Mrs.___ Rice
Capt.___ Dobbins
F.E. Flint /sic/
H.W. Brown
John P. Lawrence
L. Bishop
W.B. Gould
G.S. Cushing
H.G. Mitchell
P. Johnson
D. Owens
William Kenler
C. Gilbert
J. Chandler
B. Starkweather
O. Wilde
J. Clapp
H.P. Morse
J.W. Boynton
M.G. Robbins
P. Shottenkirk
(Continued to next page)

Mr.& Mrs.___ Johnson
W.L. Palmer
J.R. Clark
E. Townsend and
 servant
C.H. Kimball
A.N. Ebbetts
E.A. Ebbetts
Mr.___ Koschland
Mr.& Mrs. S. Francis
 and child
Mr.& Mrs. D.L. Beck
Col.___ Rhodes,
 lady and 2 chldrn
R. Singlelton /sic/
H. Manser/sic/
T. Welsh
N. Holmes
L. Parkhurst
G. Dohling
G.H. Knox
F.S. Everett
Mrs.___ Leadrum and
 3 children (?)
 (Lesdrum?)
Mrs.___ Cooney
Mrs. H. Watts
Mrs.___ Manser and
 boy /sic/
Mrs.___ Ragsdale
R.M. Russel /sic/
W.M. Green
J.D. Rollins
M. Costello
H. Silsby
T. Ewings
P.W. Caldwell
N. Gay
Robert Gray
W.W. McGoun
G. Badger
George Torney
A.B. Newhall
J.N. Wilson
W.H. Jewell
T.J. Knowles
T. Tollman/sic/
J.L. Tillman /sic/
A.J. Knowles
A. Goodrich
C. Fillebroun

C. Coney
H. Ingram
E. Brewer
H.A. Hildreth
W.F. Wright
A. Ayer
William Prossers
J. Cheeney
M. Swift
S. Averill
C. Monroe
Pat Fleming
M. Manna
G. Wonnamaker
A. Cushing
J. Cushing
James Petit
H.V. McComber
B.F. Varnum
Charles Sprague
Joseph Pearl
W.H. Silsby
A.P. Seely
D. Turner
O.B. Wyman
Thomas J. Petit
F. Brown
E.W. Shaw
C. Bacon
A. Palmer
G.T. Andrews
S.W. Gilkey
C. White
D.S. Gaines
J. Watts
C.H. Fisher
W.P. McGrath
A.A. Meyer
J.M. Evans
M. Reardon
T. Reardon
J.D. Byers
J.M. Soule
A.O. Spencer Jr.
C.H. Lungren
J. Corbyn
D.M. Kelly
A.B. Primston
H. Goff Jr.
J.W. Vandevender
C.L. Fassett

J. Spalding
John Spalding
C. Craft
W.P. Bassett
J. Schneider
G.W. Payne
J. Aurey
E. Hader
L.B. Drury
A.J. Drury
M. Hartnett
G. Carpenter
S.D. Skiff
B.F. Merill /sic/
J.C. Corey
J. Terry
L. Rounsville
G. Rounsville
O.C. Clark
S.J. Howe
D. Wales
D. Harger
W. Pendergrass
G. Willis, 2nd
J.H. Gordon
C. Twombly
T. Letskus(?)
  (Letakus?)
S. Judkins
R. Griffith
J. Buckley Jr.
M.B. Blanchard
O. Shaft
T.D. Reese
C.C. McCall
W. Ellsworth
D.H. Yeckley
  Goodlander
J.M. Fulton
D. Fitzpatrick
W. Scravendyke
W. Wilson
G.A. Hubbell
J. Tudor
J. Kinney
G. Talcott
T. Hasam and lady
J.B. Nourse
R. Nearman
R. Brown
J.A. Farmer

H. Richardson
Z. Marsh
M.M. Goff
J.M. French
P. Lewis
J.B. Mory
T.R.D. Stewart
J. Jones
T.K. Bacon
E. Burdick
F. Duffy
W. Whitney
E. Ashley
A. Ashley
H.S. Ashley
C.F. Spooner
E. Staffords/sic/
T.F. Haffords/sic/
H. Brush
John Rolie
C. Hosmer
John Carron
A. Colloton
E. Colloton
John D. Sliter
L. Croft
S.A. Downing
G. Schuster
D. Leathers
W.T. Reese
J.S. York
D. Bruckley
W.R. Griffith
James C. Drew
W.F. Graham
J. Behe (?)
A.J. Lowell
  Coningham
L.A. Corbyn
T. Sullivan
J.M. Barnes
J. Barnes
W. Coleby
S.J. John
  (Johnson?)
J.G. Post
Capt.___Midgett
D.C. James
T. O'Leary
F. Sherman
W. O'Neil

(Continued next page)

A. Pierce	H. Diamond	R.H. Hickerson
T. Bartlett	J. Graham	G. Kline
John Short	D.M. Kelly	B.V. Weeks
H.A. Bostwick	J. Stonier	J.M. Whipple
J. Heffernan	C. Blodgett	J. Turner
G.G. James	E. Coppins	Borre
A. Summerland	F. McConnell	G.W. Chandler
J.B. Ford	W. Stone	N. Rufter
Furrie	E. Thomas	G. Babb
G.T. Darling	G. Blodgett	L.C. Shepard
J. Hobbs	M. Chandler	P. Sherry
L. Griffin	E. Johnson	P. Simon
M. Williams/sic/	E. Howard	A. Wilson
M.D. Holbrook	A.H. Lilly/sic/	W. Bond
W. Powell	A. Libby /sic/	T. Bond
D. Webster	M. Libby /sic/	R. Bond
B.B. Bradbury	E. Watkins	M. Williams/sic/
G. Elkin	M. Dacon	R. Williams
A. Mayer	W. Edwards	John Duffy
T.W. McGuire	H.M. Lovell /sic/	H. Chattle
J. Heer	J. Gardiner	J. Gwinn
J. Schneider	W. Dromple	G. Wemgerde
H. Moore	L.S. Williams	Mr. Vaughn
A. Boyden	H. Hawes	G.R. Bartlett
Senor Alvarez	Peter Petit	(U.S.N.)
B.M. Moulton	M. Furniss	J.L. Smith
D. Ketirick	John McNeil	A.R. Glidden
William Dorety /sic/	A. Cunningham	Michal Kelly /sic/
E. Stone	J. Mahoney	E.A. Brown
C. Mentor	Thomas Costello	J.W. Brown
W. Barnitt /sic/	J. Sullivan	M. Derby
S. Buckingham	W.O. Brien /sic/	M. McCarty
S.B. Robinson	J. Gillman	J.C. Jordan
R. Tilton	O. Goodwin	J. Dwire
Joseph Cornelius /sic/	N. Morcom	G. Roach
B. Dawler	A. Kendall	James Reynolds
John Ring	Samuel Manly	O. Willoughby
H. Richards	James White	James Cocking
J.H. Clement/sic/	J. French	J.E. Stinson
J.H. Clement/sic/	H. Boynton	James Richards
Edmund Mitchell	Daniel Meade	R.B. Stinson
William Paul	R. Morcom	M. Ridley
R. Mitchell	D.D. Hobart	L. Allcott
A. Goodwin/sic/	J.S. Carter	W. Harbison
G. Rook (?)(Rock?)	J.H. Scott	William Turner
L. Richards	James Letcher	William Cornelious
L. Richards Jr.	A. Goodwin/sic/	/sic/
J. Richards	John Rolie Jr.	M. Cornelious /sic/
D.W. Horne	G.A. Stevens	L.B. Moulton
L.D. Easman	H. Stapleford	

- - - - - -

SHIP: WALTER CLAXTON
TYPE: Barque   FROM: Sydney, N.S.W.
ARRIVED: February 12, 1852   CAPTAIN: Goodspeed
PASSAGE: 67 days from Sydney, New South Wales. Made the land of
         Monterey, California on February 7th. Had light winds
         from Montery to San Francisco. On board are several
         families who desire to settle in California. This vessel
         brings intelligence that a very strong prejudice exists
         among the greater part of the population of the South Sea
         British Colonies towards Americans, more especially those
         who uphold the acts of the Vigilance Committee in Califor-
         nia.
CARGO: 113 bags barley, 50 boxes soap, 30 bags oats and 1 box of
       clothing.

Passengers

John Cook	Mrs. Anna S. Ross	Mr.& Mrs. J. Drum
Mrs. Mary McRoberts	Master J. Ross	Miss Sarah A. Drum
Mrs. Bridget Randel	Miss Anna Ross	Master B.J. Drum
Mrs. Barbara Rooham	Miss Rebecca Ross	Master John Drum
Miss Barbara Rooham	Miss Mary Hefferman	Mr.& Mrs. T. Carew
Miss Mary Rooham	Miss Ellen White	Master John Carew
Mr.& Mrs.___ O'Neil	Miss Leonora Scott	Master Thomas Carew
Master Andrew O'Neil	Miss Ellen Coffield	Master William Carew
Mast.William O'Neil	Mrs. Sarah Cook	Mrs. Mary T. Young
Master Michael O'Neil	Miss Isabella Cook	Miss Rebecca J.Young
Master John O'Neil	Miss Mary J. Cook	Mrs. A.S. Green
Miss Ann O'Neil	Miss Sarah Green	Miss A.S. Green

- - - - - -

SHIP: OUD ALBLAS
TYPE: Barque (Dutch)   FROM: Amsterdam, Holland
ARRIVED: February 12, 1852   CAPTAIN: Kruymel
PASSAGE: 198 days from Amsterdam, Holland, via Valparaiso, Chile,
         68 days.
CARGO: 520 tons of coal, 500 bags bran, 20 bags beans, 10 cases of
       chocolate, 2 casks wine, 36 bbls hams, over 3000 bags of
       flour, 29 pipes of gin, 20 boxes cheese, 270 bags oats and
       2890 bags of barley

Passengers

Mr.___Pescheux, lady and son   Mr.___Laurison and lady
          and 13 unidentified in steerage

- - - - - -

SHIP: VENUS
TYPE: Schooner (Mexican)   FROM: Mazatlan, Mexico
ARRIVED: February 14, 1852   CAPTAIN: Moratoro
PASSAGE: No passage time listed. From Mazatlan, Mexico, via San
         Hosea.
CARGO: 100 bbls of eggs, 10 bales of dried figs, 6 bundles of
       saddles.

(Continued next page)

Passengers

Miss Louisa Torre	Miss B. Parraso	Miss Louisa Lopez
P. Clement	J. Ortiz	P. Santilian
A. Parro	C. Morales	

and 38 unidentified in Steerage

- - - - - -

SHIP: COLUMBIA
TYPE: Steamer FROM: Astoria, Oregon Terr.
ARRIVED: February 15, 1852 CAPTAIN: C.V. LeRoy
PASSAGE: 70 hours from Astoria, Oregon Territory. The "Columbia" brings intelligence that the propeller vessel "General Warren" has been wrecked at the mouth of the Columbia River, and forty-two of the fifty-two, passengers and crew perished. Some of the survivors of the "General Warren" are returning to San Francisco on board the "Columbia".
CARGO: Not listed.

Passengers

Mr.___Goggin (Mail Agent)	Ellwood Evans	Benjamin Stark
A. Woolf	Lucien Snow	J.M. Breck
W.H. Baxter	William Geiler	Mr.___Sharp
Mr.___Wall*(of Trinidad, Calif.)	E.L. Finch*	Rev.Matthew Nolan*
	J. Van Burkier	Augustus Kip
J. Rapelve(?)	Rev.___Prelott(?)	Rev.___Roque
John W. Thompson	John Brown	William Carr
D.C. Norton	John Willis	Nathaniel Ellis
John Lyons	L.D. Duvall	John A. Mitchell
James Isaacs	E.B. Mismer	Abner Johnson
A. Husted	C.B. Sartin	F. Ball
Levi Laird	Q.M. Read	A.H. Francis
P. Raleigh	John C. Green	John T. Ricketts
A.E. Engleberry	John Johnson	R. Ralston
Thomas M. Preston	Jesse Cook	T.J. Ferguson
C.H. Fairchild	Thomas J. Biggs(?) (Blaga?)	Cyrus Cheney
W.M. Harper	H.A. Pearce	E.N. Strout
George Turner	James F. Bybee	John Mills
Mr.___Holcomb	W.H. Bliss	Mr.___Sayward
Mr.___Jolly	Mr.___Fleury	Mr.___Rigaux
William Jones*,2nd Officer of "Gen. Warren"+	Edward Beverly*, 1st Officer of "Gen. Warren"	Mr.___Fleming
		James Murray*, seaman of "Gen. Warren"
Isaac Sparrow*,seaman of "Gen. Warren"		

(*) Indicates passengers saved from the "General Warren".
(+) One contemporary source carries the 2nd Officer of the "General Warren" as "William Irons".

SHIP: FLYING FISH
TYPE: Clipper FROM: Boston, Mass.
ARRIVED: February 15, 1852 CAPTAIN: Nickles?(Nickels?)
(Continued next page)

PASSAGE: 98 days from Boston, Massachusetts. Experience light
weather during the whole passage. Passed the equator in
18½ days; to Cape Horn, 49 days; to equator on the
Pacific, 76 days from Boston. Was within 1000 miles of
San Francisco for 15 days. Greatest day's run was 336
miles; greatest speed, 15. Shortest day's run was 49
miles. Made 1194 miles the first four days out of
Boston. On December 23, 1851, in lat. 55-20S, long. 63-
57W, spoke the whale ship "Dartmouth", of New Bedford,
Manchester the master, 3½ months out. Same date, saw the
whale ship "Roscoe", of New Bedford.
> *(Flying Fish was built by Mackay, of Boston and has
> dimensions: 1505 tons; length, 220 feet; beam, 40
> feet; depth of hold, 21 feet)

CARGO: 4 looking glasses, 140 kegs white lead, scythes, drugs,
axes, 4 casks horseshoe nails, paint, vinegar, 50 boxes of
furniture, 10 tons pig iron, lead pipe, linseed oil, castor
oil, 50 casks whale oil, 8 carriage wheels, 4 pkgs of
carriage body gear, 50,000 face bricks, 6 carriages, lobsters,
safes, boiler and sheet iron, oysters, liquor and assorted
goods.

Passengers

Russell Ellis and wife	Mrs. Alborne Allen	Miss Josephine Morrow
R.F. Ellis	Mr. G.W. Webster	Mr. J. Gorham
	Charles Ellis	Mr.___Bond

- - - - - -

SHIP: SEA BIRD

TYPE: Steamer   FROM: San Diego, Calif.
ARRIVED: February 16, 1852   CAPTAIN: Haley
PASSAGE: 48 hours from San Diego, California, via intermediate
ports. Left San Diego on February 13, 1852. Called at
San Pedro, California and departed same on February 14th.
Called at Santa Barbara, California and departed same on
morning of February 15th. Stopped at Monterey, California
and departed on February 16th at 10:00AM. Weather during
latter part of voyage rainy and foggy.

CARGO: Not listed.

Passengers

Capt.___Couts	Dr.___Griffin	A. Wenthauk (?)
Lt. T.D. Johns	Major E. Barry	W. Bausman (?)
A.M. King	T.F. Keyser	(Bautman?)
J. Steele	M. Seaton	John J. Pratt
H.C. Pratt	W. Brooks	R. Tuttle
G. Miller	R. O'Neil	J. Greer
Mr.___Waite (?)	J.G. Messacks	M. Michael
(White?)	P. Monroe	R. G?isley and boy
M. Keeler	Col.___Russell	(Geisley?)
Joseph Gilman	S.M. Parsons	J.W. Bradley
R. Baker	R.T. Abbott	E.E. Porter
F.R. West	C.A. Guiqsel	J. Carroll
	(Continued next page)	

(*)Listed as in source. Refers to Donald McKay, ship-builder.

J. Filkins	D. Rouse	T.J. Sprague
Henry Filkins	J.K. Smith	Mr.___Carr
Mr.___Hill	F. Bustamente	Mr.___Beudalin,
George Beyn (?)	Josepha Bustamente	lady and son
(Seyn?)	Loreta Bustamente	Major___Bird
L. Cutter	and 4 children	General___Raines
J. Pope	E. Kambert	J.F. Spence
Miss Josephine Russell	G.M. Potter	A. Newbould
S.P. Endicott	J. Minaher(?)	E.J. Peters
J. Sullivan	(Minsher?)	S.B. Babcock

- - - - - -

SHIP: ST. MARYS
TYPE: U.S. Sloop of War   FROM: Callao, Peru
ARRIVED: February 17, 1852   CAPTAIN: George A. Magruder
PASSAGE: 34 days from Callao, Peru, lately from a cruise among the
South Sea Islands. Purpose of the cruise was to give
protection to American whaling interests and to secure
treaties with the natives of the Navigator and Fejee
(Fiji) Islands. Made the run from Ovalau, Fejee (Fiji)
to Talcahuana, Chile, a distance of 6000 miles, in 28
days.

List of Officers

Lt. James S. Biddle	Lt(Acting)T.J. Corbin	John J. Abernethy
Lt. Robert E. Watson	Purser A.E. Watson	(Surgeon)
Homer C. Blake	George R. Graham	Richard B. Tunstall
(Acting Master)	(Marine Officer)	(Asst Surgeon)
Jonathan Young	Dulany A. Forrest	John Curry
(Passed Midship-	(Passed Midship-	(Captain's Clerk)
man)	man)	James A. Green
Benjamin P. Loyall	William H. Ward	(M.S.)*
(M.S.)*	(M.S.)*	James Meads
William B. Fugitt	James Hutchinson	(Carpenter)
(Sailmaker)	(Acting Gunner)	John J.R. West
		(Acting Boat-
(*)M.S.-Midshipmen		swain)

- - - - - - -

SHIP: GEORGE WASHINGTON
TYPE: Schooner   FROM: Honolulu, S.I.
ARRIVED: February 17, 1852   CAPTAIN: Not Listed
PASSAGE: Departed Honolulu, Sandwich Islands on January 18, 1852.
Called at Lahaina, Sandwich Islands and departed same on
January 27, 1852. Sailed from Lahaina in company with
the schooner "John Allyne" for San Francisco.
CARGO: 244 bbls oil (type unspecified) and 22 tons coal.

Passengers

Mrs. E.M. Parker	Mrs. Caroline Clarke	Mr. John N. Tracy
Mr. J.W. Wadleigh	Mr. E. Keiley	George Frank Lemon
Mr. C.J. Trigler	Mr. E.G. Terry	Charles Ingraham and
H. Guyon	C. Foster	daughter
D.G. Suvey		

- - - - - -

SHIP: JOHN ALLYNE
TYPE: Schooner   FROM: Lahaina, S.I.
ARRIVED: February 17, 1852   CAPTAIN: Prattle
PASSAGE: 26 days from Lahaina, Sandwich Islands. Sailed from
Lahaina in company with the schooner "George Washington".
On February 15, 1852, spoke the ship "Emily", from San
Juan, for San Francisco. Nearly all hands on board the
"John Allyne" were sick. The captain of the "Emily"
supplied us with provisions.
CARGO: Produce (type unspecified).

Passengers

G. Bingham	T. Thomas	W.H. Johnson and
J. Ruddach	W. Miles	lady
T. O'Brien	J. O'Brien	

- - - - - -

SHIP: MATTHEW VASSAR*
TYPE: Schooner   FROM: Oregon Territory
ARRIVED: February 17, 1852   CAPTAIN: Bowen
PASSAGE: 6 days from the Oregon Territory.
CARGO: 400 sacks of wheat, 300 hogs, 20 bushels oysters, 40,000 ft
of lumber and 1 case of merchandise (type unspecified).

Passenger
Capt. O. Hall

- - - - - -

SHIP: MOULTON
TYPE: Barque (British)   FROM: Valparaiso, Chile
ARRIVED: February 17, 1852   CAPTAIN: Steward
PASSAGE: 56 days from Valparaiso, Chile.
CARGO: 600 tons of coal.

Passenger
W. Perry

- - - - - -

SHIP: CELESTIAL
TYPE: Clipper   FROM: New York, N.Y.
ARRIVED: February 17, 1852   CAPTAIN: Palmer
PASSAGE: 106 days from New York. Had a great deal of light
weather on the passage. Was 56 days from New York to the
Cape, 29 days from the Cape to the Line, 22 days from
the Line to San Francisco. Lay off San Francisco harbor
for 3 days due to light winds. Towed up to wharf by the
steam tug "Fire Fly". This is the second voyage of the
"Celestial" to San Francisco. Previous trip took 96
days.
CARGO: Liquor, butter, carpet, pumps, white and red lead, books,
hams, shovels, 6 carriages, crow bars, 3 bells, rivets,
bread, 107 tons coal, powder, iron castings, assorted goods.

Passengers
Mr.____ Hammond, lady & son

- - - - - -

(*)This vessel sometimes listed as "M.Vassar" and "M.Vasser".

SHIP: CONSTITUTION
TYPE: Steamer   FROM: Honolulu, S.I.
ARRIVED: February 18, 1852   CAPTAIN: Howard
PASSAGE: 13 days from Honolulu, Sandwich Islands. This vessel
         departed from San Francisco on January 1, 1852 to fulfill
         the contract of inter-island steam communication. Not
         having met with sufficient inducement to take up the
         contract the "Constitution" returned to San Francisco.
         While in the Sandwich Islands this vessel made the first
         trip ever made by a coasting steamer between two ports of
         the Hawaiian kingdom. She left Honolulu on January 31,
         1852, reached Lahaina on February 1, 1852 and returned
         to Honolulu on February 2, 1852.
CARGO: Not listed.

Passengers

Capt.	McLane	Mr.	Markley	Mr.	Wood
Mr.	Loring	Mr.	Dollarhide	Mr.	Otis
Mr.	Riggs	Mr.	Ring	Mr.	Eaton
Mr.	Jameson and family	Mr.	Tully	Mr.	Dinsmore
Mr.	Waller	Mr.	Sautelle	Mr.	Gifford
		Mr.	Billsby	Capt.	Clark

- - - - - -

SHIP: ORISSA
TYPE: Barque (British)   FROM: London, England
ARRIVED: February 18, 1852   CAPTAIN: Not listed
PASSAGE: 206 days from London, England, via Valparaiso, Chile,
         63 days. Got ashore on Tonquin Shoal but was towed off
         by the steam tug "Fire Fly". Experienced no damage.
CARGO: 1708 empty flasks, 10 kegs shot, 19,580 bricks, 63 tons of
       coal, 25 bbls gunpowder, guns and pistols, beer, ale, wine,
       prunes, 4 cases seed, 820 bags barley and assorted goods.

Passengers

Mr. A.F. Main	Mr. A. Stuart	Mr.	De Sassenay
Mr. Lane	Mr. Reave		

- - - - - -

SHIP: BRANT
TYPE: Ship (British)   FROM: Hongkong, China
ARRIVED: February 19, 1852   CAPTAIN: Thomas
PASSAGE: 90 days from Hongkong, China, via Mindanao, Philippine
         Islands, and 34 days from Borneo. Made nearly the whole
         of the passage in 34 days, when heavy gales were exper-
         ienced. The main topmast was carried away twice; and off
         San Francisco harbor the topgallant-mast was carried away
         and three topsails were split. Word is brought that the
         insurrection rages in North China. The revolution is
         making rapid and fearful strides.
CARGO: 2650 bags of coffee, 25 extension chairs, 40 rattan chairs,
       50 bamboo chairs, 50 rolls of matting, 8080 bags sugar, 873
       pieces of stone, 258 boxes of eggs, 77 cases of cigars, 326
       cases and 304 boxes of tea and 221 unspecified packages.

Passengers

William Atchinson	C. Breum	J.S. Ferria
Mr. Wang Ching	Miss Asee	Miss Ayum
(Chinese)	(Chinese lady)	(Chinese lady)

and 359 unidentified passengers*

(*) Probably Chinese.

- - - - -

SHIP: FANNY KINZIE
TYPE: Schooner   FROM: Bodega, Calif.
ARRIVED: February 19, 1852   CAPTAIN: Armstrong
PASSAGE: 7 hours from Bodega, California.
CARGO: 19 tons of potatoes.

Passenger
C.H. Loper

- - - - -

SHIP: VENEZUELA
TYPE: Brig   FROM: Oregon Territory
ARRIVED: February 20, 1852   CAPTAIN: Staples
PASSAGE: 7 days from the Oregon Territory. Experienced heavy gales
       on the passage.
CARGO: 100,000 feet of lumber, 17,000 laths, 326 sacks potatoes,
       174 sacks oats, 197 sacks onions and 3 cases of eggs.

Passengers

Mr. F.W. Carr	Mr. E. Vancise	Mr. J.S. Kennedy

- - - - -

SHIP: NEW WORLD
TYPE: Barque   FROM: Oregon Territory
ARRIVED: February 20, 1852   CAPTAIN: Gill
PASSAGE: 7 days from the Oregon Territory.
CARGO: 130,000 feet of lumber, 300 bushels of potatoes and 300
       sacks of oats.

Passenger
Mr. Mills

- - - - -

SHIP: OHIO
TYPE: Steamer   FROM: San Diego, Calif.
ARRIVED: February 21, 1852   CAPTAIN: Hilliard
PASSAGE: 5 days from San Diego, California, via intermediate ports
       (ports unspecified). On February 17th spoke the steamer
       "McKim", 22 miles to the northward of Santa Barbara,
       California; one of her propellers was loose, but she was
       expecting to get underway soon. The "Ohio" experienced
       very severe gales for the last 3 days of the passage.
CARGO: Not listed.

Passengers

Joseph J. Hill and	H. Charles	S. Nation
lady	S. Garvin	M. Pedro

(Continued next page)

A. Wehler and	A.M. Gavel	R. Caomden
4 daughters	Charles Waltar	A. Jenan(?)
J. Wehler	J. Brutsley	(Jonan?)
W.P. Denst(?)	C.V. Jacoby	Charles Hunting
(Deust?)	W. Homer	J. McNeil
S. Delong	M. Balou	H.C. Barbour
B.J. Gibbs	H.B. Herrick	H. Hoag
H. Millard	P. Duncombe	I. Hurst
J.B. Hutton	W.P. Daniels	C. Boggs
P. Dunn	J.S. Garrett	H.W. Custan

- - - - - -

SHIP: HOME
TYPE: Barque   FROM: SYDNEY, N.S.W.
ARRIVED: February 22, 1852   CAPTAIN: Bruemerhop
PASSAGE: Departed Sydney, New South Wales on November 16, 1851.
         Called at Honolulu, Sandwich Islands, 21 days from that
         port to San Francisco.
CARGO: 8000 bags of flour.

Passengers

A.T. Curtis and	G.J. Hayes, lady	Mrs.___Peters and
lady	and child	2 children
Mrs.___Spencer	J. Vennison and	M. Hill and wife
Mrs.___Cooke and	wife	T. George
4 children	Mrs.___Williams	Miss___Andrews
Mrs.___Wormsloo	and family	Miss___Jewell
Miss___Swan	J. Turner	W. Packer
W. Smith	L. Taylor	J. Jones
William Parker	William Kearney	William Pendergatt
J. Gadsby	William Price	William Barnett
R. Richardson		

- - - - - -

SHIP: HINDOSTAN
TYPE: Ship (British)   FROM: Glasgow, Scotland
ARRIVED: February 22, 1852   CAPTAIN: Pook
PASSAGE: 213 days from Glasgow, Scotland, via Valparaiso, Chile,
         51 days. Experienced light breezes the whole of the
         passage except the last six days. Was off the harbor of
         San Francisco for four days in heavy gales.
CARGO: 190 tons coal, 1 case knives, 8 hogs, 3 casks peaches, beer,
       butter, 16 pkgs of furniture, ale, 582 bars of iron and a
       quantity of iron plates and castings, twine, whiskey and
       gin.

Passengers

Miss___Crawford	Mr.___Roach	___Farrell
___Mowbray	N. Kirkwood	J. Kirkwood

and 110 unidentified Chileans from
Valparaiso

- - - - - -

SHIP: HANIBAL (Also known as "HANNIBAL")
TYPE: Ship   FROM: Boston, Massachusetts
ARRIVED: February 23, 1852   CAPTAIN: Kingman
PASSAGE: 213 days from Boston, Massachusetts, via Rio de Janeiro,
         Brazil. On September 17, 1851, in lat. 27-30S, long. 30W,
         experienced a severe and sudden gale, which carried away
         foremast, fore-topmast, fore and main topgallant masts,
         with all the yards and rigging attached, together with an
         entire suit of sails except mainsail. Arrived at Rio de
         Janeiro for repairs on September 20, 1851, sailed thence
         on October 31, 1851. Off Cape Horn encountered heavy
         westerly gales for 21 days. On February 17, 1852 took a
         strong gale from the NW; on February 18th, Farallon
         Islands bearing NNW 25 miles, took a pilot from the
         Pilot-boat "Sea Witch", the wind blowing a heavy gale with
         a high breaking sea running. Gale continued to blow heavy
         until the night of February 21st, since which time it was
         calm or nearly so.
CARGO: 350 boxes candles, 268 boxes saleratus, 5 boxes books, 557
       pkgs agricultural tools, 132 kegs pickles, 7 cases cloth,
       282 kegs white lead, 1 box pick handles, 50 dozen brooms, 1
       boiler, 2 wagons, 40 kegs lead, 306 pkgs glassware, 1 piano,
       60,000 ft lumber, scythe stones, blankets, whiskey, tobbaco,
       20 kegs eggs, chocolate, earthenware and assorted goods.

Passengers

Mrs. M. Simonds and daughter (both of Boston)	Mrs. McElhenny and family (of Woburn, Mass.)	John Jameson (of Lynn, Mass.) J. Whalen (of New York)

- - - - - -

SHIP: E.L. FROST*
TYPE: Schooner   FROM: Lahaina, S.I.
ARRIVED: February 23, 1852   CAPTAIN: Hempstead
PASSAGE: 18 days from Lahaina, Sandwich Islands. Experienced a
         gale from the NNW, from the 18th to 21st of February; lay
         to 3 days to leeward of San Francisco port.
CARGO: 400 bbls Irish potatoes, 18 casks sperm oil, 16 casks of
       polar oil, 3 sets wagons, 3 cases of saddlery, 4 cases of
       blackberry cordial, 42 dozen iron shovels, 18 boxes tin
       plate, 17 cases iron bedsteads and assorted goods.

Passengers

J. Breman	S.P. Chapman	S. Dodge
E.T. Young	N. Merry	W. Jones
M. Mathias		

(*) This vessel also known as the "Edward L. Frost".

- - - - - -

SHIP: EMILY
TYPE: Ship   FROM: San Juan del Sur
ARRIVED: February 24, 1852   CAPTAIN: Cole
                    (Continued next page)

PASSAGE: From San Juan del Sur, Nicaragua, via Acajutla, Salvador,
54 days from latter port. Passage time from San Juan del
Sur to Acajutla not listed. Was off the Heads near San
Francisco on February 17, 1852, at 5:00PM, when a heavy
gale from NNW to NW arose, for three days, drove us out
to sea again 150 miles distance. The following deaths
took place on the passage:
December 31, 1851 - When three days out, Captain
O.F. Fosdick, of Nantucket, Massachusetts, and
late master of the whale ship "Henry Astor".
January 5, 1852 - Reuben Ireland, of Cass County,
Missouri, of dysentery.
January 26, 1852 - William Jamieson, of Englesham,
Renfrew County, Scotland, of a liver complaint.

CARGO: In ballast.

Passengers

Mrs.___Cole	Mrs.___Allen	Mrs.___Myers
Mr. J. McGill	Mr. G. Allen	Mr. W.H. Force
Mr. J. Bell	Mr. L.L. Williams	Mr. M. Barret
Mr. C. Cox	Mr. W.S. Waterman	Mr. W.H. Miller
William Jones	Mr. E. Faregle	Mr. G. Lacey
Mr. W.S. Rollins	Mr. W.O.H. Scully	Mr. B. Rudolph
Mr. T. Mohrman	Mr. F. Allerton	Mr. S. Hendrickson
Mr. A. Sharp	Mr. G. Berteu	

- - - - - -

SHIP: GEORGE & MARTHA
TYPE: Barque   FROM: Astoria, Oregon Terr.
ARRIVED: February 24, 1852   CAPTAIN: Beard
PASSAGE: 3 days from Astoria, Oregon Territory.
CARGO: 178,000 feet of assorted lumber, 25 hogs and 20 dozen fowls.

Passengers

C. Holt	J. Fruit	Dr.___Lovejoy

- - - - - -

SHIP: INDEPENDENCE
TYPE: Steamer   FROM: San Juan del Sur
ARRIVED: February 24, 1852   CAPTAIN: Lucas
PASSAGE: 20 days from San Juan del Sur, Nicaragua, via Acapulco,
Mexico and El Realejo, Nicaragua. Left San Juan del Sur
on February 3rd and arrived at El Realejo on February 4th
(11:00AM). Left El Realejo on February 5th and arrived
Acapulco on February 10th (10:00AM), leaving there on
February 12th at midnight. No cases of sickness on board
during the passage.
CARGO: Not listed.

Passengers

R. Savage, lady,	W.H. Elliott	H. Goddard
3 chldrn & svt	J.P. Stewart, lady	E.H. Valentine
Mrs.A.M. Kance	and children	B.T. James
P.C. Dart	J.S. Thompson	Mrs.___Clark

(Continued next page)

Mrs. S.P. Goodell
and 2 children
Miss___Kidd
Miss___Somers
Dr. C.F. Ray and
lady
J. Spanner and svt
J. Totten
J.B. Menomy
E. Platcheck and svt
B. David
P. Reynolds
E. Barthelemew
J.R. Reynolds
R.S. Reynolds
R.S. Lincoln
F. Kance
N. Martin, lady
and child
H.F. Chatfield
A.F. Jones
William Edmundson
R. Smith
A. McDannele /sic/
A.G. Smith
John Clements
Richard Riardon /sic/
Robert Scott
G.W. Prescott
L.H. Hogan
W.H. Butler
James S. Mason
W.E. Donnell
S.S. Carr
John Carey
Henry F. Mosher
E. Earnest
Ignatius Eckart
I. Ayers
S. Hotchkiss
D. Houston
W.S. Dixon
E. Dixon
A. Preston
H. Overaker
B. Shucman /sic/
W. Mead/sic/
S.S. Mead
W.A. Hings
E.R. Berrey /sic/
A. Munroe

Mrs. S.C. Williams
and child
Miss___Ringgold
Miss___Threadcraft
M. Whittell
G.C. Gulick and
lady
Mrs. F. Hamisley
E. Gorham
H.A. Bogardus
B.J. Stevens
A. Danford
E. Alling
D.M. Lyons
S. Briggs
T.G. Richardson
J. Davis
J. Smith, lady and
child
John Robertson
William Birch
Robert Buckingham
Daniel Brackett
George H. Darbin
Charles Devere
Patrick Kelly and
wife
A. Brigham
C.E. Boardman
Stephen H. Creeastin?
(Crecastin?)
Michael Dougherty
Thomas O'Brien
C.D. Adams
George Louk
W. Louderback
J. Conway
F. McSorley
R. Chadwick
N. Kimberly
J. Ra???eze?
(Raffleze?)
George W. Olds
L. Olds
G.C. Henderson
J. Ryan
S. Burrell
G.A. Page
J. Gerard
C.M. Williams
C. Henderson
(Continued next page)

Miss___May
Miss___Anderson
Miss___McGuire
W.C. Hamilton
E.J. Hunter
R.B. McBride
J. Grady
Mrs. G.W. Wirts and
child
Mrs. H. Bright and
daughter
H. Woodford
George Cochran
E.H. Latham
W.O. Hanford
J. Gleason
A. Robinson
G. Lorring /sic/
Miss M.J. McMullen
Charles W. Griffith
Charles R. Worawick?
(Worswick?)
Levi Matthews
Samuel B. Goodwin
William Ray
Miss___Mahan
James Mahan
A. Brim
William Schenk
R.M. Atkinson
B.B. West
Thomas Liddy
C. Kierman
A. Legrange
L.P. Hudson
W. Stanwood
D. Crownin
H.H. Cole
C. Baldwin
D. Platt
T.H. Agnew
S. Fleming
W. Biggs
A. Metcalf
H. Kelley /sic/
James McCarty
A.A. Obin
W.A. Wilcox
W. Mead/sic/
W. Elder
N.W. Isham

H. Ligler
Haines Jewett
W.H. Hardin
J. Walton
J. Dawson
E. Spalding /sic/
C. Churchill
B.F. L??kfield
D. Alexander
L. Kingsbury
H.H. Hagen
D. Ploss
E.J. Daratt?
   (Duratt?)
A. Stebbens
William Stebbens
B.B. Elster
J.C. Elster
David Parseil(?)
   (Parsell?)
Abraham Acker
John Bowen
John Sampson
William Fuller
N.K. Sampson
W.D. de Lernmier(?)
   (de Lornmier?)
J. Little
Mrs. H.P. Breyfoggle/sic
Mrs.___Dow and
   2 children
J. Barton
B. Daniels and
   lady
G.V. Swan
G.H. Hill
M.H. Whittemore/sic/
John E. Fell
S.G. Reynolds
Ira Allen
L.O. Hudson
Alex Weiss
A.E. Wright
J.M. Wright
Mrs. E.A. White
W.B. Ransom /sic/
W.D. Blanchard
W. Hulburt
J.M. Easterly
Samuel Patterson
Simeon Pendleton

John Martin
E. Delano
E. Fannington
E. Fletcher
J. Downey
D. Campbell
P.J. Falcon
B. Hatch
J.H. Adams
E. Rowe
James Lingaur
C. Rockwell
George Parke
John Biggs
Cyrus Tyler
S.T. Sawyer
Lyman Belknap
A.P. Cooke
Joseph Colvin
Josiah Colvin
D.H. Lamorie
H.H. Butterfield
William C. Clements
Warren Ives
D.E.P. Packard
E. Knapp
Mrs.___Barlow
J.M. Cross
Mrs.M.B. Cuyler
J.O. Eldridge
H.P. Drennin
John Nicol
James Wood
A.P. Dunn
T. Plimpton
N.O. Goddell
Martin Clark
William Harris
F. Weller
B. Eckles
E.G. Salisbury and
   lady
G. Loreaux
C. Loreaux
Mrs. R. Loreaux and
   child
G.K. Terry
C.J. Morrison
R.P. Morrison
R.D. Saunders
Walton Van Loan

A. Pierce
J.B. Pierce
V.A. Kingsley
J. Grant
S.B. Houghton
William Gawn
G.E. Wilder
F. Whitney
James Chase
J. Wentworth
John F. Atkinson
H. Gilbert
J.M. Kaule
Aaron Clousen
E.C. Fairchild
Robert Hamilton
Edwin Phelps
Martin Wells
B. Wells
John Barland
D.W. Draper
H. Corey
N. Corey
J. Belt
W.B. Sawyer
John Crocker
Miss___Rogers
Henry Pitts
D.D. Henion
R. Morrison and
   lady
Horace Francisco
Charles K. Stoyer(?)
   (Steyer?,Stayer?)
J. Steadman
George Godfrey
J.B. Griffin
Edwin Bishop
S.G. Martin
H. Close
C.S. Glover
H. Burbank
Thomas Long
John Stewart
S. Breyfogle/sic/
Charles Belding
W. Colville
Wesley Jackson
A.J. Ellis
Joseph B. Lyons
B. Sailsbury?(Salis-
   bury?)

and 168 unidentified in steerage

SHIP: MAZEPPA
TYPE: Barque   FROM: Hongkong, China
ARRIVED: February 25, 1852   CAPTAIN: Paty
PASSAGE: 95 days from Hongkong, China, via Honolulu, Sandwich
         Islands, 17 days.
CARGO: 300 tons of unidentified merchandise.

Passengers

C.S. Compton and   J.A. Post and   E.G. Lewis
    servant   servant   W. Brandon
            and 33 unidentified Chinamen

- - - - - -

SHIP: CALIFORNIA
TYPE: Steamer   FROM: Panama
ARRIVED: February 26, 1852   CAPTAIN: R.L. Whiting
PASSAGE: 16 days from Panama, running time, via Acapulco, Mexico,
         San Diego, California and Monterey, California. Was
         detained 32 hours at aforementioned three ports. On board
         is a detachment of U.S. Troops, being a portion of the
         500 New York Harbor recruits, designed for posts in the
         west. Remainder of the recruits may ship aboard the
         vessel "Golden Gate",for San Francisco. On February 14th,
         in the Gulf of Tehuantepec, experienced a "norther", which
         lasted for 24 hours.
CARGO: Not listed.

Passengers

Capt. H. Day(U.S.A.)   Lt.___Mason, lady,   Lt.___Castor and
Capt.___Miller(U.S.A.)   child & servant   lady
Dr.___Crane(U.S.A.)   J. Ambrose   Mrs.___Nesbett
R. Pearce   Miss___Clark   T. Russell
J.W. Priestley   Sam Moss   J.L. Martin
J. Gallagher   Mr.& Mrs. T. Shaw   Rev. D. Deal, lady
G. Gayetche   R. Gardiner   and child
J.A. Wakeley   W. Blossom   Mrs. Mary Ferguson
Mr.& Mrs. F.J. Manley   Mr.& Mrs.___Hamilton   Mr.___Chapman.
J. Modina (?)   & 3 children   Miss Caroline Chapman
   (Medina?)   A. Bundy   J. Hammock
W. Luchsenger   A. De Widt(?)   G. Ridgeway
Rev. J. Kimberlin   (De Wiet?,   Capt.___Ricketson
   and lady   De Wiut?)
            and a detachment of U.S. Troops

- - - - - -

SHIP: MARY MELVILLE
TYPE: Barque   FROM: Oregon Territory
ARRIVED: February 26, 1852   CAPTAIN: Bailey
PASSAGE: 4 days from the Oregon Territory.
CARGO: 1000 bushels of wheat, 600 bushels oats, 400 hogs, 100
       bushels onions, 1500 bushels potatoes and 90,000 feet of
       lumber.

(Continued next page)

Passengers

Mr.___Adams   Mr.___Hildreth   Mr.___Williams
Mr.___Silver   Mr. H. Haines

- - - - - -

SHIP: GOLDEN GATE
TYPE: Steamer   FROM: Panama
ARRIVED: February 26, 1852   CAPTAIN: R.L. Patterson,USN
PASSAGE: 14 days from Panama, via Acapulco, Mexico. Left Panama
          on February 12, 1852 at 4:00PM. Arrived at Acapulco on
          February 18th, but in consequence of not being permitted
          to coal at night, was detained until the afternoon of
          February 19th. On February 22nd, in lat. 26-17N, long.
          114W, spoke the brig "Eliza Taylor" from Panama, with a
          large number of passengers, bound for San Francisco.
          The "Golden Gate" brings intelligence that a large number
          of persons bound for California are pouring into the city
          of Panama. The following deaths took place during the
          passage of the "Golden Gate":
               February 16,1852 - J.L. Kidder, aged 23 years, from
                    Alexandria, Genessee County, New York, died on
                    board, of dysentery.
               February 24,1852 - Thomas J. Blossom, aged 23 years,
                    from Turner, Maine, died on board, of fever.
               February 26,1852 - O.D. Braisted, aged 26 years, from
                    Essex, Essex County, New York, died on board,
                    of dysentery.
CARGO: Gold coin, 144 packages of express matter and 14 packages of
        unspecified merchandise.

Passengers

Mr.___Seymour	E. Cordier	Mrs.___Gray and
E. Seymour	Dr.___Todd and	family
F.H. Brown	lady	Mrs.___Denny and
Miss___Griffin	E.A. Upton	2 children
A.J. Mansfield	Mrs.___Strong	Mrs.___Stone
A.G. Beck, lady,	Miss___Grenell	Miss___Stone
neice and child	Mrs.___Torrence	___Whiting and
T. Stead	J.W. Thomas	lady
J. Stead	Mrs.___Snow	Mrs.___Leavit
Mrs.___Merserve	___Wetherby and	A.B.C. Brown
W.C. Hamilton	lady	B.F. Ferris
Mrs.___Bernard	Mrs.___Comstock and	Mrs.___Cothrin
J. Bloomingdale and	servant	Mrs.___Orus and
servant	W. Matthews	son
S. Hubbell	W. Zimmerman	W. Washburn
T.F. Durrell	N. Hill	L.F. Parker
O. Seever	D. French	J. Bryant
W. Abby	J.H. Allen	R.S. Chapman
R. Abby	W.S. Eldridge	A. Chapman
R.N. Wilcox	J.W. Fisk	D.R. Chapman
R. Lamb	J. English	A.H. Loucks

(Continued next page)

C. Martin
A. Spaker
Z. Hawkins
J. Woods
W. Woods
H.P. Murphy
Col.___Cypa?ana
   and servant
   (Cypalana?)
E.H. Boordman /sic/
   (Boardman?)
R.H. Corn
Mrs.___Dupli?
   (Duplis?,
   Duplia?)
Mrs.___Newcomb
Mrs.___Tingley
R.H. Vance and
   2 boys
G. Durkee
J. Durkee
O.E. Young
M.D.L. Brown
R. Metcalf
P. Howard
J. Evertson
D.R. Stetson
W. Stetson
J. Walsh
O.L. Stoddard
L.H. Cutter
P.C. Tarbox
J. Rathbone
S. Rathbone
N. Rathbone
J. Rathbone
H.C. Burnham
H. Tipton
D. Davis
C. Bally (?)
   (Baily?)
C.J. Darrow
C.W. Parker
   Krause
W.S. Taylor
M. McCoure
J. Cooper
D. Pentecost(?)
   (Pentecoat?)
J.N. Brown
J.M. Bean

A. Van Wie
G. Little
H. Newton
G. Briggs
J. Mailet
N. Chapman
W. Chapman
William Magnani
L. Berekzenski
E.D. Jones
M. Thompson
H. Van Read
Mr.___Crowell
Miss___Hawley
Mr.___Moukee?
   (Monkee?)
Mr.___Mullen
Mr.___Williams
S. Kent
J.C. Yagra
L. Bois
S.R. Wright
J. Efder(?)
   (Efner?)
H. Efder(?)
   (Efner?)
A.H. Sampson
R. Cushman
A. Frettz (?)
   (Freuz?)
J.R. Reynolds
L. Pepoon
W. Mould
E. Whaler
B. Dorrance
Mr.___Tracy
J.L. Yeoman
O.A. Woodey
J. Berry
J. Samuels
S. Samuels
B. O'Neil
F. Henry
   Dowd and lady
H. Hart
S. McGarvey
W.H. Sullivan
C. Mason
R.C. Clark
F. Bates
Mr.___Kelly

H. Bookson
A.W. Smith
S. Miller
A. Miller
E. Olin
L. Carrow
J.W. Field
H. McCullum, lady
   and servant
Mrs.___Maxwell
M. Hepburn
M. Lauzenbergh
Mr.___Cook
J.L. English and
   servant
Mrs.___Bergen
M. Hansom /sic/
Mrs. C. Bush
J. Autersmith (?)
   (Antersmith?)
R. Rhand
E.F. Munger
G.H. Thompson
J. Collins
W.B. Wentworth/sic/
E. Kennedy
G. Pratt
O.S. Savage
P. Roach
A.L. Coburne
S.W. Ripley
P.H. Gould
E. Patterson
J. Lawless
A.W. Rondell
L. Brown
R.L. Williamson
S. Fraser
J. Watson
W. Meyer
S.W. Patton
J. Brown and boy
J. Brown /sic/
   G?eot
J. Gore
W.M. Allen
J. Flanagan
E.S. McChesny/sic/*
Thomas Sayre
W. Young
G.H. Munroe

(Continued next page)

(*)Note J. McChesnee, page 93.

E. Perry
A. Webster
S. Goodchild
W. Currier
W. Con?it
F. Lintore
C. Bartlett
V.D. Watkins
Eli Johnson
J. McLaughlin
T.C. Patterson
W.H. Keeler
A.H. Smith
P. McGingerne
Mrs.____Kinney and
 child
Mr.____Harvey
J. Harris
D. True
L.A. Green
D. Clark
C. Foss
R. Loughman
N.C. Bedell
C. Hanson
J. Boyd
G. Graves
J. K?einsworth
 (Kleinsworth?)
____McElmse
J.S. Stiegerland
E.P. Consick
J. Eagan
G. Scroggin
P.C. Lamereux
A.H. Luck
P. Brown
C. Robertson
J. Hart
L. Cook
J. Moyle
D. Lane
F. Webster
W. Dyer
Mr.____Shufelt
 Rizuis
F. Keesey
S. Nesbit
B. Rich
G. Richards
J.H. Neal

W.E. Marsh
James Farley
B.F. Debay (?)
 (Dehay?)
A.S. Bucklin
J. Wentworth
R.R. Morey
A. Blanchard
A.S. Back?in
 (Backlin?)
J.S. Chapman
G.L. Chapman
S. Cooper
A. Stone
D. Stone
E. Stone
J.C. Clayton
C. Fowler
James Boyce
W. Holmes
F. Wells
C. Bressell(Bresseil?)
J. Rue
W.H. Richardson
P. Grouse
P. Cagan(?)
 (Cagas?)
J. Jackson
J. Malloy
R. Hardy
M.A. Cornwell
C. B???
F. Church
P. Garry
Mr.____Spooner
L. Hughs /sic/
S.K. Downing
T.P. Robertson
T. Fury
Mr.____Percy and
 lady
M. O'Neal
G. Prentice
O.T. Phelps
S. Rummel
W.C. Brown
W. Luscomb
T. Harben
T.H. Nix
C. Ellish
H. Piper
(Continued next page)

D. Weaver
O.D. Braisted
 (Died)
J. Sherman
M. Simmons
W. Haynes
D.S. Staples
J.E. Mitchell
A.A. Young
L. Wilkin
N. Newbury
L. Ross
 Drummond
G.W. Hose(?)
 (Huse?)
S. Brown
P. Kelley /sic/
D. Kelly /sic/
P. Akin
T. Perkins
E. Booth
M. Levison
J.H. Runlet
F. Campbell
J. Jewell
W.M. Harrison
W. Whitcomb
W.W. Durkee
B. Woodward
N. Toffit
F. Smith
C. Perry
H.A. Blossom
H. Kimball
A.S. Epps
B. Gartland
W.A. Wroy
J. Dugan
P. Dugan
Mr.____Spencer and
 lady
J. Blakely
E. Talbot
H. Loomis
W. Hardy
S. Watts
J. Weaver
M.P. Elmore
J. Mitchell
P.F. Davis
J.W. Dickey

H. Kelly
E.D. Wright
R. Laza(?)
J. Samuels
C. Fitch
J. Openheimer /sic/
George Hill
J.S. Dunlap
R. Conn
E. Van Heff(?)
  (Van Haff?,
  Van Hoff?)
T.G. Segur
C. Martin
A. Hall
J. Webster
D.B. Bean
J. Nesmith
J. Harben
A. Harben
J.W. Nourse
G. Gibbs
D. Whalen
L.B. Roe
B.B. Gonise
C.S. Ambleton
T. Birch
J. Daily
W.A. Shreve
J. Heard
G.F. Hule
A.W. Johnson
J. Adriance /sic/
J. Adriance /sic/
W.B. Adcook (?)
  (Adcock?)
S.G. Booth
T.D. May
Mr.____Rhodes
A.H. Maseback
B.S. Anderson
R.J. Steel
P. McCaffron
Mrs.____Bain
Miss____Bain
A.J. Kelly
Lewis Neal
R. Thompson
Alfred Scott
F. Eno
R.W. Sales

G. McDonald
J. Henry
C.J. Johnson
W.F. Weir
A. Grant
Mr.____Kuse
J. Shuner
G. Shuner
Mr.____Ault
A. Taylor
J. Mulloy
W. Knowles
J.K. Shields
G. Hewitt
S. Hewitt
Mrs.____Kelley and
  child
D. Fisk
S. Loble
A. Nix
L. Nix
T. Nix
J. Black
J.B. Wosmer(?)
  (Wormer?)
J. Parke
S.W. Chamberlain
H. Baker
John Teil
B. Page
J. Proctor
A.W. Rapelge
J.F. Campbell
J. Gordon
W. Wigat?(Wight?)
C. Wigat?(Wight?)
C. Haskell
Mrs.____Olman and
  2 children
C. Courtney
M. Villa(?)
  (Vilis ?)
Mr.____Koppehust,
  wife and 2
  children
G.W. Moore
J.P. Hughs /sic/
F.C. Frank
W.K. Spencer
R.H. Brackenridge
L. Colby
(Continued next page)

Thomas J. Blossom
  (Died)
G. Neighbor
N. Neighbor
P. McQuillon
H. McQuillon
Mr.____Ve?morel
  (Vermorel?)
Mr.____Berlew?
  (Berlaw?)
G. Cattsgat
H. Haines
W. Haines
R.P. Wells
S. Mullingsbo
A. Carruthers
F. Marr
L. Stone
B. Gairdet (?)
  (Gairdel?)
L.S. Hardy
C. Cherry
A. McFening
J. Miller
A. Remsen
B. Wheat
W. Montgomery /sic/
T.A. Bigelow
Rev. J.E. Benton
W. Clark
M.L. Goff
W. Montgomery /sic/
P.T. Gibberson
G.M. Almy
W.W. Andrews
S.G. Cone
J. Christie
Miss____Rogers
W.B. Stockton, wife
  & 3 children
N. Stockton
L. Stockton
J. Jones
T. Jones
B.M. Griffith
George Brown
W.F. Lang
F.C. Fay
L. Livingston
A.T. McLure
J. Wadsworth

D.L. Fernald
P. Morgan
George Coffin(?)
  (Caffin?)
B. Fenton
W. Evans
L. Penney
Alfred Taylor
Thomas Brady
O.P. Bellows
H. Kail
W.B. Edson
S. Wilcox
A. Phelps
D. Ellinger
D. Parsely
C. Christie
W. Christie
H.S. Delany
J. Coughron
A. Coughron
J. Hockey
H. Huntly/sic/
  (Huntley?)
J. Huntley/sic/
W. Huntley
P. McCue
F. Patterson
S. Chapman
J. Patterson
J. Proctor
R. Rhodes
J.F. Ellington
Y. Connet /sic/
C.J. Arridson
C. Hathorn
E. Keese
J. Conn
J. Farnham
Mrs.____Kelly
J. Perkins
J. Williams
F. Sefor
W. O'Neal
L. Green
T. Dyer
W.C. Dyer
W. Brown
A.G. Shepheard
H.R. Lewis
W.C. Beach

W. Smith
L. Perrin
H.P. Damreil?
  (Danrell?)
Thomas Berry
C.H. Patchin
J. Comfit
C. Comfit
J.J. Messy
James Carpenter
S.R. Curtis
S.W. Curtis
W. Foster
S. Libby
S. Brickner
H. Pollard
W. Bell
J.M.Vandenhoff/sic/
G.R. Bacon
M.W. Renshaw
W. Midgely
T. Midgely
J. Creary
J. Efner/sic/
J.H. Daggett
G.W. Robinson
C. Ramsey
D. Ramsey
C. Irwine
E. Haines
J. Benson
J. Thomas
W. Mosley
B. Ryan
D. O'Brien
G.H. Blake
J. Murray
C.M. Nix
S.E. Davis
B. Blaor(?)
  (Slaor?)
M. Cohn
P.P. Nix
W. Parker
J.T. Lawton
E. Hopkins
N. Hopkins
T. Halliday
E. Groat
J. McChesnee /sic/*
T. Smith
(Continued next page)

S. Delany
J. Baker
D. Bigelow
H.L. Bowyer
E.S. Dormon
H.S. Kellinger
L.O. Neal/sic(O'Neal?)
P.A. Serrot
F. O'Neal /sic/
A. Welman
R. Nichols
S. Smiley
G. Johnson
D. Whitehead
H. Chambers
R.C. Hodges
M. Soules
J.J. Robinson
Mr.____Mansfield
J. Connor
J.L. Kidder (Died)
W. Ryan
B. Clayton
D. Colyer
W. Thompson
R. Craig
J.B. Fogg
G.G. Cummings
Mr.____Culled
A.J. Autire
F.W. Taylor
N. Dawson
James Dervie
J. Hanson
D.G. Kennedy
J. Mullholl /sic/
B. Lally
G. Hefner
G. Mead
N. Newman
J. Grittel
S. Steinfeldt
T. Wakefield
M. Taft
A. Gould
A. Hance
John Cary
G.L. Appleton
A. Sterns
R. Borden
N. Smith

(*)Note E.S.McChesny(sic),page 90.

R. Washborne
E. Evers
D. Hardy
G. Hardy
J. Root
D.H. Yagoe
O.B. Yagoe
J.F. England
W.H. Heath
W. Harrigan
James Durie
Russel Wells
M. Rockway
A.B. Chubb
J. Van Evans
A.H. Mayer
J. Pratt
H.L. Orr
B. Ryndress/sic/
J. Becker
J.C. William
____McMurray, lady
and child
F. Solomon
Rev. E. Blockley
T.R. Cainel
J. Donaldson
J.S. Tilton
H. Burnet
George Loder
W.B. Wentworth /sic/
Thomas McGiven
W. Luston
N. Emerson
E. Bigelow
John Kelly
Thomas Doyle
P. Burns /sic/
P. Burns /sic/
E. Burns
M. Welsh
S.A. Green
C. Thayer
B.F. Dodson
A. Malloy
W.F. O'Rourke
E. White
L. Clyme
H. Everet /sic/
C. Williamson
M. Williamson

W. Thomas
W. Patten(?)
   (Patton?)
A. Leighton
P.C. Moulton
H.D. Meadows
A.H. Delany
John Boucher
George Cummings
E. Parrot /sic/
G.T. Smith
A. Farmer
C. Derrick
J.S. Wiley
C. Osborne
T. Candon
J. Smith
Robert Ford
S. Boyd
Mrs.____Olman/sic/
J.Q. Lane
____Donaldson
____White
J.B. Barker
D.B. Seyne
J.D. Harrison
F. Baker
H. Baker
W. Green
W. Cowles
W. Stevens and
   lady
J. Maxfield /sic/
J. Maxfield /sic/
J. Devon
M. Devon
E. Norris
George White
J.A. Fuller
J. Pilsbury /sic/
T. Morgan and lady
W.W. Randall
S. Allen
W. Allen
J.A. Richards
E. Chadwick
S.A. Fargo
D. Dinsmore
S. Dinsmore
J.Q. Greenleaf
W. Newton
(Continued next page)

John Perry
S. Morrison
S. Kelly
S.L. Irwin
W.D. Irwin
S. Gorman
W. Quire
M. Powers
W. Fairgrove and
   boy
Daniel Chase
J. Parker
J.F. Ramsey
B. Fanning
J. Gorham
M.S. Dewint
Thomas Allen
W. Cornelius
P. Webster
R. Cane and lady
J. King
J.C. Rogers
F. Brown
W. Simmons
J. Simmons
O. Keenan
W.E. Sibley
Robert Webb
____Grant
____Snow
S.W. Whampool/sic/
S.C. Morgan
E. Bennet /sic/
T.P. Perrean
R. Farrell
M. Connell
Thomas Norton
G. Cushman
L. Bryan
W. Madigan
D. Bomber
S.A. Stanley
C.H. Taft
A. Barr
J. Barr
H.M. Robinson
A. Weller
J. Bomber
R. Wood
J. Storer
H. Lockman

C. Cryder	John Ryan	P. Vinton
David Abby	H. Gage	S.T. Pickery
N.J. Daniels	A.T. Coombs	W. Camshan
J. Hardy	H. Coombs	James U??1
J. Cleary	T. Richardson	L.W. Noyes
W.D. Osborn	W. Miller	C. McLaughlin
W. Murray	E.A. Cameron	J. Pearce
J. Donnelly	J. McNellis	H. Pearce
W.C. Clements	R.W. Crosby	A. Pearce
A. Wright	D. Chandler	F. Carpenter
M. Yates	V. Peck	J. Hawkins
A. Rutherford	P. Cooth (?)	S.C. Pearce
G. Bishop	S. Birmingham	J.C. Andrews
J. Clapp and lady	J. Harris	D.M. Wambold /sic/
C. ???son	R. Finletter	V. Knudson
W. ???son	W. Finletter	M. Hill
John Elliott	C. Thomas	T. Sherman
J. O'Connor	C. Monar	S.A. Black
A.W. Came	J. McAller	Mrs.___Ryness/sic/
A.M. Batle (?)	J. Cathouse	Levi Korn
(Batie?)	D. Evans	

- - - - - -

SHIP: SEA BIRD
TYPE: Steamer   FROM: San Diego, Calif.
ARRIVED: February 27, 1852   CAPTAIN: Haley
PASSAGE: 3 days from San Diego, California, via intermediate ports.
Left San Diego on February 24,1852, at 7:00PM. On board
are passengers from the British brig*"Tryphene". The
"Tryphene" put into San Diego in distress. Put into
San Pedro, California and Santa Barbara, California. Last
port call was Monterey, California. Encountered strong
head winds and heavy land sea since leaving Point Con-
cepcion. Among the passengers is Mr. John A. Lewis,of the
"Los Angeles Star",and the Hon. J.R. Bartlett, of the
Boundary Commission. This vessel brings intelligence of
the death of Don Carlos Carrillo, of Santa Barbara.**
He was once Governor and he descended from one of the
most influential families in California.
(*) One source lists as "Typhene".
(**) Died February 25, 1852.
CARGO: Not listed.

Passengers

Mrs.___Fairfowl	J. Yates	S. Haley
J. Cooper and lady	A.B. Gray	Dr.___Webb
George Thurber	Lt.___Whipple	F. Weaton
Hon. J.R. Bartlett	W.A. Taylor	T.D. Johns
Capt.___Nason	F. Gonzales	T.B. Sanchez
M. Sepulva /sic/	S. Masas	A. Bedderim
D. Block	Dona Garcia	M. Bedderim
A.S. Wells	J.S. Ruth	F. West

(Continued next page)

R.D. Cutts
G. ??etter and family
Dr.___Randall
L. Bonatestee(?)
   (Benatestee?)
E. Corned
W. Wilber
E.H. Cunneff
C.C. Stevens
C. Bolener
 R.S. Smith
J.T. Maukins
S.S. Moe
Santiago Arantes
F.A. Herrick
O. Flint
W.H. Gordon
P.S. Cleariane
L. Cooper
J. Hammell(?)
   (Hameil?)
G. Murray
Joseph Love
N. Boquee
Roman Bracia
E.B. Ballinger
F. Wells
Edward Carry
Alfred Alexander
M. Woodsworth
P.J. Case
Abraham Hardenburgh
L.G. Ramsay
J.H. Kilcome
G. Greathouse
S. Eria
R. Merino
M.D. Doaer
T.T. Swain
C.C. Lyon
M. Lehman
A. Lehman
C. Cowe
J. Low
M. Burrill
H. Still
John A. Lewis

S. Newell
P. Young
M. Asavidio
R. Asavidio
F. Asavidio
A. Combs
F. Napoleon
J. Peter
R. Smith
Joseph Antoino /sic/
S. Antoino /sic/
H. Harrison
W.R. Cogswell
D. Gonzalez
George Rowell
J. Moulton and sons
John Tyler
W. Halsey
John King
G. Loucks
W. Hasting
Edward Young
T.M. Huntsman
F. Bepratt(?)
   (Bapratt?)
Henry Garrett
David Wingust(?)
   (Wingast?)
S.L. Snyder
W.D. Butler
S.S.M. Tyler
Joel Silner
Hugh Camarell
M.R. Ballinger
T.W. Shaff
    Barberi
F. Wessel and lady
George Young
J.M. Cawsey
William Elliott
L. Lever
E.H. Marcy
L. Ariva
J. Carl
E. Alvesanda
J. Ingram
Mr.___Lyons

J. Fletcher
Capt.___Cooper
W.H. Cullen
J. Levitser
E. Wilson
P. McFudder
J.J. Knap
J.E. Kaiser(?)
   (Keiser?)
H. Osbers
J. Keaver
J. Rollins
R.J. Hale
C.M. Pratt
John Higgins
J.P. Wagner
J.A. Gray
James Gow?n
   (Gowan?,
   Gowen?)
S.B. Mariao(?)
   (Marino?)
N. Gerry
S. Coverland
A. Blackman
M. Jacoby
Hugh Corrius(?)
   (Cerrius?)
J. Wingert /sic/
Frederick Wilson
William E. Stanford
Mr.___Flerness
D.C. Reed
David Smith
P. Batch
D. Argo?a
J.W. Bryant
Frederick Osborn
Bernard Riley
J.A. Lewis
C. Conrad
H. Brown
P. Nail
W. Purnell
J. Peroty
J.S. Stewart
Capt.___Bell

and 48 unidentified passengers

- - - - - -

SHIP: ALPHONSE N. CEZARD
TYPE: Ship   FROM: Nantes, France
ARRIVED: February 28, 1852   CAPTAIN: Bozec
PASSAGE: 123 days from Nantes, France.
CARGO: 43 cases of peas, 167 cases sardines, 223 bbls brandy, 100
       bbls wine, 52 cases butter, 200 cases cheese, 182,160
       bricks and 1 case unspecified merchandise.

Passengers

L. Cousin	J. Aerden	P.L. Deyaert
H. Materre	H.A. Loisel	J.C. Perrin
P. Corrot	J. Jauffenberger	L. Lagniel
M. Baille	L. Chenu	J.B. Racine
E. Garsonnas	C. Chenu	R. Bourguignon
J.J. Bertin	J. Boux	I. Flechelte(?)
J.S. Fournier	L. Maupin	(Fiecheite?)
E. Barrier	V. Sidobre	C.C. Cosnat
P. Astrac	I. Joison	A. Boisseret
M. Girardin	A. Clerentin	E. Gervats
B. Mendinat	N. Didier	A. Pommaret
P. Leflandre	F. Beaugrand	H. Dubosq /sic/*
P. Michont	H. Erneste	F.L. Calmantran
N. Jandin	J.B. Iron	D. Ortet
A. Cochereau	J. Champ	G. Vone
?.P. Jourdan	F. Beudet (?)	A. Barbier
A. Beaugrand	(Baudet?	G. Chandorat
C. Pinguet	Boudet?)	T. Boudon
V. Roux	J. Gelinaud	B. Serviat
L. Pugens	T. Lacasine	F. Betoso(?)
P. Henri	D. Co?larde	(Beioso?)
C. J?nchont	J.J. Muller	D. Chenaist
(Jenchont?,	B. Camboureac	A. Fontaine
Janchont?,	G. Lavernot	E. Jacquemont
Jonchont?)	J.B. Montabru(?)	F. Petayvis
C. Foerters(?)	(Montebru?)	A. Vignor
(Foertera?)	P. Rateau	J.G. Vol?n?
C. Benoit	J. Claudest(?)	J. Mache
E. Lu?et	(Claudeat?)	A. Myles
J.B. Chaumont	F. Caudev	D. Porreaux
J. Raquilat	J.E. Bo??frod	A. Magot
J. Nobles	F. Humblot	A.S. Oufresnoy/sic/
E. Astruck	A. Dufresnoy/sic/	L. Lareme
J. Sermet-Piu(?)	C. Verdun	A. Livenais
(Sermet-Pru?)	J. Geneste	G. Mengeot
F. Boucher	P. Rabeux	I.P. Marcele
N. P?i?o?	P. L??que?nec	P. Bernede
C. Amede	J. Huet	J. Reyasac
B. Eudeliu	F. Kopp	N. Recht
R. Fiault	P. Cremer	F. Gaignard
E. Coullon	B. Mavis	J. Clovis
J. Elliott	A. Lorvol	L. Boitet
S.V. Bourdeau	J.P. Motey	P. Salmon

(Continued next page)

(*)Note E. Duboss(?), page 98

C.Franc	A. Leger	A. Viouit(?)
F. Morin	J. Jisserand	(Vieuit?)
B. de Montfort	J.C. Straus	C. Dubray
Auguste	L. Leroux	J. Colomb
A. Mattuschka	V. Jousse	L. Frichet
P. Peyon	L. Fertin	E. Duboss?*
A. Choparr(?)	A. Le??dileur	(Duboas?)
(Chaparr?,	V. Rombro	J. Siroux
Cheparr?)	J. Lallemand	M. Blattiere
J. Clavie	H. Ouvray	A. Barie
P. Richer	A. Comminge1	E. Marque
J.B. Carpentier	A. Laveissiese	J.F. Sore1
J. Coquia	J. Coster	J. Alexandre
P. Mignan	J. Auer	P. Lacour
P. Matilet(?)	J. Fesq(?)	B. Gilles?e?
E. Lebo?gne	(Feaq?)	V. Rem?inger
A. Celerie	J. Domecq	G. Hardouin
F. Vanigout	E. Ocampo	C.C. Roux
F. Mouillard	Z. Lebrun	

- - - - - -

SHIP: COMET
TYPE: Schooner   FROM: Panama
ARRIVED: February 28, 1852   CAPTAIN: Burt
PASSAGE: 54 days from Panama, via Acapulco, Mexico, 30 days.
         Four passengers died during the voyage (the Captain
         stating, "they took their names with them").
CARGO: In ballast.

Passengers

T. Boorum	J. Ratcliff	J.B. Smith
G. Jacobs	W. Whitehead	J. Schultz
G. Goodwin	G. Bright	A. Snedecor
H. Cunningham	C.G. McCasker	J. Hogan
W. Campbell	O. Dudley	S. Hill
H.J. Ferguson	G. Fritz	D.H. Hughes
S. Moore	O. Frasey	J. Furgeson
LeCondray	G.V. Diercy	Smith O'Brien /sic/
O. Allen	S. Patten	D. Swasey
John Smith	J. Benton	E. Allen
A. Anderson	D.W. Sherlow	C. Bickford
N. Brush	H. Bird	J. P?il (Pril?,
M. Brush	F.P. Hardy	Pail?)
J. Eastbro /sic/	J. Shannon	J. Smith
W. Dunham	S.B. Knight	H.J. Knight
C. Swasey	B. Knight	

- - - - - -

SHIP: LEXINGTON
TYPE: U.S. Storeship   FROM: New York
ARRIVED: February 29, 1852   CAPTAIN: Lt.W. Radford
PASSAGE: Departed New York City, N.Y. on July 28, 1851. Called
         at Rio de Janeiro and departed there October 11, 1851.

(*)Note H. Dubosq, page 97.

Called at Valparaiso, Chile. Passage from Valparaiso to
San Francisco took 60 days.
CARGO: Not listed.
List of Officers:

Lt. William Radford (Commanding)	J. Stuart (Acting Master	J.C. Hunter (Purser)
James Suddards (Ass't Surgeon)	Thomas S. Filebrown (Passed Midship-	G.S. King (Passed Midshipman)
E. St. Clair Clark (Captain's Clerk)	man) Lt. J.C. Carter*	Charles Lever**

(*) To take command of the steamship "Massachusetts".
(**) To act as Captain's Clerk on "Massachusetts".

- - - - - -

SHIP: COLUMBIA
TYPE: Steamer   FROM: Portland, O.T.
ARRIVED: February 29, 1852   CAPTAIN: LeRoy
PASSAGE: 62 hours from Portland, Oregon Territory. This vessel
brings intelligence that the citizens of Portland had
passed a resolution disapproving of the contemplated
action by the Pacific Mail Steamship Company to remove
their depot from the city of Portland, and to stop the
direct communication between Portland and San Francisco.
CARGO: Not listed.

Passengers

Mr.& Mrs. O. Birney	Mr.& Mrs. G. Harrison	Mrs. M. Kinkle
J. Stephenson	J. McClosky	B. Jennings
T. Bagley	C.D. Maxwell	J.T. Lounsdale
A. Dibble	A.M. Starr	H.W. Corbett
R. Smith	H. Pendergrast /sic/	James Sinclair
H. McKnighton	George Brish	George R. Cooper
James Monroe	B. Grounds	C. Gatter
B.D. Caldwell	R. Spurgier	C. White
James Balch	E. Rodgers	A.W. White
William George Covington	Juba Rodgers	M.A. Bacon
A. Strong	Thomas McQuilkin	S.S. Richmond
A. Jewett	D.E. Coleman	James J. Hutton
W. Hall	B. McDonald	B. White
J.M. Howe	John Chetwood	Monroe Center(?)
	Jesse Chetwood	(Canter?)

- - - - - -

SHIP: ALERTO (Also listed as "ALERT")
TYPE: Schooner (Mexican)   FROM: Mazatlan, Mexico
ARRIVED: February 29, 1852   CAPTAIN: Randall
PASSAGE: From Mazatlan, Mexico (no departure day listed), via
Guaymas, Mexico (37 days from latter port). Miss
Rosalie Flores died during the passage on February 18,
1852.
CARGO: In ballast.

(Continued next page)

Passengers

Trinidad Balladases	Francisco Lastra	Carman Weylams
Teresa Quintans	Felipa Serabia	Carman Campa
Ursula Borgues /sic/	Dolores Flores	Refulgia Flores
(Eorgues?)	Forrefa Para /sic/	Sacrimento Roimanes
Trinidad Eorgues /sic/	(Parra?)	Refugia Garcia
(Borgues?)	Damania Parra /sic/	Francesca Garcia
Juana Borgues /sic/	(Para?)	Petra Trufilo
(Eorgues?)	Jesus Manos	Jesus Motino
Judas Trofia	Francisca Raimares	Eligia Cariel
E. Rabbes	Louisa Raimares	Jesus Cariel
J. Arenas	A. Borgues /sic/	J. Flores
Antonio Arenas	(Eorgues?)	T.M. Flores
S. Borgues /sic/	M. Borgues /sic/	M. Flores
(Eorgues?)	(Eorgues?)	P. Flores
A. Molina	C. Bernal	J.M. Frierarias
J. Marcas	Y. Cabrisas /sic/	F. Villican /sic/
F. Moto	Y.S. Cabrirera /sic/	J. Villian /sic/
J. Tapia	Manuel Flores	A. Arenas
T. Castro	B. Morceno	B. Arenas

- - - - -

SHIP: LUNA de PAITI (Listed also as "LUNA de PAITA")
TYPE: Barque (of Peru)　　　　　FROM: Paita, Peru
ARRIVED: February 29, 1852　　　CAPTAIN: Hanson
PASSAGE: 63 days from Paita, Peru. The wind had been, since
February 13th, NNE and North, light and baffling. Not
one vessel seen the whole passage.
CARGO: 16 boxes chocolate, 77 bundles cast steel, 60 bags of
cement, 190 half sacks flour, 400 bbls sweet potatoes, 100
casks onions, 24 boxes pickles and 3 cases merchandise.

Passengers

Capt. F.S. Hathaway	General Rufus McLellan

- - - - -

SHIP: ROBERT and LOUISE
TYPE: Brig (German)　　　　　　FROM: Amsterdam, Holland
ARRIVED: February 29, 1852　　　CAPTAIN: Olsen
PASSAGE: 203 days from Amsterdam, Holland, via Valparaiso, Chile,
60 days. Brings intelligence that the British ship "Cassander"(sic), Capt.___Elliott, commanding, has been lost.
The "Cassander" was loaded with coal for San Francisco
and by spontaneous combustion it took fire in lat. 15,
long. 88. Her passengers arrived at Lambisca (sic) after
being 13 days at sea in an open boat.
CARGO: Sugar, mustard, beer, gin, cordial, sherry wine, port wine,
claret wine, 6 cases segars and unidentified merchandise.

Passengers

Mr.___Leth	Mr.___Johnson	Mr.___Sellander

- - - - -

SHIP: SARAH LAVINIA
TYPE: Schooner   FROM: Santa Cruz, Calif.
ARRIVED: March 1, 1852   CAPTAIN: Scott
PASSAGE: 2 days from Santa Cruz, California.
CARGO: Lumber (type and amount not specified)
                        Passengers
Mrs.___Scott   Robert King   J. Williams
W.H. Contant

- - - - - -

SHIP: HUNTRESS
TYPE: Ship   FROM: Valparaiso, Chile
ARRIVED: March 2, 1852   CAPTAIN: Soule
PASSAGE: 59 days from Valparaiso, Chile.
CARGO: 650 tons of coal, 50 kegs of eggs and 30 cases of segars.
                        Passengers
John Champin and   W.W. Meed /sic/   W.G. Reed /sic/
   lady   P. Merie
              and 170 unidentified Chilenos

- - - - - -

SHIP: WILLIAM WATSON
TYPE: Barque   FROM: Hongkong, China
ARRIVED: March 2, 1852   CAPTAIN: Ritchie
PASSAGE: 60 days from Hongkong, China. This vessel brings word
         that nearly all the city of Hongkong, China has been
         destroyed by fire with damage at $4,000,000. The fire
         started on December 26, 1851.
CARGO: 1000 eggs, 5 cases of silks consigned to ___ Look (a China-
         man on board), 400 bags rice, 10 pkgs dried fish, 50 bags
         rice flour, 6 chests tea, 8 boxes shrimp, 1 pkg indigo, 4
         boxes eggs consigned to___Yesing (a Chinaman on board),
         20 boxes hats, 270 boxes charcoal and 117 jars and 25
         pkgs of unspecified Chinese merchandise.
                        Passengers
Mr. Jesse Southam   Peter Zacharia   F. Wallingham
   ___Look (Chinaman)   ___Yesing (Chinaman)
              and 158 unidentified Chinese

- - - - - -

SHIP: MONUMENTAL CITY
TYPE: Steamer   FROM: Panama
ARRIVED: March 4, 1852   CAPTAIN: Cressey
PASSAGE: 45 days from Panama, via intermediate ports. Left
         Panama on January 18, 1852. Arrived El Realejo, Nica-
         ragua on January 25th, arrived Acapulco, Mexico on
         February 2nd, put into Mazatlan, Mexico on February 12th
         to repair the engines. Put into San Diego, California
         on February 28th. Frederick Schartzer died at sea, during
         the passage, of congestion of the brain, no date of death
         listed. Another passenger, Isaac Gordon, aged 29 years,
         died at Mazatlan, Mexico on February 16th.

CARGO: 111 unidentified packages.

Passengers

R.W. Anderson and
  lady
Mr.   Ellis and
  lady
Norton Butler
A. McHenry, lady,
  child & svt
J. Tatt, lady
  and son
George Carpenter
James Malhom
S. Thetlow, lady
  and child (?)
  (Thetlew?,
  Thetlaw?)
Patrick Coyle
M. Hydeliff
Mr.   Sullivan and
  lady
F. Albert
T. Schartzer
W. Hubbard
J.B. St. John
P. Mulligen/sic/
George Ferby
Peter Spang
M. Rodriguez
W.H. Coleman
J. Farr
Thomas Farr
D. Philips /sic/
George Hubbard
John Stewart
John Newcomer
Benjamin F. Bower
A. Yeekley
Mrs.   Yeekley
A.D. Barker
D. Latimer
Batys Oier(?)
  (Oler?, Oter?)
L.B. Moulten /sic/
G.A. Stevens
C. Hoare
Stephen Norris
Elizabeth Norris
Sophia Norris
P. Boulden
E. McArcher

Miss   Wyatt
Masters   Wyatt
  (number of
  "Masters" not
  given)
Mrs.   Stedman and
  2 children
M.M.H. Offertt
Mrs. H.W. Sherer
G.S. Scribner
L.A. Scribner
J. Schumard
F.D. Chamberlain
Mrs. Cornelia Wilson
J. Ausrin
John Sturgeon
P.D. Wilson
Mr.   Donovan and
  lady
Henry Fisher
G. Jackson
J.T. Crane
J. Donaldson
William Browder
James Boylen
J. Hapgood
Martina M?scarro
E. Carpaux
Robert Golder(?)
  (Golden?)
B.D. Bullard
James Wilson
John Wilson
J.B. Smith
William Ewing
Mrs.   Ewing
S. Edgar
A. Shakely
M. St. Pierre
H. Fletcher
Rufus Work
F.S. Perkins
W. Bingham
M. Whitcomb
Benjamin Coxell
S.A. Pennocks
C.C. Smith
D.G. Smith
S. Lawrence

(Continued next page)

Mrs. Joana Jones
Mrs.   McDonald and
  2 children
E.P. Kennedy
Mrs.   Tengman and
  2 children
Miss   Sharr
Miss   Tweed
Mr.   Tweed, lady
  and 4 children,
  servant and 1
  child
A.G.W. Holm
William Broom
P. Broom
J. Everett
Edwin Taylor
A. Holt
P. Washburn
George Herman
William T. Rice
S. Farm
A. Block
    Banen
E.B. Casterlin
E.H. Horton
John Reader
L. Dreyton
Warren Foster
R. Walcott
Frank Kentz
J.F. Stout
John R?rt
Isaac Minor
William Massey
Mrs.   Massey
George Flint
J. Clark
F.A. Bourn
J.F. Duaster
H.A. Carter
L. Edgill
B. Skelton
G. McIntyre
W. Merritt
W.H. Woods
J.T. Woods
A. Woods
William Stone

James Connell, 3
  boys, woman and
  child
M. Goodkind
R. Huff and
  boy
J. Huff
W. M?chener
P. Keating
George Kingsley
F. Maunder
T. Alderson
Stephen Parsons
Hugh Collins
J. Jordan
J. Delap
W.E. Vancharch/sic/
  (Vanchurch?)
G. Graves
M. Boyle
Frank Joseph
E. Hawley
J. Burke
H. Beirman
S. Powell
M. Witt
W. Barber
P. Godfrey
M. Farrell
E. Sherman
H. Huntingdon/sic/
  (Huntington?)
J. Chapman
L.L. White
F. Ray, lady and
  child
A. Anderson
E. Noble
J.E. Noble
H. McArdle
A. Gomez
George Pitters
J. Murlaugh(?)
  (Murtaugh?)
P. Walden
O. Andrews
J.M. Picktel/sic/
C.H. Pecktel/sic/
M. Cahill
F. Williams
H. Marlow/sic/

J.K. Doak
J. Doak
J.R. Brading
Z. Jones
J. Broom
J. Jones
E. Chesrand
A. Wattsen /sic/
E. Hamblin
H. Stapleton
P.H. Larkin
James Holmes
Thomas Holmes
E.C. Lonoree
H.F. Bower
William Harford
E.C. Thompson
G. Hippell
W.B. Brown
Z.A. Telton and
  lady
E.G. Gilmor /sic/
H. Stockwell
A.P. Harten
A. Garcia
D. Willis
A. Knight
  ___ Clear
H. Cody
John Hapgood
A. Wills
J. Lake, lady and
  child
C. Bramner (?)
  (Bremner?)
W.D. Hensley
A. Silver
W.H. Ide
L. Parsons
G. Thompson
P.L. Shipley
S. Dickson
M. Freton
A. Joseph
M. Dillon
C.F. Healey
S. Hahs /sic/
M. Herman
Asa Taylor
W.H. Finney
F.A. Barlow/sic/
(Continued next page)

J.C. Willett
L.C. Rathbun
F. Stocktin /sic/
H.B. Bodwell /sic/
J. Martel
Mrs. ___ Martel
G. Bordwell /sic/
J. Pearson
E. Alley
S.H. Scott
Thomas Casey
Calvin Bain
H.S. Russell
H.E. Mattox
W. Warren
J. Vandergrift
John Vandergrift
George Burgarner
C. Ferrier
P. Laliaire
H. Haltimor(?)
  (Hailtimor?)
A. Reynolds
Charles Morgan
Sarah Womerly and
  2 children
S. Washburn
A. Case
A. Everton
P. Williamson
John Silver
P. Carlton
John McMaraton
J. Mayer
J. Hopkins
N.H. Hicks
J.S. Davis
E. Parkhurst
J.H. Vessel
A. Briggs
John Crawford
M. Francis
J.B. Glahn
J.D. Holmes
J. Greenham
J.H. Pray
F.M. Shirley
A. Francis
C. Jefferson and
  lady
J. Williams

James Huntingdon /sic/	S. Thomas	R. Joseph
(Huntington?)	A. Manuel	George Long
J. Goodwin	Green Victory /sic/	J. Hensley
J. Pico	T. Adams	___Meker(?)(Meket?)
Boarded at San Diego:		
C.E. Lucas	L.B. Gage	R.B. Moyer
J. Harris	W.A. McCoy	J. Woody
W.E. Watts	J. Kelly and lady	H. Craw
J.P. Flanders	J.S. Henderson	T. Osgood
J. Blackwell	F. Smith	T. Grimshaw
H. Hayward	H. Chenery	J.D. Pinkerton
C.R. Bingham	J.D. Spencer	T. Jarrett
L. Moore	J. Childers	W.M. Robb
Amos Green, wife	G.W. Childers	Dr.___Whiton
& 2 children	H. Godfrey	J. Townsend
J. Tweed	___Davis	R.P. Vanderveer
P.H. Gordon	E. Orn	

- - - - - -

SHIP: AUGUSTA
TYPE: Barque (British)   FROM: London, England
ARRIVED: March 4, 1852   CAPTAIN: Barnett
PASSAGE: 200 days from London, England, via Falkland Islands.
CARGO: 50 cases glass, 200 tons coal, 1 case flannel, 636 bags of
       oats, 900 bags barley, 100 cans oil (type not specified),
       430 casks beer, 1 safe, and a large quantity of gin, wine,
       brandy and cordial.
                    Passengers
Mrs. Elizabeth Greenwood   Mr. Charles Pace
Master John Greenwood   Mr. F. Abell   and lady
Mrs. Elizabeth Maester   R. Carter
              and 10 unidentified in steerage

- - - - - -

SHIP: CAPACITY
TYPE: Schooner   FROM: Bodega, California
ARRIVED: March 4, 1852   CAPTAIN: Driscoll
PASSAGE: 7 hours from Bodega, California.
CARGO: 85,000 feet lumber, 65 tons potatoes and 12 tons of
       machinery (type not listed).
                    Passengers

S. Smith	F. Kemble	J. Turnbull
H. Smith	H.N. Duncan	A. Gilbert
C.L. Smith	C. Perkins	W. Jones

- - - - - -

SHIP: NEW ORLEANS
TYPE: Steamer   FROM: Panama
ARRIVED: March 5, 1852   CAPTAIN: Hammersly
PASSAGE: 18 days from Panama, via Acapulco, Mexico, 10 days. The
         following deaths took place during the passage:
         February 23, 1852 - Matthew Hullerman?(Hollerman?),

aged 23 years. Buried at Acapulco, Mexico.
February 22, 1852 - E.J. Murphy, of Michigan, aged 19.
February 17, 1852 - Capt. H. Lake, jumped overboard, in a
fit of insanity.

CARGO: Not listed.

Passengers

E.J. Whitt and servant
Mrs.___Hill
P.B. Vance and servant
J.S. Stillwell and servant
L. Smith and lady
Mrs.___Thomas and 3 children
Mrs.___Mullen and child
Mrs. R.J. Howe and child
Mrs. C.J. Howe and child
Mrs. O. Reeder
T.M. Keefer, lady & 3 children
Mrs. A. Keefer and 4 children
Miss___Chapman
Dr.___Churchill, lady & svt
J. Burrington
E. Dongyear /sic/
P. Berwin and svt
R.Y. Tomlinson
J.W. Wilson
J.B. Suters
Henry Lake
Mrs.___Corbet /sic/
C.C. Howell
J. Tollensbee
J.L. Manchester
Joseph Beal
A.P. Beal
T.J. Hegtorver
H.L. Franklin
James Porter
Thomas Allen
R. McDermott
John Cummings
G. McGee /sic/
W. Brantou /sic/ (Branton?)

L.H. Brannock
W.R. Smith
Dr.___Hyde, lady and servant
___Danell
Mrs.___Desplat
P. Desplat
Mrs.___King and 2 children
J.P. Thurston and lady
G. Dalvin and lady
Anto Vogill
Mrs.___Ludwig
John Multally
Robert Hammond
J.W. Harker and lady
Dr. Hobart /sic/
Mrs.___Lewelling and 3 children
Mr.___Lewelling, lady and 2 chldrn
Mrs.___Carathers and child /sic/
W. Woods and lady
N. Hagg
Madame___Charles
G. Gurner
F.M. Hothorn
N. Roney /sic/
D.B. Gray
A.D. Lee
W.W. Lee
J.S. Lee
John Clements
David Jones
Thomas Nichols
John Goodsell
W. Moon
J.S. Bloom
L. Birmingham
Allen Tinner
Thomas Lay
Ann Lay
John Berry
(Continued next page)

T. Edgar
A.H. Denis /sic/ and lady
J.J. Westlake and lady
P. McLean and lady
Mrs.___Munell and servant
Mrs. Ellen O'Brien
Mrs. P. Cosgrove
P. Moore, lady and 4 children
Mare Hartman and child
John H. Dunn
Dr.___House
L. Ormsby and svt
P. Cosgrove
Mrs.___Doland
Mrs.___Hamilton and 3 children
H.B. Weir
D. Heath
J. Pate and lady
D.C. Freeman
O.H. Bolderston
Mr.___Hodgkins
T.J. Gareth /sic/
J. Knowlton
Miss J. Clarke
W. Bar
John Borland
James Baxter
John F. Newall
W. Daniel
Lambert Watts
W.C. Bunn
P. McQuin /sic/
Giles Bishop
Robert Ford
E. Milks (?)
G. Eager
N. Holland
J.P. Snelling

J. Leamer
Jean Desplat
Madame ___ Desplat
Benni Desplat
Mr. ___ Chapman
H.G. Stouffer
G. Bordwell
John Bowman
J. Werner
T. Kattick
George Illing
Anson J. Still
Chris Loneberger
W. Yarborough
W. Cohn
G.W. Drake
J. Vantine
Enos Drake
John Loring
John Becker
Charles Bowman
John Bliss
P. Melhearne
J. Loncriger
C. Kupper
A. Allendorf
Luke Sepro
C. Thomas
W. Williams
E.J. Evans
W.R. Williams
H.F. Davis
D. Williams
A. Davis
N. McLean
James Glaze
L.D. Wright
W. Ingram
John Coghlan
C. Linehan
J. Linehan
Jacob Brache
J.R. Underwood
J.J. Underwood
W.D. George
J. Finscher
H.A. Green
W. Taylor
Jacob New
Y.L. McLenore
James Mason

J.W. Congdon /sic/
S.M. Quin /sic/
   (Quinn?)
W.P. Love
Mr. ___ Muleen
P. Bane
D. Bane
J. Bowmaster
George Mishler
Charles Bauman
A.S. Van Neep
Francis Breeween /sic/
J. Sutter
T. Mealer
George Torney
Peter Smith
James C. Brown
W.C. Comstock
R. Kohler
John Nock
George Stample
Alex Thompson
Robert Thompson
Robert Scneider /sic/
   (Schneider?)
John Weller
Mr. ___ Bland, boy
   and svt
Owen Morgan
M. Morgan
Thomas Phillips
Benjiman Thomas
J.J. Thomas
J. Fullerton
W.A. Smith
W.P. Underwood
G.B. Reed
W. Leach
M. Geary
C. King
W.W. Worley
Ambrose Worley
E.J. Worley
Alson Worley
E. Williams
James M. Crow
J.J. Riley
Alfred Low
Thomas Low
P. Cosgrove and lady
   (sic)

Charles Bidault
J.D. Colburn
J. McNeas
M. Hamilton
Robert Dearden
W. Leonard
W.H. Murphy/sic/
T. Kneef
C. Bloeth
Charles Wedgewood
S. Howe and
   4 children
H. Stegan
D.H. Ellidge
John Nateens
W.J. Fifield
A. Packard
J.R. Taylor
B. Evans
A. Helscher
Mats Hallaran /sic/
James Simmons
Robert Bryce
James Murgroff
Michael Behler
H. Wibenoch
E. Morris
George John
John Pugh
J. Batton
Daniel Wilkinson
John Stegall
E. McCrary
J. Dishervon
Thomas Stringer
A.J. Warf
J.W. Kerbow
John Kerbow
S. Motler
E.F. Smyer
J.B. Wayne
Jesse Carroll
R.C. Emerson
Charles Man
D.H. Brannon
A.G. Brannon
Samuel King
Thomas Galt
C. Memfield
D. Hunt
James Ganinger

B. Lennon, lady
and 2 children
John Rice
Edward Block
John Davis
W. Davis
J.W. Davis
John Walsh
W.W. Goodspeed
W. Levitem
Mr.___Underoff
John Gore
H. Powell
A. Morgan
G.L. Merrits /sic/
H.H. Riker
W.J. Stedman
J.H. Glass
Isaac Hano
S. Kent
E. Sheldon
S. Wattingly
James O. Johnson
J.H. Jorden /sic/
B.A. Berry and
boy
Mr.___Hanson
J. Smith /sic/
T. Upton
D. Manley
Richard Rogers
G. Carrell
Jacob Howell
T.H. Howell
A.S. Kenner
W.R. Graves
J. Samuel
E. Samuel
F. Garcher
J. Clarke
A.A. Starkee
J. Sterling
W.T. Anderson
S. Brackett
C. Geenish
J. Smullen
E.W. Webster
W.H. Murphy /sic/
J. Roberts
A. Ray

J. Rock, lady
and child
Thomas Peaseley
George Etter
Walter Young
Robert Dearden
A. Parsons
H. Fenterhall
J.S. Leveter
H. Bingham and
lady
Phillip Wheeler
John Atkins
W.H. Lewis
J. Smith /sic/
P. Smith
L.B. Golden
E. Parker
B. Porter
J.C. Hammond
John McCune
A. Turner
A.D. McDevits /sic/
Charles Riddle
E. Walsh
George Lewis
D.N. Ellidge /sic/
A. Burns
E. Burns
W. Young
W.B. Donaldson
J.J. Westlake
W. Hunter
B. Lever
J. Dockery
J. Cunningham
R. Gilchrist
T. Kay
J. Coleman
W. Camp
R. Evans
J. Evans
H. Evans
W. Evans
Joseph Evans
Margaret Evans
G. McGee /sic/
J. Simmons
R.F. Laws
J. Forsyth

- - - - - -

John Cadman
Mr.___Cosgrove and
lady
M. Harris
W. Greenwood
J. Webster
Isaac Reed
L. Donnelly
George Jackson
John Neis and
lady
J.S. Burpee
D. Burpee
Mr.___Uhler
S. Wells
P.G. Clarke
James Smith
___Taylor
W. Wells
W. Beekman
D.C. Scott
A. McMurphy
John Ross
W.D. Dougherty
M. Roney /sic/
John Richards
J.H. Nateens
J.S. French
S.P. Sampson
J.W. Richmond and
lady
J. Mellory
J. Lovelong
J. Walsh
M. Mulheever
M. Shaver
J. Watson
J. Owens
Charles Curry
R. Berger
T.J. Heytower /sic/
(Hightower?)
T. McDonald
R. Merrill
R. Wilson
J. Moore
M. Curry
W.K. Wallace
G.H. Davis

SHIP: YOUNG AMELIA
TYPE: Brig (Mexican)   FROM: San Blas, Mexico
ARRIVED: March 6, 1852   CAPTAIN: Wallace
PASSAGE: 45 days from San Blas, Mexico.
CARGO: 400 bags corn, 750 chickens, 100 turkeys and 40 cases of
       paper cigars.

Passengers

W.T. Ewing   H. Lomer   C.D. Camp
Domingo Pesfol

and 16 unidentified in steerage

- - - - - -

SHIP: CABARGO
TYPE: Barque   FROM: Panama
ARRIVED: March 7, 1852   CAPTAIN: Barstow
PASSAGE: 79 days from Panama, via Acapulco, Mexico. The following
         passengers died during the passage (dates of death not
         listed):

         Mrs.___Swartz   Margaret Halligan
         A. Montgomery   R. Valtenbury
         E. Smith   S.D. Maxon
CARGO: 51 tons of coal and 60 bbls of molasses.

Passengers

C. Hubbell	S. Nickerson	S. Coombs
A. Steel	S.A. Braden	G.W. Gallup
J. Davis	D.P. Vickford /sic/	Mrs. D. Han
S. Laurent	D.M. Bradford	and 2 chldrn
D.D. Derhig (?)	J.Y. Cassel	J. Cupps
M. Stonemeller(?)	B.T. Sturtevant	D. Murphy
(Stonemelier?)	P. Carr	R. Eano
B.T. Ingalls	D. Callahan	P. Power
S. Boyd	A. Ewing	J.F. Daly
J.F. Gammon	L. Over	J. N. Swanzey
D. Nisser	A. Williams	R. Stone
S. Bird	D.A. Wade	G. Smith
R. Roberts	F. Mosier	L. Kemble
L.M. Norton	C. McNeal	B.S. Pendleton
W. Aldrich	W. Connel /sic/	W.H. Anderson
C. Fal?s	H.B. Chapin /sic/	M. Murphy
(Fales?)	P. Gallagher	Williams
G. Render	J. McDermott	J. Carigan
P. Kelly	T. O'Brien	H. Vogher
P. Farrel /sic/	J. Caverly	S. Farley
(Farrell?)	J. Rosena	C. Frail
S.H. Whinney	G. Stoffer	L.B. Leach
S. Jones	R. Edmar	E. Roso
J. Jones	M. Stuart	E.C. Baldrich
J. Hallegan /sic/	J. Logan	J. Brooks
Mary Halligan /sic/	H.B. Chapin /sic/	C.H. Dray
J. Leon	E. Booth	J. Daly
J. Callaghan	J.J. Ellison	J. Frost

(Continued next page)

J.A. Dangerford	J. Cutts /sic/	J. Barry
J.S. Downing	T. Kewing	W.J. Lina
W. Clinton	P. Kutts /sic/	J. Burns
J. Smalley	(Cutts?)	L.M. Elliott
J. Staffer	T. Walon	D. Mahony
P.M. Lee	H. Reed	E. Johnson
J. Driver	T. Frainer	J. Cole
J. Brown	J.B. Stone	D. Higgins
A. Montgomery	S. Booth	J. Higgins
M. Turney	G.W. Booth	D.K. Knight
R. Morrison	P.P. Lee	J. Smith
M. Durfee	R.D. Thomson	E.H. Walker
J. Collen	C. Collen	D. Wagner

- - - - - -

SHIP: OHIO
TYPE: Steamer   FROM: San Diego, Calif.
ARRIVED: March 7, 1852   CAPTAIN: Hilliard
PASSAGE: 3½ days from San Diego, California, via intermediate
         ports. One intermediate port listed as Monterey, Califor-
         nia. The brig "Victorine", with passengers from Panama,
         is reported by the "Ohio" to be laying in San Diego,
         condemned.
CARGO: Not listed.

Passengers

Dr. McKenzie	S. Sota	J. Via
J. Contreras	L. Phillips	T. Daily
B. Contreras	E. Stameill	J. Madden
O. Contreras	C.A.J. Heid	T. Hervey
R. Chappella	W.H. McConas (?)	H. Levy
J.T. Anderson	(McCouas?)	B. Malloy
A. Harvale	T. Osgood	W. Hunter
J.V.R. Erbert	Mrs. Aldrich and	J.P. Weinschronk
W. Heguman	servant	H. Baidole
D. Kutton	E.P. Compton	G.V. Chornping
W. Morrallis	M. Carraig	C. Hutch
G.O. Vannison	J. Ventran	W.C. Moriaga
R.R. Snastiga	W. Cota(?)	H. Ochoa
M. Snastiga	(Cots?)	M. Seron
N. Buteria	S. Miles	J. Blackburn
W. Garfies	J.H. Smith	M.C. Foster
D. Goodman	C.A. Narvaro	William Demfrey

- - - - - -

SHIP: COMMERCE de BORDEAUX
TYPE: Barque (French)   FROM: Bordeaux, France
ARRIVED: March 7, 1852   CAPTAIN: Get
PASSAGE: 180 days from Bordeaux, France.
CARGO: Not listed.

Passengers

Mr. D. La Grangier   M. Aribaud

- - - - - -

SHIP: NORTHERN LIGHT
TYPE: Clipper   FROM: Boston, Massachusetts
ARRIVED: March 8, 1852   CAPTAIN: Bailey *
PASSAGE: 109 days from Boston, Massachusetts.(see "Notes" Section)
CARGO: 2 boxes liquor pumps, 10 tons and 146 plates of pig iron,
       94 bars iron, 1 scale, 50 boxes lamps, 1 case steel, 6
       wagons, 1 coach, 234 boxes furniture, 62 pkgs glassware, 15
       boxes oil cloth, 63 anvils, saddlery, gunny bags, 110 tons
       coal, 3 whippletrees, 50 plough castings, 12 plough braces,
       110 bbls cement, 265 doors,1 boiler, drugs, boots, liquor,
       seeds and candles.

Passengers

J. Barstom	A. Pratt	S.D. Holman
E.H. Davis	C. Henderson, lady	Mrs. Susan D. Town
Mrs. Jane Eastbrook	and child	and 2 children
Mrs. E. Wheelwright	Mrs. Mary H. Brackett	Mr. L. Humphrey Jr.
Mr. C.O. Newcomb	Mr. W.P. Daniels	Mr. G. McFarland
Mr. H.A. Fuller	Mr. L.P. Rand	

- - - - - -

SHIP: DISTRUZIONE
TYPE: Barque (Italian)   FROM: Genoa, Italy
ARRIVED: March 9, 1852   CAPTAIN: Garalla
PASSAGE: 145 days from Genoa, Itally, via Callao, Peru, 42 days.
CARGO: Not listed.

Passengers

Capt. Joseph Del Grand*   Alexander Gort and 3
                                              servants**
               and 43 unidentified in Steerage
(*)Vice Consul of Italy.
(**) Secretary to Vice Consul.

- - - - - -

SHIP: PACQUETE de COPIAPO
TYPE: Brig (Mexican)   FROM: San Blas, Mexico
ARRIVED: March 9, 1852   CAPTAIN: Yuchaurza
PASSAGE: 22 days from San Blas, Mexico.
CARGO: 52 casks muscal wine, 18 sacks Mexican goods (unidentified)
       and one package of cards.

Passengers
                    Mr. M. Alascal
               and 11 unidentified in Steerage

- - - - - -

SHIP: STELLA del MARE
TYPE: Barque (Italian)   FROM: Marseilles, France
ARRIVED: March 9, 1852   CAPTAIN: Croce
PASSAGE: 143 days from Marseilles, France.
CARGO: 150 cases kirch water, 6 casks cheese, 1 press, 300 bbls of
       port wine, 200 bbls Madeira wine, 700 cases annisette and
       absinthe, 50 cases vinegar, 60 bags almonds, 100 casks of
       wormwood, 75 bbls of brandy, 19,000 bricks and other goods.
(*)One source states Capt.____Loring was the master.

Passengers
J.B. Bowel   C. Joseph
and 2 unidentified in steerage

— — — — — —

SHIP: TAROLINTA
TYPE: Ship   FROM: Valparaiso, Chile
ARRIVED: March 10, 1852   CAPTAIN: Cave
PASSAGE: 56 days from Valparaiso, Chile. Was off San Francisco
harbor for 3 days in thick weather and heavy gales.
Anchored off the "North Beach" area of San Francisco.
This vessel brings intelligence that the emigration from
Chile to California has amounted to nearly 1000 individ-
uals, that have taken passage from the port of Valparaiso.
Recent disturbances, both in mining and agricultural
districts, have contributed much to the movement. Some
speculators have advanced sums for paying the passage of
emigrants, taking a share in their gains in the California
mines.
CARGO: 8000 fanagas of barley.

Passengers
Mr. W.W. Snelling   H. Woodward
and 25 unidentified in steerage

— — — — — —

SHIP: JOHN ENDERS
TYPE: Brig   FROM: San Blas, Mexico
ARRIVED: March 10, 1852   CAPTAIN: Eldridge
PASSAGE: 22 days from San Blas, Mexico.
CARGO: 11 boxes paper segars, 432 kegs nails, 2 boxes flowers, 1
box clothes, 15 crates oranges, 4 turtles, 38 boxes eggs,
390 bags corn, 400 fowls, 50 pigs.

Passengers

Capt. David Goulay	Capt. H.S. Clark	W.B. Furman
F.K. Sherman	W.F. Jarboe	J.L. Murphy
S.F. Courley (?)	R.O. Lowry	S. Grant
Charles Arnold	J.T. Roberts	Manuel Sanchez
Antonio Carnalia	Carlos Argasino	Tresensia Arvilos
Pedro Velasco	Evaristo Zepida	V. McVallelasca
Thomas Pamplosa	Esocus Sanchez	Frank King
Tresensia Hernaupez		

— — — — — —

SHIP: TENNESSEE
TYPE: Steamer   FROM: Panama
ARRIVED: March 14, 1852   CAPTAIN: G.M. Totten
PASSAGE: 17 days from Panama, via intermediate ports. Departed
Panama on the evening of February 26, 1852. The emi-
gration is still on the increase with 3000 persons on the
Isthmus waiting for passage. Tickets are sold for months
ahead. Saw the steamer "North America" wrecked and lying
on her broadside with surf breaking heavily against her

sides. She appears to be a total loss and lies at a
place called Los Ramidas, near the mouth of the river
Nepa, 50-75 miles below Acapulco, Mexico. The "Tennessee"
put into Acapulco, Mexico and there obtained additional
news of the "North America". It was impossible for the
"Tennessee" to take away the passengers of the"North
America", the former being filled to utmost capacity.
Some 800-900 passengers and 100 crew members were safely
removed from the "North America" when it wrecked on the
evening of February 27, 1852. Capt.___Blethen was the
captain of the wrecked steamer. All passengers on the
"North America" were saved, among them the Hon. Judge
___Shattuck, and his partner, Mr.___Bain, and General
___Winchester and family. The passengers of the "North
America" marched from the scene of the wreck to Acapulco
in two and half days.
　　　On March 3, 1852 the "Tennessee" spoke the bark
"Elizabeth", at anchor 20 miles south of Acapulco. The
bark was 65 days from Panama and in want of water and
provisions, which were furnished by the "Tennessee".
Passengers of the "Elizabeth", numbering 120, had left
on March 3rd, by boats, for Acapulco, Mexico. The bark
was bound for San Francisco.
　　　The following passengers died on board the "Tennessee"
during the passage:
　　　　　　　C.H. Palmer (no date of death listed)
　　　　　　　O.O. Force, of Newark, Wayne County, New York
　　　　　　　(no date of death listed)

CARGO:　Not listed.

Passengers

G.T. Austin	Mrs.___Ayres, child	G. Abernethy and
George Alexander	and nurse	wife
J.C. Addison	L.S. Adams	H. Allard
Mrs.___Brown	J.C. Ayres and 3	L. Brigham and wife
Mrs.___Bowen	children	A. Barnard
Mrs.___Blitz	Mrs.___Baker	Mrs.___Brooks
J. Berford	G. Bradley	Mrs.___Benson and
Madame__Biscaccianti	Dr.___Baugh	child
E. Boydan	P. Bodley	H. Benson
W. Bolinger	G. Bartlett	J. Bull
J. Biggs	A. Broad	W. Bradford
W. Battles	Madame___Celeste	Miss___Cleenens
Miss___Clavers	Miss___Coyle and	Miss___Clarke
L.G. Chase	servant	Mrs.___Christian
J.C. Carey	J.R. Cook	J. Chester
R.C. Crane	R. Cole	Mrs.___Dayton
J. Drum	Capt.___Dupaurn	Mrs.___Dixon
J.H. Davis	Mr.___Doyle	G. Dougherty
A. Davis	S. Davidson	W. Dimrock
Mrs.___Evans and	Miss___Elliott	J. Euslom(?)
child	R. Elliott /sic/	R. Elliott /sic/

(Continued next page)

Dr.___Elliott
John Fiske
G. Grinnell
G. Gibson
H.S. Hallett
N. Helber
J. Hathaway
H. Hafleigh(?)
Mr.___Mansfield
Mr.___Mitchell, lady
& 2 children
J. Marvin /sic/
S. Martin /sic/
Mr.___Nelson and
lady
Miss___Nelson
B.F. Rawlin, lady
and child
C. Redlon
Mrs.___Swift
E.A. Shepard
Miss___Tyler
M. Jones
D.F. White
J. Wellington
S. Warren
M. Zolover
Mrs.___Brooks
Mrs.___Ferguson
P.G. Bennett
J. Fonley Jr.
M.S. Cole
Major___Ferris
Mrs.___Sutton and
3 children
S. Allen
A. Bower
H. Billings
B. Baxter
J. Bogart
J. Barley
T. Beales
J. Bowen
H. Bulbank /sic/
(Burbank?)
A. Burbank /sic/
S. Bennett
J. Baldwin
H. Bird
H. Boyles
B. Blonk

N. Evans and
3 children
A. Love
Mrs.___Haines
M. Haines
G. Heap
J. Haworth
N. Holbrook(?)
(Hollbrook?)
S.L. Masbick
E. Melwain
D. Miller
A. Norton
C. Prentiss
J. Primrost
G. Prouke (?)
(Pronke?)
S. Rice
J. Ramsdall
M.B. Stearns
G.M. Stowell
J. Tomlinsen
Mrs.___Webster
A. Weston
W. Workman
C. Walker
Miss___Greenwald
Mrs.___Griswold
Miss___Teal
H. Whyte
B.M. Noe
J. Law
Mrs.___Burns and
child
E. Agard
L. Ashworth
T. Boswell
C. Bretz
J. Berden
J. Burnes
C.S. Burr
J. Bullow
M. Bagger
D. Bradbury
A. Brown
J. Brooks
E. Bedlon
A. Burns
D. Brown
D. Bundy
G. Boss
(Continued next page)

J. Freego/sic/
L. Fensir
B. Griggs
Kate Hastings
Dr.___Hewitt, lady,
child & nurse
A. Hancock
C. Lindsay
Mrs.___McLaughlin
Capt.___Macondray,
lady and family
Mr.___Moore
F. Moore
W. Preutzer
N.R. Peters
C. Rolls(?)
(Rolla?, Rolle?)
R. Roberts
S. Sprague
T.L. Smith
L. Searle
J. Sprague
Miss___Wentworth
Miss___Wilson
A. Webster
Mrs.___Young
J. Young
Miss___Long
Mr.___Chapman and
lady
J.H. Chapman
C. Chapman
J. Atwood
F. Adams
G. Adams
E. Arnold
J. Buchanan
J. Bentley
C. Brady
J. Benedict
C. Burden /sic/
E. Burden /sic/
J. Borden /sic/
R. Benedict
J. Burnett
L. Bond
W. Baxter and son
H. Bayne
E. Bremer
J.R. Bell
W. Calmeeny

H. Chandler
W. Curtis
S. Caldwell
S. Carlton
E. Cutler
C. Crandall
J. Clark
J. Corwin
A. Drew
J. Dalton
G. Day
N. Day
S. Dunlapp /sic/
J. Eachus
M. Eastman
J. English
G.W. Emery
N. Flumer
P.S. Fogg
H.B. Hagg
J. Ferguson
G. Fairbank
D. Fay
L. Gilmour /sic/
J. Gove
J. Gatchers
G. Gatchers
C. Gifford
J. Griffin
G. Garlock
J. Hougjarros
J. Hampton
J. Hill
A. Holland
M. Randall
C. Randall
Henry Stout
F. Schott
T. Stow
J. Smith
W. Savage
W. Spray
J. Stevens
O. Stevens
G. Somerville
O.E. Stone
J. Stone
D. Sibley
S.W. Sibley
W. Thomas
Mrs.____Thomas

W. Cook
G. Cook
F. Cook
C. Coleman
J. Cochrane
A. Craig
M. Chandler
J. Davis
N. Davis
J. Daley
C. Denham
C. Davidson
O. Dunning
P. Dunning
W. Egles
J. Dewey
F.H. Fisher
R.A. Foley
J. Farrell
C.R. Fisher
J. Fitzpatrick
O. Force
W. Gray
H. Gentry
A. Gurney
F. Grobe
P. Grant
G. Gay
E. Gregory
D. Hopper
W. Henly
J. Hyde
G. Hyde
W. Holbrook /sic/
Mrs.____Sarsfield
John F. Stockton
W.G. Stearns
M. Stevens
J. Skinner
B. Shattuck
F. Silver
F. Smith
J. Scarborough
N. Lummer
O. Schaffer
A. Scott
W.W. Standish
S. Snyder
W. Taylor
J. Thomas
J.W. Thomas

S. Clapp
C. Church
W. Collins
S. Clarkson
J. Clapp
W. Cornell
S. Cannan (?)
    (Cannau?)
J. Cord
L. Dexter
D. Duane
J. Dunstan
E. Dickinson
Ed Dickinson
J. Elliott
M. Evans
J. Ferrier
R. Felderdan (?)
M. Freeborn/sic/
A. Fuller
B. Freeze
E. Fiske
B. Gardner
F. Gardner
C. Gardner
R. Graham
L. Goodall
J. Gerard
J. Griffith
J.G. Griffith
D. Griffith
R. House
P. Hoefler
W. Harris
Mrs.____Sellers
Mrs.____Stockard
M. Segfried
A. Snow
O. Stone (?)
    (Store?)
B. Seabury
H. Sanderson /sic/
M. Sandford
C. Stubbs
W. Standerson /sic/
E. Smith
B. Sellers
F. Stelby
E. Mitchell
T. Trickey and son
C.A. Thayer

(Continued next page)

F.L. Tyler
C.O. Turner
W. Tubbs
J. Wilson/sic/
C. Wells
J. Woodward
M. Wehalie
M. Whiting
F. Woods/sic/
G. Wait
L. Wakefield
L.L. Whitley
J. Walker
W.C. Weir
E. Wilbur
M. Norton
Mrs.___ Corcoran
J. Brooks
L. Brown
J. White/sic/
___ Ragsdale
H. Harrington
J. Harsen
G. Hel?burn
  (Hellburn?,
  Heltburn?)
H. Hughes
T. Reed
J. Hewitt
W. Henderson
G.W. Hollis
J. Richards
H. Harker
J. Holder
E. Harrington
O. Harris
M. Impraym
J. Moner
A.W. Moulton
J.E. Miller
J. McKenna
H. McGaw
J. McConnoly /sic/
O. Millard
R. McLaughlin
J. McNiel
S. McNiel
J. Johnston
W.R. Johnston
J. Kelley
J.A. Killer

B. Thorne
A. Thomas
D. Vincent
J. Whitcomb
S. Wheaton
J.S. Washburn
J. Williams/sic/
M. Winchester
J. Wilson/sic/
H. Wadham
J. Wolcott
C. Westfield
D.D. Weiser
S.B. Warden
H. Williams
Peter Howk /sic/
R. Drews
H. Goke
B. Klane
F. Woods/sic/
___ Wright
W.G. Harris
J. Hanson
F. Hazleton
P. Hart
J. Hathaway
S. Hull
E. Hamilton
E. Hopkins
J.V. Harris
G. Howard
C. Handall (?)
  (Haudall?)
M. Hannaberg
L. Howard
C. Hoag
John___
S. McEwen
J. Martins
C.A. Morse
R.A. Morrison
J. Morrison
J. Monson (?)
  (Mouson?)
A. McMartin
J. Nith
E. Northey
S.W. Northey
J. Kettridge
D. Kimball
J. Kimball
(Continued next page)

A. Farrell
S. Tifton
J. Williams/sic/
M. Wadleigh
E. Whitman
J. Ward
J. White/sic/
O. Wyman
J. Wilcox/sic/
G. Wagoner
F. Wooding
J. Weiser
A. Welton
J. Wilcox/sic/
N. Young
F. Young
Elizr Bell /sic/
S. Lyle
G. Chapman
W.Wilson
___ Whitlock
P. Hayden /sic/
J. Hadden /sic/
W. Hathaway
F. Harris
W. Hopkins
B. Heath
A. Hoobler
J. Howe
L.J. Howe
P. Hawes
O. Harrison
A. Harvey
N. Hill
J. Henshaw
W. Ives
G.W. Matthews
R. McCartney
B. McCartney
F. Mullin
T. McGee
G. Murray
P. McGregor/sic/
P. Moylan
George Monti
O. Noyes
J. Grainer
N. Johnson
J. Knapp
J. Keenward
W. Kenworthy

L. Konn
S.B. Kuig
W.H. Leiper(?)(Le1per?)
F.M. Leach
J.S. Love11
W. Looken
G. Lovett
G. Lane
J.H. Nelson
J.W. Nico11t /sic/
S. Martin
B.P. Jones
J.S. Jones
B.F. Jones
S. Platt
H. Platt
S.F. Parker
D.H. Potter
P. Pierson/sic/
J.G. Pearson/sic/
J. Ross
S. Ripley
J. Parker
A. Reese
J. Jellummi(?)
  (Jeliummi?,
  Jellumml?)

H. Kallander (?)
  (Kollander?,
  Kellender?)
E. Lovejoy
A. Littlefield
T. Leslie
J. Mason
Silas March
Mrs.   March
E.J. Niles
    Jenkins
I. Pardee (?)
  (J. Pardee?)
J. Pratz
J. Prior
J. Philips /sic/
S.A. Pratt
C.K. Patten
C. Peck
C.F. Putnam
P.F. Putnam
J. Richards
E.E. Richards
A. Rolls (?)
  (Rolla?, Rolle?)

B. Littlefield
J. Loveland
J. Liberman
R. Levering
A.H. Lowe
E. Lelledd(?)
  (Leiledd?)
R.R. Muner
R. McDonough
P. McGregor/sic/
M. Jocushyn
James Prune
S. Perry
O. Phillips
L. Poole
E. Pendleton
F. Preston
O. Pierce
J.L. Power
C. Palmer
J. Pollock
A. Reynolds (?)
W. Redfiele /sic/
  (Redfield?)
A. Jabon

- - - - -

SHIP: SEA BIRD
TYPE: Steamer   FROM: San Diego, Calif.
ARRIVED: March 14, 1852   CAPTAIN: Haley
PASSAGE: 4 days from San Diego, California, via intermediate ports.
Encountered very heavy weather on passage to San Francisco
but sustained no serious damage. Intermediate ports are
not listed.
CARGO: Not listed.

Passengers

Major   McKinstry
Sgt   Ferguson
Padre Juan Olby
Padre   Jose
J.S.K. Ogler
W.A. Winston
W. Wolfskill
A. Riddle
A. Matede
J.J. Spacke
R. Alexander
S. Percival
Mrs.   Bailey

Major   Patten
Capt.   Brown
Padre   Gonzalez
Padre Jose Gomez
G.P. Lebbetts
Colonel J. Williams
P. Garcia, lady and
  child
L. Morris
Capt.   Thompson
S. Chupal
J.C. Dickerman
Capt. R. Wearing

Lt.   Bond
Lt.   Sully
Padre Ant. Jimeno
M. Bacca
C.A. Gieguel
H. Hancock
D. Tuscomia
R. Gaillard
L. Luvas
T. Turner
H. Turner
Dr.   Conway and
  lady,family & svt

(Continued next page)

T. Balfour
W. Blake
C. Pierce
W.E. Reeves
W. Gavit
T. Hendricks
T.V. Eberheart
E.C. Barrett
C.J. Butter
W. Maskill
R. Johnson
W. Hurbert
W. Glowlock
W.T. Williams
N. Hawkins
G.W. McDonald
B.H. Friecker
G.W. Gray
E.M. Butler
H. Loomis
G. Huggle
J. Stebbins
L. Brewster
C.L. Cross
G.W. Ticknor
D. Decker
P.A. Brown
W. Goldsworthy
N. Truape
W. Norris
B. Horrigan
Judge___Ord
C. Lard
W. McElroy
O. Haley
H.G. Preston
William Henner
G.D. Dewley (?)
 (Dowley?)
C. Duglas /sic/

J. Hacket
A.H. Smith
C. Rolleman
J.B.T. Blaylock
M. Dillon
W. Bennett
M.G. Bennett
D. Mitchin
W. Robinson
W. Barclay
D. Dernsy
W.W. Harris
F.W. Glasgop
T. Wogenstart
B. Wilson
F. Griffin
L. Camp
J.E. Higgins
B. Smith
J. Winkleman
J. Groves
H. Groves
B. Crocker
D. Gordon
H.A. Lewis
T. Harris
J. Franklin
A. Delatour
M. Measure
H. Spencer
T. Lambert
K. Stewart
H.G.___McGelt
M. Little
E. Doolittle
A.C. Adams
A.S. Williams
P.E. Kennedy

S.W. McGinnis
W.L. McGinnis /sic/
J.W. McGinnis
W.L. McGinnis /sic/
J. Gibbs
J.J. McClusky
A.T. McClusky
D.H. McClusky
J.H. McClusky
D. Crowley
G.M. Cahen (?)
 (Cohen?)
J.G. Leonard
W. Montgomery
R.C. Montgomery
A. Henderson
J.M. Henderson
M.G. Henderson
J.L. Lewis
N.G. Griswold
J. Mitz
T. Mason
T. Struly (?)
 (Struiy?)
P. Oats
E. Bevins
L.S. Mead
J. Hodges
H. Gutner
P. Leake
M. Jirman
T. Gibbs
G.W. Bird
Mr.___Adams
H.B. Conner
T. Scranton
R. Douglas
___Stawen
J. Avery

- - - - -

SHIP: COLUMBIA
TYPE: Steamer   FROM: Portland, O.T.
ARRIVED: March 14, 1852   CAPTAIN: W. L. Dall
PASSAGE: 72 hours from Portland, Oregon Territory.
CARGO: Oats, wheat, potatoes and fowls.

Passengers

Capt. James G. Baker
Nathaniel Brown
J.E. Sweetzer

D.H. Haskell
John Ferguson
J. Kohn
(Continued next page)

Dr.___Gerry
C.D. Murray
F. Bohl and wife

118

H. Peirce
H. Burns
T.E. Webster
C. Fridenburg
W.H. Parish /sic/
S. Seivon
T.K. Osgood
Mrs. S.A. Berry
A.S. Kinle
John Larkin
Capt. S.J. Jackson
J. McCussee
George S. Barnard

Levi Anderson
Rev.M.Roberts and
    wife
Frank Browe /sic/
    (Browne?)
C.W. Cook and lady
H.C. Halter
H.G. Foster
F.A. Dickinson
Jacob S. Lisle
Peter Dean
S. Robinson

Lloyd Brooks
D. McTavish
S.F. Chadwick
James Keller
A.K. Gaines
E. Pomroy /sic/
J.M. Jordan
Eli Smith
J. Dusenbury
H. Dusenbury
David Convin
Samuel Patrick
C.D. Patrick

- - - - - -

SHIP: ROANOKE
TYPE: Schooner   FROM: Santa Cruz, Calif.
ARRIVED: March 14, 1852   CAPTAIN: Curtis
PASSAGE: 16 hours from Santa Cruz, California.
CARGO: 25 tons of potatoes.
                        Passengers
Mr.____Hodge   Mr.____Bennett   Mr.____Lean
Mr.____Holmes

- - - - - -

SHIP: JOHN DAVIS
TYPE: Brig   FROM: Puget Sound, W.T.
ARRIVED: March 14, 1852   CAPTAIN: Plummer
PASSAGE: 13 days from Puget Sound, Washington Territory.
CARGO: Piles, amount not specified.
                        Passenger
                H. A. Gouldsborough

- - - - - -

SHIP: NOBLE
TYPE: Brig   FROM: Honolulu, S.I.
ARRIVED: March 16, 1852   CAPTAIN: Robinson
PASSAGE: 18 days from Honolulu, Sandwich Islands.
CARGO: 195 bbls of polar oil, 100 half bbls molasses, 11 cases of
        turpentine, 2 cases hardware and 62 bundles of iron.
                        Passengers
Charles W. Rand   Frank Hoskins   John B. Hanff
B. Nason Jr.   W.L. Greene   A.B. Howe
Capt.____Fales

- - - - - -

SHIP: QUICKSTEP
TYPE: Steamer   FROM: Oregon Territory
ARRIVED: March 20, 1852   CAPTAIN: Tichenor
PASSAGE: 5 days from the Oregon Territory, via Trinidad, Califor-
        nia, Port Orford, Oregon Territory and Humboldt, Califor-
        nia. This vessel brings intelligence that the miners are

doing very well because copious rains are increasing the harvest of the gold materially. Preparations are underway for sluice washing on the bars of the Klamath and Trinity Rivers during the coming summer. Citizens residing on Humboldt Bay and neighboring country have appointed a committee to wait on General___Hitchcock and solicit him to establish a military post between Humboldt Bay and the Klamath and Trinity Rivers. A military force, even if it did not consist of more than twenty-five men, would preserve peace among the whites and Indians.

CARGO: 58 rolls carpeting, 50 casks chopped food, 874 bags of potatoes, 674 bags oats, 2 grizzly bears, 1 steam engine, 1 coop of chickens, 283 bags wheat.

Passengers

Mrs. B. Aspinwall	Mrs. R.A. Parker	Miss Mary Crossway
Lt. H.G. Gibson	S.C. Jayne	J. Kingsbury
J. James	W.D. Maguire	R.F. Tichenor
M.L. Wolff	J.W. McKee	J.E. Wyman
C. Morgan	S. Kelsey	W. Van Dyke
A.A. Rhodes	D. Agnew	C. Barrett
J.F. Quinn	J. McKee	C. Stanton
C.H. Gilman		

- - - - - -

SHIP: WALTER
TYPE: Barque (German)   FROM: Hamburg, Germany
ARRIVED: March 21, 1852   CAPTAIN: Drescher
PASSAGE: 165 days from Hamburg, Germany, via Valparaiso, Chile, 48 days. On January 10, 1852, off Cape Horn, experienced severe weather, lost fore-topsail yard.
CARGO: 30 cases matches, 24 pkgs agricultural tools, mill and implements, 3 wagons, 6 wheels, 1 pkg books, 120 cases of window glass, 1 case percussion caps, 8 pkgs furniture, 1588 bars of iron, glassware, cigars, 1 saddle, port wine and sherry wine.

Passenger
Mr. G. Curtis

- - - - -

SHIP: MAID OF JULPHA
TYPE: Brig (British)   FROM: Honolulu, S.I.
ARRIVED: March 22, 1852   CAPTAIN: Beauvoise
PASSAGE: Departed from Honolulu, Sandwich Islands on February 25, 1852. Experienced severe weather on the passage, sprung mast.
CARGO: 104,330 feet of assorted lumber and 12 cases of bitters.

Passengers

Mr. J. Brockway	G.A. Parks	Mr. B. Cook
H. Kinsey	Mrs.___Ellis and child	

and 6 unidentified in steerage

- - - - - -

SHIP: FAWN
TYPE: Brig   FROM: Umpqua River, O.T.
ARRIVED: March 22, 1852   CAPTAIN: Bunker
PASSAGE: 6 days from the Umpqua River, Oregon Territory.
CARGO: 1600 ft square timber and 50 cords of wood.

Passengers

Mrs.____Scott and   H.J. Kaine
   2 children

- - - - - - -

SHIP: EMMA PRESTON
TYPE: Brig   FROM: Oregon Territory
ARRIVED: March 22, 1852   CAPTAIN: Maloy /sic/
PASSAGE: Given as three days from the Oregon Territory.
CARGO: 80,000 feet of lumber.

Passenger

Mr.____Goodwin

- - - - -

SHIP: PRINCE CHARLIE
TYPE: Barque (British)   FROM: London, England
ARRIVED: March 23, 1852   CAPTAIN: Kerr
PASSAGE: 142 days from London, England, via Falkland Islands, 75
         days.
CARGO: 1 case of guns, 4 cases cutlery, 300 kegs paint, 2 pipes of
       varnish, 14 iron bottles, 50 hhds stout, 3 anvils, 4 bdls
       vices, 725 bags oats, 100 firkins butter, 73 cases oil
       stones, 50 tons coal, wine, beer, spirits and brandy.

Passengers

C. Brown	Mrs.____Bisset and	Mrs.____Tennent and
Mrs. C. Brown	family	family
Miss____Brown	Mrs.____Valverdie and	Mr.____Smith
Mr.____Rushby	family	Mr.____Newman
Mr.____Calden	Mr.____Fleming	Mr.____Marshall

- - - - - - -

SHIP: VERSAILLES
TYPE: Ship   FROM: Boston, Massachusetts
ARRIVED: March 24, 1852   CAPTAIN: Knowles
PASSAGE: 138 days from Boston, Massachusetts. On December 28,
         1851, in lat. 30S, long. 48-30 W, saw the whale ship
         "Northern Light", 38 days from Fairhaven, fast to her
         first whale.
CARGO: 200 kegs chalk, 60 bbls plaster, 150 bbls cement, 24 bbls
       butter, 30 M bricks, 100 tons coal, 9000 pickets, hams,
       shoes, tacks, furniture, 2 cases pictures, 300 doors, salt,
       37 pieces gutter, 2 carriages, 5 cases drills, files,
       cheese, 1 cask borax and assorted goods.

Passengers

Mr. A. Walker and   Mrs. R.A. Grant and   Mrs. M.S. Phillips
   family   family   and child

(Continued next page)

Mr. J.T. Eldridge   J.P. Edwards   C.H.P. Plympton

- - - - - -

SHIP: EMILY FRANCES (Also listed as EMILY FRANCIS)
TYPE: Schooner   FROM: Tahiti
ARRIVED: March 24, 1852   CAPTAIN: Freeman
PASSAGE: 36 days from Tahiti. This vessel brings intelligence
that the brig "Gen. Worth", having Rowe's Circus Company
aboard, sailed from Tahiti for the Australian Colonies.
CARGO: 100,000 oranges, 2500 limes and 25,000 cigars.

Passengers

T. Hinigan	S. Bertrand	C. Maxant
M. Dubinard	T. Cauze	

- - - - - -

SHIP: SUSSEX
TYPE: Brig   FROM: Oregon Territory
ARRIVED: March 24, 1852   CAPTAIN: La Dieu
PASSAGE: 8 days from the Oregon Territory.
CARGO: 92,000 ft lumber, 21,000 laths, 76 sacks wheat, 100 sacks
oats, 25 bushels turnips, 25 bushels potatoes, 28 hogs, 13
dozen fowls and 130 dozen eggs.

Passenger
B. M. DuRelle

- - - - -

SHIP: OHIO
TYPE: Steamer   FROM: San Diego, Calif.
ARRIVED: March 25, 1852   CAPTAIN: Hilliard
PASSAGE: 4 days from San Diego, California.
CARGO: Not listed.

Passengers

Charles Moore	N. Howard	N. Alden
Miss Mary Moore	J. Herns	W. Workmer
Lucretia Moore	J. Alexander	A. Puirta
J. Moore and	R. Dria	M. Sexton
lady	W.D. Bradshaw	C. Baum
J. Myer	William Weinschink	Mr.____McClellan
Capt. J.D. Nason	J.A. Bennett	A. McKennrn /sic/
J. China	C.W. Williams	(McKennan?)
C.H. Johnson	J.P. Davis and	A. Bil /sic/
Mr.____Little	daughter	(Bill?)
H. Cummins	H. Stuss	J. Rodgers
D. Price	N. Cottle	W. Konsha
J. Doom	J. Sharp	J. Windorf
J. Adams	A. McDonald	F. Rostigo
J. Gilbert	T. Cavano	C. Burk
J. Phillips	J.H. West	D. Powers
W. Rayvor /sic/	S. Miller	S. Higbee
P. Smith	J. Rumsey	W. Cummings
J. Ryder	J.P. Wallace	J. Scott

(Continued next page)

M. Curm /sic/	J. Wilkes	J. Simmons
A. Leonard	J. Sahlver	M. Kellogg
J. Wright	J. Flood	P. Burns
T. Burr	W. Cunningham	

- - - - - -

SHIP: J.W. HAVENER
TYPE: Brig   FROM: Valparaiso, Chile
ARRIVED: March 25, 1852   CAPTAIN: Staples
PASSAGE: 47 days from Valparaiso, Chile. On March 22, 1852 saw
       the barque "New World" in lat 36, long. 127-40, bound for
       the Oregon Territory.
CARGO: 2929 fanegas barley, 15 hogs, 35 pigs, 5 dozen chickens and
       10 sacks of bran.

Passengers

Mrs. Rosa Alvarez and	Miss C. Garcia	Miss J. Vilarel
2 children	P. Munoz	A. Myers
A. Parra		

and 8 unidentified in steerage

- - - - - -

SHIP: HENBURY
TYPE: Ship (British)   FROM: Hongkong, China
ARRIVED: March 25, 1852   CAPTAIN: Clark
PASSAGE: 63 days from Hongkong, China.
CARGO: 77 bbls tar, 300 mats cassia, 800 bags rice, 1000 boxes of
       tea and 250 packages unspecified merchandise.

Passengers

Mr. R.P. Wood	Mr. B.F. Moses	Mr. S.P. Goodale

and 236 unidentified Chinamen

- - - - - -

SHIP: FRANKLIN ADAMS
TYPE: Brig   FROM: Puget Sound, W.T.
ARRIVED: March 26, 1852   CAPTAIN: Felker
PASSAGE: 10 days from Puget Sound, Washington Territory.
CARGO: 13,000 feet of piles.

Passenger
The Duke of York*

(*) An Indian chief, known at Port Townsend, Washington
    Territory, as "The Duke of York".

- - - - - -

SHIP: BALTIMORE
TYPE: Brig (Hawaiian)   FROM: Honolulu, S.I.
ARRIVED: March 26, 1852   CAPTAIN: Thorpe
PASSAGE: 15 days from Honolulu, Sandwich Islands. This vessel
       brings intelligence that a great eruption on the Island
       of Hawaii has taken place. The crater of Mauna Loa
       erupted, commencing February 19, 1852, throwing cinders
       and ashes in the air and discharging streams of lava.
       The eruption is said to be the most extensive that has

ever taken place on Hawaii within the memory of man.
CARGO: 48,950 feet of lumber and $12,000 in money.

Passengers

Capt. C. Prentiss	Capt. E. Wakeman	Mrs.___Rowland
Miss___Garvey	Lewis Smith	L. Meyers

- - - - - -

SHIP: FREMONT (Also listed as COLONEL FREMONT)
TYPE: Brig   FROM: San Pedro, Calif.
ARRIVED: March 26, 1852   CAPTAIN: Erskine
PASSAGE: 8 days from San Pedro, California.
CARGO: 1000 sacks corn, 600 sacks potatoes.

Passengers

Mr. P.S. Miller   C. Shields

- - - - - -

SHIP: EAGLE
TYPE: Brig (Hawaiian)   FROM: Honolulu, S.I.
ARRIVED: March 26, 1852   CAPTAIN: Newell
PASSAGE: 30 days from Honolulu, Sandwich Islands.
CARGO: 54 grindstones and 75,000 feet of lumber.

Passenger

Mrs. Capt. O. Hard

- - - - -

SHIP: PACIFIC
TYPE: Steamer   FROM: San Juan del Sur
ARRIVED: March 26, 1852   CAPTAIN: Lefevre (Le Fevre?)
PASSAGE: 15 days from San Juan del Sur, Nicaragua, via Acapulco,
          Mexico. Sailed from San Juan del Sur on March 10, 1852
          at 8:00PM. On March 15th, about 40 miles to the south-
          ward of Acapulco, Mexico, stopped and attempted to board
          the wrecked steamer "North America", but in consequence
          of the heavy breakers did not succeed. Arrived at
          Acapulco, Mexico on March 15th at 6:00AM. Departed
          Acapulco on March 16th, at 9:00PM. Experienced a strong
          southeasterly current on the coast, and from the Island
          of Cerros (Ceros?) to Point Concepcion the weather was
          thick and foggy. From Point Concepcion to the Heads
          experienced a heavy northwester and the seas were very
          rough.
CARGO: Not listed.

Passengers

J.R. Rollinston, wife 2 chldrn & svt	Mrs.___Burr, 3 chldrn & svt	Mrs.___Richardson
C.R. Ladd	Clara Burr	J.W. Ruggles and wife
J. Hathorn	W. Burr	J.J. Stewart and wife
N. Nevans	L.B. Gilman	J.P. Raynan
Charles Wood	W.M. Peters and wife	J.W. Moor (sic) and wife
W.J. Dickman	James Brooks	
J. Charter		

(Continued next page)

Elenor Gayson /sic/
Laura Gayson
Emily Gayson
Elizabeth Gayson
H.L. Dodge and wife
J. Parker, wife,
   2 chldrn & svt
L.A. Holmes
C.W. Langley
R.W. Hasthorne /sic/
Mrs. L.E. Shutleff/sic/
Mrs. E. Shutleff /sic/
J. Hetherington
Mrs.____ Campbell
Mrs.____ Barnes and
   child
E. Ginnell
D.C. Farble
S. Edgerly
J. Harris
Dl. Van Cleef/sic/
   (Daniel Van Cleef?)
N.L. Polk
B.W. Todd
Charles Elling
G.J. Stebbe
J.H. Crane
U.S. Whitcomb
J. Whitcomb
S.L. Clifton
J.C. Frost
E. Frost
W. Washburn
J.P. Courtier
S. Burrell
E.P. Burrell
J. Babcock
W.M. Green
G.D. Powers
W. Main
L. Main
Thomas Gardner
J. Clark
B. Allen
N.B. Ried /sic/
B.D. Haithany
F. Mitchell
G.G. Brown
John E. Foster
J.F. Randolph
M. Randolph

N.D. Thayer, wife
   and child
G.C. Moor (sic) and
   wife
M. Bryan, wife and
   servant
H.L. Scranton and
   servant
C.J. Newcomb
D.W. Burnside
C.J. Morgan
S.H. Morgan
Mrs.____ Whitney
H. Whitney
Miss H. Conly /sic/
J.T. Mills and wife
D. Cole
Mrs.____ Casy /sic/
J.S. Trout
Mrs.____ Trout
C.O. Brigham
J.B. Benjamin
A.M. Fuller
L. Eddy
J. Cushing
M. Whilston
M.O. Laughlin
William M. Gaffien(?)
   (Gaffen)
S.M. Leonard
E. Leonard
William Sheldon
C. Chamberlin
J. Williams
S. Elliott
D. Elliott
C.W. Lewis
W.L. Lewis
A. Lewis
M. White
D. Wilbour /sic/
N.C. Story
M.E. Letts
D.T. Daggott /sic/
L.F. Moulton
W.E. Overton
N.M. Prescott
B.M. Prescott
P. Glenn
F. Walker
A. Flagg
(Continued next page)

Mrs. H. Cross and
   3 children
D. Clark
A.C. Thompson
R.M. Townsend
G.W. Grimes and
   wife
G.L. Allen
J. Lippincott
A. Stebbins
C. Stanford
T.W. Stanford
H.J. Hall /sic/
Capt. J.T. Wright
Mr. H.J. Hall /sic/
H. Cawards
D. Haskell
A. Haskell
N. Curtis
William Haskell
S.M. Stack
A. Vinton
G.W.H. Davis
I. Clapp
A. Pinson
M. Harnson
William Casey
T. Hall
A. Chase
J.J. Carpenter
S. Turner
L. Bartlett
A. Laurunce /sic/
R.E. Elliott
N. Mullikin
A. Adams
T.C. Collins
N. Lucas
B. Lucas
Thomas Clark
C. Sanders
E.O. Calhune /sic/
William Darnund
J. Scott
E. Scott
J.M. Varnum
Thomas Sprague
F. Carr
A.A. Relpatrick
Charles Martin
S.E. Perkins

S. H. Johnson
L. Carpenter
J.M. Manany
G. Scott
J. Spencer
E. Trattery
L. Wallace
F.A. Vandercook
A.L. Waygeman
J.L. Dutton
W.D. Carter
Alex Miller and
   wife
J. Smith
M. Parker
S. Joyce
H. Sanborne
C.S. Sanborne
S. Ram
V.N. Sanborne
D. Leonard
J.S. Whiting
J.D. Whiting
W.H. Shaw
J.T. West
A. Wright
S. Haas
E.H. Everett
J. McClew
P. Collins
A. Balon
George Ewing
J.A. Brown
J. Watson
J.R. Baker
P. Brennan
M. Durgon
D.L. Stewart
O. Kilbourne
J.R. Congdon
William P. Brooks
H.B. Fowler
Daniel Barnes
S.A. Southwick
J.B. Elliott
L.W. Dodge
J. Kearney
R. Hogan
W. Gwynn and
   2 boys
J. Barney

D.A. Hough
W. White
George Kelly
J. Gill
William Prebble
W.R. Wells
B.W. Marts
J. Ralston
H. Ralston
J.A. Tredwell
A. Goodman
Miss Mary Lee
D. Johnson
J.V. Bolen
Mr.___ Bell
T. Foley and wife
J. Shaw
E. Lum
E.C. Jones
O.T. Hill
J. Kimball
C. Ferris
R. Drake
J. Wagstaff
J.W. Woodward
W. Hill
N. Bowden
A. O'Niel /sic/
P.W. Tracy
E. Talbot
G. Bishching /sic/
P.F. Palmer
P. Hall
R. Inland
J. Fowel /sic/
H. Given
William Holt
J.F. Smith
B. Pearl
E.S. Moody
G.W. Mitchell
J. Mitchell
Samuel Hale
A.H. Proctor
J. Northrop
J.O. French
C.E. Cook
B. Bullard
Mrs.___ Foster
J. Foster
F. Foster
(Continued next page)

R. Cole
W. Murray
T.M. Clark
L. Restine
J.L. Beadle
J.F. Misk
J. Torrens
J. Stewart
E. Smith
C. Quig /sic/
C.W. Kirtland
M. Dorman
D. Cunfield
I. Hall
A.J. Chase
J.L. Noyas
A.G. Gill
G.G. Putnam
J.B. Hunkins
C.N. Brooks
E. Burnham
J. Lean
J.S. Brady
G.K. Swan
G.A. Abbott
J. Strong
H. McAskell
A. Coles
J. Bonvee
S.B. French
J.D. French
L. Lester
J. Butterfield
S. Hutchinson
E. Perkins
G. Sampson
P. Clough
A.B. Brown
S.L. Thompson
J.B. Thompson
J.M. Hall
C.B. Hall
L.G. Sullivan
E. Vose
H.J. Briggs
Albert Green
A.S. Vail
N. Glass
Mrs.___ Thrill
M. O'Brien
D.S. Sheldon

D. Carpenter	E.L. Cary	J.M. Colwell
J. Armstrong	A. Brown	W.A. Sampson
Mrs. J. Armstrong	H.H. Bostwick	P. Sampson
& 3 chldrn	J.S. Wilkinson	H.A. Eaton
J.A. White	J.J. Parshley	A.P. Nutter
M. Bremans	M. Glazier	T.W. Nutter
A.D. Lathrop	G. Hubbard	S.M. Collins
Noah Dodge	George Scott	G. Washbourne
L.G. Cole	P.T. Pitkins	J.D. Clogston
D.T. Cole	E. Moss	D. Kindel
J.A. Hudnot	M. Frink	M. Ligonnery
A.P. Stanford	Capt. R.G. Cruttenden	John M. Hubbard
M. Davis	(sic)	A.S. White
D. Mitchel /sic/	(Crittenden?)	O.E. White
(Mitchell?)	D.J. Apthup	J.D. Lane
S.M. Cook	G.W. Barker	M.T. Lane
J.D. Van Buren	J. Briggs	Joseph Potter
L.E. Shitleff /sic/	R.N. Hewlett	G.S. Ashmead
E. Shurtleff /sic/	M. William	T. McBride
J.M. Woodruff	Luke Jones	J. Finney
B. Alvord	J. Bennett	D.S. Mosier
J.M. Anderson	L. Sharp and boy	Sam Brigham
S.A. Tower	E.F. Horton	J. Kellogg
H.P. Edwards	J.L. Bennett	John C. Fisher
C.H. Damon	G. Locke	T. Gone
R. Sweet	D. Corken	W.R. Peters
B.T. Barlow	F. Spencer	A.T. Johnson
W. Cole	S. Moss	H. Johnson
C. Almy	C. Roe	L. Babbott
R. Denmark	M. Talmer	F. Shaffer
A. Flint	J.H. Preston	M. Aikin
J. Gallagher	J.R. Buffington	J.P. Gregg
C.W. Payne	A.V. Dougherty	W. Watt
W. Gallagher	J.H. Reed	J.J. Danin
W. Duncan	J. Mackey	J. Tanes
R. Reed	W. Shermoy	A. Underhill

- - - - - -

SHIP: ORLEANS
TYPE: Brig   FROM: El Realejo, Nicaragua
ARRIVED: March 27, 1852   CAPTAIN: Seaman
PASSAGE: 36 days from El Realejo, Nicaragua, via San Juan del
         Sur, Nicaragua.
CARGO: In ballast.

Passengers

Mrs. ___ Alexandra	N.F. Howard	William Forbes
& 2 children	Mrs. M. Grew and	Mrs. ___ Forbes and
Mrs. Maria Smith	3 children	child
John Smith	Mrs. John Smith and	Henry Darland
Charles H. Graham	child (child died)	George Hobsan /sic/
L.J. Limerlin & svt	J.M. Hamilton	J.B. Cook

(Continued next page)

W.S. Cook
Archibald Turner
Mrs. Archibald Turner
   & child (child
   died)
A.P. Bell
D.M. Singletan (?)
   (Singleton?)
Wesley Pitsford
J.R. Campbell
William Berkmere
J.W. Thames
J.C. Fincer
J.J. Janes
Isaac Watkins
H. McClellan
A. Stanley
J.W. Mace
H.A. Thalley
H.H. Krull (died)
Margaret Ann Smith
   and child

John H. Pickering
Mrs. John H. Pickering
E. Carney
W.M. Carney
Daniel McCormick
   (above party died)
   Pendgins
W.R. Crissan
John Stowers
James E. Graves
James M. Graves
Charles Mendleman
J.A. Nelson
S. Nelson
William Thrasher
A.H. Johnson
J.F. Johnson
J.H. Huggins
Isaac Cram
A. Cram
Tarlton Turner

Alden S. Gage
Mrs. Alden S. Gage
   & 4 children
S. Jones
M. Hammand /sic/
E. Hope
J.B. Eatan /sic/
   (Eaton?)
William Eatan /sic/
   (Eaton?)
William Eatan Jr.
   /sic/ (Eaton?)
Samuel Eatan /sic/
   (Eaton?)
J. Uttan
Thomas Cusade
J.D. Cusade
E. Mull
Joseph Mull (died)
Richard Dorland
   (died)

- - - - - -

SHIP: ELIZABETH NEWELL
TYPE: Brig   FROM: Honolulu, S.I.
ARRIVED: March 27, 1852   CAPTAIN: Smith
PASSAGE: 22 days from Honolulu, Sandwich Islands.
CARGO: 170 bars iron, 137 tons coal, 10,557 ft lumber, 10 bbls
       dried apples and 10 packages of coffee.

Passengers

J.S. Kidder   Mr.____Richards

- - - - - -

SHIP: COLUMBIA
TYPE: Steamer   FROM: Oregon Territory
ARRIVED: March 28, 1852   CAPTAIN: Dall
PASSAGE: 60 hours from the Oregon Territory. Left Astoria,
       Oregon Territory on March 26, 1852 at 8:00AM. This vessel
       brings intelligence that the Pacific Mail Steamship Com-
       pany have established their general depot at St. Helens,
       (St. Helen), Oregon Territory, to which point the "Colum-
       bia" will hereafter run. The "Willamette" will connect
       with the "Columbia".*
CARGO: 1250 sacks oats, 797 sacks wheat, 202 sacks potatoes, 40
       casks onions, 54 sacks bran, 50 sacks flour, 55 sacks of
       barley, 60 boxes eggs, 2 bbls butter and 1500 chickens.

Passengers

Mrs.____Ingalls and   Sidney A. Jewett   W. Pomeroy
   2 children   F.N. Blanchet   S. Howe
Joseph Marx   Mr.____Robinson   Mr.____Purcell
                  (Continued next page)

(*)Willamette(sic). Vessel might have been the "Williamtic" or the
    "Williamantic".

Richard Berry	Mr.____Biglow	C. Robinson
J.J. Williams	H.E. Hawley	Mr.____Saunders
Samuel Dow	Alfred Dibblee	J.D. Cannon
L. Boom	Mr.____Kennedy	Mrs. L. Williams
W.H. Smart	T. Pritchard	Mr.____Caldwell
H.H. Tickner /sic/	H.C. Ames	C.H. Childs
William Copley	J.M. Clark	E.W. Eddy
Thomas Scott	C. Hamlin	J.F. Burdick
J.W. Kalfus	Isaac Wyatt	M. Harpole
William Young	O.R. Fuller	O.H. Cone
M.P. Brown	G.W. Wolf	W.H. Means
H.L. Miller	J.L. Bromley	E. Lewis
R.W. Coles	Robert Stewart	S. Sweetzer

- - - - - -

SHIP: ABYSSINIA
TYPE: Barque (British)   FROM: Valparaiso, Chile
ARRIVED: March 29, 1852   CAPTAIN: Gordon
PASSAGE: 48 days from Valparaiso, Chile. Experienced very severe
          weather for the last three days of the passage; lost
          quarter boats, split sails, etc.
CARGO: 116 kegs shot, 71 boxes preserved meats, 257 bars iron,
        2786 bags barley, 5 boxes candles, 3 bbls eggs, 87 bbls
        cement, 100 bbls beer and assorted merchandise.

Passengers

Mr. J. Leadbeater	Mr. A. Girell	Mr. G. Boye
Mr. S. Goodwin		Mr. L. Seaver

and 12 unidentified in steerage

- - - - - -

SHIP: SEA BIRD
TYPE: Steamer   FROM: San Diego, California
ARRIVED: March 30, 1852   CAPTAIN: Haley
PASSAGE: 6 days from San Diego, California, via intermediate ports.
          Experienced very severe head winds during the passage.
          After leaving Monterey, California on March 27th, a gale
          from the Northwest became so strong as to force the "Sea
          Bird" back to Monterey. Remained in Monterey for 36 hours
          before putting to sea.
CARGO: Not listed.

Passengers

Capt.____Hunter	J.J. Overstreet	Capt.____Whittel
Capt. J. Buhl	H.H. Manson	W. Hunter
J. Myers	Mr.____Gallan	M. Vallesco
H. Swartwout	H. Chussman	G.W. Senine
Mr.____Miner	Q.J. Sparks	J.W.P. Davis
L. Lake	L. Fontellsilla	M. Pallow
B. Lauter	P. Mooney	W. Demfroy
J. Murray	H. Davidson	E. Lazard
Mr.____Pauli	J. Osio	M. Mallasin
G.A. Rodriguez	J. Vallejo	B. Vasquez

(Continued next page)

R. Pinto

Dona Issabel Gomez
   (Issabel-/sic/)

Dr. J. Stoakes

J. Bleecher

R. Leese

Dr.___McKee

J.W. Baker

Mrs.___McKinley

D.C._Smith

Mr.___Corrigan

E.C._Wilson

S.A. Pollard

Mr.___Little

- - - - - -

D. Spence and lady

Charles Canfield

W. Gilbert

H.G. Gibon (?)
   (Gihou?,Gibbon?)

William Blackburn

SHIP: PANAMA

TYPE: Steamer   FROM: Panama

ARRIVED: April 1, 1852   CAPTAIN: James Watkins

PASSAGE: Departed Panama on evening of March 12, 1852. Arrived
   Acapulco, Mexico on March 19th at 3:30PM. At this port
   found about 500 of the passengers who had been on board
   the wrecked steamer "North America". Received on board,
   of the foregoing number, 37 persons, including 16 ladies
   and 10 children, the ship being so crowded no more could
   be taken on board. Previous to arrival of the "Panama"
   some 200-300 of the wrecked passengers had left in sailing vessels for San Francisco. Departed Acapulco on
   March 20th, at noon. On March 23rd, off Cape St. Lucas,
   passed the steamer "New Orleans", bound south. On March
   26, at 2:30PM, passed within a mile of a rock, on which
   the sea broke occasionally, southeast end of Martin's
   Island, N.E. by E., Point Vergenes E.S.E., compass bear-
   ings; with a smooth sea the position of the rock would
   not be seen.* Arrived at San Diego, California on March
   27th at 9:00AM; left San Diego at 7:30PM that evening.
   On March 28th, at noon, in consequence of a very heavy
   gale from the westward, anchored under the lee of Cata-
   lina Island, and remained there upwards of six hours.
   Arrived at Monterey, California on March 30th at 9:00PM.
   Experienced very heavy weather from San Diego to Monterey.
   Departed Monterey at 9:00PM on March 31st.
       The following death took place during the passage:
           March 30,1852, at sea - Mr. N.C. Potter, of dysentery,
               of New London, Connecticut, aged 22 years. Buried
               at Monterey, California.
   Upon arrival in San Francisco the following marriage
   took place on board the "Panama":
           April 1, 1852 - Frederick J. Thibault, of San
               Francisco, married to Emma M. Horstmann, of
               Philadelphia, Pennsylvania, daughter of the
               late William H. Horstmann. Ceremony performed
               by Rev. Flewell S. Mines.
       The "Panama" brings intelligence that the stream of
   passengers for California seems to be increasing in volume at Panama. It is reported that $18\frac{1}{2}$ miles of the
   Panama Railroad are completed. The name of the new town
   at Navy Bay, the Atlantic terminus of the Panama Railroad,
   is to be called "Aspinwall City".

(*)Point Vergenes(sic).

CARGO: Mail, trunks and packages. Five packages for Madame Eliza Biscaccianti. The small passage boat "Wooley Moon". This boat was discovered by the "Panama" on her downward trip to Panama. The "Wooley Moon" was found adrift, outside the Golden Gate, picked up and taken to Panama and returned to San Francisco. The owner was located in San Francisco and the boat returned.*

(*) Owner:- Charles Mayo.

Passengers

Capt. W. Hutching and lady
Miss Emma M. Horstman
Mrs. M.E. Andrews and child
Mrs. F.H. Wooster
Mrs. M.B. Smith
J.R. Hewitt and lady
Thomas C. Coombs and son
J.J. Dimon and lady
D. Gihon and svt
Capt. W.C. Waters
F. Bye
B. Richmond
H. Schenck
E.T. Sangster
G.H. Vose
E. Caldwell
A. Caldwell
S. Barstow
J. Rudolph
W. Dawson
R.F. Tooma
A. Hoag
C. Jewitt
J. Arnold
A. Lambeth and svt
A.B. Lessing
L.E. Reardsley /sic/ (Beardsley?)
J.F. Bassett
J.W. Oakley
J. Canfield
C.B. Simmons
J. Lucas
Z. Swift
C.J. Warren
J. Gearcs /sic/ (Gearce?)
J.N. Caldwell

Mrs. E.A. Wheaton
D.W.C. Thompson and lady
Mrs. L. Hansbrow
R.F. Hall and lady
L.O. Goodrich
T. Smith
Mrs. J.E. Ober (?) (Oher?)
T. Grimes, son and servant
J.G. Evan and son
A.A. Cohen and servant
H.B. Malone
W.C. Annan
E. Brown
H.A. Parker
W.T. Pool
A. Carroll
G.W. Hamilton
R. Beck
L. Goss
B.C. Williams
W.N. Stoddard
E. Mount
A. Markwall /sic/
J. Sherwood
J.S. Dimon
D. Cueth
C. Wheeler
J.C. Bowman
C.N. Smith
G.L. Henry
J. Fall
A.F. Potter
J. Blorer
J. Savory
P.B. Ferrill
R. Lovegrove
W. Smith
H.H. Bancroft
(Continued next page)

Mrs. J.E. Davenport
Mrs. M.H. Yates, 3 children & svt
H.H. Howe and lady
Mrs. A.P. Swift and 4 children
Mrs. C.F. Hussey and 4 children
Miss M. Copeland
H. Gillingham and lady
Capt. R. Maguire(R. N.)
J.A. Hull (R.N.)
Dr.___ Simpson (R. N.)
E. Jago (R.N.)
J. Patee
M. Furman
H. Blossom
C. Hallett
C.D. Talmadge
H. Seaton
J. Walker
S. Hance
C.R. Tyler
J. Ricketson
W.F. Jones
G. Hugell
J.B. Purdy
W. McNutty /sic/
P. Ford
S.H. Ford
R.S. Ellis
C. Langley
J. Sherman
W.H. Bliss
B.V. Babcock /sic/
B.V. Frazer /sic/
G.W. Dennison
J.R. Hammond
J. Reynolds

T. Moyer	Thomas Jackson	J.F. Root
J.R. Smith	Joseph Wiggin	G. Smith
C. Jack	J. Shear/sic/	C.B. Jurks
J.M. Hammatty	N.B. Parker	C. Tompkins
P. Birmingham	J. Barrett	J.F. Narrin
J. Rynd /sic/	G. Woods	P. Laho
J. Spear/sic/	O.A. Sandam	J.D. Webster
G.G. Chase	H. Featherson	J.J. Walker
G.P. Cole	T.L. Hickson	M. Van Horn
J. Geddes	L.B. Brown	E.D. Bliss
B.G. Atkinson	T. Wakeler /sic/	J. Clark
W.E. Phillips	G.N. Ellis	E. Burrows
M. Green	J.S. Ellis	P. Mahew
E. Hardy	W. Knapp	W.S. Bailey
F.H. Spear	L. Cross	J. Hager
J.A. Wilcox	J.W. Whitney	A. Morgan
D. Goldbacher	H.G. Andrews	Y. Jones
L.D. Thompson	B. White	J.B. Bennett
G.W. Howlitt	S. Conklin	D. Murray
J. Andrews	W. Donley	M.D. Seeley
J. Mortland	C.D. Broock	K. Ferry
J. Webster	H.R. Smith	S. Hinman
R.C. Negus /sic/	N.C. Butts	D.M. Sanborn
G.D. Simmons	J. Beach	A. Blackman
P. Disnor	L. Jones	J. Rising
P. Vassta	J. Laescamp	M. Wilson
B. Kuteed	R. Sprookelcamp	D. Smith
J.H. Malcolm	P.C. Noyes	M. Perkins
George Martin	D.D. Seymour	J.J. McNeery /sic/
W.B. Miller	J.A. Jackson	A.D. Linthican
L. Simons	J.H. Ashley	C. H. Perkins
J. Baird	E. Dennison	J.A. Benham
S. Eastman	J. Rodenberger	J. Ackerman
H.H. Ingraham	A.J. Waterman	J. Moran
E. Briggs	J. Mansor	T. Hickey
T. Crawley	R. Ainsworth	L. Green
J. Lombard	C. Halleck	R. Ward
H. Van Geiser	Q.J. Latham	B. Meanz/sic/(Means?)
A. Ward	J. Robinson	C.D. Morgan
R. McDonald	R. Bryer	W. Marshall
W.P. Moffat	C. Goodell	B.E. Egbert
A. Heath	H.M.J. Richardson	William Read
J.R. Heath	E.A. Wadhams	J.H. Seabury
P.J. David	P. Barrie	M. Darouss
J.C. Berry	A.E. Wadhams	S. Darouss
W. Greggs	L. Baryie /sic/	P. Soule
J. Dimon (?)	R.F. Thinbee	G. Whitford
C. Gordon	M. Yager	G. Berang
W. Baiseley	L. Snow	L. Mayer
H. Helferty	J. Spear/sic/	J. Walker
W. Averill	J. Kenney	A.R. Bates

(Continued next page)

A.R. Benedict
S.H. Tyler
A. Hancock
A. Spear
A. Sawyer
C. Howe
J.H. Grant
J. Phillips
C. Parrott
S. Wilson
D.R. Cobb
G.L. Jenkins
G. Simmons
E. Taber
J. Etchels
H. Spear
E.H. Smith
G.R. Lester
G.A. Field
W. Tyler
J. Simpson
J. Beasely
J. Henricks /sic/
T. Birmingham
P. Kent
J. Kenna
J.M. Jayne
H.T.Storne
J. Jenkins Jr.
J. Chase
W.H. Brown
G. Chase
D. Billings
J.W. Whitlock
A. Clinton
W. Pierce
D. Wilson
T. Kirk
G. Sargent
F.H. White
B.N. Tuttle
G. Smith
J. Loots
N. Ransing (?)
   (Rensing?)
G.E. Williamson
H. Rodering
J.M. Williams
A. Pohler /sic/
B. Kibblee
M. Martin

P. Kenney
C. Merriam
A.P. Bessey
C.W. Kineman
W. Cunningham
J.W. Hunt
P. Taff
H. Kartman
J. Lebe
H.H. Welch
W.W. Reed
H. Pelling
W. Chapman
M. Cook
J.W. Wood
A.C. Edwards
J. Foster
J. Black
S.P. Smith
D. Murray
J.J. Lowell
J. Tirrill
W. Harding
W.P. Hasken /sic/
J.C. Dramer
G.V. Chandler
J.K. Chandler
E. Taft
P.D. Garrett
S. Barber
P. Sprague
G.E. Eddy
N. Howard
T. Andrews
W. Sholdor
A.H. Newell
J. W. Parker
G.W. Bowles
A.C. Thompson
W.M. Thompson
R. Cummings
G.H. Marsh
J. Bloomer
J. Learing
E.P. Harwood
B. Menker
H.M. Coburn
W.R. Wheelock
P. Alcock
L. Scharton
J. Kuhler /sic/
(Continued next page)

J.F. Young
H.H. Heidson
R. Wheeler
G.A. Cheney
J. Marsh
F. Kinsman
S.C. Washburn
J. Tower
H.T. Harris
J.A. Deming
G.L. Roberts
F. Keney /sic/
J.G. Strouben
T.L. Jacson /sic/
   (Jackson?)
W.M. Reese
M. Titworth
G.H. Wiggins /sic/
M. Horre
J. Waterhouse
M. Burk
C.W. White
A. White
G.W. Littlefield
C. Spider
G. Meldron Jr.
W. Parmalee
R. Brail
L. White
B.D. Hutchins
L.P. Smith
A. Seeley
J. Wilson
J.T. Hanks
L. Brown
J. Smith /sic/
J. Smith /sic/
C. Leland
H. Bates
A.S. Myrick
R.W. Kellogg
P. Fletcher
J.R. Dugan
W.W. Dugan
J.C. Walker
F. Ames
J. Lord
W.Muir
P.M. Mossenny
J. Linepheh /sic/
H. Peck

J. Limpech /sic/
E. Burt
M.L. Cushing
J.H. Allen
E.J. Hawks
B. Heaton
A. Alden
J.A. Bruce
J.R. Cate
W. Clapp
J. Fletcher
C.A. Mory
H.C. Hollister
J. Herman
W. Norman/sic/
R. Aitkin
J.B. Burkle
J.C. Hawks
G.M. Woodman
T.R. Paddock
C. McDonald
A. Warner
E.H. Ward
J. Warner
J.W. Russell
J.S. Smith
J. Mooney
T. Doe
C.R. Brundage
W. Hall
W. Parsons
R. Blood
P. Sullivan
?. Forbx /sic/
  (Forbe?,Forbes?)
M. Osborne
W. Thornton
J. Valentine

W. Tinker
E.N. Lincoln
E. Walker Jr.
B. Lincoln
C.H. Ball
J.W. Thurston
A. Knox
R.W. Knox
L.L. Reed
H. Gossert
B. Boss
J.M. Towle
N. St. John
D. Mechelson /sic/
D.B. Denny
A. Seymour
J. Bardor
R.H. Sibley
H. Sibley
N.P. Moore
J. Fisher
B.M. Schultz
A.M. Spaulding
L.H. Nay
W. Terrilligu /sic/
  (Terrillign?)
H. Leoney
S. Blair
H.W.G. Terry
H. Fent
D. Torrio
J. Deldine
F. Felling
Mary Itzel
J. Thomas
A.C. Sangstee
T. Mosley

J.J. Clarke
R. Alexander
D. Lee
G.W. Simpson
A.C. Green
T.B. Green
G. Nerman /sic/
W. Richardson
R.F. Fowle
G.W. Spring
R.M. Sweet
H. Stratton
H. Clark
D.R. Cable
E. Wilcox
W.H. Andrews
C.P. Birge
E.M. Dubois
W.W. Orr
G.W. Heiman
G. Myers
W. Brandor
W. Marshall
J.Duff
J.M. Tidd
T. Corkill
B. Bates
J.T. Olercland /sic/
  (Cleveland?)
M.P. Clereland /sic/
  (Cleveland?)
C.W. Lorre
J. Edgar
H. Mehr
C. Britt
M.E. Andrews
P. Lywson

Passengers from wreck of "North America", received on board at Acapulco, Mexico:

Thomas Hunt and
  servant
Mrs. C.A. Shattuck
  & 6 children
Mrs. E. Thompson
Miss A. Martin
Miss G. Coker
Mrs. R. Wheeler
C.J. Dempster
J.B. Crockett

J. Winchester, wife
  and 2 children
J. McDougal and
  lady
Mrs. H. Myers
A. Dickinson and
  lady
Mrs. M. Kerr
Thomas George

D. Norcross, wife
  and daughter
H. McCormick and
  lady
Miss S. Abbott
Mrs. S. Smith
P. Moody and lady
Mrs.___ Lyons and
  daughter

- - - - - -

SHIP: FREMONT (Also known as "COLONEL FREMONT")
TYPE: Steamer   FROM: Panama
ARRIVED: April 1, 1852   CAPTAIN: J.M. Dow
PASSAGE: Departed Panama on March 7, 1852. Called at intermediate
          ports. Departed Taboga on March 7, 1852 at 10:00PM.
          Arrived Acapulco, Mexico on March 16th and departed on
          March 17th, at 5:00PM. Saw the brig "Clarita", Captain
          ___ Holmes commanding, at Acapulco. Said brig had a
          number of passengers of the wrecked "North America" and
          would sail soon for San Francisco. The "Fremont" exper-
          ienced constant northerly gales during the passage to San
          Francisco.
CARGO: Not listed.

Passengers

Dr. H.P. Bostwick	Mrs.___ McDonough and	Mrs. B. Duffy and
Mrs.___ Foster	boy	boy
Miss S. Asbury /sic/	Miss E. Gibbons	Miss___ Moore
and servant	Miss___ Simpson	Miss E. Burnstein
Mrs.___ Donos (?)	T. O'Dul /sic/	Mr. E. Burnstein
(Donoa?)	G.J.H. Sanders	B. Burnstein
Mrs.___ Crane and	F.P. Harrison	Dr. T.W. Birkey
child	Mrs.___ Harrison and	Mrs.___ Alford and
Mrs.___ Rosenberg	child	child
Mrs. S. Maddox	Mr.& Mrs.___ Stokes	J.G. Moore, lady
Rev. S.W. Davies	W. Stokes	and boy
Miss A. McLlean/sic/	Mrs.___ Jackson/sic/	George Mack
(McLean?)	Mrs.___ Jackson/sic/	J.P. Haynes
Miss C. McLean/sic/	R. White	P. Sessivns /sic/
L. McLean /sic/	Mrs.___ Stith /sic/	(Sessions?)
H. Koster	W. Kenan	J.Powell (M.D.)
J.D. Jordan	William Weatherspoon	John Hassell
W.W. Baugh	S. McGuire	J. O'Donnell
Washington Baugh	J.A. Chase	Dr.___ Crane
J.E. Vanmeter /sic/	H. Miller	K. Day
I. Isel	M. Patten	J.S. Allen
M. Jordan and lady	D. Shepherd and	B. Ritchie
H. Jordan and lady	sister	D. Holdenborg and
Rosenberg	J. Shepherd and	lady
R. Patten	sister	H. Browse
L. Flemming	G. Shepherd	J. Currie, lady and
J. Foley and lady	James Freelove	child
Edwin Norwood	J.W. Tritipo	S. Harrison
W. Riley	P.B. Demming	J.J. Boggs
E.F. Clarke	A.J. Durfy	P. McGinnity
William Green	A. Abrams	J.A. Davenport
L. Lokoloske	A.B. Mock	F. Donohue
S. Haws	R.O. DeWitt	J. O'Brien
J. Greenbaum	N.D. Mount	N.W. Snyder
J. Levy	A. Racenfild/sic/	T. Morgan
John Kantzer	(Racenfield?)	Samuel B. Drake
S.H. Parker	G. Lamb	Mr.___ Demster

(Continued next page)

W.H. Wade
H.A. Johnson
Mrs.___ Funk
W. Ives
A. Weill
W. Atison
S. Gilkie
J.L. Daly
P.F. Conger
P. McLean
W. Rippey
R. Curtis
A. Wattles
S. Tritips /sic/
Pat Donnell
George Elliott
L. Martin
A. Parke
A. Donaldson
N. Stephens
E.S. Moody
J.L. White
___ Robb
G.T. Powell
G. Delsen
J.M. Peters
J. Justice
George Buckley
Mr.___ Baldwin
R. Houston
H. Bigelow
E. Brinskill and
lady
O. Quackenbush
W. Quackenbush
O. Lightfoot
C. Kister/sic/
P. Koster/sic/
Mr.___ Brush
S. Down and two
boys
___ Eliza (servant)
A. Bazer
J. McKnight
Mrs.___ Dunniker
S.C. Stuart
J. Peck
J. Buckley
E. McPherson

J.O. Dennison
Mrs.___ Dunn/sic/
Miss___ Fretz
Miss H. Fretz
M. Werger
J. Werger
Mr___ Asbury /sic/
A. Cramer
___ Bradley
H.J. Chinn
William R.___
P. Taft
J. Griffin
J. Crank
F. Kelley /sic/
William Hughes
T. Dunn
Mrs.___ Dunn/sic/
B. Strauss
W.A. Gray
M.C. Martin
J.W. Thurman
Louis Monroe
J.M. Pelon
F. Koster
J.M. Henderson/sic/
J.M. Milliken
D. Shonkwiller
John O'Connor
L. Swaggerty
J. Hart
T. Cummins
G. Reddish
E. Shinn
A. Birckley /sic/
Z. McPherson
J. Green
J. Brooks
R. Oscer/sic/
P. Niess
C. Zeiter
A. Stuart
A. Douglass
S. Hall
Mrs.___ Rantzer
George A. Peters
L. Detee
James White
A. Henderson

- - - - - -

J.C. Dunn
Miss___ Heiser
W. Johnson/sic/
G. A. Carnahan
C. Meyer (?)
(Mayer?)
F. Newton
P. Dayton and wife
B. Murphy
P. Smith
A.W. Kelly
J.H. Dickinson
P.S. Underhill
T. McQuade
J. Conlan
M. Keuan
J. Hilan
M. Foley
A. Young
D. Gittings
J.R. Vance
G.W. Hays
J.J. Singleton and
3 servants
Thomas Greene
A.C. Heeth /sic/
W.M. Buel
H. McKinley
H. Wilson
J. Salles
J. Cash
John Hughes
W. Johnson/sic/
J.J. Peck
W. Waterhouse
J.M. Henderson/sic/
C. Schwartz
G. Wayne
G. Forbes
J.H. Spencer
A. Injanni
B. Injanni
F. Injanni
D. Daley /sic/
H. Johnson
Thomas Creamer /sic/
J. Ferrance
G.F. Whitmore

SHIP: AURORA
TYPE: Ship (British)   FROM: Valparaiso, Chile
ARRIVED: April 2, 1852   CAPTAIN: Cottier
PASSAGE: 70 days from Valparaiso, Chile.
CARGO: 850 tons of coal.
Passengers
Mr. A. McFarland   John Basquier   Mrs.___Rossas and
                                                       2 daughters

- - - - - -

SHIP: AGATE
TYPE: Brig   FROM: Tahiti
ARRIVED: April 2, 1852   CAPTAIN: Johnson
PASSAGE: Departed from Tahiti on March 5, 1852.
CARGO: 250,000 oranges and 200 coconuts.
Passengers
Capt. David Dring and   Mr. E.P. Adams   Mr.___Clawbot
    lady   Mr.___Pigant

- - - - - -

SHIP: VINCENNES
TYPE: U.S. Sloop of War   FROM: Astoria, O.T.
ARRIVED: April 4, 1852   CAPTAIN: W.L. Hudson
PASSAGE: Departed Astoria, Oregon Territory on March 31, 1852.
         This vessel brings intelligence that the schooner
         "Juliet" had gone ashore a short distance below the
         mouth of the Columbia River in lat. 45-15N.(+)
CARGO: Not listed.

List of Officer of the "Vincennes":

Dominick Lynch (First Lt & Executive Officer)	Lt. J.N. Barney	Lt. M.C. Perry, Jr.
O.C. Badger (P.M., Acting Master)*	Lt. J. Wilkinson	Edward J. Rutter (Surgeon)
G.M. Hand (M.)**	W. Stokes (Lt of Marines)	S. Allen Engles (Ass't Surgeon)
John W. Hudson (Captain's Clerk)	Walter O. Crain (P.M.)*	J.C. Sullivan (M.)**
T. Tatem (Sail Maker)	W.B. Forister (Boatswain)	Eugene Mack (Gunner)
	W.F. Laighton (Carpenter)	

- - - - - -

SHIP: LAURA BEVANS (or LAURA BEVAN?)
TYPE: Schooner (Whaling)   FROM: Lahaina, S.I.
ARRIVED: April 4, 1852   CAPTAIN: Pierce
PASSAGE: 14 days from Lahaina, Sandwich Islands.
CARGO: 500 watermelons, 1800 pumpkins and 450 bbls of potatoes.
Passengers
         Mr. H.H. French   Capt.___Griffin

- - - - - -

(*) Passed Midshipman   (+)"Juliet" sometimes listed as
(**) Midshipman   the "Juliette".

SHIP: ELIZA TAYLOR
TYPE: Brig   FROM: Panama
ARRIVED: April 5, 1852   CAPTAIN: Eldridge
PASSAGE: 80 days from Panama, via Acapulco, Mexico and San Diego,
         California; 10 days from latter port. Experienced severe
         gales on the coast and was off San Francisco harbor for
         eight days.
CARGO: Not listed.

Passengers

S. Rule	C.O. Parker	B. Sachs
B.M. Babcock	W.W. Garlock	E. Schiffle (?)
J. Thompson, lady	J. Whitteridge	(Schiffie?)
and son	J.P. Lane	F. Cutts
D. Frasier	T. Frasier	Mrs.___Clark and
		son

and 6 unidentified in steerage

- - - - - -

SHIP: OREGON
TYPE: Steamer   FROM: Panama
ARRIVED: April 7, 1852   CAPTAIN: R.H. Pearson
PASSAGE: 15½ days from Panama, via Acapulco, Mexico. Departed
         Panama on March 22, 1852 at 7:00PM. Passed Point Mala
         on March 23rd at 4:00AM. On March 27th, at 7:00PM spoke
         the steamer "California", bound to Panama, all well.
         Arrived at Acapulco, Mexico on March 29th at 1:00AM. At
         Acapulco found a number of the passengers of the wrecked
         steamer "North America" anxiously awaiting the arrival of
         a vessel from San Francisco for them. The "Oregon" took
         eighty(+)of the passengers and the "Northerner" an equal
         number; all of the ladies of the wrecked vessel had left
         in the former steamers and in various sailing vessels.
         Mr. William L. Newell, with many of the "North America's"
         passengers have boarded the "Oregon" for passage to San
         Francisco.* On March 31st, at 9:00AM, passed the steamer
         "Isthmus", standing toward San Blas, Mexico. At 8:00PM,
         on the same date, Mrs.___Cruey, a cabin passenger, died
         of congestion of the lungs. At midnight of April 1st,
         passed Cape St. Lucas. On April 5th, at 11:00AM, passed
         San Diego, California. A child of Mrs.___Cruey, born on
         board, died at 7:00PM on April5th. Experienced strong
         head winds nearly the whole passage. The health of the
         passengers was unusually good during the voyage.
CARGO: Not listed.

Passengers

Mrs.___Bond	Mrs.___Baker	Mrs.___Hierre,
Mrs.___McKnight	Miss___Richardson	child & svt
and child	Mr.___Leech, lady	B.E. Smith
C. White	& servant	Lt.___Magaw (of
Mrs.___Boullett	Mrs.___Turner	U.S. Army)
and boy	Mrs. A.B. Petty	Mrs. P.H. Holley

(Continued next page)

(*)Listed on page 141 as "W.L. Newall", per source.
(+)Figure as per source.

Mrs.___ Reese and
    infant
Mrs. C. Wright
Mrs.___ Donaldson
Mrs.___ Pierce /sic/
Senor___ Peisa
A.M. Sickley
Frank Powers
Nicholas Prsons/sic/
    (Parsons?)
James Minturn
John Ludan
Mrs.___ Minturn and
    child
A.S. Paul
J. Morgan
C. Peck
Samuel Mathews /sic/
J. Allison
J. Thomas
J.B. Ulrich
H.C. Perkins
J. Francis
M.M. Brockman
W. Harris
J.W. Ring
A. Golinger and
    lady
J. Earl
J. Coward
R.W. Davis
Miss Eliza Davis
J.K. Bowman
S.R. Groom
E.P. Davis
P.H. Vizzy
S. Prion
D.C. Tarbler
T.B. Moore
T. Wallace
S.J. Arnold
E. Boyle
F. Mason
J.E. Smith
___ Trestler and
    lady
Mrs.___ Ainsworth
Mrs.___ Ogleby
C. Latapie
C. Baker
L. Creesey

Miss___ Pierce
P.R. Ringstrom
    DeMers
___ Ward and lady
Mrs. S. Pratt and
    boy
John Lanior/sic/*
D. Johnston
David Jones
J. Gartrell
H. Gartrell
Martin Whalen
Mrs.___ Whalen and
    5 children
Wilford Allen
William Cashner/sic/
H.C. Moseley
D. Castner /sic/
J. Strafford
D. Fairchild
W. Martin
W.C. Richmond
R. Kendall
J. Kendall
A. Sinclair
W.G. Lawrence
J.A. Lawrence
Max Miller
J. Potter
G.P. Derry
Miss Mary Hale
S.S. Pierse/sic/
J. Boyle
M.H. Bucher /sic/
C.M. Simmons
W.Y. Gage
A.D. Arnot
D. Dorrity
E. Gage
J.Q. Blinn
G.W. Shotwell
W.B. Moore
W.M. Lent and
    servant
I. Sherman
A. Holbrook, lady
    & 3 children
Capt.___ Harron and
    2 boys
W. McKnight and boy
J.G. Doane
(Continued next page)

R. DeShanc(sic),
    lady & boy
    (DeShane?)
P. Pavon and lady
Mrs.___ Stewart
W. Murray, lady and
    child
M. Brady
J. Brady
J.W. Kennan
Charles B. Toole
Lindsey Aikens
W.R. Hart
James P. Hart
J.B. Wilson
J. Marsen
S. Marsen
O.H. Hardy
Samuel Joy
Stephen Joy
A.S. Foss
W.Y. Clark
E.W. Sales
Thomas Marn
W.C. Porter
W. Rider
J.C. Tranbly and
    lady (Traubly?)
J. Hackett
Charles Hoofniere
M. Moody
M. Smith
J. Glass
H. Hussington
G.H. Haspeth
N. Osborne
W.H. Mead
T. Flanagan
G.W. Packard
P. Arbuckle Jr.
A. Champbell /sic/
    (Campbell?)
H. Ernst
Samuel Breck (?)
    (Brock?)
Mrs.___ Couch and
    3 children
J. Van Vorhees
J.L. Bond and boy
J.V. Gilbert
H. Wells

(*)Note "W.B. Lanier",page 140.

A.M. Tymerson
A.G. Pierce
W.B. Wier
N.O. Keefe
M. Plummer
Mrs.___Whalen
H. Larkin
Mrs. J. Stevens
R. Threlfall
J. Bilby
J.W. Ralston
J. Ralston
J. Whalen
J.G. French
A.D. Grambette
A. Ferguson
P. Wilson
A. Asbrand
J. Benselman
L. Thomas /sic/
G. Thomas
L. Thomas /sic/
L. Thomas /sic/
B. Kinney
A. Laing /sic/
B. Barker
B.F. Goodman
John Mertyn
J.B. Sturdevant
J.G. Elliott
W.T. Ford
D. Craft
William Leach
T.G. Singleton
F. Cook
John Dunn
T. Phieffenberger
Orin Hicox
David Patten
O.H. Woodward
C. Levereaux
H.F. Beckwith
C.O. Foote
M. Coates
T. St. John
Peter Snyder
F. Wiger
R.G. Story
John Story
___Hutchinson
T. Leeds

C.C. Williams
J.H. Williams
G.W. Turner
Charles Wright
R. Murphy
J. Hall
U. Booth
J. Davis/sic/
T. Morgan
N.M. Baxter
O. Short
G. Mills
A. Glode
Y.S. Ruddock
E. Bower
J.H. Fuller
J. Dresha
A.B. Paine
T. Marual
E. Banys /sic/
E. Banks /sic/
H. Buchanan
William Stickney
F. Dickhouse
A. Huffnagle
J. Huffnagle
___Hendricks
W. Jordan
F. Jordan
R.F. Hubbard
W. Porter and
4 children
F. Haine
G. Smith and son
H. Amidon
Lewis Hember
James Anthony
M. Rountree
Mary A. Robinson
James Ahrens
T.L. Smith
Water King /sic/
George Mehl
E. Chisholm
J. Windell
C. Beebe
A. Worden
J.T. Abel
S. Weeks
N. Sawyer
L.J. Hart
(Continued next page)

J.D. Turner
W. Warwick
William Owen
A. Keese
G. Treneux and
lady
R.B. Hazard
J. Bamber
D. Craig
J.H. Jones
W. Fowler
J. Keese
P.W. Sterling
N. Chipchase
F.H. Fisher
F. Clayanore
S. Dolan
P.H. Young
J. Davis/sic/
T. McNair
D.A. Patterson
J. Lindley
James Noyes
R. Dyuglass /sic/
J. Fisher
R. Cross
Thomas Early
P. Criddell
Hugh Green
H. Devagney
J. Carney and
lady
J. Spencer
A. Sherman
G. Morgan
John Gose
W. Hooper
N.P. Rowell
S. Penny
Mr.___Merchant
A. Rogers
Robert Herbert
John Call
J.B. Goodman
M. Levi
D. McKeever
T. Thornton
S. Milliard
P. Coorech /sic/
A.W. Porter
J. Yherkser

J. Valentine
T.C. Dowell
W.H. Campbell
H. Johnston
S. Idy
B.D. Myers
R.A.W. Fraser
N. Otis
H. Sinclair
A. Powers
E. Cassy
L. Dodlear and
   lady
A. Martin
J.H. Challens
L. Chance
D. Kenyon
S. Zanes
   ____ Wardwell
W.A. Howsell
J.H. Brooks
W.B. Lanier/sic/*
J. Stevenson
J. Mara
T. Bell
M. Dougherty
H. Isaas (?)
   (Isaac?)
Joseph McGinniss
E.B. Humphreys
G. Millard
C. Cottermeyer
E. Smith
J.C. Griffith
J.H. Griffith
P. Leary
L. Martin
H. Holly
P.H. Holly
H. McClusky
J.Q. Adams
P. Holly
T.B. Thomas
A.J. Thomas
B.D. Thomas
F.M. Thomas
J. Wallace
J. Batt
W. Wilkes
J. Carman
William Jameson

S.R. Deth
J. Steinman
P.S. Tracy
W. Nichols, lady
   & 3 children
C. McNeil
C.F. Carroll
J.M. Pecker
W. Stillwell
P. Cassidy
Mrs.____ Cross and
   child
P. Huyskill
S. Sackett
W. Sharpe
B. Witton
W. Gardner
Mrs.____ Wilson
J.G. Vingen
A. Irway
J.E. Thompson
G. Martyne /sic/
A. Sutro
P. Bodey
R. McMunamee (?)
   (McManamee?)
H. Church
J.W. Snyder
William Neeley
H.S. Shurland
C. Van Sautford
A. Driesback
J. Sherwin
J.W. Ballard
C. Hoff
J. Ward
M. Nichess
G.Y. Bedford
D.R. McLellan
A.G. Bird
H.M. Bernard
W.W. Jenkins
J. Manghan
Mr. A. Hall
J. Black
J. Baker
J. Carson
W.G. Bothwell
James Barrack
J. Fulton
H. Putman
(Continued next page)

W. Winger
   ____ Foegley
C. Allen
W. Dunning, lady
   & 3 children
W. Buck
A. Kiddell
J. Davenport
James Scott
C. Knepsion /sic/
Mrs.____ McNair
   ____ Whyte
N. Cuthbertson
J. Guard
W. Dent
D. Kyle
J. Partier
B. Martin
D.G. Sherrill
R. Foster
J.G. Rittenhouse
J. Covidge
J. Capelet
T. Cook
J. Shawl
C. Christophe/sic/
C.J. Peters
L. Tripp
A.B. Webster
J. McGee
F. Bernhardt
S. Van Dusen
P. Grisseti
J. McKnight
William Baker
M. Zernerwich
R.C.R. Petty
J.N. Petty
J.W. Williams
W.R. Deese
L.H. Stephens
C.C. Otis
J. Thompson
W.G. Ames
J.M. Percy
M. Phillips
J. Samuel
S. Day
J.L. Lamb
W.H. Lee
T. Brown

(*)Note "John Lanior", page 138.

C. Randall	D. Tullech	A. Gates
P. Schower	W. Searles	E. Cuyler
W. Miner	W. Forshay	J. Paul

--Boarded at Acapulco, Mexico:(From wreck of "North America"?)

J.T. Hoffman	E.B. McCrea	H. Rice
J.G. Smith	G.H. Davis	S. Sharpe
F. Genian	A.F. Randolph	W. Webster
Mr.___ Omev (?)	E. McClane	G.J. Reed
(Omey?)	J.W. Bronk	A.B. Evans
D.P. Shattuck	C.C. Miles	E. Chamberlain
J.S. Shattuck	E. Burbank	A. Landon
J. Clough	A. Dumarhart	J.A. Bradshaw
G.W. Stevens	T.R. Brown	William Glaskin
B.F. Pollard	E.H. Wade	W. Rankin
J. Mills	J.A. Emery	E.B. Dover
Dr.___ Carroll	L. S?ott	A. Wait
F. Spotts	J. Ramsey	J. Weaver
S. Taunton	J.L. Wakefield	W. Dickinson
A.S. Newall*	L.F. Sowles	M. Bymes
E. Dunn	R. Sanches	J.H. Gorton
J. Burbank	Mr.___ Sanches	S. Kilbure /sic/
L.D. Butler	W. Stoll	J. Berry
___ Amidon	J.F. Hall	J. Olds
William Carleton	J.B. Wells	Dr. F.H. Pickney
M. Sharpe	W.L. Newall*	D. Norris
D. Shotwell	W.S. Newall*	J. Crandall
J.S. Eaton	E. Avery	A.G. Williams
T.A. Morse	F. Crane	J. Smith
A.A. Gore		

- - - - - -

SHIP: OHIO
TYPE: Steamer   FROM: San Diego, California
ARRIVED: April 7, 1852   CAPTAIN: Hilliard
PASSAGE: 5 days from San Diego, California, via intermediate ports.
        Put into Santa Barbara, California and Monterey, Califor-
        nia. Departed latter port on April 6, 1852.
CARGO: Not listed.

Passengers

Mr.___ Woods and	Major___ Sevalla	Major___ Rollin
lady	J.M. Brady	O. Bulluck /sic/
H.H. Harrington	A.B. Knowlson	G.L. Wadsworth
Charles Johnson, lady	G. Thurston	L.G. Wadsworth
& sister	J. McKinnon	M. McVoy
D. Donovan	J. Raiman	B. Atkinson
R. Porter	M. Cornelius	G. Crander
J.B. Staats	M. Cornelius Jr.	R. Mitchell
M. Straus	B.B. Brooks	G.W. Payne
J. Brown	E.P. Brooks	J. Hamilton
W. Herman	S. Cornelius	S. Vanderslip
E.H. Draper	S. Nerepass	R. Spinerling

(Continued next page)

(*)W.L.Newall listed as Wm L. Newell on page 137, per source. Note
    other Newall's on page 141.

A.B. Spaulding	J.B. Taylor	A. Laird
G. Sraswasha /sic/	C.S. Taylor	E.M. Ingraham
E. White	S. Spaco	L. Gregory
J. Rice	C. Desler	M. Moch
A. Hickey	D. Mason	E. Porter
S.B. Steele	S. Newton	D.J. Caulkins
D. Mansfield	S.P. Cary	P.H. Clough
R.A. Finnel	D. Goddard	P.G. Bailey
S. Edson	J.H. Stebbins	R.H. Blood
J. Nerve	D. Collins	A. Roland
A. Nerve	C. Collins	A. Prickley
P. Finity	J. Duncan	J. Harrie
G. Whild	J. Randall	D.F. Hammond
A. Updike	J. Whisp /sic/	J. Reinhart
R. Ramport	J. Wistch /sic/	A. Dealer
O. Blake	A.J. Reynolds	M. O'Brien
S. Field	G.A. Brown	J. Bennett
J. Duffau	J.W. Brown	A. Luther
C. Munroe	J. Sheppard	B. Grissett
T. Harris	C.F. Goodrich	A.D. Onley
T.W. Six	H.P. Ambrose	S. Miller
R.D. Six	S.L. McCann	W.B. Foster
W. Brown	W. Kinney	B. Mallory
G. Bosworth	G.C. Hanson	G. Penrose
A. Mitchell	H.J. Cox	M. Cornelius /sic/
B. Beole	P. Bearde	W.R. Smith
A. Fuller	A. Cox	J. Haley
E.W. Chase	S. Manning	B. Fisk
C.R. Carlton	G. Beale	A.F. Sapher
J. Currnel	Charles Walters	Joseph Boston

- - - - - -

SHIP: ENVELOPE
TYPE: Barque (British)   FROM: Valparaiso, Chile
ARRIVED: April 8, 1852   CAPTAIN: Tomlinson
PASSAGE: From Valparaiso, Chile, via Guayaquil, Eucador. Passage
from latter port was 60 days, no passage time listed from
Valparaiso to Guayaquil. The "Envelope" sprung a leak in
her lower bow port a few days out from Valparaiso, and
was compelled to put into Guayaquil to repair.
CARGO: 450 tons of coal, 350 deal plank, 286 bags of flour, 2019
half-bags of flour, 818 quarter-bags of flour, 82 kegs of
eggs and 12 boxes of spices.
                    Passengers
        Mrs.____Tomlinson   Mr.____Butt
                - - - - - -

SHIP: ARCHIBALD GRACIE
TYPE: Barque   FROM: Manzanillo, Mexico
ARRIVED: April 9, 1852   CAPTAIN: Peters
PASSAGE: 30 days from Manzanillo, Mexico, via San Blas, Mexico.
                (Continued next page)

CARGO: 1400 bags corn, 40 boxes eggs, 22 sacks beans and 1000 lbs of chiles.

Passengers
Mr. R. Leech   A. Wood
and 36 unidentified in steerage

- - - - - - - - -

SHIP: INDEPENDENCE
TYPE: Steamer   FROM: San Juan del Sur
ARRIVED: April 10, 1852   CAPTAIN: Lucas
PASSAGE: From San Juan del Sur, Nicaragua, via Acapulco, Mexico, 12 days. Passage time from San Juan del Sur to Acapulco not listed. This vessel brings intelligence that John Foster, Esq., the British Consul for the Republic of Nicaragua, died at El Realejo (Realejo) Nicaragua. Date of death not listed. Consul Foster, according to a contemporary source, died on March 6, 1852. He had lived in that country since 1824. The "Independence" also brings intelligence that the Nicaraguan government issued an edict prohibiting the export of corn, owing to the unusual number of locusts that have lately appeared in that country. The corn crop of the season was "nearly destroyed".
     The following deaths took place during the passage:
          April 2, 1852 - Henry Bush, on board the "Independence" of Exxex County, New York
          April 3, 1852 - James Carburg, on board the "Independence", of Massachusetts, of concussion of the spine.*

CARGO: Not listed.

Passengers

C. Cornell, lady and child	Mrs. J. Hawley and 2 children	Mrs. D. Kerliff and 2 children
Miss Ellen McLaughlin	H. Tenbrook	Mrs. C. Turner and 2 children
R.P. Bateman	H. Castle	A. Robertson, lady & 2 children
S.B. Middlebrook	M.L. Barker	Mrs. C.G. Howard
J.M. Middlebrook	D.F. Butt and lady	O.A. Clark
H.G. Middlebrook	E.R. Wadsworth	C.C. Clark
N. Gray, lady and child	A. Marsey and lady	C.S. Preble, lady & 2 children
H.M. Gray	H. Laughlin	J.S. Dole, lady, infant & svt
E.A. Burr and lady	A.J. King	T. Gallagher
N. Bartholomew	L.P. Converse	E.B. Lane
T.E. Miles	H.G. Randall	W.L. May
H. Olmstead	J.D. Cartwright	J.M. Thompson
J.S. M'Cain	A.T. Green	C. Carpenter
Mrs. R. Garrabrant and child	E. Brookshire and lady	A.D. Personett
William Burbridge	Miss H.C. Massey	G. Choate
Miss M. McCool	Miss A. Kent	J.M. Hopper
H.P. Caulkins	J. Tallman	
D.E. Wellman	J. Dunn	

(Continued next page)

(*)See "Notes", page 243 and entry for "James Carbury", page 145.

William White
George Cooper
D. Myers
J.B. Hatch
S.P. Spearin
S. Spearin
A. Wakefield
J. Moore
L. Moore
A.W. Bumps
I. Carr
I. Abbott
R. Farrille /sic/
J.C. Richardson
H. Faville /sic/
W.R. Richardson
I. Blakeman
T. Venables
A.L. Lochlin
J.L. Lochlin
N. Moore
T. Smith
J.M. Enton
J.C. Duncan
J. Dougherty
M. Dougherty
U.L. Goodwin
J.W. Kneeland /sic/
R.E. Clark
S. Sharp
J. Farman
J. Manning
L.L. Dickinson
John Tillison
G. Delget
John A. Holbrook
W. Higley
H. Miner
H. Perry
D. White
John Walter
Charles Richmond
W. Bateman
R. Bateman
P.G. Bateman
Henry Ehle Jr.
N. Bishop
T.B. Stewart
S.G. Tisdale
George Hope
J. Down

H. Wood
William Fletcher
W.R. Stanley
M. Marston
W. Lamb
D.P. Chase
D. Wortley
A.B. Tilton
J. Appleton
C. Severance
I.N. King
J. Libbey
T. Coleman
B. Allen
A. Goodyear
T. Tuttle
W.B. Garland
W. Baker
J. White
W.L. Higley
N. Mickham
John Welch
Jacob Welch
J. Peake
C. Sharp
J.A. Mocatti
T. Carey
G. Good
B. Morris
J.B. Lane
H.M. Bush
J.M. Bennett
Joseph Colvin
T. Colvin
S. Paine
J.B. Truesworthy
B. Loring
S. Ashley
Martin Ashley
Dr. N.J. Wilson
Dr. H.C. Bagg
W.S. Bumo and lady
Austin Walrath
J.H. Walrath
William Blair
C.C.P. Severance
G. Stoutenburg
John Sylabor
John G. Pitkin
E.N. Harswell
N. Flanders
(Continued to next page)

A. French
Thomas Jennis
W.F. Babcock
D. King
P. Gillman
M. Varney
D.B. Coleman
H. Coleman
R.D. Bosworth
J. Wood
A.W. Carey
A. Ludwig
R. Ludwig
H.R. Austin
W.C. Pressey
C.B. Pressey
B.B. Wheatryl
R. Foster
P. Lynch
F.L. Espanier
W. Phelps
S. Davidson
R. McCabe
B. Whittaker
J. King
W. Davidson
J. Harl /sic/
L. Sulliff
Henry Brown
E. Edmonds
J. Bucklin
J.W. Adams
F.L. Bishop
Charles Wilcox
N. Kingsley
Abraham Hall
W.W. Wilson
Pohn Page /sic/
   (John Page?)
C. Raymond
C. Lockrow
F. Shear
N.J. Wells
C. Crater
N. Heath
G.W. Frink
Charles Smith
James Hind
C.H. Rap
Z. Butterfield
William Sturgis

N. Roberts
M. Sullivan and
   lady
Rodney Smith
Thomas Murray
_____Sanderson
William Griffith
N. Van Rankin
A. Hubbard /sic/
A. Hubbard /sic/
J. Hubbell
M.M. Patridge
N.J. Walcott
D. Stannard
G.A. Morse
G. Stannard
A. Allen
Alden Morse
John Duke
H.H. Smith
E.O. Tompkins
A. Collins
Thomas Garfield
J.J. Paige
James Carbury/sic/*
W.F. Thayer
J. White
J.H. Coumb/sic/
E.A. Hall
M. Burdick
E.J. Vincent
R. Walker

H.L. Hinman
N. Spencer Jr.
Daniel Giles
Austin Martin
Mr.____Myers
_____Bellinger
M.W. Rosebeck
R. Jewett
M. Orent
A. White
E.D. Percival and
   lady
A.H. Hubbell
Lyman L. Gorham
D. Fowler
A.S. Hart
R.H. Cooper
Roland Loomis
William Green
H. McKean
G.D. Northrop
B. Murphy
W.B. Wilder
E.A. Perry
H.J. Osgood
J.D. Cremer
G. Carson
Francis Hart
John Page
Charles McGraw
Joel Harris
F. Hule

J. Carr
D. Donnivan /sic/
Benjamin E. Brown
D. Carpenter
_____Christie
Franklin Palmer
D.H. Robinson
D. Ferris
A. Gardner
P. Gardner
E. Gardner
F. Tudsbay and lady
J.H. Craigmiles
C.B. Judd
C. Judd
J.N. Canfield
Henry Bagg
J.D. Col?er
J. McBridge
P. Bowers
John Garfield
James Sweet
Ezra Snyder
William Conner
J.P. Ford
C.C. Bagg
G.E. Weller
L. Peirce
A. Griffith
J.D. Patter
J.P. Wallace
Joseph Wheeler

--Boarded at Acapulco, Mexico; following passengers from
   the wrecked steamer "North America":

Mrs.____Bain, 4
   children & svt
Miss____Carr
Mrs.____Durfee
Miss L.A. Miner
Mr.____Winni and
   lady

E.D. Smith, lady,
   sister and 2
   neices
Mrs.____Pouell and
   4 children /sic/
   (Powell?)
J.P. Buckley

G. Flint, lady and
   5 children
Mrs.____Fogerty
Mrs.____Morse and
   3 children
J.Q. Adams

- - - - - -

SHIP: SEA BIRD
TYPE: Steamer   FROM: San Diego, California
ARRIVED: April 11, 1852   CAPTAIN: Haley
PASSAGE: 3½ days from San Diego, California, via San Pedro,
     California, Santa Barbara, California, San Luis Obispo,
     California and Monterey, California. Encountered strong
     NW winds and heavy head seas from San Pedro.
CARGO: Not listed.

(*)See "Notes", page 243

146

Passengers

James S. Lawson   H.W.G. Clements   George Coggins
N.C. Covington   John Taylor   Mr.____Tillitson
Henry Murdock   John Macy   Andrew Miller
M. Clark   Juan Arando   A. Sanchez
John McElroy   J. Schultz   Dr. H.R. Nyles
John Homer   W.S. Moran   J.H. Hubbard
A. Devour   Mrs.____Tucker and   Jose Machada
B. Sharp   2 children   W. Saunders
G. Hall   G. Hackamyer /sic/   James Johnson
M. Katz   John Sanfranco   Dr. E.B. Shaw
E. Leis   D. Anderson, lady   Capt.____Deering
Henry Jones and   & servant   Mr.____Hubbard
   lady   W.E.P. Hartnell   John Danante
Capt.____Cooper   J.E. Hartnell   M. Acevido
A. Tresconi   Col.____Russell and lady

- - - - - -

SHIP: INVINCIBLE
TYPE: Clipper   FROM: New York
ARRIVED: April 13, 1852   CAPTAIN: Johnson
PASSAGE: 114 days from New York (one source states 110 days), via
         Rio de Janeiro, Brazil, 79 days. On January 3, 1852
         put into Rio de Janeiro for water, having lost ship's
         supply by rivets loosening in iron tank, causing 8 days
         loss of time.
CARGO: 260 iron bars, 292 boxes soap, 14 bundles of shovels, 1
         cask borax, butter, chains, 1 wagon, 3 cases sails, red
         lead, boots and shoes, furniture, 77 bbls whiskey, 26 pieces
         of iron shutters, seeds, 10 bbls plaster, 35 barrels of
         cement, acid, copper, steel, vices, 105 grindstones, 2 boxes
         scythe stones, 1 box gold leaf, scythes, horseshoe nails,
         scales, 15 boxes coffee mills, gin, brandy, apples, hats,
         mill cranks, 24 doors, carpeting, 20 kegs shot, 1 organ,
         1 piano, 160 boxes oysters and assorted goods.

Passengers

Benjamin F. Foyen,   Mrs.____Osborne   Mr.____Wallace, lady,
   lady and child   R. Whiting   child & servant
Mrs.____Sheppard   Miss____Durie   Oliver Kimberly
Mrs.____Johnson*and   Wilmarth Waller   Miss____Eardley
   child   Henry Tuthill
(*) Wife of ship's captain

- - - - - -

SHIP: ROANOKE
TYPE: Schooner   FROM: Santa Cruz, California
ARRIVED: April 13, 1852   CAPTAIN: McAlmond
PASSAGE: 2 days from Santa Cruz, California. Left at Santa Cruz,
         California,the U.S. Surveying Steamer "Active", Lieut.
         ____Alden commanding, which was bound for Monterey,
         California.
CARGO: 70 tons of dry goods and groceries, 31 tons of potatoes and

1200 feet of lumber.

Passengers

| Capt. | Tuttle | Mrs. | Castro and | Mr. | Cole |
| Mr. | Stillman | son | | Mr. | McPherson |

- - - - -

SHIP: NORTHERNER
TYPE: Steamer   FROM: Panama
ARRIVED: April 14, 1852   CAPTAIN: Randall
PASSAGE: 15 days from Panama, via intermediate ports. The "Northerner" left no passengers on the Isthmus awaiting passage.
The agent, on the day of sailing, put the price of passage at so low a figure that all wishing to were able to
procure passage. There were not over 50 individuals left
in Panama, and they were mostly holders of tickets on
some independent line. On April 3rd passed the wreck of
the steamer "North America" on the beach some 40 miles
south of Acapulco, Mexico. The sea was making a breach
over her, and she appeared to be broken in two forward of
her engine, and the bow to have fallen seaward.
Arrived at Acapulco, Mexico on April 3rd at 9:00PM, and
sailed at 1:00PM on April 4th, taking the balance of
passengers from the wreck of the "North America" that were
able to raise the small amount charged by the agent of the
Pacific Mail Steamship Company at that port. There were
from 175 to 200 passengers of the wrecked steamer still at
Acapulco, living on the charity of the citizens, awaiting
the arrival of the clipper reported to have been dispatched by Vanderbilt's agent to their relief.*
Arrived off San Diego on the evening of April 10th, but
did not run in until 10:00AM next morning, being prevent-
ed by dense fogs. Found the steamer "Isthmus" in port, all
well, waiting for fresh provisions. Sailed at 3:00PM. On
the night of April 11th lay-to for five hours in the Santa
Barbara Channel, on account of fog, being unable to see
across the ship. Experienced head winds and gales from
Cape St. Lucas up, and made the passage through in 15 days
and 20 hours running time. During the passage there were
many cases of sickness among the passengers, but not any
deaths.
The following marriage took place on board the "Northerner" on Wednesday morning, April 14, 1852:
Horace P. Janes, Esq., Counsellor at Law, of San
Francisco, to Miss Julia M.H. Hall, of Nashville,
Tennessee, performed by the Rev. Dr. Boring.
CARGO: Mail.

Passengers

Miss Julia E. Hall**	Mrs.	Hawley	Mrs.	Pinto
Mrs.	Janes	Mrs.	Lanbeux	Mr. R.H.	Waterman
Miss	Brown	Mrs.	Austin	Mrs.	Bell
Mrs.	Maxwell	Mrs. S.	Dehaig	Mrs.	Draper

(Continued next page)

(*)Clipper dispatched was the "Northern Light".
(**)Sic. Note "Passage" resume listing for "Miss Julia M.H.Hall!"

Mrs.___Cravatt
Miss___Doty
Mrs.___Jones
Mrs.___Duck
Miss___Duck
R. Tunis
F.E. Pinto
B. Tunis
Rev.___McCoy
A.H. Ringgold
J. Spear
J.O. Watkins
J. Shoemaker
M. Delgado
S. Cowles
Rev.___Butts
G. London
S. Littlefield
J.V.A. Lansing
C. Wellsgang
E. Hall
D.P. Conklin
J. Allard
G. Algers
C. Pra?ley
D. Lenterbanne
W. Hawley
J.C. Maynard
N. Searles
S.P. Webb
J. Weltre (?)
W. Cline
E. Schupler
C.G. Taylor
W.J. Dinsmore
W.B. Fletcher
M. Lazinski
A. Myers
J.R. Fennell/sic/
M. Isaacs
J. Georgette
P. Houser
J. Fay
W.A. Reese
B. Banker
J. McGrath
J.C. Sonkie
J. Wright
A. Thompson
H. Morris
D. Faus

Mrs.___Ezekiel
Mrs.___Ruggles
Mrs.___Farish and
    6 children
Mrs.___Saroni and
    child
W. Craig
J. Heiss
H. Tinkham
C. Pike
W. Wiggins
H. Pike
A.C. Anderson
J.C. Morrison
J. Brown
N. Worrell
R.H. Evans
W. Timpson /sic/
H. Johnson
M. Reed
H. Tay
Mr.___Saroni
W.J. Taylor
M. Vedder
E.G. Winne
M. Auger
J.L. Janes
H.W. Theal
C.W. Mulford
Mr.___Austin
H. Ketchum
H. Green
J. Eckhart
J. Fuller
C. Freeland
H.S. Hall
P. Fanin
G. Wontrode
E. Gireney
L.B. Dubois
W. Sanders
J. Goothill
D. Thompson
G. Morton
H. Brinneman
W.M. Braton
R. Phillips
L.B. Freer
P. Nourgion
J. Sullivan
M. Gouldman
(Continued next page)

Mrs. J.B. Besscott
Miss___Knox
Mrs.___Lane and
    child
J.M. Freeman
James A. Gilbert
E.B. Mastic
J. Lane
G. Cullum
E. Barnam
M. McCormack
R. Denton
J.S. Remsen
B. Talman
M. Duck
J. Littlefield
G. Brewster
E.B. Dunham
J. May
J.P. Flint
R.S. King
S.B. Goodman
J. Adams
J. Wakefield
L. Johnson
R.H. Sterling
J.W. Sterling
J.W. Huntington
James Cole
H. Brown
E.D. Thomas
F. Luty
J. Jones
B.F. Jones
E.B. Varney
D. McKee
J. Alby
Mrs.___Donovan
J. Ingraham
J. Hiller
J. Langin
M. Langin
A.J. Vagalee
G.H. Deekniper
A. Johnston
J. Wilson
C. Ackerman
J.H. Ackerman
L. Hush
Mrs.___Langin
J. Brothers

Mary Donovan
J. Bernhardt
C. Ferry
L. Gale
J. Donovan
M.L. Nelson
F.M. Hughes
D. Bellen
S. Lorestorn
J. Butler
S.W. Reed
E. Thomas
R.H. Shoot
J. McGill
V. Huitze
M. Hennessy
E. Evans
C. Cook
W. Filey
J. Dash
J. Mier
P. Spohn
D. Cochran
P. Newell
Mrs._____Newell
C.F. Holbrook
J. Mooney
E. Ever
J. Ross
B.J. Benton
Mrs._____Collins
L. Hush
J.G. Rice
M. Eagan
Mrs._____Eagan
Miss_____Eagan
W.A. Mansfield
C.J. Auton
J. Dyce
J.T. Thornton
W.A. Jyalls
Miss_____Collins
J. Peigle
A. Mellin
P. Look
B. Vaughan
B.B. Rewdon (?)
    (Rowdon?)
Miss_____Langin
F. Reynolds
M. Walker
J. Morton

C. Sherman
J. Bigelow
C. O'Neil
J. Litchfield
C.W. Scott
James Barnett
H. Sheppard
J.C. Hilton
J. Murphy
S. Wade
B.C. Pratt
J.J. Leuce/sic/
Mrs._____Hunden
H. Louts/sic/
O. Forbos /sic/
    (Forbes?)
H. Taylor
P. Gaston
C. Simonds
J. Marshall
C. Short
R.S. Thompson
W.W. White
H. Davis
D.W. Colton
G. Seebold
J. Mitchell
J. Pitcher
J. Schwartz
J. Hughes
J. Nicoll
Mrs._____Waters
J. Hurges/sic/
Mrs._____Hurges/sic/
G.F. Hon
P. Sykes
J. Carey
L. Stewart
W.W. Garrison
O.K. Stampey
B.B. Woodward
J. Brown
J. Petrie
Miss_____Honges
F.M. Fennill/sic/
J.G. Loomis
Josiah Fitze
A. Sansagras
B. Gorman
W. War
W. Miller
W. Jennings
(Continued next page)

M. Evans
H. Morrison
O. Myers/sic/
J. Forbes
C.K. Ferguson
M. Maltbro
    (colored)
J. Wyman
W. Jackson
L. Murphy
F.A. Chase Jr.
E. Kopka
Mrs._____Kopka
L. Rehelan
J. Thomas
E.H. Pratt
R. Johnston
J.J.B. Hamblin
J. Collins
E. McGee
R.T. Frost
R. McMillan
H. Fitzpatrick
Mrs._____Fitzpartick
Mary Riley
Miss_____Riley
M. Araby
E. Best
J. Weible
J. Loring
A. Franklin
J. Cosgrove
J. Taylor
J. Henry
J. Jackobs/sic/
F. Darkin /sic/
D.F. Luffkin
Mrs._____Luffkin
Miss_____Luffkin
O.H. Smith
H.L. Ewing
W. Huntress
J.A. Cowan
W. Cardwell
J. Decker
M.C. Higgins
J.C. Childs
W. Sharp
J.W. Summers
L. Lewis
B. Reardon
W. Kitteridge

F.C. Davis
George Finney
J.M. Hanford
G.W. Bedell
E. Bedford
W. Ford
J. Ford
J. Simonds
G.W. Davis
P. Fiber
G. Morey
O.A. Davis
M.M. Marsh
J. McCulloch
M. Sweetland
J.J. Ross Jr.
L.W. Simonds
C.A.P. Stevenson
M. Holmes
J.D. Vingarden
W. Vingarden
J. Nelson
M. Ritz
C. Steamyer
W. Shenkin
G. Mart
D. Brown
   (Colored)
J.W. Jenkins
S. Hagus
H. Buck
A. Frasin
E.E. Hughs /sic/
L. Wilkins
J.G. Brown
Milley Harrison
   (Colored)
M. Sprague
Mrs.___Sprague
M. Blanchard
Patrick___
   (Colored)
M. Phillips
J.P. Merrill
P. Teft
G.D. Buffum
C. Johnson
C.A. Chapin
A.G. Parmeter
R.P. Monnell
Bernard O'Neil

L. Marsh
C. Lucas
J. Atkinson
H. Mitchell
A. Wood
J. Van Walkenburg
G. Newton
W. Prouty
E. Adams
J. McFarland
H.F. Waters
J.H. Barlow
F.B. Smith
H. Botsford
P. Bedell
D.F. Bailey
J.W. Harris
J. Harris
W. Mahoney
A. Schribner /sic/
W. West
S.H. West
P. Schmind
J. Ritter
F.M. Spears
E. Eaton
A. Judson
E.L. Russ
S.H. Barber
R. McCracken
J. Torrey
   Hamilton
   (Colored)
W. Skiels
Stephen___
   (Colored)
G.M. Monten
F. Charles
P.W. Brown
G. Wilden
Charles Shakelford
   /sic/
   (Shackelford?)
A. Van Dyne
C.O. Sheldon
R. Merrill
L.G. Merrill
A. Wheeler
H. Beach
E. Rush
Charles O'Neil
(Continued next page)

L. Cadwick /sic/
J. Thomas
E. Miller
J.B. Green
G.W. Ayers
A. Snow
H.H. Barnes
D. Hogan
J. L. Schwartz
P. McQuade
H. Bancroft
C.E. Barnes
J.H. Norton
J. Sherburn
G. Condit
L.D. Braman
A. Newton
C.W. Ellitt /sic/
   (Elliott?)
M. Conig
M. Borden
J. Zimmer
C. Demmis
J. Myres /sic/
H.M. Tice
E.G. Tice
J. Tice
J. Humphreys
E.W. Much
C. Corbitt
W.S. Bennett
W. McPherson
D. Griffith
Charles Slaven
Roger Finn
W. Atkins
W. Bank
J.B. Easley
Abram Past
D.C. Haycroft
Daniel Davis
O.C. Harris
John Cole
W. Watkins
F.A. Wheeler
J. Doroty Jr. /sic/
E.E. Swift
John Eaton
M. Sullivan
F.B. Lansing
J.H. Bard

W.H. McDonald
James McGinnes
J.H. Turk
J.J. Lane
Henry Marshall
R. Stoneham
Martin Burroughs
Mrs.___Burroughs
M. Canney
J. Slaven
Mrs.___Slaven
J. Mannch
J. Gellespi /sic/
B. Johnston
E. Skinney
L.R. Cole
W. McDonald
J.C. Hensakee
F.N. Leonard
Adam Mendall
W. Riley
C. Neahl /sic/
W.M. Palmer
H. Wolf
J. Plymonds
B. Stemburg
J. Bowman
E. Rockfellow
F.A. Chase
Mrs.___Kulman
R. Lausenburger
A. McGill
J. Walch /sic/
J.E. Norton
J. Rock
J. Riglee
F. Sampson
W.G. Barnes
H.C. Benson
H. Johnson
M.D.L. Gaines
J. Rose
W.H. Fredenburg
J.E. Smith
J. Huffmaster
J.R. Power
A. Dodge
M. Dillon
Peter Miller
W. Thompson
H.J. Thompson

R.S. Duff
Peter Seyser
Mrs.___Seyser
Mrs.___Keton
Mary Keton
H. Fountain
P.A. Wolf
H. Wiggett
S. Johnes /sic/
R. Eddis
C. Ashley
J. Bush
A. Edwards
John Cunningham
F. Wilson
J. Stevenson
J. McAlindon
George Kielman (?)
Mic Martin /sic/
H.H. Brundige
A. Blommar (?)
   (Blommer?)
F.M. Worley
G. Roberts
J. Smith
James Murphy
W.F. Stein
J. Black
G. Robinson
A.M. Holloday
Mrs. A. Temmany
Rufus Coolidge
D. Brace
H.G. Brown
M. Lawton
A. Morris
G. Sorewood
M.S. Burdick
H.W. Toucy
D. Finn
J.A. Beard
E. Harris
W.W. Spencer
F. Tribon (?)
   (Trihon?)
J. Carr
W.J. Weed
___Slocum
J.J. Steward
W. Hughes
James Fuller
(Continued next page)

Smith Campbell /sic/
James Smith /sic/
B.J. Mills
Henry___
   (Colored)
J.E. Kane
H. Hand
A. Blair
A. Bannell/sic/
W.H. Ever
H. Banner/sic/
A.J. Peck
J. McConnell
Stifano Brusans
W. Surtger
A. Pe?kley
J. Hillman
Mrs.___Kaseka
Hans Eas /sic/
C. Hunck
R. Johnston
Susan Johnston
Henry Bond
J.G. Blackstock
John Dougall
M.W. Burnett
P. McGee
A. Humphries /sic/
P. Weisenhamer (?)
C. Hender
P.R. Maxon
Thomas A. Shedd
G.W. Jane
L. Bacon
G. Lippett
N. Gilbert
P.K. Moore
W.W. Bardwell
E. Sweetland
B.B. Green
J. Cloque
R. Burnell
A. Barnes
H.M. Faber
S. H?rtapples
D. Osgood
J.T. Hagin
A.S. Grinnell
H. Emery
James Finney
F. Thompson

S. Gamgas	William Myers	M. Gagly
J. Cassani	W.F. Hoffman	B. George
Mrs.____Sweeney and 3 children		

--From San Diego, California:

Peter Gentenes	Capt.____Spinney	Mrs.____Camduff
Mrs.____Eaton and child	F.W. Shattuck	H. Martin
Dr.____Williams, wife and child	Dr. H. Pujas	L. Handford, wife and child /sic/

- - - - - -

SHIP: COLUMBIA
TYPE: Steamer   FROM: Oregon Territory
ARRIVED: April 14, 1852   CAPTAIN: Dow
PASSAGE: 64 hours from the Oregon Territory, via Port Orford,
          Oregon Territory. Departure port in the Oregon Territory
          was Astoria. This vessel brings reports from Queen
          Charlotte's Island confirming the accounts of extensive
          quartz gold mines there, but the discovery is not as val-
          uable as first represented, and the difficulties encount-
          ered in working the mines, from the hostility of the
          Indians and the inhospitable nature of the place, present
          serious obstacles to mining parties.
CARGO: 134 sacks feed, 68 sacks chopped wheat, 5 packages of
          beaver skins, 43 boxes eggs, 18 tins lard, 5 packages of
          butter and 9 boxes unidentified merchandise.

Passengers

J. Wolf	C. Homer	B. Schloss
S. Norris	G.L. Story	C. Foster
J.R. Howard	J. Lovett	W.C. Holman
J. Lockwood	D.D. Loring	E. Guthrie
P.G. Hamilton (?) (P.O. Hamilton?)	M. Farley	Mrs.____Newman
H.H. Francis	Four Sisters of Notre Dame	Mrs.____Stewart and daughter
Q. Dubois (?) (O. Dubois?)	S. Dinsmore	H. Yesler
M. Cunnell	J. Waters and wife	C. Dumal
C. Ames	J. Ashcraft	William Fields
	E.T. Ashcraft	

- - - - - -

SHIP: WILLIAMANTIC
TYPE: Schooner   FROM: Astoria, O.T.
ARRIVED: April 14, 1852   CAPTAIN: Vail
PASSAGE: 8 days from Astoria, Oregon Territory. Experienced heavy
          gales, which carried away part of the bulwarks.
CARGO: 38,503 ft lumber consigned to Jones & Eldridge and 90,000
          ft of lumber consigned to Charles Hopkins.

Passengers

John Miller	N. Lambert	J. Foster
J.W.____		

- - - - - -

SHIP: ISTHMUS
TYPE: Steamer   FROM: Panama
ARRIVED: April 15, 1852   CAPTAIN: Harris
PASSAGE: From Panama, via intermediate ports. Departed Panama on
         March 14, 1852.
CARGO: Not listed.

Passengers

Mr.___Verdier	Mrs.___Walker	E. McLean
___Bonneson	A. Gravenporst /sic/	___Luck
___Myrtle	Mrs.___Russell and	L.F. Boley, lady and
Rev. J.W. Casper,	4 children	son
lady & son	Miss P. Lewis	___Walker
Miss___Casper	Madame___Trouette	H. Pritch
___Callahan	& child	G.D. Philips
H.H. Hicks	Rev. J.W. Kelly,	E.S. Mendels, lady
___McGee and lady	lady, 3 chldrn	& 4 children
D.P. Vail	and servant	S. Reed
Mrs.___Griffin	Mrs.___Callahan	Rev. J.B. Hill
Mrs.___Tichnor and	and 2 children	J. Van Riper and
3 children	___Russell	lady
Mrs.___Williamson	H. Fullam	C. Pippert /sic/
H.O. Preston	P. Parsons	J. White
E. Piper /sic/	J. French	A. Mahoney
S. Hardie	C. Penoyer	W.E. Field
N. Mitchell	W.S. Newman	G.B.R. Wade
A.A. Light	H. Griffith	Z. Bowman
H. Walman	A. Mitchell	L.W. Fee /sic/
H. Hovey	A.H. Colvin	N.H. Lee /sic/
F. Straper	C. Case	J. Hevener
C. Marsh	W.J. Newell	W. Hevener
A.E. Wadhams	P.D. Merriam	W. Sampson
W.S. Sanford	A.D. Merriam	T.E. Morgan
E. Richards	J.H. Hull	J.C. Loville
W.F. Baley /sic/	W.E. Hull	S.H. Sargent
J. Runde	J. Stoops	A. Brown
R. Murphy	W.H. Walcott	E. McCray
E. Brown	C. Potts	E. Platt
O.O. Slayton	D. Bartlett	J. Robinson
E.C. Graff	E. Huyck	J. Fisher
E. Scarborough Jr.	D.K. Bilding	J. Faber /sic/
G.C. Slayton	D.L. Brainard	O. Bevier
J.C. Tabor /sic/	S.L. Brainard	C. Van Arne
M. Clery	A. Sylvester	J.M. Gould
P. Reach	P.W. Baker	W.R. Mitchell
S.S. Gould	J. Kempf	J. Wright
S.J. Worrey	P.M. Medford	D. Walker
H.H. Worrey	C.W. Dotsen	J.R. Henry
R. Jack	B. Curran	G. Bolton
J. Hutchinson	G. Carter	T.S. Parvin
W.F. Hutchinson and	G.D. Sutherland	J.H. Ware
2 servants	N.H. Moson/sic/	H.G. Fiske

(Continued next page)

E. Fiske
R. Waltham
J. Wrede
E. Dunlap
J.G. Austin
D. Cook
C.W. Luck
C. Arvis
___ Dorsey
H. Fiske
H. Saltmach
F. Flaherty
J. Stearns
A. Sprague
J. Tucker
E. Lott
S. Harrington
E.C. Rockwell
E. Thomas
D. Wood
L. Wood
A. Wood
S. Wood
L. Luce
E. Pridly
E. Lathrop
P. Comstock
S. Van Trump
Samuel Van Trump
Jacob Keese
F.H. Bryan
J. McKnighton
S. McKnighton
A. Schumack
Henry Sande
W. Johnston
J.L. Avery and
   12 servants /sic/
A.H. Erwin and
   7 servants /sic/
A.J. McDowell and
   5 servants /sic/
C.A. Young
Mrs.___ Young
J.M. Wood
J.W. Wood
B.F. Bates
L. Martin
Mr.___ Griffin
F. Lallier
F.W. Hood

W. Scott
William Georget (?)
   (Georgei?)
J. Everell
D.L. Bartlett
W. Gordon
A.S. Nichols
A. Lunchback
___ Webster
___ Webster II
T. Derbyshire
B.H. Crowell
H. Hartshorn
J.H. Richmond
H. Kross
P. Glover
P.V. Fox
J. Stevers
G.W. Coteman
J. Young
V. Pinkham
C.E. Curtis
G. Shaw
H. Furry
N. Long
H. Pulver
W. Hilt
S. Uppeck
W. Harper
R.A. Wright/sic/
J. Terry
D. Molody
E. Manley
P. Burkhard
J.C. Evans
J. Henry/sic/ (Henrys?)
William Henrys /sic/
   (Henry?)
M. Winters and
   servant
C. Warlic
L. Baker
James Munroe
M. Bosca and lady
E.L.C. Smith
N. Johnston
S.S. Brick
Daniel Cluffy and
   lady
R. Salter
J.R. Hood
(Continued next page)

J.A. Criswell
M. Limberl
M. Shonholl
D.T. Lufkin
A. Leonard
G. Case
J. Harris
___ Burke
C. Baron
G. Baron
J.L. Weeks
D. Bacon
B. Longly
J.R. Hall
C. Cordes
T. Sampson
E.F. Nitcote
J.B. Condray
L. Smith
H.M. Way
G. Frost
H.A. Carm?n?
   (Carmans?)
W.T. Iron
H. Kewick
L. Bissell
R. Harper
W. Smith
C. Nichols
N.H. Richardson
R. MCabe /sic/
   (R. M'Cabe?,
   R.M. Cabe?)
P.P. Schenck
George Elliott
S. McMurray
W. Murdock
L. Dougall
W. Bright
L. Mostellay
D. Houch
G.W. Dam
M. Seaman
John Lisey and lady
B. Freeman
George Adams
E. Giles
William Cluffy
James Cluffy
D. Lanman
D. Hamilton

James K. Wright
J.M. Chastano
R.A. Wright /sic/
S. Aldridge
J. Conner
L. Thompson
L. Griffith
G.A. Crane
G. Graham
Mrs.___Godfrey
J. Alexander

N.P. Harber
H.F. Richardson
J.M. Perry
L. Mooney
J.M. Thompson
H. McCarty
H. Hurlburt
D. Hurlburt
M. Halsey
E. McLean
L. Pope

J. Jackson
M. Braswell
J. Crane
T. Weaver
G. McCreary
W. Hodgkin
P. Kelly
T. Delaney
J. Durey
R. Berhard
Mrs. M.A. Graham
    and child

--Boarded at Acapulco, Mexico:

P.B. Tompkins
W.H. Sharp
J.H. Furney
Mrs.___Harris
E.G. Cheney
F. Ulrich
D. Van Winkle

J. Bailey
C.H. Morris
Capt.___Cram
Miss___Martin
G.M. Sheridan
Col.___Stephens

E. Pollack
J.C. Stevens
Mr.___Dolds
Capt. S. Moody
P. Van Amburgh
R. Stephens

- - - - - -

SHIP: HURRICANE
TYPE: Clipper   FROM: New York
ARRIVED: April 15, 1852   CAPTAIN: Verry(?)(Very?)
PASSAGE: 120 days from New York, via Rio de Janeiro, Brazil, 61
         days. Passage run from Rio de Janeiro to San Francisco
         made in excellent time. On January 2, 1852, in lat. 17-
         58, experienced a white squall, carried away fore and
         main topmasts, mizzen topgallant mast. Bore up for Rio
         de Janeiro, arrived there on January 28th. Sailed from
         Rio on February 9, 1852. The U.S. Sloop-of-War "St.
         Lawrence", from New York, bound for San Francisco, sailed
         from Rio on February 8, 1852, and the U.S. Sloop-of-War
         "Portsmouth", bound for San Francisco, sailed on February
         7, 1852.
              (The "Hurricane" has the following dimensions: 1697
              tons; length, 227 feet; breadth of beam, 41 feet;
              depth of hold, 26 feet. Her builder was Mr.___
              Smith, of Hoboken, New Jersey).
         Greatest distance by the "Hurricane",during this passage,
         was 400 miles in 24 hours and greatest speed was 18 miles
         per hour.
CARGO: 100 boxes tomato catsup, 25 boxes pie fruit, 895 boxes of
         syrup, 24 boxes coffee mills, 35 boxes tobacco, twine,
         candles, 3 carboys vitriol, spices, cherry brandy, matches,
         4 bbls of ten pins and balls, butter, steel iron, 20 bbls
         crushed sugar, iron, steel, 2 iron safes, 20 kegs shot, 20
         bbls sal soda, hams, 8 iron lamp posts, glassware, gin, 4
         bbls mess pork, 5 iron columns, 1 billiard table, 4 pumps,
         lemon, seeds, oysters, 104 tons coal, pickles, boots and
         shoes, earthenware and assorted goods.

Passengers

Mrs. Harlow and 3 children	Mrs. Gallagher Mr. Hull	Mr. C. Davidson Mr. H. McDonald

- - - - -

SHIP: WYANDOTT
TYPE: Brig   FROM: Hawaii, S.I.
ARRIVED: April 17, 1852   CAPTAIN: West
PASSAGE: 27 days from Hawaii, Sandwich Islands.
CARGO: 228 bbls oil, 620 fowls, 262 turkeys, 50 pigs, 20 bbls of
       sweet potatoes.

Passengers

Capt. Heren	M. Austin	A. Kirchner

and 3 unidentified in steerage

- - - - - -

SHIP: CRESCENT
TYPE: Ship   FROM: New York
ARRIVED: April 18, 1852   CAPTAIN: Forbes
PASSAGE: 140 days from New York.
CARGO: 2 boilers and machinery, 3 couches,, 100 bbls cement, 1
       coach,one wagon, shovels, 4 cases sheet iron, boots, 404
       boxes tin, 5 cases copper, 6 pigs block tin, paper, ale,
       1289 bbls oats, 65 tins hams, 1 case cigars, wine, 312 tons
       coal and assorted goods.

Passengers

D. Hall Pat Brenan	W. Armstrong H. Armstrong Jr. and lady	J. Armstrong G.H. Armstrong H. Rowe

- - - - - -

SHIP: VANDALIA
TYPE: U.S. Sloop-of-War   FROM: Honolulu, S.I.
ARRIVED: April 19, 1852   CAPTAIN: William H. Gardner
                                                        (Gardiner?)
PASSAGE: 18 days from Honolulu, Sandwich Islands, where the vessel
         had been stationed for last five months. Brings intell-
         igence that the great eruption of Mauna Loa has greatly
         abated. News is also brought of the thirty-ninth
         anniversary of the birth of his Majesty Kamehameha III.
         His Majesty reviewed a large number of Hawaiian troops.
         The review was highly satisfactory and reflected great
         credit upon Lieut. Jacob Read, of the"U.S.S. Vandalia",
         who had been indefatigable in his efforts to drill this
         first levy of Hawaiian troops. The drill proved that
         Hawaiians are capable of being disciplined into a
         soldier-like appearance under competent officers.
CARGO: Not listed.
Officers of the "Vandalia":
Lt. Robert E. Johnson   Lt. Reed Warden   Lt. T.Herman Patterson
James C. Palmer(Surgeon)Robert Carter (Assistant Surgeon)

(Continued next page)

John P. Bankhead (Acting Lieut.)	John V.B. Bleecker (Purser)	Walter V. Gillias (Acting Master)
Jacob Read (Lieut. of Marines)	John B. Stewart* H. St. George Hunter* Stephen B. Luce*	A.W. Habersham* Charles H. Cushman** Ottokar Henkel**
Zachary Whitmarsh (Boatswain)	John D. Brandt (Gunner)	Robert M. Bain (Carpenter)
John W. North (Sailmaker)	John Robbins (Captain's Clerk)	John M. Warrington (Purser's Clerk)

(*) Passed Midshipman
(**) Midshipman

- - - - - -

SHIP: DESDEMONA
TYPE: Barque   FROM: Astoria, O.T.
ARRIVED: April 20, 1852   CAPTAIN: Ritchison
PASSAGE: 6 days from Astoria, Oregon Territory.
CARGO: 186,000 feet of lumber.
                        Passenger
                        J.B. Pritot

- - - - - -

SHIP: ZOE
TYPE: Brig   FROM: Honolulu, S.I.
ARRIVED: April 21, 1852   CAPTAIN: Pearsons
PASSAGE: 20 days from Honolulu, Sandwich Islands.
CARGO: 210 casks and barrels of polar oil, 24 barrels of tar and
        pitch, 15 hogs and 1231 packages of unspecified goods.
                        Passengers

L. Swan and lady	Capt. ___ Long, lady and servant	H.O. Weed R.W. Benedick
J.H. Force	W.C. Yarwood Jr.	Capt. A. Rogers
A.R. Arnott	Dr. J.W. Bay	D.M. Weston
A.J. Cartwright	R.S. Bay	W.E. Alny Jr.

                and 5 unidentified in steerage

- - - - - -

SHIP: EMMA PACKER
TYPE: Schooner   FROM: Huanie, Society Is.
ARRIVED: April 21, 1852   CAPTAIN: Buckley
PASSAGE: 34 days from Huanie, Society Islands.
CARGO: 150 oranges, 1000 cocoanuts and 24 hogs.
                        Passengers

P. Techeres	John Meterius	Alve Techeres

- - - - - -

SHIP: PICARD
TYPE: Brig (British)   FROM: Sydney, N.S.W.
ARRIVED: April 21, 1852   CAPTAIN: Bowden
PASSAGE: From Sydney, New South Wales, via Tahiti, and Honolulu
        (26 days from the latter port).

CARGO: 50 hhds Tooth's ale, 10 hhds Taylor's London porter, 10
casks Byass' ale, 367 bars flat iron, 6 bales printed
cottons, 1 case drapery, 1 bale blue shirts, 6 tons coal,
12 kegs honey, 11 gross ginger beer bottles, 15 hhds sugar
house molasses, 44 boxes window-glass, 2 cases quinine, 15
casks fire-proof paint, 9 parrots, 9 cockatoos, 1 case
millinery and assorted goods.

Passengers

S. Tams   Mrs.___Robb and   Miss___Lucas
                           child

- - - - - -

SHIP: J.B. LUNT
TYPE: Brig   FROM: Portland, O.T.
ARRIVED: April 21, 1852   CAPTAIN: Dagget
PASSAGE: 8 days from Portland, Oregon Territory.
CARGO: 6000 bushels potatoes, 138 bushels onions, 100 bushels of
oats and 39 hogs.

Passengers

R.C. Smith   H.D. Clarke   N.B. Powell
Mr.___Jones

- - - - - -

SHIP: ECLIPSE
TYPE: Clipper   FROM: New York
ARRIVED: April 22, 1852   CAPTAIN: Hamilton
PASSAGE: 104 days from New York, via Valparaiso, Chile, 39 days.
Made the run from New York to Valparaiso in 64 days, and
was several days off Cape Horn, in calms and light winds.
Left at Valparaiso the ship "Seaman's Bride", from New
York, bound for San Francisco. It had put in in distress,
with loss of foremast, and would sail in 20 days. The
"Eclipse" had light, baffling winds north of the equator.
Best day's run was 325 miles. The first night out from
New York the jib-boom was carried away.
CARGO: 1 reaping machine, 100 wheelbarrows, 2 spring carts, 6
carts, 89 stoves, 200 pieces of stoves, 16 casks of brass
kettles, 8 wagons, 3 carriages, 4 cases paper hangings, 200
bbls cement, 3 boats, 23 iron posts, 15 boxes tin plates,
1000 bbls flour, iron plate, iron bars, gin, wine and
assorted goods.

Passengers

Capt.___Robertson   Mrs.___Cummings and   ___Hussey and lady
Dr.___Turnbull   3 children   Mrs.___Collins and
Dr.___Crane   Dr.___Thorne   4 children
___Birdsall   ___Morris   ___Tallman
___Fisher   ___Jolly

- - - - - -

SHIP: CHALLENGE
TYPE: Clipper   CAPTAIN: John Land
ARRIVED: April 22, 1852   FROM: Hongkong, China
PASSAGE: 33 days from Hongkong, China. This marks the quickest
passage between the coast of China and North Western
America yet recorded in the annals of modern voyages (as
of April 22, 1852). Departed from Hongkong on March 19,
1852, and the coast of Japan on April 5, 1852, making the
run from the latter country in 17 days. The greatest
distance run by log in 24 hours was 360 knots; and the
greatest progress made in a direct line was 335 knots.
The highest speed attained was 16 knots per hour. The
average log of the whole passage was 10 knots; and the
average on a straight line, 9 knots per hour. Whilst in
the China Sea made the distance between two islands, which
were 42 miles apart, in two hours and a quarter.
CARGO: In ballast.

Passengers
553 Chinese emigrants*
(*) All unidentified, all in good health, no deaths during passage

- - - - - -

SHIP: WHITON
TYPE: Barque   FROM: Sydney, N.S.W.
ARRIVED: April 23, 1852   CAPTAIN: Smith
PASSAGE: 70 days from Sydney, New South Wales. Departed Sydney on
February 13, 1852. This vessel brings intelligence from
the gold fields of the British colonies. Conditions at
the gold fields are anything but favorable. Heavy rains
and floods, disease and crime, are reported to prevail in
almost every mining province. Swollen rivers carry away
works and stored goods and gangs of desperadoes infest
some of the mountainous districts.
CARGO: 250 tons of coal.

Passengers

W. Thurgood	Capt. E. Bond	Capt. C.A. Falken-
Mrs. Thurgood	Miss Fitzgerald	burg
P.R. Blight, lady	Boyden, lady	Riley, lady and
& daughter	& 3 children	3 children

- - - - - -

SHIP: BENJAMIN HOWARD
TYPE: Ship   FROM: Boston, Massachusetts
ARRIVED: April 23, 1852   CAPTAIN: Shrene(?)(Shreve?)
PASSAGE: 120 days from Boston, Massachusetts. On March 16th, in
lat. 23-18S, long 90W, spoke the barque "Alpha", from
Callao, Peru, bound for Liverpool. In the Straits of La
Maire, passed the ship "Mechanics' Own", from New York,
bound for San Francisco.
CARGO: 150 tons ice, 1 ice house, 1 ice wagon, 80 tons coal, 173
bbls charcoal, 68,000 ft lumber, 78 dozen chairs, 235 boxes
preserved meats, 2 carriages, 5 express wagons, 10 boxes of

mattresses, 6 bales gunny bags, 50 dozen pails, 100 boxes of medicine, 50 kegs Stoughton's elixir, 53 boxes oysters, 252 boxes of candles, harness, glassware, furniture and assorted goods.

Passengers

Miss Sophia Moulton	Miss___Johnson	Miss___Newhall
H.J. Johnson and	E. DeLaroy and lady	J. McInsp and lady
lady	F. Nutter	G. Harley
J. Harley		

- - - - - -

SHIP: OHIO
TYPE: Steamer   FROM: San Diego, California
ARRIVED: April 25, 1852   CAPTAIN: Hilliard
PASSAGE: 5 days from San Diego, California. On April 22nd encountered a severe gale of wind off Point Conception. This
vessel brings intelligence that the wharf at San Diego,
new town, has been purchased by the Pacific Mail Steamship Company for ten thousand dollars.
CARGO: Not listed.

Passengers

John Wilson	R. Pacheco	Capt. F. Steele
Miss R. Wilson	A. Weinschunk	M. Torres
Miss J. Wilson	M. Cota	P. De la Guerra
M. Penchard	J. Kays	A.S. Taylor
D.M. Noe	W.R. Stokes	M.D. Bundridge
J. Jackson	A.T. Pierce	J. Pacheco
M. Taluas	J.A. Post	T. Pacheco
T. Whalay	Capt.___Kennedy	W.S. Avis
Capt.___Williamson	M. Monson	W.M. Foster and
Miss___Cummins	J.G. Sichel	lady
Mrs.___Kohler	J.P. Davis, wife	J.P. Jones
J. Luis	and sister	W.H. Graves
J.W. Crawley	W. Sanspall	W. Brown
A. Fontalrosa	R. Jorquna	T. Cardenas
A. Arroya /sic/	J. Vergena	J. Ligorda
(Arraya?)	P. Vendicia	F. Corudo
P. Arraya /sic/	V. Velis	Jose Gallardo
(Arroya?)	T. Velis	T. Martin
A. Achoa	J.C. Velis	C. Rajas
C. Brown	J. Escoba	J. Feliciana

- - - - - -

SHIP: COLONEL FREMONT
TYPE: Brig   FROM: San Pedro, California
ARRIVED: April 26, 1852   CAPTAIN: Erskine
PASSAGE: 11 days from San Pedro, California.
CARGO: 50 bbls sugar and 53 bbls of oranges.

Passengers

J.B. Lynd   A. Nesi

- - - - - -

SHIP: CURLEW
TYPE: Schooner   FROM: Santa Cruz, California
ARRIVED: April 26, 1852   CAPTAIN: Brown
PASSAGE: 48 hours from Santa Cruz, California.
CARGO: 48,000 feet of lumber.

Passengers

J.L. Cooper   A. Trust   D. Kirby
S.S. Cobly

- - - - - -

SHIP: CERES
TYPE: Brig (Dutch)   FROM: Panama
ARRIVED: April 27, 1852   CAPTAIN: Devries
PASSAGE: 63 days from Panama. Following deaths took place during
          the passage:
                March 4, 1852:- H. Turner
                March 6, 1852:- G. Hinton
                March 8, 1852:- J.W. Shelton
                March 9, 1852:- E.L. Shelton
CARGO: In ballast.

Passengers

H. Werner	C. Relingden	W. Kenheer
T. McGuird /sic/	T. Keger	C. McCauley
(McGuire?)	A.T. Duner	J.C. Wright
J. Davis	N.M. McGill	J.M. Danagan
S. Lot	J.M. McGill	L. Levy
W.V. Steward	T.W. Harris	___ Rueff
J. Barman	A.C. Hall	D.A. Dyer
W. Weathering	G. Mead	J. Sherry
E. Burke	R. Mead	D. String
F. Downing	J. Rominger	T. Chumbolles
C.A. Graham	R. Crowing	W. Thersher /sic/
W. Escewner	R.M. Staner	R. Thresher /sic/
T. Simeon	M.M. Frost	E. Shaw
T. Turton /sic/	C. Bear	G. Loth
D. Hauser	W. Stranchter	Charles Dainley
C. Middle	F. Adskins /sic/	W. Williams
T. Werthey	J. Maitoe	M. Pollock
R. Steward	M.W. Sunders /sic/	J. Hope
A. Euger	F. Hudson	J.W. Hope
H.Y. Mars	F.F. Allen	J. Conner
J. Calven	H. Stowell	J. Lundley
James Calven	J. Stops	L. Pumish
R. Brooks	C. Gilliam	J.W. Keves (?)
J. Pand	J. Hull	(Keyes?)
W. McGilvery	W. Hull	W. Bayley
___ Gamlich	J. Kirk	J. Deckerman
E. Palmer	A. Taylor	E. Church
J. Brower	P. Hanson	G.M. Yager
P. Grimen	H. Toy	T. Coil
C. Halland	J. Toy	J. Rugley

(Continued next page)

A. Boyd   G. Conner   T. Cramer

Mrs. S. Mason and   Mrs. C. Umber and
    child   2 children

- - - - - -

SHIP: ELLEN NOYES
TYPE: Barque   FROM: Boston, Massachusetts
ARRIVED: April 27, 1852   CAPTAIN: Lewis
PASSAGE: 178 days from Boston, via Talcahuana, Chile, 60 days.
CARGO: 173 tons coal, 136,000 ft lumber, 50,000 shingles, 500 bbls
       cement, 100 kegs nails, 75 bbls hams, 200 kegs lard, 500
       reams wrapping paper, 100 hf bbls mackarel, 49 cases of
       furniture, 10 cases agricultural tools,19 casks raisins, 15
       casks liquor, 1000 kegs gunpowder, 3 kegs fuse, chocolate
       and assorted goods.

Passengers

J. Auld, lady   S.H. Rounds, lady   W. Bell
   and child   and child   A. Cook

- - - - - -

SHIP: SABRINA
TYPE: Barque (British)   FROM: Auckland, N.S.W.
ARRIVED: April 27, 1852   CAPTAIN: Kemp
PASSAGE: 58 days from Auckland, New South Wales. Left in Auckland
       the schooner "Falmouth", bound for San Francisco in two
       weeks.
CARGO: 3100 boxes potatoes, 1200 baskets and 200 boxes of onions.

Passengers

         P. Levesley   Mrs. Kemp

- - - - - -

SHIP: "ANITA"
TYPE: U.S. Transport Barque   FROM: San Diego, California
ARRIVED: April 28, 1852   CAPTAIN: Not listed
PASSAGE: 8 days from San Diego, California.*
CARGO: U.S. government stores.

Passengers

Lt. Stoneman and   Lt. Frasier and   Troops of Company
  troops of Company   troops of Company   "C", Second
  "A", First Dragoons   "F", Second Infantry   Infantry
(*) The "Anita" proceeded to Benicia, California after arriving
   in San Francisco. Stores and troops were landed at Benicia.

- - - - - -

SHIP: "ACTIVE"
TYPE: U.S. Surveying Steamer   FROM: San Pedro, California
ARRIVED: April 28, 1852   CAPTAIN: Lt. Alden, U.S.N.
PASSAGE: Departed from San Pedro, California on the afternoon of
       April 26, 1852 in consequence of the arrival at that port
       of the steamer "California", which was in distress. The
       "California", under command of Captain Whiting, with
       nearly 500 passengers bound for San Francisco, broke down

on the evening of April 24, 1852, off the Island of Santa
Cruz. Under canvas (sail) the "California" made San Pedro
on the evening of April 25, 1852. The "Active" took on
board the mail agent of the "California", 100 mail bags
from the steamer and the following passengers from the
distressed vessel (see below passenger list).

CARGO: 100 mail bags (from the "California").

Passengers

From the "California":-

Charles Sutton (Mail Agent)

Lt.___Ammen (U.S.N.)
___Jackson (Mid-Shipman,U.S.N.)

Capt. R. Clary (U.S.A.)

Mr.___Gallaer (Collector, of Benicia, Calif.)

Commodore___Sloat, (U.S.N.), Pres. of California Dock & Navy Yard Commission

Mr.___Green (Deputy Collector, San Francisco)

Edward Jones, Esq. (of San Francisco)

Commander___Ogden (U.S.N.)

Lt.___Blunt (U.S. N.)

T. Sanger, Esquire (Engineer to the Commission)

Hall McAllister,Esq.
___Hamilton (Ass't Engineer of the "California"

* * * * * *

The following passengers of the "California" were reported to
be at San Pedro, California, awaiting passage to San Francisco:

G.F. Smith, lady & servant
J. Baxter
J.S. Butrick
Dr.___Brown
E. Martin
Mrs. A. Jenkins
N.C. Hall and lady
W.G. Goodrich
H. Hurd
J.H. Hilands
E. Stone
W. Ryerson
D. Hogeland
A. Fowler
H.A. Vaughan
H. Carter
P.H. Tebbetts
S.W. Ladow
F. Flanegan
C.B. Phillip
R. Sherman
W. Grischen
R.G. Soule
D.J. Davies
J.R. Newton

A. Smith, lady & servant
B. Utter
L.M. Alverson
William Potter
S. Mead
B. Newton
Miss___D'Orsay and servant
J. Miller
O.G. Fowler
H.H. Coleman
C.W. Smith
P.C. Hoff (?) (P.O. Hoff?)
W. Henwood
N. Payne
E. Crowell
R. Macdonald /sic/
R.J. Wager
J. Martin
W. Reed
G.S. Schuyler
Mrs. W.E. Ransted and 2 children (?) (Ranstod?)
J. Kating
(Continued next page)

A.P. Rankin, lady & servant
W.H. Hall
D. Rose
L. Coons
G.N. Norton
Mrs. S.H. Dexter
Miss___Letcher and servant
A. Smyth
H. Smyth
J. Gleeson
V. Faber
J. Campbell
J.F. Bryron /sic/
W.R. Swin
W.F. Coulton
A.E. Coulton
J.W. Spear
P. Duffy
M.E. Estee
H. Brown
T. McCain
G.F. Rogers
W. Sutton
H.O. Soule (?) (H.G. Soule?)

J.H. Greenhart
T. Reading
A. Gray
W. Bartlett
P. Dunnigan
J. Nute
C. Calahan /sic/
J. McCrossen
D.J. Howell
H.B. Arnold
C.R. Stowery
John Taylor
L. Johnson
J. Kidder /sic/
H. Barnes
E. Bigelow
M. Lapoint (?)
  (Lupoint?)
J. Levey
A. Pease
R. Brangon
J. Dupery
F. Muir
S. Haggart
D. Gibbs
E. Gibbs
N.K. Saffer
J. McCarty
J. Nelson
George Allenham
T. Booth
W. Burling and
  lady
W. Patten
A.B. Crane
N. Taylor
Z.W. Keyes
T. Cornell
M. Honnud
H. Darlume
W.R. Parkhurst
J. Lowner
F. Levison
J. Frinkbos (?)
  (Frinkbon (?),
  Frinkbou (?),
  Frinkboa (?)
A. Burrow
W. Ford
R. Braid
G. Giles

Mrs. C. Dugan /sic/
D. Sinclair
W. Catlin
M. McKendrick
J. Kirkade
A. Camburn
D. Thomas
D. Janes
J.W. Baker
Mr.____ Slade, 4
  children & svt
S.D. Jones
J.D. Willcutt
H. Darling
J.J. Sutton
D. Devlin
J.C. Make
L. Pebbell
W. Davis
R. Green
D. Forlie (?)
C. Whitney
W.H. Dennison
G. Lewis
S. Ferguson
G. Feulon
J.E. Thompson
L. Winser
A. Marsh
R. Marsh
J. Smith /sic/
B. Downey
J. Smith /sic/
E.H. Campbell
H.G. Burr
J.L. Sperry
W.B. Hansbrown
J.W. Tongue
J. Hackett and son
H. Redding
T. Ryan
W. Bainhamer
W. Sherla
J. Stounes /sic/
T. Cunningham
J. Kidd /sic/
J.A. Jones
William Jones
J. Murch
R. Allen
(Continued next page)

Mrs. C. Dugan /sic/
Mrs.____ Ripley and
  3 children
P. Kennedy
S. Donahoe
C. McKenzie and
  lady
D. Bostwick
Dan Bostwick
J.W. Holt
S. Twell
William Hays /sic/
S. Willard
J. Brown
S. Hodges
P. Farnsworth
A. Winser
E. Green
P. McKim
M. Burns
W.W. Farnham
P. Carrolane /sic/
L. Smith
C.D. Stearns
J. Hill
J. Reinhart
W. Sadler
J. McCann
W.B. Smith
R.T. McCann
E. Foley
J. Burke
H.M. Thompson
J.A. Brown
Mrs.____ Cook and
  5 children
Miss Amelia Cook
Miss Maria Cook
D. Knight
W. Dudsler
W. Fawcett
L. Greene
T. Billon
F. Scott
J. Scott
W. Fullon
R. Smith
T. Hannell
R. Beard
G. Breed
O. Lewis

J. Wildey
J. Myers /sic/
George Myers
T. Thompson
H.F. Rawson
A.R. Clark
C. Monroe
John Kille and
    lady
Patrick Sexton
J.B. Mackie
H.T. Hewett
F. Citteridge
Thomas Brookes
James Wilson
J.S. Bloom
J.M. Egbert
W.G. Egbert
J.F. Dmith /sic/
    (Smith?)
R. Connelly
W.H. Miller
J. Hartman
P. Blake
G. Stonebrook
W.K. Lament
S.C. May
P. Geiger
D. Flickenger
A. Cook
G.W. Gibbs
F. Lombard
Joseph W. Knox
H. Shepard
J. Gundon
J. Calkins
G. Calkins
A. Everett
D.A. Everett
B. Phelps
    Benlon
Miss Mary Reeves
M.A. Nell, lady and
    2 children
A.P. Vining
S. Bownmaster/sic/

M. Lane
A.S. Schuyle /sic/
G. Loyall
S.S. Loomis
R.S. Loomis
G.H. Moore
J.V. Browne
J. Darling
J.K. Reed
J. Norden
A.P. Cook
S.M. Thompson
W. Morrison
J.B. Schermerhorn
W. Ingraham
A.E. Cox
D.A. Cox
Joseph Sherron
John Sherron
John Pew
C.H. Jardan /sic/
J.J. Morton
J. Bongey
L. Manot
James Willcutt
R. Strong
G.W. Lewis
J.B. Galloup /sic/
L. Rowley
S. Popham
M. Forsham
L. Patterson
J. Myers /sic
J. Walwarth
John S. Baker
N.G. Hewett
J.H. Cook
G. Warner
C. Ladd
G.G. Lumbert
J.C. Pennell, lady
    & 2 children
C.V. Gray and lady
Mrs.___Brown and
    infant
P. Thayer
- - - - - -

B. Ferris
J. Ferris
J. Freelove
C. Freelove
G. Kidder /sic/
J.F. Souther
E. Chunk
T.E. Douglass
A. Chamberlain
L. Gull
G. Geppord
J. Jones
D.A. Townsend
Joseph Jones
J. Faul
F.C. Peters
A.R. Champlin
A. Parsons
J. Rausaey /sic/
M. McCullough
J.R. Lang
John Lawby
W.H. Kuster
A. Wynsted
J.C. Fuller
G. Marsden
S. Johnson
H.P. Burr
L. Buchard
S. Thayer Jr.
A.A. Braman
Richard Geer
H. Crandall
O. Mayew /sic/
H.D. Carpenter
J.H. Keyes
J. Steven
P. Fitzpatrick
T.S. Wheelock
R.H. Belden
Mrs. Sarah Horrell
Miss Rebecca Horrell
Miss Mary J.
    Horrell
S. Hillman

SHIP: WINFIELD SCOTT
TYPE: Steamer   FROM: New York, via Panama
ARRIVED: April 28, 1852   CAPTAIN: Couillard
PASSAGE: Arrived at Panama on April 1, 1852, having made passage
to that port from New York in 66 days, including all
stoppages. Running time, New York to Panama, 48 days and
10 hours-the quickest trip on record. Called at Acapulco,
Mexico, passage time from Panama to Acapulco being 6 days.
Passage time from Acapulco to San Francisco was 8 days.
Passage time from Panama to San Francisco would have been
shorter if the vessel had not experienced head winds and
very heavy weather.

> Officers of the "Winfield Scott:
> Captain: Kenney Couillard
> Engineer: Samuel Perry
> Purser: Edward K. Shed
> Ass't Purser: Walter G. Smith
> Surgeon: John W. Busterd
> First Officer: H.I. Tompkins
> Following deaths took place during the passage:
> April 18, 1852:- Colon Tomb, of Wisconsin, aged
> 63 years, disease remittent fever, conges-
> tion of the brain.
> April 25, 1852:- Mary Dowell, consort of Thomas
> Dowell, of Ohio, aged 30 years, disease was
> dropsy.
> Following birth took place during the passage:
> April 24, 1852:- Rachel Dunn gave birth to a boy.
> He was named Winfield Scott Dunn.

CARGO: Not listed.

Passengers

J. Vandelier	P. Jessie	J. Russell
M. Hallenbeck	B. Watkins	C. Hathaway
J. Stevens	A.W. Burns	Mrs.___ Livingston
___ Clark and lady	___ Cribbs and lady	___ Bee and lady
___ Mains	Miss___ Cribbs	Mrs.___ Williams
M. Mellvaine	J. Finley	F. Knox
J. Maddox and lady	L. Lemon, lady and	Mrs.___ Gurley
___ Culbertson	3 children	M. Spear
Mrs.___ Culbertson	E.D. Lawrence	A.D. Gawtell
E. Jones	E. Kelly	Mrs.___ Fish
Mrs.___ Philips	Mrs.___ Smith	Mrs.___ Fox
J.H. Scranton	J. Martin	D. Dryden
W. Morton	Mrs.___ Miller	Mrs.___ Carter and
Mrs.___ Clark	___ Hunt	4 children
Miss___ Clark	___ Reford	A. Thompson
W. Anderson	M. Carothers /sic/	___ Fielding
S. Caltun	D. Wallace	___ Menser and
___ Sayre	R. Wallace	___ lady
___ Bodaron	___ Ball	___ Abrams
L.D. Wickes	J. Worcester	D.W. Miller

(Continued next page)

C. Martin	Miss___Prior	Miss___Williams
S. Adams	M. Daggett	C.P. Field
C. Powell	B.W. Clark	J. Hon /sic/
J. Williams /sic/	G.M. Works	Miss___Bowstead
O.M. Knapp	M. Virgin	Mrs___Home /sic/
J. Edwards and	B. Lincoln	J.R. Adams
lady	J. Smith /sic/	M. Nicholson
S.A. Pierce	R. Dodson	C. Hill
S. Young	H. Cowan	L. Mence
H. Sorge	W. Tatum	L. Vansickles
S. Horton	A.M. Williams	J. Church
___Scales	A. Bradley	___Peck
C. Griffins	R. McNaught	W.W. Fatin
G. Beck	A. Bliss	S. Bender
L. Shield	A. Wellker /sic/	M. Mood
M. Mould	B. Bordwell	E. Denham
D. Braslin	E. Powers	C. Frazer
H. Strong	N. McMullen	A. Mayer
___McLain	J. Wilcox	W. Gedd
J. Williams /sic/	A. Smith	J. Miller /sic/
E. Thomas	J. Anderson	P. Gleeman
C.H. Tanan	T. Leech	J.K. Hanson
M. Swett	C.H. Bosth /sic/	J. McComy
O.K. Reese	G. Roebaum	W. Guy
R. Robinson	J. Levitt	J. Stonesepper
P. Lynch	M. Fahey	E. Knight
J. Snyder	C. Goldsbro /sic/	P. Furgel
W. Snyder	W. McDonald	P. Shea
J. Lynch	F. Ehler	J. Walker
W. Blancher	C.J. Garden	W.E. Wood
W. Davis	J. Savage	J. Walters /sic/
E. Burke	M. Rodger	C. Walters
Lewis Davis	W. Jackson	J. Walters /sic/
J. Miller /sic/	C. Halsted	Mrs.___Walters
A. Brown	R. Mitchell	P. Drasseur /sic/
L. Brown	L. Lavallette	L. Desereus /sic/
J. Brown	G. Holman	A. Lasseur
M. Hosack	G. Hudibras	J. Holbrook
H. Anderson	S. Timanus	L. Lovejoy
P. Hornbeck	N. Bronson	B. Morrill
J. McGubbin	F. Willets	C.A. Bryant
R. Rooch	Mrs.___Willets	C. McLain
W.D. Kane	P. Mason	A. Vanbrent /sic/
G. Wilson	J. Hillsa /sic/	F. More
H. Horseman	J. Smith /sic/	William Kerr
G. Peterson	N. Brown	J. Hughes
A. Sullivan	M.D. Roussett	A. Babcock
J. Shook	G. Emerson	A. Robertson
H.A. Hines	S. Hauna	J. Dunningan
H. Major	E.W. Prince	W. Thoms /sic/
E. Ellis	W. Slade	O. Dudley

(Continued next page)

J. Barbour
J. Glessuer
F. Francis
J. Rosenbann
L.C. Daniels
C.H. Crippen
   Reiglau
W. Young
M. Keshlan
Mrs.   Bordur /sic/
J.P. Riffet
Martin Auguste
Robert Goudon
M. Kelly
A. Coburg
   South
F. Quigley
L. Doumel
James Dunn
Mrs.   Garrow /sic/
W. Henderson
W. Tinker
D. Davis
T. Frankheimer
   Ellersly /sic/*
Adam Weaver
E. Sawton
P. Kuch
A. Lewis
Charles Rosing
E.B. Green
E.R. Brandon
J. Lyman
D.J. Green
D.S. Buduor /sic/
J. Johns
P. Gringle /sic/
Peter Haffle (?)
   (Haffie?)
T. Burkhard
M. Visaler
S. Wagner
J. Wagner
Jim Wagner
C. Henkle
D. Gray
S. Gowdy
J. Gowdy
H.M. Percival
G. Deterling
W. Winard

W. Mergarden
E. Hart
W. Wentworth
J. Wentworth
W. McCord
C. Fox
F. Wigler
A. Litchfield
Mrs.   Malloy
D. Hahan /sic/
John McLean
John Fulton
D. Osborne
D. Dempsey
W. Launer
S. Knockloft
S. McCoy
John Bagan /sic/
M. Obagan /sic/
John McMullen
John Stille
A. Stille
John Croger
T. Hicky /sic/
E. Pinsey
B.J. Ellery /sic/*
C.L. Hill
P. Dutchman
G.W. Gomarrow /sic/
F.J. Brown
F. Dunbar
A. Whanger
J. Ryan /sic/
J. Jones
W.A. Dublee
G. Gribbs
G. Linerce (?)
   (Lineree?)
Peter Schmit
John Rahirg
William Large
W. Handt
B. Venier
S. Worling
F. Felix
D. Strong
C. Strong
J. Fogarty
L. Gowas
J. Ryan /sic/
M. Ryan

H. Eude
J. Cunningham
B. McBride
W. Cunningham
J. Henderson
   Deisman
   Kungler
J. Kingbaum
B. Eggin /sic/
S. Sheffer
A. Duval
Ezra Foster
J. Pullhumeff
A. Sterne
   Tocsin
E. Handford
John Fitch
George Gavie
John Phalon
Mrs.   Hayes
J. Cuchusag
E. Mackinaw
Jacob Zitter
Nector Ellis
W.H. Hunt
C. Trehan
J.W. Bosque
P. Cemate (?)
   (Comate?)
J.H. Williams
O.R. Butler
F. Hughes
D. Cerf and lady
J. Patten
W.H. Williams
John Fry
P. Gnugle /sic/
Carl Voss
M. Wagner
A. Schender
Antonio Kerr
H. Kaly
John Kaly
J. Martin
S. Fowler
J. Carey
J. Baltimore
J. Allen
W. Ellis
S.S. White
R. Gelling

(Continued next page)

(*)Note similar surnames, "Ellersly" and "Ellery".

John Johnson
P. Vauthorn /sic/
(Vanthorn?)
W.P. Roberts
H. Way
D. Abrams
N.G. Thomas
J.F. Higgins
C.C. Henry
J.B. Hall
N. Valentine
J. Craigh /sic/
Thomas Dowell
Mrs.___Dowell
(died in passage)
C. Currie
J.B. Killian
J. Licomb
W. Greene
D. Ella /sic/
A. Hartsack
W.M. Mitchell
S. Jenness
R. Rapp
J. Good
P. Smith
M. Sayres
E.M. Finch
G. Collins
R. Winslow
J. Allen
T. Dodge
O.S. Rice
C. Chase
W. Malloy
W. Karson
M. Sullinghon
C. Blackburn
R. Round
Mrs. C. Dunn
W. Right
C.W. Moulthrop
A. Moulthrop
W. Willis
R. Lilly /sic/
M. Welsh (?)
(Welch?)
H.M. Grieman
S. Wheelock
W. Wheelock
J.P. Evans

N. Bren
J. Bren
W. Dillingham
George Wilkinson
H. Arrow
W. Monghar
Thomas Kine
J. Leach
L. Lewellyn
W.P. Newell
E. McLaughlin
J. Culbertson
H. Wilkinson
Mrs.___Louise
W. Staples
A. Brown
L. Turlybybee
R. Lilley /sic/
E. Valee
J.B. Brown
C. Shaney
A. Bolton
___Austin
J. Menton
P. Singer
J.H. Pierce
L. Bailey
A.M. Mason
W.G. Hull
D.J. Wright
J. Denning
O. Chase
E.A. Low
J. Billings
S. Hill
S. Brown
H. Rolfe
P.J. Antis
A. Petrie
P. Benjamin
J. Kelly
J. Beckwith
D.L. Conner
H. Crooker /sic/
H. Murray
P. Murray
L. Murray
J. Musgrave
J.D. Wright
H. Locke
A. Jones
(Continued next page)

J. Wallace
T. Watson
Mrs.___Watson
W.A. Moore
R.W. Folks
J. Smith
J. Bannister
J. Crebler
B.Bowell /sic/
Philip Frany
J. Horseman
L. Foley
J. Chatellin
Mrs.___Gellie (?)
(Gallie?,
Gollie?)
H. Crooker
H. Ellis
J. Thompson
A. Ellis
J. Johnson /sic/
Charles Johnson
J. Johnson /sic/
J.G. Freeman
A. Stores
E. Dempthey
D. Bartlett
C. Grant
A.A. Doe
J.E. Fisher
J. Hanfield
D. Kennedy
R. Baw
W. Tender
H. Thayer
H. Daniels
D. Colburg
A. McKennet
M. Weills /sic/
G.L. McKnight
J.P. Israel
J. Bayle
J.B. Lustiff
J. Liscomb
J. Hamilton
S. Callcott
R. Dunn
J. Martih /sic/
(Martin?)
D. Bowman
J. Savage

E. Savage
H. Rice
J. Howard /sic/
M. Higgins
R. Clotz
J.P. Holmes
H. Joseph
Mrs.___ Joseph
M. Lord
A. Bill
J. Laflin (?)
(Lafin?)
J. Hartsup /sic/
R. Hedge
M. Miller
J. Spaniard
Z. Coznac
M. Davis
G. Morse
R. Monk
J. Foster
M. Selighon
D.A. Rodger
N. Kelly
E. Darling
P. Henkum
P. Eckhart
A.P. Sterling
E. Ella
F. Lambert
J. Rollins
C. Swatch
A. Thomas
C. Rutck
G. Wills
C. William
J. Hugh
C. Anthony
N. Monday
J. Miller
J. Champin
A. Ferguson
J. Howard /sic/
G. Smith
J. Dowell
E. Rumick
V. Ruse
H. Crane
L. Benner
D. Weltz
S. Weltz

P. Moulen (?)
(Moulon?,
Moulan?
Moulun?)
J. Myer
D. Dyer
W. Westweather
Mrs.___ Workman
Colon Tomb
(died during
passage)
M. Lyman
J. Scott/sic/
J. Cull
H. Osman
T. Blanchard
M. Murphy
H. Miller
G. Hutton
C. Russell
F. Maccabee /sic/
M. Luvel
W. Gilmore
D. Cummins /sic/
L. Dow
J.M. Ferguson
A. White
J. Kingsley
W. Lamont
J. Frickett
L. Goodhue
J. Campbell
C. Taylor
W. Fanike
James Fair
H. Dumfrees (?)
(Dumfress?)
S. Simmons
J. Marks
J. Smith
J. Heddley /sic/
C. Wedgwood
Ch. Jones
(Charles Stone?)
D. Robbins
V. Hila /sic/
S. Morgan
J. Gibson
E. Sprague
S. Benner
A. Holmes
(Continued next page)

C. Grimes
J. Casey
E. Blamont
M. Hopkins
S. Freeman
J. Fenner
John Smith
James Smith
A. Nelson
J.H. Patrick
J.H. Wilson
P. Lyon
J. Porter
J. Sickle
Pat Villon
J. Coster
M. Jennings
J. Stephens
J.B. Irwin
J. Brand
T. Graft
S. Stedman
N. Knapp
Z. Mitchell
P. Durkee
J. Frost
L. Lifkin
J. Scott /sic/
T. Kennedy
G. Penwan
F. Myer
A.B. Jump
J. Thorn
M. Green
J. Dress
James Maker
J. Shaw
J. Mathew /sic/
C. Snell
J. Welch
J.P. Crall
A. Sherbourne
E. Brackett
M. Hines
William Caffan
D.T. Hobet /sic/
J. Tagert
A. Wilde
J.B. Close
C.B. Stone
H. Flanders

A. Sabine
M. Rose
G. Smith
L. Wilsey
E. Tompkins
A. Bemis
J. Middleton
John Billings
B. Hurd
A. Cole
J. Edington
H. Scales
J. Foleat (?)
  (Folest?)
J.S. McNeil
E. W?lma?th
  (Wilmarth?)
R. Gelmore /sic/
J. Monteray
J. Bloomfield
S.M. Whiting
J.T. Cross
P. Dlaly /sic/ and
  lady (Daly?)
P. Morton
J.S. Barber and son

J.E. Somely (?)
  (J.E. Semely?,
J.B. Somely?,
J.B. Semely?)
W. Gilsy
C.H. Everett
C.H. Bresia (?)
E. Virgin
A. Rose
J. Hermon /sic/
W. Loring
P. Pisser
M. Holt
W. Ford /sic/
E. Baw
R.A. Sayles
J. Baw
J.C. Sadue
E. Kines
E.W. Slater
J. Fair
J.S. Messman
P. Cazadon (?) and
  lady (Cazaden?)
J. Cain
J. Parmenton

Rob Robinson
  (Robert Robinson?)
W. Grealing
A. Britain
W. Ford /sic/
W.R. Anna
C.B. Comstock
S. Stone
George Martin
A. Beavy
S.N. Gumsy
L. Guildheimer
L. Sinclair
J. Chapman
E. Brigham
J. Kenney
J. Macklin
J. H. Allen
H. Close
J.C. Murphy
D.M. Murphy
John Cain
M. Delany
P. Martin
P. Shaw

- - - - - -

SHIP: JOHN DUNLAP
TYPE: Schooner   FROM: Acapulco, Mexico
ARRIVED: April 28, 1852   CAPTAIN: Ellis
PASSAGE: 36 days from Acapulco, Mexico.
CARGO: In ballast.

Passengers

Benjamin Weeks
C. McKenzie
S.G. Lewis
C. Elliott
H. Butler
George W. McElrath
W. Kirkpatrick
A. Fox
John H. Dickinson
H. Pearce
J. Baskeen
J. Rogers
W. Baskeen
J. Barrett

James M. Neal
Judson de Golia
J.A. Hudnol
W. Bennett
G.S. Norris
H.E. Ranison
Alex Vance
W.B. Philips
W.F. Norcross
W. Barrett
R. Holman
J. Reynolds
R. Stevens
T. Jobb

P. Waddington
F. Smith
John O'Donnell
W. Heath
C. Straight
Z. Straight
J.W. Hunter
L.D. Perney
W.P. Hendrickson
M. Harris
S. Thomas
J. Evans
H. James

- - - - - -

SHIP: DOROTHEA ERNESTINE (also listed as DOROTHEA EANESTIN)
TYPE: Brig (German)   FROM: Panama
ARRIVED: April 28, 1852   CAPTAIN: Main
PASSAGE: 64 days from Panama.
CARGO: In ballast.

Passengers

C.A. Martin	T.N. Canfield	T. Ryan, lady and
J.H. Vinnan, lady	W.M. Livingston	3 children
& 5 children	E. Cowles	E. Howell
W. Barnes	W. Vance	S. Howell
G. Gray	N.H. Osborne	G. Jellet
L. Carver	E. Swain	M.C. Canfield
D. Gorman	R. Jones	C.L. Canfield
J. Caruthers	E. Cutter	H. Evans
S. Marshall	J. Nesbitt	J. Dodd
C. Kelly	A. Gardner	E. Woodruig /sic/
J. Gerrard	J. Miller	(Woodring?)
P. Welsh	J. Bradly /sic/	J. Mead
J. Scherlock	J.M. Sanborne	A. Raymond
D. White	J. Brier	G. Raymond
W.A. Townsend	H.M. Hulbert	

- - - - - -

SHIP: MALOUIN
TYPE: Ship (French)   FROM: Havre, France
ARRIVED: April 28, 1852   CAPTAIN: Danuel
PASSAGE: 180 days from Havre, France, via Rio de Janeiro, Brazil,
         120 days.
CARGO: 60M bricks, 1 case books, 25 pkgs cotton, 100 cases of
       champagne, 5 wheels, 2 axles, 100 baskets of champagne,
       200 cases of wine, 733 quicksilver bottles and 1500 cases
       of red and white wines. Several packages of unidentified
       merchandise.

Passengers

Mr.____Lontance
and 78 unidentified in steerage

- - - - - -

SHIP: FREDERICK VII
TYPE: Ship (Dutch)*   FROM: Hamburg, Germany
ARRIVED: April 28, 1852   CAPTAIN: Boysen
PASSAGE: From Hamburg, Germany, via Rio de Janeiro, Brazil and
         Valparaiso, Chile. Fifty-two days from the latter port.
         Anchored off North Beach in San Francisco.
CARGO: Vinegar, oats, tobacco, segars, woolen goods, bottled beer,
       sperm candles, pipes, sherry cordial, books, pearl buttons,
       10,220 bars iron, 12 iron barrows, 5 iron safes, wine, gin
       and assorted goods.

Passengers

Mr.____Sontag, lady, family and   Mr.____Hogle
    servant
  (*) One contemporary source states the "Frederick VII" was a
      Danish vessel.

SHIP: COURSER
TYPE: Ship   FROM: Boston, Massachusetts
ARRIVED: April 28, 1852   CAPTAIN: W. Cole
PASSAGE: 108 days from Boston, Massachusetts.
CARGO: 1700 bbls flour, 3614 bags barley and oats, 5 crates earthen-
       ware, 189 boxes oysters, 500 kegs nails, 45 tons pig iron,
       47 sheets iron, 60 cases borax, 6 pigs tin, 26 boxes tin,
       75 rakes, 20 casks soda, 1051 boxes soap, 150 tons coal,
       2 coaches, 3 wagons, 73 bundles clapboards, 25,000 ft plank,
       114,000 ft lumber, 15 casks lignum-vitae, 1 pianoforte, 10
       bells, apples, coffee and assorted goods.

Passengers

Mrs. W. Cole (wife of the ship captain) and two children	S. Hooper W. Amory	L.L. Thorndike ____Mellen and lady

- - - - - -

SHIP: BLONDE
TYPE: Barque (British)   FROM: Panama
ARRIVED: April 29, 1852   CAPTAIN: Soutter
PASSAGE: 67 days from Panama. The following deaths took place
         during the passage:
             February 23, 1852:- Dennis Racer, of Delaware County,
                 Indiana
             February 23, 1852:- Thomas Pearson, of Nova Scotia
             March 1, 1852:- Charles Dazotell
             March 2, 1852:- Gurley Russell, of Monroe County, Ohio
             March 3, 1852:- Parcus E. Shelden
             March 4, 1852:- Evelin J. Randall, Greenboro, Vermont
             March 4, 1852:- J.S. Tompkins, Cayuga County, N.Y.
             March 8, 1852:- Francis Pargman, New York City
             March 9, 1852:- George W. Meade, Belmont County, Ohio
             March 13, 1852:- Orlando J. Mitchell, Delhi, N.Y.
             March 13, 1852:- James H. Houston, Philadelphia, Pa.
             March 16, 1852:- Soren P. Fairman, Albany, N.Y.
             March 18, 1852:- Henry Hagadon, East Palmyra, N.Y.
             March 22, 1852:- C.B. Morton, Augusta, Maine
             March 24, 1852:- Cornelius Neal, Wheeling, Virginia
             March 29, 1852:- Charles P. Bartleson, Will County,
                 Illinois
             March 31, 1852:- Ambrose Jagger, Wayne County, N.Y.
             April 2, 1852:- William M. Cooper, Fountain County,
                 Indiana
CARGO: 500 tons of coal.

Passengers

A. Hendricks	David Kennedy	W.T. Hungerford
J.S. Tompkins	W.A. Scott	J.B. Sugee
R. McGinigans /sic/	H.E. Burlew /sic/	C. Dozotell*
W. Depuy	W. Mason	M. Fleming
M. Prow	D. Monroe	O.W. Doolittle

(Continued next page)

(*) Listed as "Charles Dazotell" under deaths.

174

S. Allen
James S. Roberts
J.M. Gaston
J. Early
_____ Beach
James Wright
W.R. Parkhurst
D. Barrkan /sic/
A. Barrkan /sic/
J. Gibson
S.B. Shabber
R. Tiblett/sic/
James M. Coombs
A.C. Handon
Gilbert Smith
G.M. Philips /sic/
J.D. Hoff
J. Carlisle
J.W. Clark
Charles Bonnemort
J. Younce Sr.
J. Younce Jr.
W. Holdren
W.J. Jewett
J.M. Jewett
D. Fitzgerald
S.G. Davis
S.F. Rody
A. Kelgore
G.C. Dockunn
D.J. Cheavey
C. Kraws
T. Bates
E. Knight
J. Jones
C. Morris
J. Winemiller
G. Hendricks
J.S. Tompkins/sic/*
    (died)
N. Mason
F. Galehouse
A. Carduff
J. Selleck
P. Teimley
C. Hunter
D. Wellard
S. Sailsbury
M. Curtin
W. Mein
J. Kennedy

John Chapen/sic/
J. McCauley
E.J. Howard
John M. Murren
G. Griffin
Joseph Mann
A. Farnham
J. Losey
G.S. Alford
James Short
M.J. Bennett
A.C. Holloday
G. Wadleigh
James Sprow
Isaac Baldwin
Patrick Tierney
James Pempler
J.H. Gamble
James Boaker
John McManus
S.B. Harrison
J. Cornett
D. Racer
R. Racer
N.W. Busarde
A. Saw
J. Saw
Joseph Wyman
J.B. Winckley
D.D. Reynolds
M. Simmons
A.J. Edwards
D.A. Hammond
W. Buckner
E. Shipman
S. Graham
John C. Rose
D. Kennedy
W.A. Scott*
R. McGinnigan/sic/*
J. Chapin /sic/
W. Turner
J.A. Swart
John S. Little
J. Gorman
C. Chaffee
Joseph Widdowson
T. Failey
R.S. Friend
E. Vanryper
M. Donahoe

James R. Porter
George Burke
J. Baker
D.M. Gates
John Smith
J. Bantz
E. B. Blowers
W. Day
Charles Wickham
N. Goddard
A. Scott
A. Hinckley
Samuel P. Thompson
A. Baldwih /sic/
    (Baldwin?)
W.J. Franklin
R. Osborne
W.G. Andrews
George M. Bacon
J.W. Call
A. Semmett
R.S. Ward
S. Slusher
G. Deltling
S.S. Hardy
H.S. McVicker
Henry C. Robey
H. Haggadon
Ambrose Jagger
    (died)
A. Filbrich
J. Ticknor
W. Nicewonger
J. Kent
G. Russell
A. Hasket
W. Huff
W.T. Hungerford*
Robert Wilson
H.E. Burlew /sic/*
R. Cuyler
James McCorkhill
R. Vanbergen
A.J. Brand
J. Long
J. Knowlton
D. Houk
J. Sloan
A. Hadley
George Proctor
O.J. Mitchell

(Continued next page)

(*) Names repeated twice in passenger list by original source.

J. Stacy	F. Pargman (died)	J. Kipp
W.H. Parker	J.C. Tibetts /sic/	M.H. Vhitney /sic/
D. Campon	Thomas Clerk /sic/	(Whitney?)
A.A. Campon	J.W. McCall	R. Watson
W. Rowell	Soren P. Fairman	D.S. Watson
T. Rowell	(died)	G. Hovey
E. Barnwell	J. Lewis	J.H. Houston
R. Hill	___Boljer and	J.A. Cunningham
Charles Fisher	lady	B.D. Burnheart
F. Cripp	H. Cummings	G.B. Hoyt
N.D. Fray	W. Greenwood	E. Woodworth
E. Vaughan	A. Sibley	J. Bingham
G. Gale	E.S. Harter	J.D. Gistroute
J. Gale	C. Cooper	A. Cook
S. Metcalfe	B. Philips /sic/	Thomas McAndrews
T.H. Burns	M. Orr	R.L. Williamson
J.L. Morgan	W. Biscit and lady	P. Whalen
___Mayres	W.E. Doane	J. Murray
J. Clement	D. Doane	G. Ray
J. Taylor	J. Mitchell	A.M. Mabie
L. Keith	L. Wachtenjusen	A. Murray
W. Fulton	J.L. Gillespie	J.L. Lathrop
T. Trefy	Pat Maley	C.A. McIntire
H.M. Heuston	L. Pinnes	B. Swartz
J.S. Frazier	J. Osborne	E. Irwin
F. Riddle	A.M. Osborne	R. Craham /sic/
E. Jones	E.M. Targo	(Graham?)
W.H. Powell	A. McConnell	J. Sylvester
L. Davis	D. Hutchins	T.G. Gifford
H.W. Larrabee	T. Courts	T.M. Wilby
G. Corsod	J. Scott	J. Emblem
A. Walker	C.G. Craft	G.M. Graham
J. Lowery	C.S. Goddard	P. Taine /sic/
H.B. Taylor	J.C. Whitehouse	T.C. Hoyt
J.H. Palmer	W. Hawes	A. Morton
A.E. Slokum	G.O. Wheeler	S.P. Randall
J.T. Palmes /sic/	J. McClure	W. Dow
W.G. Standish	J.M. Sweeney	A. Douglass
D.F. Osborne	J.B. Stringham	J. Lacy
W. Scott	G. King	S.F. Armstrong
R.M. White	J. Grier	T. Edwards
R. Mitchell	A. Campbell	D. Edwards
J. Thompson	R. Thompson	

- - - - - -

SHIP: NEW ORLEANS
TYPE: Steamer   FROM: Panama
ARRIVED: April 30, 1852   CAPTAIN: ?
PASSAGE: 19 days from Panama, via Acapulco, Mexico and San Diego,
California. On April 23, 1852, Nathaniel Kendrick Ray-
mond, son of I.W. Raymond, Esq, of San Francisco, died
during the passage. Deceased was aged 4 years and 5

months.

CARGO: Not listed.

Passengers

Mrs. J.W. Raymond, 3 children & servant /sic/
H.G. Hanks /sic/
S. Caw
M. Caw and servant
Mrs.___ Graham and child
H.G. Hanks /sic/
Miss___ Arbuckle
Mrs.___ Foster and child
Mrs. J. Newby
R.M. Moore
Rufus Hitchcook /sic/ (Hitchcock?)
A. Donaldson
J.J. McEwen
John Anderson
J.O. White
J.B. Stevens
C.D. Davenport
T.A. Gardnee /sic/ (Gardner?)
W. Davis
D. Comstock
J.R. Stewart
S. Ewings /sic/
W. Ewings /sic/
S. Ewing /sic/
E. Kimball
H.G. Graham/sic/
B. Deawitt /sic/
J.W. Kelsey
A.A. Lindskoy /sic/
J.E. Stover
William Stoon
H.A. Peck
A. Davidson
H.C. Nichols
G.H. Brown
Samuel Hustice
J.L. Brown
G.W. Coffee and lady
T.A. Warbass, lady and child
Mrs. C.B. Benjamin

Mrs. J.B. Leonard
J.O. Seymour, lady and child
W. Merton/sic/
Mrs. C. Dubo
Mrs.___ Warren
Mrs. J. Hall
R.R. Carrington
Mrs. L.B. Lathrop
Mrs.___ Oorham /sic/
G. Quimby
E. Hopkins
A. Thompson
Col. P.B.W. Stockton, lady and son
Levi Estis
J.J. Laring
J. Carothers and friend
S.B. Gray
S.W. Crittenden
D.H. Dryden
J. Smith
W. Brownet /sic/ (Browner?)
A.A. Williams
P. Flanagan
H. Warson
G.C. Hutchinson
H. Linch
W. Hull
J. Newsham
William Clements
W.T. Willis
W.W. Wolfenburger
P. Wolfenburger
W.P. Gordon
G.P. Hunt
A.H. Randall
F.R. West
P.Q. West
T.R. Higgins
Mrs.___ Row (?) and 2 children (Rew?)
C. Tarbox
A.G. Tarbox
Mrs. G.P. Hunt
(Continued next page)

___ Adams, lady, 3 children and servant
J.A. Martin
Mrs. M. Bartwell and child
W.W. Starr
L.H. Lechtensteim, lady, child and servant
A. Frierson
T.J. Davenport
Mrs. D.F. Mourton/sic/
J.H. Lappens and lady
Charles Weller
D.S. Stimpson
J. Merrill
P. Braister
Mrs. J. Gammon
D. Stearns
A. Stearns
J. Fellett
P. Ewett
R. Whitney
___ Ridgeway
W.E. Parker
L. Burrs
J. Lovell
D. Sargent
M. Butts
B.B. Gage
M.P. Warren
John T. Patrick
J. Steffe
J. Johnston
R. Mitchell
J.A. Humphraville
J. Lintefield
H. McCranken
M.V. Ream
J. Bailey
Mrs. S. Eaton
A.P. Tompkins and lady
N. Loring
E.C. Bronson
A. Bronson

Mrs. W.K. Benjamin
T.A. Gardener /sic/
D.C. Alden
N. Martin
William H. Lang
John F. Lang
C.F. Cutter
S. Hull
O. McMahon
D. Dregg
J. Akin
T. Rollins
C.D. Deitch
W. Wi?khouse
(Wilkhouse?
Wickhouse?)
H. Stephens /sic/
H.S. Stevens /sic/
A.M. Nichols/sic/
N.M. Plower
J.L. Miller
B. Hurricane
M. Bulia
D. Bulia
J.T. Adams
C. Pattersen /sic/
Z. Pinkum /sic/
W.H. Campbell
J. Stephens /sic/
T. Nichol /sic/
J. Baker
W. Kibbe
F. Daggett
James Hunt
M. Moore
C. Tellen
W.F. Blumheard
W. Musson
H.B. Young
W.S. Low
W. Morgan
Isaac Williams
Josiah Williams
H. Lewis
Thomas McMullen
J.J. Hallock
J.H. Fowler
M. McGuin
D. Slain
F.C. Tyler
C.H. Ward

Mrs. ___ Humphraville
J.A. Clark
J.C. Stone
R. Day
F. Hosely
B.F. Gardner /sic/
F.M. Munson
G.S. Ennis
G. Ennis
W.S. Snow
B. Wilfull
D. Trask
D. Midger
W. Ingham
J. Cleret
C. Cleret
J. Kelley
J. Dowerson
B. Dimond
A. Dresser
J. Comstock
T. Hunt
J. Norton
J. McLaughlin
H. McLaughlin
F. Dodge
W. Adams
G. Adams
T.A. Goodall
Levi Newcomb
Theodore Smith
T. Driscoll
M. Driscoll
G.W. Briggs
A. Casey
M.M. Newcomb
W.W. Williams
H.B. Green
W. Denman
B. Murphy
J.A.S. Benedict
Thomas Bell
John Jones
James Sutcliff
C.E. Brownel /sic/
John Colbert
J.A. Chattendon
M. Coffes /sic/
(Coffee?)
S.R. Pearce
Richard Robinson
(Continued next page)

S.E. Alden
E.C. Thompson
E. Thompson
A.W. Parke
D. Munson
E.H. Shepherd
B. Wiswell
G. Nutlen
P. Cannaghan /sic/
M. Canaghan /sic/
W.P. Griffin
G.S. Cummings
G.W. Ingersoll
J. Webb
S. Lawyer
Charles Caney /sic/
H. Dargarty
G.S. Terry
J. Canen/sic/
C.E. Evens /sic/
F. Bennett
T. Bennett
R.J. Skidmore
J. Teylor /sic/
(Taylor?)
T.K. Willson
M. Hall
W. Hall
R. Snowden
P. Jones
E. French
A. Haverill
L. Buckland
P. Simmons
W. Dunning
E.L. Simmons
H. Hotchkiss
James Lathrop
A.H. Lathrop
Alden Lewis
Samuel Fainley
Thomas Culberson
/sic/
William Todd
J.H. Murphy
C. Denton
A. Davidson
J. Ranistive
C.F. Beard
S. Gleason
C. Belknap

A. Richardson
C. Myrick
L. Newton
H. Chandler
Albur Earl
M. Dixon
M. Townsend
L. Jenkins
B.F. Haight
B. Harding
S. Remorat
A. Linsey
W. Bond
John Bond
John Schembly
J. Ruffell
J.H. Wright
P. Huchings /sic/
     (Hutchings?)
J.L. Burr
G.F. Bagley
Squire Gorham
W.H. Haskins
J.H. Wilson
George Lyon
O.G. McDonald
T.B. Reynolds
J. Kiltby
L. Osborne
W. Berrey /sic/
R. Dunkerton
J.K.H. Lindsonan
Thomas Gilbert
G.W. Chase
James Gaddis
George Harman /sic/
E. Harmon /sic/
W. Munson
J. Halleran
H. Lund
B.H. Green
W.H. Green
W.O. Burley
J.K. Dickinson
J. Waugh and son
James Waugh
John Waugh
J.R. Roxbury
H. Part /sic/
     (Hart?)
E.J. Hart /sic/

M.P. Harrington
D.F. Warner
J. Clark
George Carpenter
P. Aba
R. Brighten
J. Lee
H. Lee
John Wilsey
George Bemdage
R. Bemdage
Thomas Chisholm
A. McIntosh
J. McMullen
B. Erwin
J.W. Lemee
W.J. Plummer
W.H. Smith
A.C.P. Manchester
J.M. Stockwood
William Sweed /sic/
     (Sweet?)
S.C. Little
J.F. Swain
George Reynolds
J. Ottengen
E. Harlow
L. Toussereindot
Daniel Clevland /sic/
     (Cleveland?)
James Sellers
Henry Gardner /sic/
A.H. Harrison
J. Wiveley
E.P. Bates
D.W. Severny
W.W. Cadis
Jere Phoulkan
W. Cullan
J. Betson
D.D. Stanton
R. McDougal /sic/
S.S. Clark
R.C. Rollins
B. Oliver
P. Reed
J.E. Whitford
A.L. Johnson
N. Chenery
H.T. Blakesly
F. Smith
(Continued next page)

W. Crandall
H.N. Hill
J. Bosworth
G. Crandall
W. Davis
J.A. Huddock /sic/
     (Haddook?)
S. Haddook /sic/
     (Huddock?)
J. Towsend
W. Van Gorden
M.W. Cole
Robert Hewitt
B.B. Williams
M. Vicker
J.H. Little
Henry Adams
J.L. Adams
William Reed
George W. Fisk
N. Latimer
John Hannox
R.H. Piper
G.W. Haskins
J.C. Hinkley
J. Garring
John Smith
W. Headly
Eli Knapp
W.H. Scott
G. Dorry
P.G. Gatch
A.H. Harman /sic/
M. Harman /sic/
Charles Cox
J.M. Cox
C.A. McThetis
M.O. Cornell
J.A. Butterfield
W.J. Cunningham
H. Bachus
G. Gardiner /sic/
C.S. Alis
J. Gammon
James Gammon
G.W. Munroe
C.E. Stowe
D. Daghert
R.M. Colburn
D.S. Miller
_____ Wright

L. Barker
W.H. Maine
J.D. Sheperd
F. Brown
L. Greely
H.C. Leavitt
F.B. Little
J.P. Plumer
H. Carvil
R.M. Draper
C.H. Chapin
P.R. Binon
D. Bush
A.H. Goodstein
A. Donaldson
W. Pierce
J. Dodge
D. Munn
A. Munn
J. Wise
R.B. Wilson
E. Beihl
J.B. Bayley /sic/
W. Hall
A.G. Ramsey
N. Snyder
H. Ea?ling
  (Earling?,
  Easling?)

R.W. Bailey /sic/
R.W. Bailey /sic/
W. Spring
J. Hunter
J.M. Pratt
J.H. Loring
A.J. Harris
F. Wells
R. Vinal
A. Bowie
S. Badger
P. Warfield
F. Barton
L.B. Lathrop
E.T. Mulford
A. Mayer
W. Irwine /sic/
J. Orr
James Orr
L. Orr
J. Ragy
T. Carr
W.A. Culow
G.W. Bartholomew
H.S. Bartholomew
H. Dibson
J. Brower
J. Springer

_____ Wright
H.S. Ricker
A.W. Cole
J. Smith
T. Francis
J. Ham
W. Thompson
S. Eaton
C.A. Swift
A. Swift
W.F. Swindley
J. Newberry
G.H. Woodward
A.F. Foster
A.R. Biggs
T. Biggs
N. Kurtz
J. Kurtz
O. Duck
A. Fuller
C. Merrill
H. Cahone
H. Binon
L. Norton
D. Hadley
B.F. Stone
H.G. Graham /sic/
O. Neskins

and 17 others, names unknown

- - - - - -

SHIP: COLUMBIA
TYPE: Steamer   FROM: Oregon Territory
ARRIVED: April 30, 1852   CAPTAIN: William L. Dall
PASSAGE: 4 days from the Oregon Territory. This vessel brings
         intelligence that rich gold discoveries are said to have
         been made on DeShute's River. Vessel departed from
         Astoria, Oregon Territory on April 26, 1852. Experienced
         a constant succession of strong southerly winds since
         leaving the bar.
CARGO: 1081 sacks potatoes, 22 packages butter, 66 boxes of eggs,
       15 coops of chickens and 23 packages unidentifed goods.

Passengers

F.M. Warren
A. Beeser
D. Flannery
B. Biglow
C.W. Bradley
B.P. Anderson
J.W. Medley

J.S. Sherman
H. Clark
H. Failing
E.L. Finch
J.B. Allen
G.B. Knowles
G. McCarty
(Continued next page)

T. Lowe
James Chambers
J.B. Goddard
T. Reese
N.S. Abernethy
William H. Taber
N.P. Rust

T. Bouton	J. Dukes	W.R. Smith and wife
R.L. Daniel	William Foster	J. Smith
W. Snow	G. Vezey	A.W. Herrick

- - - - - -

SHIP: CLARITA
TYPE: Brig (Mexican)　　　　　　FROM: Acapulco, Mexico
ARRIVED: May 1, 1852　　　　　　CAPTAIN: Holmes
PASSAGE: 31 days from Acapulco, Mexico. *
CARGO: 2 bundles of saddles and bridles and 27 boxes and bales of
　　　　unspecified merchandise.

Passengers

Mrs. J. Dolby	E. Jones	C. Ho?t
Miss A. Dolby	S.F. Mathers	C. Alden
G.H. Moon	J.N. Smith	Mr.___McIntire
W.R. Rober	J. Balstein	P. Jeeks
Mrs.___Gonzales and	N.L. Munroe	Mrs. G. Herron
3 children	A. Jones	G.N. Carson
R.A. Baxter	J. Iram	E. Castilla
R.N. Haser	C.A. Everett	J. Hameron (?)
S. Berry	C.W. Herd	(Hameran?)
M. Mintfort	G. Ryes	J. Longford
G.A. Fairchild	A. Schesell	J. Giorge /sic/
Mr.___McHenry	C. Gray	G.W. Miles
P. Piesch (?)	D. Ryes	J. Stevens
(Piasch?)	M. Yonder	M. McMahon
P. Beard	B. Badran	A.W. Norton
A. Greer	J. Hinckley	A. Calwell /sic/
J. Berrer	F.E. Frank	L. Chusen
H. Mead	H.F. Hasbourne	W.P. Baker
S. Finch	C. Resey	W.H. Baker
F. Ward	J. Starr	W. Fulton

- - - - - -

SHIP: GEORGE WASHINGTON
TYPE: Schooner　　　　　　　　　FROM: Honolulu, S.I.
ARRIVED: May 1, 1852　　　　　　CAPTAIN: Cary
PASSAGE: 20 days from Honolulu, Sandwich Islands.
CARGO: 5200 gallons of sperm oil and unidentified sundries.

Passengers

Mrs.___Delancy and	Mr.___Statenhorst	W.E. Bright
3 children	Capt. W.F. Crowell	J. Ramsay
A. Coffin	C.E. Delover	J. Gootry

and 5 unidentified Chinamen

- - - - - -

SHIP: JOHN M. MAYO (also listed as J.M. MAYO):
TYPE: Ship　　　　　　　　　　　FROM: New York
ARRIVED: May 1, 1852　　　　　　CAPTAIN: Reed
PASSAGE: 138 days from New York.
CARGO: 100 bales oakum, 150 dozen pails, 100 tins crackers, 200
　　　　dozen brooms, 120 casks oats, 55 firkins butter, 31 reels
(*)On board are a number of passengers from the wrecked "North
　　America".

of lead pipe, 40 boxes tine plates, 10 cases of copper, 889 cases red wine, 961 bbls flour, 109 M ft lumber 441 tons of coal and assorted goods.

Passengers

Mr.___Foster and son   Miss___Foster   Miss___Foster
                              Miss___Foster

- - - - - -

SHIP: GEORGE EMORY
TYPE: Brig   FROM: Port Steilacoom, W.T.
ARRIVED: May 1, 1852   CAPTAIN: Wilson
PASSAGE: 16 days from Port Steilacoom, Puget's Sound, Washington
         Territory.
CARGO: 9000 ft piles, 45,000 lbs potatoes, 300 lbs of feathers and
       90,000 shingles.

Passenger
Cyrus Palmer

- - - - -

SHIP: SATELLITE
TYPE: Ship (British)   FROM: Valparaiso, Chile
ARRIVED: May 2, 1852   CAPTAIN: Markham
PASSAGE: 53 days from Valparaiso, Chile.
CARGO: 680 tons coal, 100 boxes tin, 4198 bags barley and 277 pkgs
       of unidentified merchandise.

Passengers

Mrs.___Cole and son   Miss___Simpson   10 unidentifed in
                                                steerage

- - - - - -

SHIP: CAPE BRETON
TYPE: Barque (British)   FROM: San Antonio, Chile
ARRIVED: May 2, 1852   CAPTAIN: Reed
PASSAGE: 80 days from San Antonio, Chile.
CARGO: 6512 bags barley

Passengers

J. Gray   E. Holden   W. Folks

- - - - - -

SHIP: VELASCO
TYPE: Schooner   FROM: Huaina, Society Isls.
ARRIVED: May 2, 1852   CAPTAIN: Worth
PASSAGE: 36 days from Huaina, Society Islands.
CARGO: 200,000 oranges.

Passengers

M. Jackin   J. Jackin Jr.   W. Parker

- - - - - -

SHIP: M. VASSAR (also listed as MATTHEW VASSAR and M. VASSER)
TYPE: Schooner   FROM: Oregon Territory
ARRIVED: May 2, 1852   CAPTAIN: Bourne /sic/
PASSAGE: 10 days from the Oregon Territory. Departed from Astoria,

Oregon Territory. This vessel brings intelligence (from Astoria) that a party of overland immigrants arrived at Fort Vancouver (previous to the sailing of this vessel). The party of immigrants had left Fort Hall six weeks before and they had no difficulty with Indians while in the mountains.

CARGO: 360 hogs and 60 tons of coal.

Passengers

J.Y. Wilson   J.B. Campbell

- - - - - -

SHIP: LEONESA
TYPE: Brig   FROM: Puget Sound, W.T.
ARRIVED: May 3, 1852   CAPTAIN: Howard
PASSAGE: 9 days from Puget Sound, Washington Territory.
CARGO: 10,000 ft of piles.

Passengers

L. Terry   Mrs.___O'Meara

- - - - - -

SHIP: G.W. KENDALL
TYPE: Brig   FROM: Port Steilacoom, W.T.
ARRIVED: May 6, 1852   CAPTAIN: Not listed
PASSAGE: 6 days from Port Steilacoom, Puget Sound, Washington Territory.
CARGO: 600 bushels potatoes and 11,000 feet of square lumber.

Passengers

W. Packwood   W. Legard

- - - - - -

SHIP: UNICORN
TYPE: Steamer   FROM: San Pedro, California
ARRIVED: May 7, 1852   CAPTAIN: Lapidge
PASSAGE: 5 days from San Pedro, California. The "Unicorn" was dispatched from San Francisco, on April 30, 1852, to San Pedro, California. Purpose of trip was to pick up the stranded passengers of the steamer "California" and bring them to San Francisco. The "California" had put into San Pedro in distress.* The "Unicorn" took on board the passengers and brought, in tow, the disabled "California".
CARGO: Steamer "California" in tow.

Passengers

(See pages 163 to 165 for list of "California" passengers)

- - - - - -

SHIP: GRECIAN
TYPE: Brig   FROM: Oregon Territory
ARRIVED: May 7, 1852   CAPTAIN: Crosby
PASSAGE: 4 days from the Oregon Territory.

(Continued next page)

(*) The "California" had set out from Panama, bound for San Francisco (see pages 162-163).

CARGO: 140,000 feet of lumber.

Passengers

Mr.____Marlin   Mr.____Hunt   Mr.____Wright
Mr.____Boston

- - - - - -

SHIP: OHIO
TYPE: Steamer   FROM: San Diego, California
ARRIVED: May 9, 1852   CAPTAIN: Hilliard
PASSAGE: 5 days from San Diego, California, via San Pedro, California. Sailed from San Diego on May 4, 1852. Experienced
fine weather during passage. Left the steamer "Constitution" in San Diego with a large load of passengers from
Panama. The "Constitution" arrived in San Diego on May
3rd but was unable to proceed on her voyage to San Francisco by reason of the non-arrival of supplies of coal.
She was expected to sail for her destination on May 10th.
The "Constitution's" purser, Dr.____West, had intelligence
that some sixty or seventy Texans are at Mazatlan, Mexico,
having crossed the country, and are now waiting passage up
the coast. On the afternoon of April 10, 1852, a boat conveying passengers from the steamer "Panama" to the steamer
"Constitution", was swamped in a heavy rolling sea, and
nine persons were drowned. Their names were: P. Auronico,
M. Fry (or Fri), M. Gianine, M. Bullette, A. Felipi, P.
Pedrini, A. Lumbardi, G.O. Olipi and A. Lumbardi, Jr. The
"Constitution" had left Panama on April 10, 1852, arrived
at Acapulco, Mexico on April 19th and sailed on April
20th, arrived at San Blas, Mexico on April 24th, sailed
on same date and arrived at Mazatlan on April 25th. The
"Constitution" departed from Mazatlan on April 26th, experienced heavy head sea and strong winds until it arrived
at San Diego on May 3rd, at noon.
The "Ohio" reports that the British brig "Tryphina" (or
"Trypeina") and the brig "Christiana" are being detained
by the sheriff of San Diego, California, to satisfy judg-
ments for supplies, wages, pilotage, etc.*
The "Ohio" reports that during the temporary stay of the
steamer "California" at San Pedro, about a hundred of the
"California's" passengers took occasion to visit the city.
Several of the passengers were highly pleased with the
appearance of the country and it is possible that some of
them will return and locate permanently at San Pedro.
Captain Hilliard, master of the "Ohio", reported that
the U.S. Revenue cutter "Frolic", Captain____Ottinger
commanding, was at on San Pedro, California. The "Frolic"
was bound on a cruise and all hands reported well.
CARGO: Not listed.

Passengers

G.W.P. Bissell   J.P. Mott   J.P. Haven
J.J. Ames   Mr.____Rand   Capt. R.H. Haley

(Continued next page)

(*)Vessel also referred to as "Tryphenia", "Tryphene" and "Typhene".

Judge___Sutherland	Judge___Wetherby	J. Botaris
W. Douglass	A.H. Wilcox	P. Smith
E. Brady	C. Williams	J. Mann
Mrs.___Brady	R. Atkinson	J. Bordman
J. Edward	D. Block	M. First
V. De Flis (?)	J. Armath	M. Childs
(De Flia?)	M. Hick	H.A. Hatch
T. Donlyn	Col.___Johnson	T.A. Herder
J. Volck	C.E. Hanson	F. Hilnes
C. Bickford	A. Jacoby	A. Daly
M. Raccellat and	S.K. Robinson	W. Fisher
sister	J. Simonsfield	J. Anchavis (?)
J.R. Mason	T. Needham	(Anchavia?)
Senor___Estudilla	Mr.___Sexton	Mr.___Curtis

- - - - - -

SHIP: OXNARD
TYPE: Ship   FROM: Boston, Massachusetts
ARRIVED: May 9, 1852   CAPTAIN: Hinckley /sic/
PASSAGE: 150 days from Boston, Massachusetts.
CARGO: 44 kegs lead, 50 bbls and 200 tins rice, 25 boxes oysters,
       122 tons coal, 25,000 bricks, 400 casks nails, 359 bbls
       cement, 11,000 ft oak plank, 30 white oak knees, 2187 ft
       oak timber, 100,000 shingles, 20 pair doors, 40 sash doors,
       butter, cheese, tea, hams, 25 bbls pitch, 25 dozen shovels,
       pick and axe handles, 10,000 pickets, 30,000 lath, 4200
       sash light and assorted goods.
                         Passengers
              *Mr.___Hinckley   Mr.___Appleton

- - - - - -

SHIP: POMONA
TYPE: Schooner   FROM: Shoal Water Bay, W.T.
ARRIVED: May 9, 1852   CAPTAIN: Terry
PASSAGE: From Shoal Water Bay, Washington Territory, via Trinidad,
         California (4 days from latter port). This vessel brings
         intelligence that packers are coming in from the Upper
         Klamath, Scott's and Salmon River diggings, bringing not
         only good returns in gold dust, but most cheering news of
         good prospects for the future. Hundreds of miners are
         flocking in upon the Salmon and Klamath from all directions,
         and damming, sluicing and long toms are doing work to
         perfection. The trail from Trinidad to the mines is now
         being improved and shortened. Indian disturbances are
         reported to be frequent in the area. The Indians have
         threatened to kill white people in the Klamath River
         area.
CARGO: 1000 bushels of oysters.
                         Passengers
Col. A.J. Butler   E.S. Sayls   Mr.___March

- - - - - -

(*)Sic. Note name of Captain of vessel (Hinckley).

SHIP: TENNESSEE

TYPE: Steamer	FROM: Panama
ARRIVED: May 10, 1852	CAPTAIN: Lt. George N. Totten

PASSAGE: 14 days from Panama. Departed Panama at 7:00PM on April 25,1852 with passengers and mails. Three deaths occurred during the passage, and those were from diseases contracted previous to the persons coming on board. Sanitary regulations imposed by the ship's surgeon, Dr.___McNaughton, were effective. The "Tennessee" arrived at Acapulco, Mexico on May 1st, where she found the "Monumental City", which arrived three days previously from San Juan del Sur, Nicaragua, with nearly 500 passengers, many of them sick. Five persons had died on the "Monumental City", and of thirty-two who were sick and had been conveyed on shore, five had died also. On May 2nd the "Monumental City" left for San Francisco.

The "Tennessee" took on board 63 passengers at Acapulco, leaving there on May 2nd. Arrived at San Diego, California on May 8th and found the steamer "Constitution" in port, with passengers, waiting for coals. Departed from San Diego on the same day, and arrived at Monterey, California on May 10th. The following deaths occurred on the passage to San Francisco:

James Small, fireman, of Panama fever
John Watson, of Delaware County, Ohio, of Panama fever
J. Van Valkenburg, of Michigan, of dysentery.

The following are the names of some of the parties having died on board the "Monumental City":

Mr.___Caldwell
Mr.___Brown
Mr.___Rich
Mr.___Kemp

CARGO: Mail

Passengers

O. Cross (U.S. Army)	C.D. Blanchard	C.H. Corser
W.M. Rockwell	J.B. Legay	H.B. Lathrop and servant
J.H. Abbott	R. Howlrnd /sic/ (Howland?)	M. Lathrop and lady
D. Johnson	A.S. Dungan (?) (Duncan?)	J.B. Sandbern (?) (Sandborn?)
T.D. Johnson		
M.H. Chaplin	D.A. McDermot (?) (O.A. McDermot?)	T. Hawes
T. Sanderman		R. Scott
F. Fenny	J.H. Bowman	A.H. Chaplin
___Josephson	___Openheim	___Granmen
___Samuel	John Coley	N. Wykoff
P. Levalleg	D.A. Fostea /sic/	A. Dickenson and son
William Pearmain	G. Foster /sic/	
Miss C. Burton	J. Lewis	Dr. E.M. Patterson
___Birdsall (Mail Agent)	O.H. Pierson, lady & 3 children	Rev. George S. Pierson and lady

(Continued next page)

Miss M. Pierson
W.D. Foley
Rev. H.B. Sheldon (?)
   (Shelden?)
Rev. J.A. Swaney, lady
   & 2 infants
Rev. T. Caldwell
Mrs. E. Platt and
   child
Mrs. S. Simon and
   child
G. Brown and lady
Mrs.___ Hazelett and
   child /sic/
William Collyer
Miss A. Jaggers
G. Baker
W.T. Collyer
Valentine Almy /sic/
Charles Almy /sic/
L. Wadhams
Mrs.___ Edwards and
   servant
   ___ Spear
H. Z?dtmah, lady,
   2 children and
   servant
   (Zadtmah?
   Zedtmah?
   Zidtmah?)
J.D. Mahan
Thomas Hodges
Joseph Whitmore
J. Beason
J.B. Beason and
   servant
W.B. Beason
S. Beason
J. Regan
J.C. Miller
J. Madasa /sic/
W.S. Rapp
J. Medasa /sic/
J. Joseph and
   son
R. Joseph
William Blanck
T.V. Scott and
   2 servants
J.A. Brooke
P. Smith

John Darrington
Rev. W.J.M. Clay
Rev. D. Merchant
Rev. John Mathews
Rev. J. Hunter and
   lady
Mrs.___ Totten,
   2 children and
   servant
Mrs.___ Korlkumpf and
   servant
Mrs.___ Ross
Mrs.___ Hoffman,
   child & servant
D. Stutts
J. Van Houten
B.O. W?r??n
   (Warren?)
Theodore Lawton
H.P. Day
William Roberts
Mrs. G.B. Newell
Mrs. F. Tower
Mrs. J.L. Riddle
   child & servant
W.D. Harrington,
   lady, 2 children
   & servant
H. Shipman
C. Simpkins
A.S. Easton
A. Wescott
Jacob Ewalt
A.S. Moss
D.A. Candee
E. Houghtaitlng /sic/
   (Houghtaitling?)
J. Ghort
A.S. Allen and
   son
J. Eve?ding
   (Everding?)
S. Head
J.E. Wol?e
   (Wolfe?)
   ___ Barnard
Thomas Cassidy
John R. Clock
W.H. Bates
S. Stowbridge
R. McGowan
(Continued next page)

Mrs. A.T. Beals,
   child & servant
Rev. J. Dillon
Rev. P.G. Buchanan-
   an /sic/ and lady
Rev. A.S. Gibbons
   and lady
Mrs.___ N?vitt and
   daughter
   (Nevitt?,
   Navitt?
   Nivitt?)
W. Madusa /sic/
John L. Keeler
C.B. Preble
Benjamin Emerson
James Fannerskill
E.C. Norman
A.D. Norman
John Peck
J. Bishop
Mrs.___ McBryan
Mrs. A. Hall
A. Hall
Mrs.___ Hickey and
   4 children
John M?dden
   (Madden?,
   Medden?)
J.J. Ball
W.W. Ball
F.N. Ball
A. Wilson
S. Sond /sic/
   (Bond?)
John E. Beecher
G.B. Newell
H. Fluat (?)
   (Fliat?
   Fleat?)
E. Spahn (?)
   (Spehn?
   Spohn?)
O.H. Dewey
S.M. Shelton
G. McGinnis
S. Adams
I.W. Montgomery
P. Sherridan /sic/
   (Sheridan?)
H. Rabe

C. Spe??y
J. Basler
B.K. Bell
A. Garrett
J.M. Garrett
Mrs. ___ Carr?il
  and 2 children
M. Coeragan /sic/
A. Farrell
S. Price
A. Cartowich
S. Devraux
C. Murray
D.O. Mott
James Grant
J.B. Birjohn
J. Salerdet
L. Salerdet
H. Swanker (?)
  (Swenker?)
J.H. Ottman
James Acott and
  lady
N. McNeil
P. Laughlin
W. Draefo?
L. Mara
A. Leonard
R. McLeod
John Grimstone
S.H. Crarey
R.H. Brisefield
M. Williams
J. Waddell
J. Elias
J. Watson
J.S. Taylor
E. Emery
N. Sylvester
W. Kennedy
F. Boggiand
S.B. Rolfe
A.N. Tyrell
J.D. Jones
J. Reily /sic/
J. Simpson
D.B. Wright
J.D. Colton
M. Gross
M. Sanford
C. Sanford

P.C. Johnson
B.W. Johnson
J. Creed (?)
L. Johnson
F. Coorman
T. Clark
H. Watts
J. Scharf
J. Crasson
A.H. Severs
M. McNamara
J. Elandson
A.H. Stewart
E.A. Wilson
H.M. Empey
P. Riasko
John Riasko
  ___ Hillsman
L. Timper
J.H. Farlicke
H. Bullman (?)
  (Buhman?)
O. Mahon
G. McAnnally
W. Grothers
M. Gleason
L. Currier
John Powley
R. Garrish
B. Garrish
H. Phillips
W. Moorse /sic/
  (Morse?)
  ___ Bi?gs
  (Biggs?)
A.G. Corning
G. Ault
A. Lafamer /sic/
C. Scott
T. Nall /sic/
T.J. Doomis /sic/
A.C. Woodruff
N.A. Fell
W.C. Hart
P. Leddick
T. Asharth
W. Harlin
W. Harper
M. Wheolan /sic/
  (Wheelan?)
S. Van Volkenburgh /sic
(Continued next page)

H. Bailey
W.T. Rice
J.P. Bouch
F. Nill /sic/
Mrs. ___ Atkinson and
  child
W. Atkinson
W.R. Hurst
E.B. Thomas
F. Klusman
L. Arat
James Cassidy
H. R?hn
  (Rehn?, Rohn?)
E. Giraldin
J. Geneveloc (?)
  (Genaveloc?)
J. Penri
H. Sarrmahler (?)
  (Sarrmehler?)
W. Smith
W.M. Smith
M. Keenard
Miss P. Smith
W. Struve
S.V. Flint
C.C.N. Hotwell (?)
  (Hotwall?)
F. Cunningham
Mrs. ___ Sutton
J. Weir
H. Corker
J. Pincas
L. Pragher
S. Jacobie
P. Quigley
A. Griffin
T. Labeux
P. Heinrich
W. Scott
W.J. Beard
B. Thompson
A.C. Brainard
E.H. Skinner
W. Ronald
J. Noble
W. Galbraith
G. Stoops
G. Mills
D. Hunter
G. Biffa

T. Stevenson
M. Whitcomb
J. Caree
J. Conrad
E. Kellogg
E. Ingersol /sic/
A. Ingersol /sic/
S. Van Loan
L. Van Loan
T. Lewis
R. Henry
J.R. Still
A. Misseler
D. Cameren /sic/
J. Dewitt
C. Dewitt
C. Whitford
A.S. Pickett
John Ellis
N. Green
D. Toomey
Edwin Knapp
F. Guiseppi
D. Trnmbull /sic/
  (Trumbull?)
H.M. Smith
H. Curtis
R. Hallanbeck (?)
  (Hallenbeck?)
W.E. Cline
B. Rolett
G. Bronell
J. Shaw
J.W. Walbridge
C.D. Kellum
S. Harris and lady
A. Harris
D. Lathers
D. Carlin
J. Mooney
W.O. Williams
J. Carter
G. Hollman
G.F. Brown
Mrs. C. Alpy /sic/
C. Hoppin
O.B. Sturtevant
C. Van Houten
T. Rawlings
D. Snyder
A. Hall

A. Albertine
T. McGriere
J. Sullivan /sic/
J. Rapp
P. Rapp
A. Horton
T. Bishop
W. Clough
G. Out (?)
  (Ont?)
W. Barnes
J. Long
J. Murphy
A. Rappler
L. Rappler
J.H. Jacobs
William Sames
R. Tyler
James Tyler
J. Falkner
R. Fife
G. Baptiste
C. Gendetti
John Smith
S. Plympton
G. Edwards
D.H. Kammerly
J. Van Schaick
D. Packard
G. McMurray
Mr.___ Maguire
John Walker
John Davis
R. Ollefson
A. McPhail
O. Bigelow
H. Buhe
S.B. Lewis
R. Leonard
J.A. Trainer
P. Basler
L. Knox
T.P. Howland
G.B. Macey
D.F. Macey
J.W. Watkins
S. Thomas
A. Darrah
R.O. Harmon
L. Lehm
H. Hodges
(Continued next page)

A. Hubbard
S.A. Hubbard
R. Seegfried /sic/
M. Leonard
J. Butler
M.H. Wright
A. Jeromes /sic/
S. Jeromes /sic/
J.H. Hardenbeck /sic/
F.T. Chase
R. McGlammery
A. Heaftaling
T. McNeely
H. Jeraux
A. Berti
W. Shawl
G. Shawl
A. Shawl
M.C. Tubbs
T. Entrister
J. Sullivan /sic/
G. Padelli
S. Mirhole
A. Hiler
J.W. Hiler
J.R. Rannely
R.W. Guthall
R. Walker
J. Walker
J.C. McDonnell
E. Davis
W.S. Kelly
Thomas E. Miller
S. Jonson /sic/
L. Wood
E. Barnes
E. Norton
H. Scamahorn
H.C. Herrick
A.R. Merideth /sic/
R. Hodge
D. Searl
R.S. Smith
E. Lewis
O. Buckman
C. Carrol (?)
  (Carrel?)
J. Cromwell
E. Scanlan
M.M. Prichitt /sic/
N. Cahan /sic/

J. Sock
George Winsor /sic/
J.G. Nelson
P. Hibbard
William Kelly
I. Scoles
Mr.___Wakefield
J. Condon
R. Delasandri
F.M. Bowman
J. Chandler
S. Donaldson
G. Gozert
G. Hall
F.P. Hall
J. Hiken
J. Lewis
J. Mumford
C. Myers
J. Richardson
A.H. Ingersoll /sic/
G. Street
A. Simon
G.W. Pepper
G. Brinckerhoff
G.A. Hall
H. Butler
William Dampourer
F.A. Shaffer
B.T. Marble
P. Tachout (?)
   (Tacbout?)
G.T. Walker
J. McDonald
G. Bachelder
G.W. Hungerford
W. Averill
J. Lefevre
A.G. Helfman (?)
   (Holfman?)
O.N. Howard
E.H. Howard
E.H. Williams
James Williams
J.C. Vosburg
S. Lane
William Laesman
Daniel Laesman
John Wright
J. Larkin
James Larkin

R. Burgess
E.C. Johnson
H. Philfrick /sic/
   (Philbrick?)
H.C. Gaskill
Sam Stuart
J. Benard
G.C. Dolpheim
G. Brown
J. Bruce
P.P. Corning
B. Davis
F. Davis
G. Hillge /sic/
F. Franes
J. Kelly
W.P. Lee
J. Miller
J. Peabody
P. Plaeson
William Gallagher
J. Gallagher
J. Sanders
M. Woodruff
J. Mannersmith
H. Snyder
S. Baker
W. Lemon
J.W. Fielding
W. Johnson
R.O. Johnson
A. Johnson
J. Johnson
N.H. Twichton
N. Nall /sic/
O. Hemis
S. Sharp
S. Paddock
B. Dowling
H. Norcross
A. Norcross
E.C. Walton
H.P. Derrick
John Dewer (?)
   (Dower?, Dawer?)
J.B. Norris
D. Graham
D.L. Davis
W. Sp?eene
J. Rycraft
A.M. Allbe /sic/
(Continued next page)

F. Faught
J. Davis
S.T. Turner
G.E. Hale
A. Titus and son
Pat Keefe
J.C. Holmes
G. Berts
E.P. Boardman
D. Curtis
H. Chambers
T. Donlan
H. Henshaw
M. Hoogs
C. Johnson
G.W. Kirken
C.S. Mathews
E. McFarlan (?)
   (McFarlen?)
W. Palmer
F. Schover
W. Scott
S. Peel
D. Percival
A. Weiss
J. Cannon
L.C. Palmly
H. Arman
T.R. Goodhart /sic/
   (Goodheart?)
J.S. Goodheart /sic/
   (Goodhart?)
R.S. Carter
William Block
W. Brown
J. Fisher
W. Malfto (?)
W.H. Howard
J. McInery
S.A. Burpee
W.B. Cushing
C. R?nny
   (Ranny?, Renny?,
   Ronny?)
T. Baldwin
N. Baldwin
A.C. Wilson
P. Fisher
W. Baker
R. Hick
J.G. Reed

James ?arder
J.N. Slonisker
Mrs.___Anderson and
    daughter
G.B. Anderson

William U?ter
    (Utter?, Uiter?)
John H. Judy
L. Donigan

J.C. Swift
J. McCumisky
J.D. Lawson
D. Dewitt

- - - - - -

SHIP: ROBERT SMALL
TYPE: Ship   FROM: Hongkong
ARRIVED: May 11, 1852   CAPTAIN: Small
PASSAGE: 53 days from Hongkong, China.
CARGO: 8500 tiles.

Passengers
Mrs. Capt___Small,   Dr.___Hunter
    child & servant
    and 375 unidentified in steerage*
*(Believed to be Chinese)

- - - - - -

SHIP: CYCLOPS
TYPE: Brig   FROM: Oregon Territory
ARRIVED: May 12, 1852   CAPTAIN: Perkins
PASSAGE: 5 days from the Oregon Territory.
CARGO: 70 tons of potatoes and 130,000 feet of lumber.

Passengers
M.S. Smith   Aaron Coleridge   John Matlack

- - - - - -

SHIP: PACIFIC
TYPE: Steamer   FROM: San Juan del Sur,
ARRIVED: May 13, 1852   Nicaragua
CAPTAIN: Lefevre (also listed as Lafevre)
PASSAGE: Coaled at El Realejo, Nicaragua on April 28, 1852 and
    departed from San Juan del Sur, Nicaragua on April 29,
    1852 at 8:00PM. Arrived at Acapulco, Mexico on May 3rd
    and sailed again on May 4th. Found the American barque
    "Ann Smith" in distress at Acapulco. This vessel was
    45 days from Panama with passengers for San Francisco.*
    The "Ann Smith" was out of provisions and could not sail
    until relief could be obtained. The sum of $1500 had
    been raised and some provisions purchased, but not enough
    to guarantee a supply to San Francisco. A subscription
    was raised among the passengers of the "Pacific", amount-
    ing to $125. Passengers by the "Ann Smith" had purchased
    through tickets of Palmer & Haight, and were driven to
    this extremity, on account of frauds practiced upon them.
       The following deaths took place during the passage of
    the "Pacific":
            May 4, 1852:- Wareham Pomeroy, of congestion of the
                brain, of East Hampton, Massachusetts, aged
                42 years.
            May 5, 1852:- John J. Haas, of congestive chills, of
(*) One contemporary source states "Ann Smith" 55 days from Panama.

Dorchester, Massachusetts and late of Springfield, Massachusetts, aged about 40 years.
   May 11, 1852:- James W. Burton, of Castalia, Ohio, of dysentery, aged 21 years.
   May 11, 1852:- William Strain, of Bridgeport, Conn., of dysentery.

CARGO: 22 boxes of unidentified goods, 15 trunks, 3 sacks, 1 bale, 2 diamonds and mail.

Passengers

S. Katz
C.W. Davis
H. Voorhis
Mrs. S. Boston and infant
G.N. Frederick and lady /sic/*
Mrs.___Abdal (?) and child (Abdel?, Ahdal?, Ahdel?)
C.A. Baldwin
Mrs. H. Benchl, child & svt
H.R. Murray
Mrs.___Kendall and child
Miss___Disbrough (?) (Dishrough?)
John Esehenbergh (?) (Eschenbergh?)
John R. Esehenbergh(?) (Eschenbergh?)
O. Unz and servant
R.W. Van Sychles (?) (Van Syckles?)
Mrs.___Carpenter
D. Drew
Mr.___Nye and lady
W. Pamberthy (?) and lady (Pemberthy?)
Mrs. M.A. Thompson
Mrs. L. Alson (?) (Alsen?, Alsop?)
G.W. Chase and lady
J. Duffield
W. Sprague
J. Manning
T. Dean /sic/

D. Knapp, lady and child
Mrs. C. Cady and child
Mrs. Mary Stone
G.H. Martin, lady and child
Mrs.___Jervey
Mrs. G.W. Sagar (?) and 5 children (Segar?, Sugar?)
Mrs. James Patterson
Mrs. C.V. Homer
W.A. Henry
Dr. T.L. Megguin and lady
George Diety /sic/
Mrs.___Woff /sic/, 5 children and infant
N. Cranes (?) and servant (Crapes?)
N.W. Sanbaury
Mrs.___Langdon
Mrs.___James
J.C. N?les(Niles?) (NaTes?, Noles?)
Mrs.___Collins
L.G. Carpenter
J. Ferguson
J. Clark and lady
T.S. Hall
E.W. Hopkins
D. Davis
F.W. Chapman
G.B. Reid
W.J. Warner
T. Redfield
W. Webster
H.P. Rollins

James S. Deans /sic/ and lady
W.S. Place
Mrs. M.A. Johnson and child
Miss Julia Johnson
G.W. Douglass
G.F. Bragg
J.C. Marrians and lady
N.H. Woods
Mrs. H.M. Harvy /sic/ and 4 children (Harvey?)
S. Mandlehamer (?) and lady (Mandlebamer?)
Thomas W. Duty /sic/
J. Lanier
Mrs.___Myers
Miss___Myers
S.S. Johnson, lady and servant
Mrs.___Gallagher and children
Mrs.___Vincent
Mr.___Elliott
Mrs.___Douglass
Mrs.___Howard
M.J. Dunstany and lady
P. Grove and lady
Miss___Grove
Miss___Grove
Mr.___Grove
Mr.___Grove and servant
B. Tuthill
C. Van Ness
J. Miner
F.G. Glass
W. Gibbs

(Continued next page)

(*)Note listing for A.J. Fredericks, page 192.

L. Hill
W. Reed
G.W. Lorkner
W. Zigler
J. Leehner
J.H. White
H. Stoughton
W. Kingman
J. Peaks
W.T. Ellis
T.G. Kingsland
W. Bigham /sic/
J.W. Victory
J. Coles
C. Rastner (?)
   (Bastner?)
J. Freeman
A. Duane
R. Bowles
P.C. Turner
J. Turner
F.C. Wissman
J. McMullen
R. Morris
J. James and child
W. Vincent and
   3 children
Mrs. H.R. Gates
E. Holmes
F.B. Howes
Mrs.___ Rowe, child
   & infant
Miss___ Rowe
Mrs.___Barton
W.B. Van Sykles/sic/
S.F. Burt
S.T.F. Winslow
C. Hovenaugh
G.F. Davis
R. Montague
F. Williams
William Williams
N.D. Traphagen
D. Mason
R. Crandal /sic/
G. Beattie
J.W. Gordon
Mrs. M. Kuven and
   2 children
C.B. Preble
G.S. Preble

W.A. Benjamin
J. Wells
J. Liese /sic/
E. Gushart
S. Spink
W. Spink
O.V. Kinney
H. Washburn
A.L. Smith
T.C. Washburn
J.J. Norris
R. Blood
D. Disbrough /sic/
E.R. Wright
J. Larne
D. Bowles
C. Bowles
A. Boynton
D.W. Cook
E.V. Gilman
Mr.___King
G. Storms
A. ElWood /sic/
   (A. Elwood?,
   A. Wood?)
T. Carpenter
F.A. Foster
J. McDonald and
   lady
F.B. Taber
J. Cloud
J.W. Burton
Miss___Thurry
J. Harter
S.S. Dovoner and
   servant /sic/
A.S. Hall
H.L. Tupper
Mrs. T. Phair and
   infants /sic/
T. Phar /sic/ and
   sons
H. Phair /sic/
J.P. Hobert /sic/
   (Robert?)
O.R. Armstrong
A.J. Fredericks*
S. Templeton
J. Doyle
S.H. Bennett
J. Bennett

W. Bullard
N. Lindesmith
W. Stupp
J. Shaffener
R. Ramsey
J. Ward
C.O. Taylor
W. Patterson
S. Olson
G.W. Veatch
A. Holmes
C.H. Holmes
J. Bassler
B.F. Barstow
E. Bamm
P.G. Peck
W. Peck
E. Robertson
W. Dunlan (?)
   (Dunlap?)
O. Hyde
J. Armstrong
J.H. Rogers
J. Dudley
S.H. Winterbottom
J. Bennett
Mrs. P. Place
Mrs. S. Katy
Mrs.___Irvin
T.J. Poulterer
J.H. Condir
Rev. J.D. Blain,
   lady, child and
   servant
G. Tenny and
   servant
R. Holden
J. Case
M.H. Robinson
N.J. Rouser
C. Woodruff
P.D. Elmendorf
A.J. Harrison
Maria Ruins
J. Brotter
F. Cole
C.R. Goodman
W. Beattie
W. Leonard
J.M. Swain
J.H. Abbott

(Continued next page)

(*)Sic. Note G.N. Frederick and lady, page 192—minus "s".

J.H. Mudgett
B.T. Woods
J.B. Henry
J. Patterson
F. Moss
W. Coffinger
Mr.___Roach
C. Mathews /sic/
L.G. Reno
W. Snowden and
    child
T.A. Provost
J.B. Walker
N. Holmes
George H. Swininton
    /sic/
    (Swinington?)
J.H. Temant and
    boy /sic/
Mrs.___Nicholas
C. Nicholas and
    boy
W.E. Brooks
Mrs.___Brooks
B. Kimberly
S. Dickerman
A. Kirchner
A.S. Moore
B.L. Bartlett
W. Koosten (?)
    (Kopsten?)
W. Ordney
C.L. Jackson
E. O'Neil /sic/
G.D. Crocker /sic/
W.B. Fuller
M. Morton
J.C. Owens
George Sargent
J.M. Wilcox
E.B. Davidson
J.E. Davidson
Thomas Magillon
G. Nicholl
T.B. Dalrymple
S.M. Hannards
M. Ehlinge
M. Riley /sic/
E. Kiley /sic/
    (Riley?)
L. Riley /sic/

E. Choar
J. Baldwin
A. Roid
H.M. Harvey
J.W. Robinson
L.C. Cutter
C. Robinson
G. Lubolt
W. Hendershot
I. O'Neal /sic/
John Donver/sic/
W.F. Erit
S. Hayne
J. Hague
W.S. Benson
B. Crooker /sic/
O. Detuck
J. Mins
G.W. Sanders
Mrs.___Rowe
W. Rowe and
    brother
J. Briant
W.H. Temple
Mrs.___Brown
B.C. Sturgis
J. Brownell
S.E. Buchanan
H.L. White
B. Bramhull
J.C. Stevenson
P. Stevenson
D.T. Meigs
C.A. Meigs
J.J. Way /sic/
L.S. Gay /sic/
J.L. Carnaghan
L. Kingsley
L.Biucksley /sic/
    (Buicksley?
    Bucksley?)
G.E. Powell
S.S. Parsons
L. Wolff
S.B. Cook
George Yale
A. Yale
E. Pendleton
M. Owens
B. Hill
F. Beardsly
(Continued next page)

J.B. Emerson
H. Hays
J. Hays
J.P. Treadwell
S. Palmer
M. Palmer
C.P. Corbin
S. Smith
John Fitger (?)
    (Pitger?)
C.G. Borkins
R. Swift
D. Lifford
J. Goodspeed
E. Chamberlin/sic/
W.R. Frink
A.M. Coy
S.H. Goodman
H. Gillman
A. Beach
J.A. Hull
J.H. Lee
C.M. Foster
W.F. Daggett
A. Hull
A. Schnider /sic/
E. Chamberlin /sic/
J. Chapman
S. Dyer
H. Benjamin
W. Toll
N. Saxton
J. Hasdick
John A. Faas
L. Billings
J.H. Mellechop
M.H. Mahan
J.R. Day
S.B. Hoxie
E.M. Clark
J.C. Robinson
William Murphy
W. Wait
S.B. Cooper
D.S. Morrison
S. Moore
C. Johnson
W. Johnson
P. Grimes
S.D. Elliott
P. Brady

B.W. Robinson   J.B. Brubaker   J. Johnson
C.B. Underwood   E.P. Brubaker   C.P. Burrows
D.C. Knight   N.R. Kimball   C. Orvis
    Warton /sic/   S. Swain   Mr.____Straine
R.A.S. Barton /sic/

- - - - - -

SHIP: ARCHITECT
TYPE: Clipper   FROM: Hobart Town, V.D.L.
ARRIVED: May 14, 1852   CAPTAIN: Caspar
PASSAGE: 77 days from Hobart Town, Van Dieman's Land. This vessel
      brings intelligence relative to the gold seekers in the
      colony. Most of the gold districts in the colony are
      abandoned on account of the weather and the health of the
      diggings. The new gold mine on the Mitta Mitta, it is
      believed will be successful. The want of water, the heat
      and sickness, blight and flies at Mount Alexander, have
      caused many of the diggers to turn their attention towards
      the Omeo diggings.
CARGO: 4500 boxes potatoes, 1500 boxes onions, 70 tons of coffee,
      25 boxes apples and 80 bags barley.

Passengers

Mrs.____Osborn, two   Two passengers un-
   children & svt   identified in
                       the steerage

- - - - - -

SHIP: FOI
TYPE: Ship (French)   FROM: Havre, France
ARRIVED: May 14, 1852   CAPTAIN: Hebert
PASSAGE: 130 days from Havre, via Callao, Peru.
CARGO: 4 cases tree plants, 10 cases sardines, 1 case tools, 87
      cases absynth, 6 cases perfumery, 1 case needles, 3 cases
      smoking tobacco, 1 steam machinery, 2 cases playing cards,
      red wine, brandy, vinegar and assorted goods.

Passengers

Mr.____Devan and   175 passengers un-
   lady   identified in
                       the steerage

- - - - - -

SHIP: ORTOLEON*
TYPE: Schooner   FROM: Umpqua River, O.T.
ARRIVED: May 14, 1852   CAPTAIN: Ratcliff
PASSAGE: 3 days from the Umpqua River, Oregon Territory. This
      vessel brings intelligence that everything was quiet at
      Umpqua, no trouble with the Indians for some time.
CARGO: 10 cords wood.

Passengers

E. Jones   C. Bipend   E. Walker

- - - - - -

(*) This vessel listed as the "Ortolean" in Volume I.

SHIP: NOBLE
TYPE: Schooner   FROM: Honolulu, S.I.
ARRIVED: May 15, 1852   CAPTAIN: Robertson
PASSAGE: 18 days from Honolulu, Sandwich Islands. This vessel
brings intelligence that a severe earthquake was experienced on Hawaii on the night of April 14, 1852. On April
15th, a new volcanic eruption broke out about 3 miles to
the northward of the eruption that took place in February,
1852.
CARGO: Not listed.

Passengers

Capt. Dean	Capt. Leach	Mr. Roberts
Mr. Gilbert	Mr. Bishop	Mrs. Aeroc

- - - - - -

SHIP: GUADALOPE PREMERE (also listed as "GUADALOPE")
TYPE: Schooner (Mexican)   FROM: Acapulco, Mexico
ARRIVED: May 15, 1852   CAPTAIN: Abrams
PASSAGE: 66 days from Acapulco, Mexico, via Mazatlan, Mexico.
Have on board passengers from the wrecked steamer "North
America".
CARGO: In ballast.

Passengers

*-From the wrecked "North America":-

H.G. Kendrick and 2 others (names not known) /sic/**	G. Bently Winreich	B.P. Moore
	John Parry	Samuel Head
John K. Hoxie	D. Moore	O. Daniels
A. Morse	J.C. Wingate	J.J. Morton
E. Morse	T. Friguarter	P. Hanton
W.S. Morse	C. Matthews and	J.A. Jamison /sic/
John Stafford	lady	C. Marriott
P. Ayres	P. Woodhouse	W.J. Armstrong
S.B. Whipple	S. Hart (or S.	H. Kendricks /sic/
S.A. Jamison /sic/	Fert) /sic/	(note listing for
E.A. Burben	James Wood	H.G. Kendrick)
Thomas G. Andrews	E.R. Wolcott	W.B. Kendricks /sic/
John Chan	Jonathan Jones	(note listing for
W.P. Fowler	Abram Cole (3	H.G. Kendrick)
D. Naftel	tickets) /sic/	Austin Smith
Joseph Porter	F. Farkey	D.S. Ely
William Porter	Thomas W. Palmer	Thomas Laka/sic/
Lloyd Porter	C. Shandreu	William Curtis
Charles P. Morgan	H.G.W. Cole	A. Houghton
F. Garlin	W. Blackwell	C. Bravo
Ira Berry	Levi Sears	J.M. Mathews
S.A. Scott	S.H. Olman	Joseph Loopen
James Ely	James Harvey	J. Baker
G.B. Drury		C.C. Bergman

(*) List based on report from Mexico.
(**) Name might be "H.G. Kendricks". Note listings for H.
Kendricks and W.B. Kendricks. Conversely, latter names
could be "H. Kendrick" and "W.B. Kendrick".

SHIP: ROBERT BRUCE
TYPE: Brig   FROM: San Jose, Mexico
ARRIVED: May 16, 1852   CAPTAIN: Charon
PASSAGE: 27 days from San Jose, Mexico.
CARGO: 20,000 pounds of sweet potatoes.

Passengers
Dr.____Lane
and 1 unidentified in the steerage

- - - - - - - -

SHIP: CORNELIA
TYPE: Brig (Mexican)   FROM: Mazatlan, Mexico
ARRIVED: May 18, 1852   CAPTAIN: Bustas
PASSAGE: 48 days from Mazatlan, Mexico, via Santa Barbara, Cali-
         fornia.
CARGO: 119 boxes eggs, 15 dozen fowls and 12 hogs.

Passengers
A. Arcalarias
and 47 unidentified in the steerage

- - - - - -

SHIP: CURLEW
TYPE: Schooner   FROM: Santa Cruz, California
ARRIVED: May 19, 1852   CAPTAIN: Brown
PASSAGE: 40 hours from Santa Cruz, California.
CARGO: 60 tons of potatoes.

Passengers
Mrs.____Tuttle   L. Goodchaux   W. Wire
T. Clarke

- - - - - -

SHIP: COLORADO
TYPE: Brig   FROM: Humboldt Bay, Calif.
ARRIVED: May 21, 1852   CAPTAIN: White
PASSAGE: 4 days from Humboldt Bay.
CARGO: 100,000 feet of lumber, 18,000 laths, 50 tons coal, 1 steam
       engine and $40,000 in gold dust.

Passengers
William S. Clemens	Mrs.____Favry	G. Kohner
and lady	R. Humphrey	Edward Ryley /sic/
William R. Duff	William E. Dwyer	T. Graham
J.A.C. Moore	J.C. Stratton	H.A. Warren
William Scott	S.H. Grubler	Capt. James McMahon
William Hathaway	D. Pickard	C.H. Holmes
C.B. Ferguson	P. Pelkasen	A.H. Abbot /sic/
C. Christiansen	M. Ferramoth	D.G. McCotter
J.R. Perkins	T.M. Kirkpatrick	J.N. Dow
Captain____Winnett		

- - - - - -

SHIP: REINDEER
TYPE: Brig (Hawaiian)   FROM: Shanghai, China
ARRIVED: May 22, 1852   CAPTAIN: Morrison
PASSAGE: 40 days from Shanghai, China.
CARGO: Eggs and barley (consigned to J. Hooper, on board).

Passengers

| J. Hooper | ____Parker | ____Hays and lady |

- - - - - -

SHIP: OHIO
TYPE: Steamer   FROM: San Diego, California
ARRIVED: May 23, 1852   CAPTAIN: Hilliard
PASSAGE: 5 days from San Diego, California, via intermediate ports
          of San Luis Obispo, California and Santa Barbara, Cali-
          fornia. Experienced strong head winds from Santa Barbara
          to San Francisco.
CARGO: Not listed.

Passengers

Mr.____Fletcher	D.C. Robinson	J. Lard
W. Steward	Mr.____Nichols	J. Hull
J. Machada	N. Mauzey	P. Banning
T. Dolons /sic/	Mr.____Eddy	C. Sanford and svt
J.M. Yndart /sic/	J. Larco	J. Morgan
(Yudart?)	L. Lake	L.A. Mora
A. Lainsworth	A. Ray	J. Arthur
P. Carroll and wife	G. McDougal	M. Myers
E. Block	P. Morong	C.J. Culberton /sic/
B.S. Lippincott	H.C.M. Ely	(Culbertson?)
____Vance	M. Keller	____Hooper
____Skinner	____Barry	____Cehn /sic/
T. Ocio	J. Cook	Dr.____Vallick and
D. Ivarra	J. Boston	boy
R.E. Raimond /sic/	J.A. Cullen	____Mitchell
P.A. Roach	____Wall	____Liest

- - - - - -

SHIP: MANUKU
TYPE: Schooner (Hawaiian)   FROM: Lahaina, S.I.
ARRIVED: May 24, 1852   CAPTAIN: Merrill
PASSAGE: 27 days from Lahaina, Sandwich Islands.
CARGO: 90 bags pula, 96 bbls salt, 1 case matches, 600 bbls of
        potatoes, 1500 squash, 28,000 roa (sic) lumber, 400 fowls
        and 35 turkeys.

Passengers

P. Cummings	S.B. Alding	S.C. Jones
M. Richardson	W. Morgan	J.B. Thomas
T. Goodwin		

- - - - - -

SHIP: FAWN
TYPE: Brig   FROM: Umpqua, O.T.
ARRIVED: May 24, 1852   CAPTAIN: Bunker

PASSAGE: 3 days from Umpqua, Oregon Territory.
CARGO: 3000 ft of piles, 2000 ft square timber and 40 cords of wood.

Passengers

Miss Mary Hogan	Miss M. Chadwick	Miss M. Schofield
Miss Helen Hogan		

- - - - - -

SHIP: VESTA
TYPE: Brig   FROM: Morea, Society Islds.*
ARRIVED: May 24, 1852   CAPTAIN: Simpkin
PASSAGE: 43 days from Morea, Society Islands.*
CARGO: 180,000 oranges.

Passengers
G. Thatcher and lady

- - - - - -

SHIP: CARIB
TYPE: Barque   FROM: Valparaiso, Chile
ARRIVED: May 24, 1852   CAPTAIN: Ripley
PASSAGE: 57 days from Valparaiso, Chile.
CARGO: 3800 bags barley

Passenger
C.S. Clapp

- - - - -

SHIP: RUTH
TYPE: Brig   FROM: El Realejo, Nicaragua
ARRIVED: May 24, 1852   CAPTAIN: Hilton
PASSAGE: 30 days from El Realejo, Nicaragua.
CARGO: 800 sacks of corn and unidentified merchandise.

Passengers
William Banister*
and 19 unidentifed passengers
(*) Died of measles during passage

- - - - - -

SHIP: BRUTUS
TYPE: Ship   FROM: Panama
ARRIVED: May 24, 1852   CAPTAIN: Mitchell
PASSAGE: 57 days from Panama.
CARGO: In ballast.

Passengers

H. Hicks	W.C. Collins	H. Dennis
A.D. Edwards	J.B. Callio	J. Smith
J. Rodgers	P. Callio	C. Laciana
A. Smith	E. Callio	D. Crombie
A.H. Smith	F.G. Russell	N.G. Boyd
E. Hartman	J.H. Trible	H.C. Wright
C. Polk	J. Lanier	C. French
A.S. Williams	J.M. Causland	A.F. Chapman
W.R. McMillen	J.M. Williams	W.F. Gudt

(Continued next page)

(*)Morea(sic). Moorea.

P. North

E. Lockwood

M.D. Garner

R. Garner

M.C. Bovey

C. Thomos /sic/
 (Thomas?)

J.H. Thomas /sic/

G. Hillman

V. Parker

J.A. Watts

R.D. Galyon

L.R. Davis

B. Pleasant

H. Beauchamp

A.P. Gorgen

V. Kean

W.T. Davison

S. Russell

R. Clarke

G. Ellison

J.M. Smith

J. Barlow

W.P. Flack

J. James

J. Hargott

V.P. Browne

J. Heal

H.G. Smith

L. Milner

V.J. Van Dour

W. Gordon

W. Franklin

W. Meyer

D. Praser /sic/
 (Fraser?)

J. Fry

G. Fry

J.S. Hallum

D.H. Walton

H.A. McLean

W. Twiner

B. Wellingham

H. Wellingham

E. Osborne

J. Watson

G. Mann

D.N. Ford

A.J. Foster

A. Lease

R.T. Slaughter

W.J.P. Slaughter

E. Townan/sic/

R. Dunney

A. McWilliams

J. Hutchings

J.M. Daner

J.T. Simpson

A.T. Anderson

P.T. Anderson

B.W. Anderson

H. Halman

V. Shiffer

T. Hart

A. Davison

E. Wall

J. Nicholson

P. Whitcomb

J. Morgan

S. Senilan

H. Johnson

F. Jane

C. Kerntal

W. Leslie

J. Curtis

J.H. Toon

F.C. Munly

C.P. Jackson

W. Baker

E. Knapp

R. Fulton

J.G. Thomas

G.H. Snyder

W.E. Hartman

E.G. Hartman

W.W. Webb

W.D. Crouch

P.C. Aplin /sic/

E.B. Jago

M. Bobo

F.H. Dunbar (?)
 (P.H. Dunbar?)

W. Bonas

P. Hoffman

M. Light

W. Drummond

J. Taylor

S.Y. Douglas

J. Bradley

J. Martin

H.P. Woods

S.D. Frost

P.C. Appling /sic/

R.A. Appling /sic/

H.W. Hall

W.Y. Hall

J.D. Davis

C. Strong

D. Midway

A. Chamby

A.W. Deane

G. Kin

A. Wilcoxson

W.T.S. Burns

G. McLean

A. Martin

J. Evans

C. Evans

A.A. Jordan

W.H. Shed

R. McDonnell

A.P. Harrison

T.J. Hogan

A. Hogan

R. Kemphall

E. Thirk

W.T. Mock

C.M. Henstein

W.H. Smith

A. Eaton

E. Day

R.G. Mooney

J. Goen

J. Bates

W. Rasil

J. Smith

S.H. Collins

A.P. Chevalier

(In researching the passenger list of the "Brutus", the author
located a contemporary source document which reflected names
of some of the passengers booked as "steerage". In comparing
the steerage list source with the basic passenger list it was
apparent that there were discrepancies in the spelling of

200

some of the given names and surnames. The below list represents passengers traveling as "steerage" on the "Brutus".
Where the spelling entry differed with the basic research
source it is so noted)

R.N. Turner	E.R. Appling	W.F. Smock
J.C. Ellison	W.H. Hudson	R.J. Anderson
R.A. Kempstead	R. Clark	M.D.K. Berring
John Agovout	J.C. Smith	W. Russell
C.E. Day	Thomas C. Nunnally	A. Willing /sic/
William Borrest /sic/	B.S. Murray	A. Willing /sic/
B. Anderson	W. Hall	B. Willing
J.H. Appling	Louis Lepage	W.C. Robert
John Horton	A.A. Mack	Samuel Sinclair
W.F. Trow	D.M. Henderson	Joseph Burleson
S. Martin	R.J. Simpson	R.D. Kilgrove
J.N. Bobo	A.G.P. Thomas	George McCaw
Solomon W. Hill	Thomas Schaffer	

John Morgan (note "J. Morgan" listed on page 199)
Charles P. Jackson (note "C.P. Jackson" listed on page 199)
A.W. Denn (note "A.W. Deane" listed on page 199)
J.H. Snider (note "G.H. Snyder" listed on page 199)
A.J. Anderson (note "A.T. Anderson" listed on page 199)
Jackson Goins (note "J. Goens" listed on page 199)
A.F. Chapindor (note "A.F. Chapman" listed on page 198)
James C. Watts (note "J.A. Watts" listed on page 199)
B.H. Walton (note "D.H. Walton" listed on page 199)
Charles Polk (note "C. Polk" listed on page 198)
James Taylor (note "J. Taylor" listed on page 199)
Andrew J. Harrison (note "A.P. Harrison" listed on page 199)
J.M. Nicols (note "J. Nicholson" listed on page 199)
J. Hallom (note "J.S. Hallum" listed on page 199)
James Fry (note "J. Fry" listed on page 199)
W.E. Hartmann (note "W.E. Hartman" on page 198)
H.W. McLean (note "H.A. McLean" on page 199)
Timothy H. Hart (note "T. Hart" on page 199)
V.J. Van Doren (note "V.J. Van Dour" on page 199)
D. Frazier (note "D. Praser"/sic/ (Fraser?) on page 199)
Thomas Fleck (note "W.P. Flack" on page 199)
O. Strong (note "C. Strong" on page 199)
Vincent Parker (note "V. Parker" on page 199)
A. Chomley (note "A. Chamby" on page 199)
G.W. King (note "G. Kin" on page 199)
V. Korm (note "V. Kean" on page 199)
Henry Johnson (note "H. Johnson" on page 199)
E. Hartmann (note "E. Hartman" on page 199)
R.F. Slaughter (note "R.T. Slaughter" on page 199)
George Mann (note "G. Mann" on page 199)
George Fry (note "G. Fry" on page 199)
W.J.T. Slaughter (note "W.J.P. Slaughter" on page 199)
J. McCauslin (note "J.M. Causland" on page 198)
W.H. Shea (note "W.H. Shed" on page 199)

- - - - -

SHIP: INDEPENDENCE
TYPE: Steamer   FROM: San Juan del Sur,
ARRIVED: May 26, 1852   Nicaragua
CAPTAIN: T.D. Lucas
PASSAGE: 18 days from San Juan del Sur, Nicaragua, via intermediate
         ports. Departed San Juan del Sur on May 7, 1852 at 6:00PM
         and arrived at Acapulco, Mexico on May 14th, at 7:00AM.
         Departed Acapulco on May 15th at 2:00AM. The following
         deaths took place during the passage:
              May 11, 1852:- J.R. Edsall, at 8:00PM, of fever,
                 taken on the Isthmus, of the Washington Terri-
                 tory.
              May 18, 1852:- J.T. Smith, of congestion of the
                 bowels.
CARGO: Not listed.

Passengers

Miss Mary Ladd	Mrs. G.H. Williams	L.A. Booth
Mrs.___Stephen	E.R. Waterman and	Mrs.___Levi, child
Mrs. N. Fales	lady	& servant
J.B. Green and	R.M. O'Brien and	C.M. Cherry and
lady	child	lady
J.C. Kilbourn	L. Pollock	H.B. Bruikman
J.W. Sigourney	P. Hendrickson	J.W. Webster, lady
H.P. Depoff and	Mrs.___Clark and	and child
servant	child	P.S. Grant
Miss___Hillyer and	H.B. Morrill, lady	P.H. Owens
servant /sic/	and child	W.W. Stone
B.B. Barnes	Mrs. H.H. Robinson,	E.B. Cahoon
Mrs.___Ellis	child and servant	A.C. Beckwith
S.H. Woolsey/sic/	Mrs.___Tappen, two	Mrs.___Backus and
B.J. Ray	children & svt	two children
Mrs. L. Hermance	Miss H. Ferris /sic/	W.B. French and
and child	J.S. Friend	lady
W. Tingle	Miss M.J. Fisher	Mrs. J. Hagan
Mrs. S.A. Moulthrop	J.A. Hiller /sic/	R. Howes and lady
C.G. Whitcomb	J. Liscocki	Mrs. A.M. Baggs
C. Ford	John L. Polhemus	Z. Crowell and
S. Strauss	W.J. Smith	lady
S.B. Lee	H. Garrett	L. Moriceu
S. Hatch	J.E. Galloway	J. Collins
L. Sherwood	J.T. Smith	J.D. Brower /sic/
S.A. Lindsley	W.R. Smith	William Baldwin
O.P. Lindsley	A.W. Brainard	S. Baldwin
W.J. Tomlins	J. Blumance	T.W. Marshall Jr.
L. Dawson	D. Collins	A.T. Cooper
A. Deerick (?)	C. Grimskey /sic/	J. Campbell
(Doerick?)	C.H. Rumrill	A. Crane
Mrs.___Grumsky /sic/	Miss___Pegot	W. Smith
J.C. Lafayette	J.M. Wiley	H. Smith
G.C. Jewell	J.C. Worth	H. Conklin
P.J. Gilbert	A. Daggett	G. Beach

(Continued next page)

M.D. Hakins (?)
    (Haskins?)
G. Kincaid
G.G. Ellis
S. Mosher /sic/
William Daggett
B. West
W.L. Kilbourn
J. Kilbourn
B. Fales
L. Miller
J.W. Cherry
R. Booth
C. Kingsbury
J.B. Walker
J. Smith
William Smith
D. Cutting
C.B. Cutting
B. Hermance
John Hillman
J.R. McCloud
S.E. Peacock
J. Peacock
A. Peacock
E. Peacock
J.H. Burdett
C. Honfton (?)
    (Houfton?)
A.B. Irvin
S.B. Fowter /sic/
    (Fowler?)
T. Hild
A. Hild
J.H. Parlin
L.B. Prindle
J.D. Parker
P.H. Mitchell
J.G. Maxwell
J. Dayton
C.B. Miles
S. Pierce
C. Atkinson
J. Stillman
F. Barber
R. Rutcliffe /sic/
J. Hoyle
P. Brady
E. Overstetter
W. Walbrend
H.H. Watts

G.W. Augier (?)
    (Angier?)
G.H. Williams
E. Stansbery
R.R. Stevson /sic/
    (Stevenson?)
A. Stratton
E. Booth
P. Reed
H. Brinkwedd /sic/
J.W. Tollett
P. Veasey
H.P. Barnum
B. Nichols
I. Lee
H. Kimball
A. Sleeper
D. Dennisan /sic/
    (Dennison?)
J.H. Benham
William Singart
E. Robinson
J.L. Dickinson
H.B. Crawford
S.S. Mursey /sic/
    (Murfey?)
H. Murfey /sic/
    (Mursey)
J.G. Quigley
M.R. Jackson
W.H. Hovey
C. Moore
S. Moore
J. Givens
J. Blake
J.W. Braley
T. Moshier /sic/
E.S. McCormick
J. Jamison /sic/
D. Starr
C.A. Belknap
P.B. Knapp
L.A. Sterry
C.W. Moxon
J. Smith
N. Davis
H.L. Bissell
J. Walker
J. Hart
P.L. Mattheson /sic/
C. Kelsey
(Continued next page)

J.D. Merrick
M.T. Joyce
M. Lincoln
W.H. Fleming
J. Wanger
D.W. Smith
J. Stearns
M. Dunne /sic/
H.E. Johnson
T. Bigley
J. Stanton
A. Lockwood
S. Blodget
C. Blodget
W. Van Wyck
G. Davis
N. Hoyt
E. Smith
J. Rapaljo
J.L. Smith
J. Frans /sic/
L. Barber
William H. McClung
W.A.L. Paulp
L.D. Webster
William Ellis
R.J. Bemis
W.D. Fisher
William Lawrence
C. Sheldon
W. Sneaton
D.H. Bisbee
G.C. Thompson
S. Chandler
N. Judd
J. Judd
J. Farris /sic/
J.G. Williams
W.H. Palmer
J.H. Courtelyou
E. Stapleton
B. Ladd
P. Ladd
H.H. Patterson
R. Ray
L. Beajan
J. Ray
W. Walton
D. Davis
E. Cameron
S. Hermance

T. Hermance	J.A. McFarland	M. Farley
J. Taylor	D.B. Dingman Jr.	W.H. Soniden
W.R. Wmite /sic/	P. Gilman	J. Stevens
(W.R.W. Mite?)	R.J. Richards	J. Davis
H. Jones	R. Williams	J.B. Fitch
T.F. Jones	P. Burns	E. Clinton
T.A. Jones	William Anderson	J. Clinton
W.H. Gains	William Gant	Nancy Lewis
C.J. Dutton	Mrs. L. Guyant	S. Isaac
J. Visiberg and	J.H. Hobson	J.D. Minor
servant	A. Martine	G. Durand
M. Braden	D. Thompson	T. Irvin
J. Luth	W.L. Beach	C.W. Holdridge
W. Edwards	D. Davis	C. Hollis
E. Richards	R. Woolley /sic/	P. Philip
J. Morris	G. Williams	J.Davis
T. Lloyd	D. Howels /sic/	J.A. Marriner
J.L. Seymour	S. Gilbert	R. Fullerton
J. Tappen	R. Kent	Scott
Wood	Chapin	G. Worth
J. Coleman	G.W. Cook	T. Worth
O. Leveridge	S. Pontiers /sic/	J. Sprague
B. Cook	T. McLean	J. McKee

- - - - - -

SHIP: PANAMA
TYPE: Steamer   FROM: Panama
ARRIVED: May 27, 1852   CAPTAIN: R.H. Pearson
PASSAGE: 17 days from Panama, via intermediate ports. Left Panama
         on May 10, 1852 at 6:00PM. Arrived Acapulco, Mexico at
         2:00PM on May 17th. Left Acapulco on May 19th at 9:00PM
         and arrived at San Diego, California on May 25th at 5:30
         PM. Departed San Diego on same day at 12:00M. But one
         death occurred on board during the passage- a Frenchman,
         who died suddenly (name not listed).
CARGO: 177 packages of merchandise (goods not specified) and 40
         packages of baggage.

Passengers

Mrs. Burnham	Mrs. Galloway &	W.P. McCurry, lady
& servant	3 children	& child
Mrs. Danewald	Mrs. C. Straus /sic/	J.M. Fox
P. Pettinas	W. McGungle	Miss Strong
J. Hess, lady, two	H.N. Atting, lady,	Miss Lord
children & svts	child & svt	Miss Allen
J.B. Halford & lady	W.S. O'Connor	Miss M.A. Burns
Dr. J.T. Vaiden	M. Sevins and	Mrs. Claughney
M. Eder & lady/sic/*	nephew	Mrs. J.D. Carr,
Master Labath	Rev. J. Rider	daughter & svts
Miss Lawrence	G.S. Martell	Mrs. Mack and
A.L. Boms	Capt. Milligan	daughter
M. Trader	J.W.Brooks & lady	M. Comstock
	(Continued next page)	

(*)Note D.M. Eden, page 204

Mrs. T. Payne and child
B. Wands
James Riley and lady
Mrs.___Clarivele and daughter
Mrs. E. Reid
H. Ortman and lady
G. Kraine and lady
Mrs.___Adset and child
E.B. Mott
Henry Child
W. Smith
J.C. Miller
P. Kelly
William F. Colter
H.A. Kraul
L. Duplin and boy
C.C. Rand
D.M. Eden /sic/*
M. Tibbetts
J.P. Bradley
E.T. Ruse
J. Satterlee
S. Miller
H. Carpenter
G. Skellenburgh
W.H. Mack
H.A. Bills /sic/ (Mills?)
S. Mills /sic/ (Bills?)
R.R. Swain
A. Lipset
G. Bush
T. Burket
And. Henn (Andrew Henn?)
L. Douglass /sic/ (Douglas?)
G. Douglas /sic/ (Douglass?)
A. Conch
C.J. Hilliard
F. Genderman
T. Cannason
F. Slater
G. Kissane
M. Hickley

Mrs.___McDougald
Miss E. Gardner
J.S. Church
Mrs.___Church and daughter
Mrs.___Atchison /sic/
B. Kirby (Berford & Company's Messenger)
J. Jackson
Mrs. N. Sleeper and child
G.W. Hoglin
S.B. Stroup
W. Brown
William Welsh
G. Baker
S. Atchisen /sic/
H. Reynolds
O. Steiger
A. Winley
L.B. Adset
S. Heveman Jr.
J.W. Cole
T. McManus
J. Lipple
S. Mathney /sic/
R.C. Bigelow
E.P. Marley
M.W. Calkins
C.A. Belden
J.B. Hutchinson
W. Matthews
M. Collins
G.P. Crocker
G. Barnes
W. Northrup
J. Benson
A. Benson
W.H. Whitney
T.M. Manus /sic/
C.R. Maxin
P. Kennedy
J. Kean
A.J. Giles
J.P. Westgall
R.O. Porterfield
J. Porterfield
J.L. Thomasson /sic/
B.B. Dunham
J. Sutton
(Continued next page)

Miss___White
C.F. Mersh
J. Howland and lady
Mrs.___Lombard
Mrs.___Sowles and child
Mrs.___Nuttal /sic/
W.L. Miller
Capt.___Lawrence
A. Steward
J. De Puton and lady
G.W. Jewell
C. Foot
J.P. Doremus
D.D. Fairchild
J. Baird
John Jansen
H. Heirsh
D. Simon
John Winer
N. Sleeper
R.P. Lewis
N.R. Tavener
M. Wesserman
H. Rolson
M. Frost
H. Malley
A. Reirshul
N.G. Simond /sic/
J.R. Allen
W.H. Bailey
H. French
L. Demenstroy
H.D. Whipple
S. Cook
J. Hargraves
G. Hasbrouck
A. McDonald
D. Haly /sic/
D.A. Weston
G.M. Alden
O. Phillips
T. King
R.F. King
N.S. Atwood
J. Stephenson
W.H. Plummer
J.G. Plummer
S.D. Willis
W. Lawless

(*)Note M. Eder and lady, page 203.

J.O. Butler
F. Barnes
M.L. Warren
T. Howes
J. Wheeler
P. Cross
J. Carey Jr.
Mrs.___Hays
E.B. Ryan
Mrs.___Bayer
R. Stinger
D. Loper
J.J. Osborn
F.P. Rhodes
J. Baker
T.A. Jones
J.A. Bandt
J.L. Wood
W. Wood
J.K. McLeod
J.B. Flood
W.C. Duff
___Daffycy /sic/
L. Butts and dog
J. Butts
Daniel Walton
D. Barker
L.C. Waldo/sic/
M. Scorro and son
Mrs.___Norton and
   child
M. Olier /sic/
Mrs.___Bills
H. Duval
M. Dingler
J. Walbro /sic/
J. Woodlaw
John June
H. Jackson
J. Jackson
R.A. Doyle
T.B. Hall
S. Ricketsen
Alex Flanigan
E. Flanigan
A. Card
J. Farnham
J. Laurie
G.A. Picket /sic/
J. Nuttal /sic/
S. Leitner

E.F.M. Dykes
H. Henshaw
F.A. Halliburton
S. Preston
J.M. Preston
W.R. Goodnaugh
C. Myers
Miss___Sims
U. Kinney
L.R. Henderson
M. McAfee
J.E. Ingraham
W. Howell
J. Eskinger
W.F. Bastinger
L.J. Manro /sic/
G. Hughes
J.A. Rogers
W.C. Thomas
W. Fortune
___Kinnsly & lady/sic/
Dr.___Todd
W. Widden and
   brother
W. Emmett and
   brother
R. Forizey
M. Morehouse Jr.
M. Dabas
W. Patten
L. Chapilin /sic/
   and friend
   (Chaplin?)
F. Orr
M. Good
D. Pempelli
A.C. Dexter
M. Beckwith
J.R. Styles
R. McDaniel
W. Shade
E. Croden
J. Keyes
J. Johnson
M. Murray
C. Little
H.McCullough
J. Slaght
S. Hallagan
W. Stewart
J. Gaier
(Continued next page)

J. Guess/sic/
J. Tiern
B. Tiern
B. White
M. Hall
G. Van Hagen
Mrs.___Dunlap
J. Bowon and lady
   /sic/
E.E. Holden
J. Gaden
J.S. Haines
J.J. Sutton
W.W. Todd
W.A. Hill
J.W. Hill
F.M. Farmer
C. Wade
J. Wade
W.H. Wade
Mrs.___Carter
___Martin
D. Cometti
M. Cometti
F. Hanse and son
L.N. Burns
G.A. Wood
Martha Snow
A.F. Hogan
B. Gribble
M. Peggard and
   friend
O. Alamondie
G.W. Dennison
G. Rinkham
A. Allison
James Moore
F. Disterdeck
H. Shroeder /sic/
W. Shroeder /sic/
T. Maher
W.H. Jacobs
James Woodrow
J. McFarland
William Hays
D. Woolf /sic/
S. Bishop
T. Lewis
M.P. Dorsh
T. Cade
E. Meiley

H. Harrison, wife
& 5 children
R. Dudley
R.W. Cromwell
J.H. Harrington
L. Killin
M.H. Hermstan
W.N. Hart
S. Tilton
J. Mayall
E. Mayall
L. Weyterman
Mrs.____Weyterman
Mrs.____Shephard /sic/
M.E. Davock
C. Younker and
lady
J. Genage
J.N. Palmer
J.C. Baker
D. Healy
Charles Fowler
A. Clark
F. Creme
H. Stedman
J. McNear
I. Hall
J. McMaster
D. Carpenter
G. Sukosi
O. Piciani
J.M. Beers
G.W. Bryant
J. Bean
A.G. Blake
A. McKie
C. Henscher
J. Shepherd /sic/
T. Evans
A. Evans
J. Davis
V. Jahant
R. Rurgess /sic/
(Burgess?)
G.R. Little
S. Yocham
S.J. Poston
C. Roy
N. Roy
J. Clark
Z. Guest /sic/

M.O. Hanna
L. Parish
W.H. Rowe
E. Platt
C.J. Pegg
J.F. Hughes
J. Blake
J.B. Stratton
D.W. Brown
J. Ocho
L.W. Wells
Mrs. S. Montrose
Mrs. B. Montrose
J. Keely and lady
J. Teal
A. Dotta and lady
M. Dotta
L. Solarie
C.H. Graham
E.A. Hopham
M. Dugan and two
children
M.P. Dunn
H. Ruder
C.W. Whitman
C. Surkemp
J. Wilsen /sic/
S. Miller
C. Johnson
F. Stopauli
L. Laeosi
W. Back
J.W. Roberts
E. Henley
J. Gue /sic/
A. Barber
L. McDonald
W. Earnest
D. Earnest
H. Hopkins
J. Dunn
E. Dunn
P. McKeen
A.D. Brownell
W.L. Parker, lady
and child
A. Wiley
R. Wiley
Dr. E. Shield
T. Hopkins
C. Hopkins
(Continued next page)

G. Bates
W. Ingals /sic/
J. Earle
T. Rankin
M. Donovan
J.R. Henfield
H. Rockwood
F. Weaver
C. Edwards
R. Sewall
J.J. Welben
A. Joseph
A.J. Saben
L. Samuel
M. Fadget and lady
J. Fitzpatrick
L. Guse
J. Pine
C. Hemstreet
W.J. White
A.D. Wells
M.J. Barber
A.W. Wright
H. Halsen
J.H. Welsh
W. Knapman
J. Orten
A. Brabende
B.F. Wade
L. Morse
A. Johnson
A. Powers
C. Spaulding
H. Wells
J. Hathaway
F. Rabe
L. Banks
L. Banks II
D.D. Thomas
J. Thomas
W. Danforth
L.H. Brown
G. Shaffer
R. Parsons
Mrs. M.L. Moore
Mrs.____Corrigan
and child
R. Cuney /sic/
J.W. Kelton, lady
and 2 children
E. Valentine

J.H. Ensworth	F.H. Hewlett	J.H. Tourtelette
H.B. Moore	L. Goodwin	W. Van Logan
D. Sealy	J. Carty	A.S. Kenyon
J.R. Jacobs	W. Wright and lady	P. Hitheard
W. Hitchcock	Dr.___ Russell	W. Thompson
S. Waller and lady	Z. Fell	J. Tapiano
N. Tapiano		

- - - - - -

SHIP: GULNARE
TYPE: Brig   FROM: Sydney, New South Wales
ARRIVED: May 27, 1852   CAPTAIN: Nosworthy
PASSAGE: 90 days from Sydney, New South Wales. This vessel brings
intelligence that nearly 40,000 people are congregated at
Mount Alexander gold field and although the weekly trans-
mission of gold continues to be large in the aggregate,
the average of each digger's gains is far less than that
earned by the miners of the Turon and Meroo.
CARGO: 1320 tons of coal

Passengers

L. Hamlin and lady	M.A. Perries, son	Miss___ Bellingham
T. Curtagne	& 2 daughters	R.G. Kenny /sic/
Mrs.___ Galvin, son	J. Coleman and	Mrs.___ Simmons and
and daughter	lady	child
M. Cotton	O. Sprinks	Mrs.___ Whitfield
Miss___ O'Donnell/sic/	J. Keena /sic/	& 3 daughters
M. Connell and	J. Blackington	Henry Davis and
wife /sic/	John Swaine	wife
Thomas Facy	W. Fitzgerald	Mrs.___ Glasson and
Mrs. Charlotte Jones,	Mrs. L. Weir and	daughter
son & daughter	3 daughters	Thomas McKeon
Patrick Freeman and	John Connor	P. Dillon
wife	M. Riley and son	T. Dillon
Margaret Cherry	J. Sullivan and	D. Dillon
Maria Cherry	wife	Rebecca Harper
Mrs.___ Goodridge		

- - - - - -

SHIP: ISABELLA
TYPE: Barque   FROM: San Juan del Sur,
ARRIVED: May 28, 1852   Nicaragua
CAPTAIN: Miller
PASSAGE: 89 days from San Juan del Sur, Nicaragua, via Lahaina,
Sandwich Islands, 25 days. This vessel brings the in-
telligence that James Kalhakalaui, aged 16 years, died
in Lahaina, Sandwich Islands, on April 21, 1852. He was
the son of Kanekea(spelling?) and Keoho Kalole, and great
grandson of Keaweahulu, the High Priest, when Captain
James Cook lost his life at Kealakekua. The following
passengers died during the passage of the "Isabella":
March 11, 1852:- Walter Rutherford, of Delaware County,
New York, aged 40 years.

March 16, 1852:- W.P. Denman, of Washtenaw County,
Michigan, aged 35 years.
March 16, 1852:- Abel Crossman, of Berrien County,
Michigan, aged 50 years.
March 28, 1852:- Okftt Depew, of Washtenaw County,
Michigan, aged 26 years.
April 4, 1852:- J.D. Marshall, of St. Marks, Texas,
aged 2 years and 3 months.
April 7, 1852:- Frederick Bher, of Germany, and late
of Illinois, aged 45 years.

CARGO: 8 boxes of Irish potatoes, 1200 pumpkins, 500 melons and
10 bunches of bananas.

Passengers
39 unidentified passengers*
(*)In addition to those indicated as dying during passage.

— — — — —

SHIP: HOOGLY*
TYPE: Clipper   FROM: Boston, Massachusetts
ARRIVED: May 29, 1852   CAPTAIN: Chadwick
PASSAGE: 127 days from Boston, Massachusetts, via Rio de Janeiro,
Brazil. When three days out from Boston the fore and
main topmasts were carried away and had to put into Rio
de Janeiro for repairs.
CARGO: 1 horse power, 1 wheel, 1 thresher, 1 separator, 1 fan
wheel, 223 bundles of iron, 55 chairs, oysters, tar, 635
kegs molasses, 200 bbls oil, 2500 bags oats, 5 boxes of
agricultural tools, boots and shoes, rivets, anvils and
bellows, soap, 7 carriage bottoms, 50 wheels, 6 pair of
springs, cream tartar, furniture, iron safes, 2 crushing
machines, marble, 184 iron doors, shingles and assorted
goods.

Passengers

D.W. Pinkham (of
Maine)
Mrs. Melissa D.
Pinkham & infant
(of Augusta,
Maine)
B. Pinkham (of
Augusta,Maine)
Rev.Benjamin Brierly
(of Brandon, Vt.)
Mrs.F.M. Brierly
(of Brandon, Vt.)
B.C. Brierly
(of Brandon, Vt.)
M.B. Frost (of
Groton, Conn.)
Benjamin McKendry
& lady (of Boston)

Mrs.Mary B. Taylor
& child (of
South Boston,
Mass.)
Miss E.J. Taylor (of
South Boston,
Mass.)
Master___Taylor (of
South Boston,
Mass.)
J.R. Brierly (of
Brandon, Vt.)
W. Miner (of Groton,
Conn.)
E. Newton (of Groton,
Conn.)
T.D. Wilson (no town
listed)

Mrs. R.S. Taylor (of
South Boston,
Mass.)
Miss M.F. Taylor (of
South Boston,
Mass.)
Miss M.A. Taylor (of
South Boston,
Mass.)
J. McLand (of Dexter,
Maine)
D. McLand (of Dexter,
Maine)
Mrs. M.E. McLand (of
Dexter, Maine)
F. McLand (of Dexter,
Maine)
J.B.Ruelle(no town)

(Continued next page)
(*)This vessel also known as the "Hoogley".

J.T. Haskell (of Waldoborough, Maine)	G. Gardner (of Boston, Mass.)	S.B. Mayhew (of Charlestown, Mass.)
Samuel Hamlin (or Hamlen?)(of Providence-no State listed)	J.L. Roberts (of Boston, Mass.)	W.Q. Brown Jr. (no town listed)
	H.W. Taylor(of South Boston, Mass.)	A. Merritt (of Quincy, Mass.)
D.L. Perkins (of Boston, Mass.)	F.D. Williams (of Boston)	

- - - - - -

SHIP: BALTIMORE
TYPE: Brig (Hawaiian)   FROM: Waimea, S.I.
ARRIVED: May 28, 1852   CAPTAIN: Thop /sic/
PASSAGE: 18 days from Waimea, Sandwich Islands. This vessel brings
         intelligence of the death of John S. Owens, in Honolulu,
         Sandwich Islands on April 30, 1852. One contemporary
         source lists the death as "John L. Owens". Owens was one
         of the pioneer settlers in San Francisco, from whence he
         moved to Stockton, California. He went to the Islands to
         regain his health.
CARGO: 10 casks sperm oil, 90 boxes soap, 754 bags brown sugar, 20
       20 casks whale oil, 48 coils manila rope 88 kegs butter, 46
       bbls syrups and a number of barrels of dried apples.

Passengers

C. Baulker and daughter	H.A. Latoesan and lady	Capt.___Hill (U.S. Army)
Capt.___Hanna	Miss___Partridge	Carolina Goodyear
Mr.___Peabody	D.L. Lanhallan	

- - - - - -

SHIP: POTSDAM
TYPE: Ship (German)   FROM: Valparaiso, Chile
ARRIVED: May 28, 1852   CAPTAIN: Wolf
PASSAGE: 58 days from Valparaiso, Chile.
CARGO: 98 cases dried fruit, 1800 bags barley, 205 boxes candles,
       350 cases wine, 331 boxes vermicelli, 1250 bags flour,
       9 cases of boots and shoes and assorted merchandise.

Passenger
Don Hosea De Kalma

- - - - - -

SHIP: MARY MELVILLE
TYPE: Barque   FROM: Oregon Territory
ARRIVED: May 29, 1852   CAPTAIN: Bailey
PASSAGE: 5 days from the Oregon Territory.
CARGO: 90,000 feet lumber, 244 bundles laths, 10 bbls butter, 20
       kegs butter, 13 packages eggs, 47 sacks potatoes, 1 bbl
       lard, 3 coops chickens, 47 hogs.

Passengers

B.G. Durett	S. Walker	___Hoxis
___Stansbury		

- - - - - -

SHIP: JOHN HENRICH
TYPE: Barque (Dutch)   FROM: Amsterdam, Holland
ARRIVED: May 29,1852   CAPTAIN: Not listed
PASSAGE: Total passage time not listed. From Amsterdam, Holland,
         via Valparaiso, Chile, 50 days from latter port.
CARGO: 10 casks cement, 2840 bars and 160 bundles of iron, 362
         boxes glass, 45 pipes gin, 4 pkgs white lead, 600 packages
         of lead in oil, 1 cask lime juice, 300 casks butter, 1 case
         pictures, cheese, wine, vinegar, vermicelli, beer, 26 casks
         of verdigris, 36 casks of blue and assorted goods.

Passengers

E.A. San Melligan   F. Birley   J. Morrison
A. Buch   L. Grossoro

- - - - - -

SHIP: J.C. LEGRAND
TYPE: Brig   FROM: San Juan del Sur,
ARRIVED: May 30, 1852   Nicaragua
CAPTAIN: Gregory
PASSAGE: 34 days from San Juan del Sur, Nicragua. On May 25, 1852,
         saw the British schooner "Hurricane" in lat. 30N, long.
         130W. The "Hurricane" was 46 days from Valparaiso, Chile,
         bound for San Francisco.
CARGO: In ballast.

Passengers

E.D. St. Cyr and	Mrs. ___ Milligan	Thomas Burns
lady	J.S. Martin	W. Polly
P.S. Colgrove	Charles Young	S.A. Burns
J. Callaghan	E.E. Perkins	E.C. Belding
G.A. Swaynay	J.E. Perkins	J.F. Morrell
H. Strain	T. Bailey	L. Lynder
T. Birney	H. Brown	Leo Bume /sic/
J. Mitchell	B. Collins	C. Pierce
L. Wright	L. Frayer	J. Gardiner
J.W. Tyler	P.M. Taft	J. Beebee
D. Perkins	C.B. Eastman	A. Christian
C. Perkins	D. Fox	P. Mantier
N. Morton	J. Igram /sic/	A.F. Wallace
N. Truim	T. Putnam	J.W. Hall and svt
J.W. White	L. Dodd	C.H. Emerson
P. Crossman	S. McKittrell /sic/	E. Snyder
H. Mendolhon /sic/	H. Rockmahn /sic/	D. McKay
M. Schoffer	J. Hayton	J. Khurur /sic/
J. Muntack	J. McKittrick /sic/	G. Hanson
O.M. Warren	E.H. Reefman	J. Ewing
J. Nichols	T. Edward	C. Anderson
J. Daymon	J.S. Hardy	J.C. Stewart
J.W. Peirce	J.W. French	R.C. Lonogen
O.C. Eaton	H. Crane	W.J. Smith
J.W. Claxton	G. Claxton	E. Claxton
J. McMann & lady	G.N. Power	D. Brooks

(Continued next page)

The following deaths took place during the passage of the "J. C. Legrand":

> May 1, 1852:- G. Jones, of Pennsylvania, aged 30 years, of diarrhea.
> May 1, 1852:- Griffiths Pew, of Utica, New York, aged 30 years, of diarrhea.
> May 6, 1852:- Michael Miller, of Surrey County, England, aged 30 years, of diarrhea.
> May 9, 1852:- J.S. Maston, of Poughkeepsie, New York, aged 24 years, of diarrhea.
> May 17,1852:- Thomas Burns, of New Haven, Connecticut, age unknown, of diarrhea.
> May 29, 1852:-John Bright, of Utica, New York, aged 30 years, of diarrhea.

- - - - -

SHIP: LOWELL
TYPE: Brig   FROM: Talcahuana, Chile
ARRIVED: May 30, 1852   CAPTAIN: Mann
PASSAGE: 58 days from Talcahuana, Chile.
CARGO: 300,000 apples.

Passengers-

Mrs. R. Elmasaria and   Miss Clara Aregaro   S. Gonzales
   3 children   and child   N. Ray
Miss Louisa Harrison
              and 49 unidentified in steerage

- - - - -

SHIP: EXACT
TYPE: Schooner   FROM: Puget Sound, W.T.
ARRIVED: May 30, 1852   CAPTAIN: Folger
PASSAGE: 7 days from Puget Sound, Washington Territory. On May
         22, 1852, off Cape Flattery, saw the British frigate
         "Thetis", 40 days from Callao, Peru, bound in.
CARGO: 92,000 laths and 200 bushels of oysters.

Passenger
H.A. Bailey

- - - - -

SHIP: LEVERET
TYPE: Brig   FROM: Oregon Territory
ARRIVED: May 31, 1852   CAPTAIN: Davis
PASSAGE: 5 days from the Oregon Territory.
CARGO: 150 tons potatoes, 100 sacks wheat

Passengers

Mr.___ Rhodes and   J. Masterman   P. Child
   lady   O. Guernsey

- - - - -

SHIP: LAURA BEVAN(or LAURA BEVANS?)
TYPE: Schooner   FROM: San Luis Obispo,Calif.
ARRIVED: June 1, 1852   CAPTAIN: Not listed
PASSAGE: From San Luis Obispo, California, via Monterey,California
         (36 hours from latter port). The "Laura Bevan" brings to
         San Francisco five passengers from the steamer "McKim"
         (at Monterey), all the other passengers of the steamer
         had left previously.
CARGO: Pine wood.

Passengers

Capt.___Osborne   P. Miller   C. O'Leary
J. Cloutman, M.D.   W. O'Leary

- - - - - -

SHIP: SHERIFF
TYPE: Schooner   FROM: Bodega, California
ARRIVED: June 2, 1852   CAPTAIN: Tibbey
PASSAGE: 11 hours from Bodega, California.
CARGO: 50,000 feet of lumber and 60 tons of potatoes.

Passengers

Mr.___Giddings   Mr.___Tibbey and   J. White
   and lady   child   J. Nye
W. Scripton   W. Gaurr /sic/   L. Torress

- - - - - -

SHIP: POMONA
TYPE: Schooner   FROM: Trinidad, California
ARRIVED: June 5, 1852   CAPTAIN: Terry
PASSAGE: 2 days from Trinidad, California. The master of the
         Pomona reports that the brig "John Clifford", Captain
         ___Leming commanding, was wrecked in attempting to cross
         the bar coming out of Humboldt Bay, California. The "John
         Clifford" carried a full cargo of lumber destined for San
         Francisco.
CARGO: 36,000 feet of lumber.

Passengers

Col. A.J. Butler,lady,   Mrs.___O'Meara and   Major___Sales
   2 children & svt   child   Mr. L.B. Gilkey

- - - - - -

SHIP: SARAH LAVINIA
TYPE: Schooner   FROM: Santa Cruz, California
ARRIVED: June 7, 1852   CAPTAIN: Norway
PASSAGE: 4 days from Santa Cruz, California.
CARGO: 36,000 feet of lumber, 125 boxes lime.

Passengers

W. Cutell   Capt.___Whitney   J.L. Marshall
Mr.___Jones

- - - - - -

SHIP: WILHELMINA
TYPE: Brig (Hawaiian)   FROM: Lahaina, S.I.
ARRIVED: June 7, 1852   CAPTAIN: King
PASSAGE: 25 days from Lahaina, Sandwich Islands.
CARGO: 400 bbls potatoes, 200 bbls sweet potatoes and 90 hogs.
                        Passengers
            Mr.____Niles   Mr.____Pollard
                  - - - - - -

SHIP: TRIUMPH
TYPE: Brig   FROM: San Juan del Sur
ARRIVED: June 9, 1852   CAPTAIN: Rogers
PASSAGE: 61 days from San Juan del Sur, Nicaragua.
CARGO: In ballast.
                        Passengers
Mr.____Gharky, lady   Mr.____Stewart, lady   Mr.____Ogden, lady
   & 2 children   & child   & child
Mr.____Waters, lady   Mr.____Collins, lady   Dr. A.D. Ferguson
   & child   & son   Capt.____Blackstone
Capt.____Blasdell   Mr.____Curtis
Mrs.____Blasdell
                  and 64 unidentified passengers
                  - - - - - -

SHIP: TARQUINA
TYPE: Brig   FROM: Oregon Territory
ARRIVED: June 9, 1852   CAPTAIN: Willett
PASSAGE: 4 days from Oregon Territory.
CARGO: 2000 bushels potatoes, 12 tons butter, 400 chickens, 35
       hogs and 103,000 feet of lumber.
                        Passengers
R.H. McNear   J. Stewart   L. Rousseau
O.J. Backus   G.M. Reed
                  - - - - - -

SHIP: HERON
TYPE: Sloop (British)   FROM: Tahiti
ARRIVED: June 9, 1852   CAPTAIN: Lyons
PASSAGE: 50 days from Tahiti, via Maui, Sandwich Islands.
CARGO: 60,000 oranges, 100 citron, 100 lemons.
                        Passengers
Capt.____Harrison and   Mr.____Walch, lady   Mr.____Clinet and
   lady   & child   lady
                  - - - - - -

SHIP: EMMA
TYPE: Brig (French)   FROM: Tahiti
ARRIVED: June 11, 1852   CAPTAIN: Redic
PASSAGE: 53 days from Tahiti.
CARGO: 110,000 oranges and 1 cask of limes.
                        Passengers
            Mr.____Lamonie   Mr.____Mullimer
                  - - - - - -

214

SHIP: SUCCESS
TYPE: Barque   FROM: Oregon Territory
ARRIVED: June 12, 1852   CAPTAIN: Fairley /sic/
PASSAGE: 3½ days from the Oregon Territory.
CARGO: 110,000 ft of 3 inch plank, 16 cases of unidentified
       merchandise.

Passengers

J.C. Lewis   L.B. Brown   C.H. Clark
J.S. Somers

- - - - - -

SHIP: WINFIELD SCOTT
TYPE: Steamer   FROM: Panama
ARRIVED: June 15, 1852   CAPTAIN: K. Couillard
PASSAGE: 14 days from Panama, via Acapulco, Mexico. Departed
         Panama on May 29, 1852 at 9:00PM. Arrived at Acapulco on
         June 5, 1852 and departed on the evening of June 7, 1852.
         Encountered very heavy weather all the voyage. This
         vessel brings intelligence of the appointment of Major
         Pearson B. Reading, of California, to the office of
         Superintendent of Indian Affairs for California.
            Two passengers died at sea during the passage, both
         were sick when they came on board. Deceased were:
            June 8,1852 - Nelson Asten, of Springfield, Mass., of
                          dysentery.
            June 14,1852- J. Costello, of Mobile,Alabama, of
                          dysentery.

CARGO: Not listed.

Passengers

D. Shoemaker and   B.B. Wallace   J. Dunken
   lady   Mr.___Heskell   Mrs.___Fuller
Mrs.___Driver   Mrs.___Saunders   Miss___Ayers /sic/
Th. Plank /sic/,   T.J. Stonagle,lady   James Hogg, lady
   lady & 5 chldrn   & 4 children   & 3 children
   (Thomas Plank?)   J.C. Smith, lady   J.J. Monoue /sic/
Mr.___Massbaum   and child   John Copeland
Charles Bader and   W. Denegan, lady   Mr.___Robinson
   lady   & 2 children   D.L. Libbey
Sam Howe   A.J. Drosser   Thomas Lane
Montgomery House   R. Pray   W. Stiles
D.B. Blake   R. Monsell   W. McAllister
F. Moone /sic/   J.W. Rucker   George Dwight
D.N. Sloan   J. Roberts   S. Utley
H. Sesulman (?)   H. Mergen   Peter Town
   (Sesuiman?)   M. Hallett   Jacob Stone
D. Carpenter, wife   A. Jones   Charles Burg
   & 2 children   David Letz /sic/   T.S. Harrison
W.T. Hunt   Andrew Letz /sic/   Mrs. Donerly /sic/
James McConger (?)   Lawton Letz /sic/   H.M. Nichul /sic/
   (James M. Conger?) Henry Letz /sic/   (Nichol?)
Samuel Weller   William Cole   William Starvey
                       (Continued next page)

James Mone /sic/
H. Cocknell
Mrs.____Owens
George Findley
James Barnes
J. Papois
E. Conner
Mrs.____Hewlitt
William Jibb
W. Meyers/sic/
L.A. Barington /sic/
G. Hicken, lady
  and child
P. Poida /sic/
M.J. Keenan
J.H. Robinson
Mr.____Wickerden
H. Shield and lady
D. Getz and lady/sic/
W. Hoagland
J. Hoagland
H. Neil
Dr.____Hallenbush
John Conner
Mrs.____Vangeddes
Miss____Messervy /sic/
M.J. Van Amen
M.W. Watson
M.W. Messer
Mr.____Wolf and
  lady
Mr.____Brading
Mr.____Berford
Mr.____Laurens
L.A. Davis
C.C. Davis
E. Andrews
J. Donohue
J. Pintoven
H.B. White
W. Sallman
B. Nelson
P. Savity
E. Miller
M. Marble
A. Hergan
J.W. Feyshler
W. Barsten
J. Stephens
J. Higgins and wife
A.L. Eddy

James Champion
M. Hubbard
Perry Levene
M. Jaller
John Spinney
John Moore
B. Moore
J. Loud
James Loud
W. Wingler
P. West and lady
Mrs.____Blangy
A.S. Patterson and
  lady
C.M. Chase
A. Ayres /sic/
O.H. Ayres /sic/
J. Ayres/sic/
J.E. Kade
A.B. Kade
D. Fuller
A. Runnell
Stuart Smith
E.C. Hall
Mrs. A. Seeley
H.G. Addison
Robert Duke, lady
  & servant
J.S. Reed
A.B. Ashen and
  lady
C. Littlejohn
Mr.____Atheam
A.F. Dudley
L. Cahn
William Hewlitt
H.M. Cal /sic/
J. Worden
F.J. Andrews
W.J. Felix
L. Duffey /sic/
H. Paganilly
F. Meyer /sic/
G.D. Foster
B. Driver
J. Hannington
Martin Kelly
W. Denstone
J. Walker
J. Manning
T.P. Hutchings
(Continued next page)

N. Boughton
M. Smith
J. Durand
J. Pervan
Peter Strickland
T.L. Wellington
H. Smith
E. Hass, lady and
  servant
Rev. A.D. Loring
Mrs.____Howard
R. Lewis, lady and
  child
W. Scott
J.C. Smith
E.R. Dudley
R. Lee
H.G. Kilgour /sic/
Mr.____Halloway
O.F. Blackburn
Mr.____Lask and lady
B. Peanut
John Hudson and svt
Dr. J.G. Morgan
Mrs.____Tilden and
  daughter
Mrs.____Ticoy /sic/
Mrs.____Worth
M.L. Winn, lady and
  2 children
Mrs. M. Preston
Mr.____Graham and
  lady
J.C. Lauhton /sic/
  (Laughton?)
B. Roberts
J. Duffey /sic/
J. Pollock
D. Crockett
P. Levnau /sic/
J. Roper
S. Cromlin
J. Cunningham
M. Fellet
T. Clerk
A. Friend
Thomas D. Wade
W. Wright
M. Hartney
G. Saunders
S. Dakin

216

F.W. Feild /sic/
  (Field?)
J. Horner
J. Collington
J. Reiley /sic/
T. Birmingham
C.M. McDonald
E. Fitzgerald
C. Crocker
W. Crocker
J. Cartwright
F. Hardie
G. Johnson
E.H. Walker
M. Meyers /sic/
D. Wright
A. Wise
R. Virgun and 24
  others (not
  identified)
H.D. Herman
A. Mays
C. De Graff
J. Mullay
F. Hilton
A. Hilton
Mr.___Theller
E. Hubbard
W. Carpenter
C. Martin and son
J. Haster /sic/
William Hasser /sic/
W. Kaster /sic/
Will Rahn
J.T. Hiblen
R. Salem
G. Hoa /sic/
J. Fredericks
T. Kneeland /sic/
J. James
W. Cordray
P. Hays
W. ?eyer and wife
  (Reyer?,Beyer?,
  Meyer?)
J. Starkey
T. Vandeken
J. Field
J.H. Wood
G. Roth
C. West

G.L. Bliss
W. Squires
N. Swan
J. Mulligan, wife
  & 2 children
J. Belden
E. Robinson
J. Elliott
J. Smith /sic/
B. Shaw
B.F. Skillman
L. Fitch
G. Fearner
T. Asher
G. Scholdt
W. Frame
J.R. Carponter /sic/
  (Carpenter?)
J. Tader
R. Belfore /sic/
Ann Butler
J. Doyl /sic/
  (Doyle?)
William Catelon
W. Wininger /sic/
  and lady
  ___Somenly
G.W. Mannor
A. Hansel
J.W. Gaulkner
H. Schultz
Thomas Bant
Mrs.___Becking
P. Bram
  ___Malcom /sic/
  (Malcolm?)
E. Griefe
A. Ravel
W. Thomas
P. Engle
J. Crawley
F. Haffmister
W. Sanyard /sic/
J. Maynard /sic/
A. Pitcher
J. Mellody /sic/
S. Wetland /sic/
E. Monnesey
H. Tibbits /sic/
J. Wallace
S. Highme /sic/
(Continued next page)

J. Cook
W.L. Lawton
M. Till
R. Goodyall /sic/
P. Harris
H. Haskie (?) and
  wife (Haskle?)
  ___McMentor and
  wife
H. Sturke
J. Thompson
A. Huldfelt
H. Ackerman
G. Hide
W. Hodge
J. Brown
C. Brown
W. McNight /sic/
D. Tittle
D. Enson
A. Enson
J. Street
J. Park
I. Park
G. Park
R. Pyam
G.B. Hoffman
F.E. Clay
F. Duprie
J. Smith /sic/
William Stone
E.T. Ettington /sic/
Mrs.___Hunting
M. Hunting
A. Etting /sic/
C. Liverham
N. Miller
A. Canfield
L. Lloyd
J. Lynch
S. Parker
G. Thunderhouse and
  wife
T. Friend
A. Lander
T. Brown
W. Bantine
N.W. Ellis
J.W. Ellis
F.T. Ellis
P. Cody

R. Ayers /sic/
A. Ayers /sic/
S. Ayers /sic/
J.A. Rogers
G.H. Rogers
L. Daly
W.H. Jones
W. Bleakley
S.P. Parsons
M. Lingle
Mrs. A.L. Brownlee
B. Beckwith
D.M. Vanberg
P. Corris
R. Hayes
G. Hayes
S. Cockamore
G. Hubbard
W. Freind /sic/
  (Friend?)
E. Welch
A. Meyer
H. Russell

W. Greensdale
C. Smith
D. Howell
J. McCollen and
  lady
T. Donaghu /sic/
  (Donaghue?)
C. Collins
G. Miller
W. Scott
   Tinkindale /sic/
L.B. Dowing
P. Osgood
P. Douglass
Mary Lyon
T. Lyon
N. Elder
G. Samson
F. Reiken
Mrs.____McKune
John Bader
J. Welsh
D.G. Rouse

J. Perry
W.H. Post
O. Fordham
J.H. Fordham
D. Shoemaker
William Mix
N. Antone
T.B. Merridith /sic/
W. Greek
Mrs.____Brisch and
  3 children
H. Hest /sic/
J. Minch
J. Sweet
J. Johnson
L. Waters
J. Walker
J. Mitchell
J. McClure
T. Reed
F. Goris
M. Schroder

- - - - - -

SHIP: NORTHERNER
TYPE: Steamer   FROM: Panama
ARRIVED: June 16, 1852   CAPTAIN: J.B. Isham
PASSAGE: 19 days from Panama, via intermediate ports. Sailed from
Panama at 11:00PM on May 27, 1852. From Point Mala to
within 80 miles of Acapulco experienced strong winds and
gales from the north-west, and heavy head seas. Arrived
at Acapulco, Mexico on June 4th. Sailed from Acapulco on
June 5th and experienced strong head winds until June
12th. Arrived at San Diego, California on June 13th and
sailed same day. Arrived at Monterey, California on June
15th and sailed same day. The below passengers died during the passage:
        Levi Scoffield (sic), 23 years of age, of Mount
        Awarot, Vermont; of dysentery.
        Joseph Crawford, 25 years of age, of New York City;
        of dysentery.
        Robert Masters, 21 years of age, of Wisconsin; of
        dysentery.
        Elisha Root, 27 years of age, of Rochester, New
        York; of dysentery.
CARGO: Not listed.

Passengers

Capt.____Knight and
  family
Miss____Jeffers

W. Whitney and
  family
Mrs.____Wright

H.M. Newhall and
  family
Mrs.____Downs

(Continued next page)

218

E.H. Watson and
  family
Miss___Bevin
Mrs.___Bevin
Miss D. Bevin
A. Leonard
J.W. Bubous
Mrs.___Varney
Mrs. L. Deal
Mrs.___Bookstaver
Mrs.___Clare
Mrs.___Hutchings
Mrs. B.F. Smith
S. Satro /sic/
J.J. Cooke
D.C. Gardiner
J.A. Cole
J.B. Kelly
James de la Montayne
O. Satro /sic/
J.S. Burton
O.H. Dibblee
A.B. Dibblee
Capt.___Codman
H.W. McNay
G. Boyce
T. Boyce
Dr. J.F. Hornsby
W. Willis
A.S. Swearinger
W.R. Stephens
D. Blair
W.E. Lippincott
J.W. Martin
H. Moorhouse
G. Moorhouse
Helen Tracy
W.M. Strand
W. Pierce
T.H. Atwood
F. Pattani
Julia Grisby /sic/
  and wife
C.W. Corner
A. Black
A. Rurgess /sic/
  (Burgess?)
C. Gennata
Martin Curtiss
W. Garfield
J.B. Mortimer

E. Hall and family
Mrs.___Eldred and
  child
Mrs.___Dougherty and
  2 children
G. Sweeney
Mrs. C. Jones
Mrs.___Raymond
Miss___Dunlap
Mrs.___Lyon and
  family
Mrs.___Warner
Mrs. J.W. McCabe and
  infant
H.B. Williams
E.S. Matthisson /sic/
L.P. Sage
D.W. Swift
P.A. Pa?view
  (Panview?,
   Parview?)
A. Sweat
R. McCright
H. Foster
L. Bean
R. James
James Greinstead
J.H. Marks (?)
W.C. McElroy
H. Seymour
James Norgues /sic/
W.S. Phillips
E.A. Phillips
A.W. Gallier
William Kelley
B. Sprague
C. Sprague
W. Kain
Charles T. Perry
N. George
C. Phillippini
R. Handy
C. Seiderman
Mary Ryan
H.D. Krondahl
W.D. Brown
Ira Conant
J. Vartigus
J. Springer
H. Scaffer
S.D. Perkins
(Continued next page)

J. Smiley and
  family
Mrs.___Tompkins,
  2 children & svt
Miss L.J. Roatner
O.F. Gilter
Mrs.___Josselyn
Mrs.___Hodgedon
Mrs.___Middleton
  and family
Mrs.___Scofield
Mrs. E. Dorr
Mrs.___Irvine
Mrs.___Stone
H. Harwood
J.B. Bames /sic/
B.O. Williams
A.L. Williams
A.L. Williams Jr.
S.W. Stearnes
J. Mennoy
E.P. Barker
J.L. Hepburne /sic/
L.P. Pope
Thomas Patton
J.H. Moray
H. Livingston
L.W. Wright
H.Y. Addison
J. Stone
D.H. Stone
J.A. Stone
J. Potts
J.B. Barton
L. Bard
J.C. Howard
John Dougherty
T. Collins
James Tilfer
E. Penney
L. Blanc /sic/
J. Van Faltgas/sic/*
Mary Dougherty
Dr.___Challoner
W.B. Bailey
S. Collier
J. Tonella
L. Martin
Miss___Hart
A. Garfield
William Tobin

(*)Note F.Vanfithgas, page 218.

P. Burnham
M. Burger
John Newell
Mr.____Delarau
Mrs.____Delarau
A. Hoffman
G. Hoffman
A. Dyer
A.M. Greenleaf
E.W. Saunders
J.M. Otis
B.B. Philbrick
John H. Wells
W.R. Malone
Mr.____Kellogg
B.S. Saunders
L. Hall
L.D. King
J. Robinson
P.P. Hartt /sic/
   (Hart?)
A. Pina
W. Hooper
D. Reed
V. Beffa/sic/
C. Longi
George Green
A. Pendall and
   six brothers
John Howard
G.W. Stevens
J.N. Lansing
James McKinsey
Betsey Burnes /sic/
John Albut
W.A. Perkins
J. Beffa /sic/
A. Beffa /sic/
A.D. Whitcomb
T. Folley
J.N. Queen
P. Gyor /sic/
P. McLane
J. White
S. Myers
R.A. Wick
H. Wilcher
P. Leiby
T.N. Springer
G.O. Baldwin
F. King

Henry Fogg
James Druyer
N.G. Hart
G. Metze
L. Hatch
A. Hatch
William Donaldson
D.S. Sartwell
David Young
C. Underwood
Thomas Campbell
Abner Campbell
H.H. Foster
Mr.____Frink
Mr.____Oneil /sic/
W. Finney
C. Finney
D. Crowley
D. Frazer
S. Patterson
J.B. Guntze
J. Hicks
R. Brook
P. Patlari
George Orr
G. Briggs
G.B. Davis
John H. Davis
J. Shipton
H.H. Frees
A. Beall
G.C. Hutchinson
L. Tonnella
P. Patis
James Martin
S. Pillsbury
Thomas Ryan
John Mass
George Cohen
A. Cracken
Mr. & Mrs.____Burnham
   and 2 children
G. Flint
A.E. Bates
S. King
A.J. Mear
C.W. Brown
Fras Clare /sic/
   (Francis Clare?)
Miss____Conway
J. Beeman
(Continued next page)

J.J. Omstott
J. Coleman
D. Kingsbury
D. Bolger
E. Davis
A. McLean
H.W. Wilson
Thomas Wilson
J. Evans
L.B. Ferries
George Pearce
H.P. Remicle
L. Martin
W.H. Martin
E. Hinckley
R.H. Webster
D.S. Marble
J. Ruse
E. Pearson
M. Picoli
J. Benoise
A.A. Caldwell
M.F. Hoyt
S. Baley /sic/
R. Martin
P. Boldman
E. Wellman
G.B. Allin
George Schly /sic/
   (Sehly?)
Isaac Leight
D. McKinnon
F. Vanfithgas/sic/*
John Sullivan
George Cole
S.A. Rollins
John Weyloff
Lewis Wolf
W. Silk
C. Smith
J. Lawyer
C.D. Nichols
A. Wells
R.M. Burne
D.J. Swab /sic/
F. Norton
J.E. Pierce
M.B. Pickett
B.A. Drinkhouse
Ellen Montes
G. Morgan

(*)Note J. Van Faltgas, page 218.

H.W. Whitney
Aug. Kroft /sic/
   (August Kroft?)
John Sweeney
H. Saulsbury
J. Bowers
M. Finney
W.H. Stubblefield
B. Moared
J. Stone
S. Hunter
T. Glasskin
B. Bantesta /sic/
P. Jabiller
P.V. Dean
William Vicory
A. Ashton
C.F. Pearce
E. Ballard
J.V. Lewis
C. Enos
S. Leiby
F.W. Schaburger
D.W. Long
C. Johnson
E. Moor
F. Smith
G. Simmons
P. McBride
E. Bryant
D. Lanison
L. Dennison
J.L. Fish
C. Weary
J.F. Hamlin
J. Dilley
A. Waltemath
R.R. Wick
P.F. Finney
J. O'Donnell
J. Wyman
A. Beffa /sic/
Emily Grossman
J. Hill
L.B. Murphy
A. Frawgine
J. Cattoe
T. Sken /sic/
G.W. Lawson
C. Lawson
Jane Laddy

John Smith
W. Hendee /sic/
J.H. Park
J. Stoddard
M. Josephi
A.S. Hill
Mr.____Taylor
J. Bockee
P. Perez
P. Prince
Thomas Cheeney
W. Ryan
J. Dickson
W. Thoyall
J. Broas /sic/
C.L. Wilcox
C.H. Patterson
M. Watson
D. Benjamin
A.W. Wick
W. Crummells
O. Chickering
G.S. Routh
J. Matthews
C. Weisner
E. Bent
J. Waterman
J. Morrell
J. Biglow /sic/
L.N. Scofield /sic/
P. Harned
D.D. Root
G.A. Jones
E. Claflin
J.D. Everett
J. Falmer /sic/
J.M. Bissel /sic/
D.W. Koch
R.E. Pierce
J. Sherman
A.L. Russ
D. Sire
R. Josselyn
W. Johnson
N.F. Wood
C. Betta /sic/
B. Hellion
J. Brundy
Mrs.____Rook
J.P. Williams
A.E. Meany
(Continued to next page)

B. Walze
C. Smith
P.H. Owens
M. Haley /sic/
C. Clark
S. Beck
M. Burgin
E. Tobin
M. Zell
F.L. Campbell
B. Haney
F.C. Whaley
T. Dacy
Susan Felsortar
W. Dyke
W. Perkins
E. Peekins /sic/
   (Perkins?)
A. Root
O. Bennett
R.W. Collier
J. George
G. Hoke
J.J. Miller
E. Root
R. Burham /sic/
   (Burnham?)
A. Miller
H. Nichols
M. Rickenbock
Pat Doyle
D. Thomas
C. Forbush
J.L. Gassert
A. Rose
Mr.____Miller and
   wife
W. Henry
A. McKever /sic/
A. Simpson
J. Dotta
J. Schwing
P. McCormick
F. Burges /sic/
A. Garney
G. Daston
J. Long
N. Lock
Mrs.____Shubert
J.D. Barby
M. Mellovoisse

J. Fox	R. Allen	B.L. Hibbard
H. Milner	W. Serogie	T.W. Benton
W. Audray	J.J. Gray	R. Huck
J. Franfini	N.R. Tonella	T. Becker
Mary Pendergast	J. Charles	P. Schoring
Mrs.___Childers	M.B. Howard	C.J. Duncan
E.J. Drugy	N. Elliott	E. Panton
D. Hoegg /sic/	E. Abell	O. Buregon and two
D.D. Leeper	J. Craig	brothers
D. Scranton	J. Duncan	J. Legg
J.Q. Brigham	A.H. Gurnsey	A. Hack
C.E. Blackman	C. Crawford	M. Haley /sic/
G. Cadiex	F. Percy	J. Baxter
A. Gerhald	G. Loomis	E. Charles
D. Brown	W. Berry	J. Hays
C. Strong	A. Shastell	D. Smith
W.F. Steele	J. Broas /sic/	C. Dacy
N. Bernard	G. Monotti	W. Richards
M. Gillett	Mary Thomson	J. Graffe /sic/
J. Casey	H. Wittenbrock	M. Hustin /sic/
G. Seitze	J. Perez	E. McCan /sic/
J.K. Fahey	J. Taylor	F. Nicole /sic/
J. Alexander	R.C. Calvin	T. Stevenson
J. Barrett	J. Botsford	J. Crawford
J. Winter	J. Patrick	F. Basheiri
M. Manni	J.F. Hanland	W. Powell
G.F. Chester	P. Graff /sic/	P.O'Brien
C. Leonard	J.H. Huston /sic/	M. Cockie
P. Holly	A. Bantestor /sic/	J. Deck
J.H. Gillman	H. Smith	J.B. Insco /sic/
Susan Baley /sic/	W. Gage	D. Camosey
J. Jallalie	J. Werner	James Flannerly
M. Tomion	M. Srlma /sic/	M.E. Stearns
S.S. Lencomb	(Srima?)	C. Stone
B. Alexander	S. Osborne	S. Keating

- - - - - -

SHIP: PAQUET de La PAZ
TYPE: Brig (Mexican)   FROM: Mazatlan, Mexico
ARRIVED: June 17, 1852   CAPTAIN: Forga
PASSAGE: 32 days from Mazatlan, Mexico.
CARGO: 30 bbls of eggs and 400 fowls.

Passengers

J.G. Newman	J.S. Jones	J. McKnight
L.B. Newman		John Thomas

- - - - - -

-- PASSENGER LISTS CONTINUED TO NEXT VOLUME --

NOTES

Data contained in this section has been incorporated into the index of this book. Primarily, the following citations deal with variations in the spelling of passenger surnames and given names or expansions on the identity of passengers.

Page 10-11 - (Ship/Typhon, "furniture of various types"):- A secondary source identified the furniture as: "one set of superior rosewood, purple plush, consisting of one tete-à-tete, six chairs, one armchair, and marble-top centre table, glass door wardrobes, with column and plain, rocking chairs, mahogany bedsteads and hair mattresses". The "Typhon" was from New York.

Page 13 - (Ship/Monumental City, from Panama, "J. Lincolns"):- Aforementioned passenger name listed as found in original source. Note "W. Lincoln" and "W.N. Lincoln", same vessel, same page. "J. Lincoln" should be considered alternative.

Page 15 - (Ship/Golden Gate, from New York, "A. Powers, "E. Power"):- Aforementioned passenger names listed as found in original source.

Page 18 - (Added Ship Arrival):- The following vessel arrived in San Francisco on January 13, 1852:

SHIP: COMET   FROM: New York
ARRIVED: January 13, 1852   CAPTAIN: E.C.Gardner(Gardiner?)
PASSAGE: 104 days from New York (port to port or anchor to anchor). Made the Heads on January 12, 1852 with all sails set, including three skysails, with a light breeze from the West. The tide made ebb and the wind died away with the vessel drifting out to sea, but not before communicating with the shore. Stood out to sea and then, with good wind, made San Francisco on January 13th, anchoring below Clark's Point.
CARGO: 30 kegs horseshoes, 5 kegs horseshoe nails, 3 omnibuses and fixtures, 3 piano-fortos, 316 kegs nails, 99 kegs peaches, 9 casks shot, 10 anvils, 208 crowbars, 986 bars iron, 55 sheets boiler iron, 1 case pistols, tobacco, 3 carriages, shovels, bedsteads, 18 wagons, 6 lumber wagons, 16 wagon tongues, 24 carriage wheels, 10 kegs litharge, 50 plough moulds, 86 plough castings, 2 iron wheels, 180 tons of coal, 111 cases powder, 1 case percussion caps and assorted goods.

Passengers

Mrs.____Speckles and 2 children	W.H. Appleman and lady	Mrs. U.H. Vollee and 2 children
C.H. Clark	Mrs.____Washburn	A.F. Brander
J. Gage	J. Coddington	Mr.____Perry

(Continued next page)

Rev. E. Corwin and lady (Chaplain of the American Seaman's Friend
   Society, San Francisco).

- - - - - -

Page 22 - (Ship/North America, from San Juan del Sur, Nicaragua,
   "N.P. Hopkins"):- Aforementioned passenger name carried
   twice in the passenger list of the "North America".
   Author unable to determine if this was double entry (error)
   in original source.

Page 23 - (Ship/Quickstep, from Mexico):- Shortly after arriving in
   San Francisco the "Quickstep" was chartered for the purpose of conveying volunteers to San Diego, California to
   quell an Indian uprising. On the day before the vessel
   was to sail (December 10,1851) word was received that the
   uprising had ended. The volunteer group, known as the San
   Francisco Rangers, were, nevertheless, eager for adventure.
   They set sail for San Diego on December 13, 1851, this
   time aboard the vessel "North Bend".

Pages 20-21 -(Ship/North America, from San Juan del Sur, Nicaragua,
   "Mr. & Mrs. Joseph Proctor):- A contemporary article
   notes that both Mr. and Mrs. Proctor would appear at the
   Jenny Lind Theatre in San Francisco. Mr. Proctor was an
   impersonator and the reference revealed the fact that "his
   fame preceded him to our shores". Proctor was well known
   in New York, Philadelphia and Boston. The couple opened on
   December 22, 1851 in a moving performance of "Damon and
   Pythias". As this was Mrs. Proctor's first appearance on
   any stage her ability was unknown. However, she received
   an enthusiastic receiption for her role as "Calanthe", even
   though being "deficient" in voice.

Page 25 - (Added Ship Arrival):- The following vessel is believed
   to have arrived in San Francisco during the last week of
   November 1851:

SHIP: CORSAIR
TYPE: Brig   FROM: Honolulu, S.I.
ARRIVED: November,1851(?)   CAPTAIN. William S. Neal
PASSAGE: From Honolulu, Sandwich Islands. Passage time not known.
CARGO: Unknown.

Passengers

| William D. Folger | E.M. Clissold | Charles H. Noyes |
| J. Brown | W.H. Wilson | |

- - - - - -

Page 26-(Ship/California, "Judge___ Hall):- Aforementioned passenger identified as "Hiland Hall" in another contemporary
   source. Hall was one of the U.S. Land Commissioners for
   California whose arrival was eagerly awaited. Californians were harrassed by disagreements over land titles
   and it was the projected duty of the Commissioners to
   study the title questions. Hall was seriously ill during
   the passage and had still not recovered when the "Califor-

nia" arrived in San Francisco. Another member of the
board, Judge Harry J. Thornton, was also expected to come
to California. The delay in the arrival of these individuals, according to a contemporary source, was "seriously
retarding the permanent prosperity of the State". On
December 15, 1851, word reached San Francisco that Judge
Thornton was dangerously ill in Washington, D.C. During
a personal rencontre in an election campaign he had cut
his hand and an inflamation set in, resulting in an am-
putation. His recovery was considered doubtful. Thornton
did recover and he arrived in San Francisco aboard the
"Northerner" on January 1, 1851. The passenger list of
the "Northerner" is listed in Volume I, pages 125-128.
However, the name of Judge Thornton is not reflected in the
foregoing source. The fact that he was aboard this vessel
is only substantiated by a passing remark in a secondary
contemporary source. The name of another Judge, one Judge
_____Townsend, is listed as being a passenger on the steam-
er "Northerner".

Page 28 - (Ship/Valparaiso, from New York; "G.J.H. Ballard"):- One
1851 source carries this passenger as "J.H. Ballard".

Page 29 - (Ship/New Orleans, from Panama; "W. Stuart"):- Note
passenger "J. Stuard", same vessel, same page. Given
initials have been cross-referenced to the two surnames.

Page 30 - (Ship/New Orleans, from Panama; "W.H. Hoage" and "Miss
_____Hooge"):- Aforementioned surnames are listed as found
in original source. Author believes original source was
in error and reader should consider "W.H. Hooge" and "Miss
_____Hoage" as alternatives.

Page 31 - (Ship/Augusta, from London, England):- The cargo of this
vessel also included three 12-foot mahogany framed billiard tables with cues and pool balls. The foregoing was
manufactured by Thurston & Company of London, England.

Page 32 - (Ship/Pacific, from San Juan del Sur, Nicaragua; "Antonio
Garro", Indian Chief):- A reference to this Indian chief
will also be found in the passage notes of the "Sea Bird",
pages 41-42. In this latter reference, the chief is carried
as "Antonio Garra". Other contemporary sources reflect the
chief as "Antonio Garru".

Pages 32-34 - (Ship/Pacific, from San Juan del Sur, Nicargagua):-
A secondary contemporary source adds the following individuals to the passenger list of the "Pacific":

J. Shaw	E. Blanchard	R. Basher
J.A. Shaw	G. Storer	D. Dodge
J.S. Barrett	Mrs. L.B. White	C.G. Garrett
W.K. Brown	E. Meather	B. Gratrol
Mrs. L. Pratt	J. Selby West	Mrs. Sarah
Mrs. Hannah Grover	Miss Anne Griffin*	Colburn

(*)Miss Anne Griffin was sick during the passage and
died in San Francisco on December 12, 1851. She was
aged 35 years at death and from Salem, Massachusetts.
The secondary source reflected a number of different sur-

name and given name listings which were in conflict with
the passenger names listed on pages 32-34. The following
enteries cite the name used in the primary research source
(with page number, this volume), followed by the secondary
source listing, noting conflicting spelling:

Miss Lucy White (page 32) as "Miss Lucy B. White"
James L. Groves, wife & 2 children (page 32) as "James L.
 L. Groven, wife & 2 children"
P.L. Chansley (page 32) as "P.L. Chanoler"
E.K. Elend and wife (page 32) as ".E.K. Elrod and wife"
J. Davilbies (page 33) as "J. Davilbiss"
C. McFalon (page 33) as "C.B. McFalon"
A.B. Mareton (page 33) as "A.H. Mareton" (note below name)
N. M??reton (page 33) as "N. Moreton" (note above name)
 (Note: Reader should also consider alternatives of
 "A.B. Moreton" and "N. Mareton" in view of this secon-
 dary source).
J. Scovera (page 33) as "J. Seovern"
B.F. Hucsey (page 33) as "B.F. Huesey"
W.P. Michner (page 33) as "W.P. Michnor"
B. Hilton (page 33) as "S. Hilton"
D.H. Robinson (page 33) as D.S. Robinson"
N.P. Read (page 33) as "N.P. Rose"
F.N. Whitney (page 33 as "F.X. Whitney"
J. Ash (page 32) as "Israel Ash"
Mrs. D. Williams (page 32) as "Mrs. L.D. Williams"
Mrs.___ Thing (page 32) as "Mrs. M. Twing"
Mrs. L. Stevenson (page 32) as "Mrs. W.S. Stevenson"
Mrs. E. Whally (page 32) as "Mrs. Emily Whalley"
E. Hamilton, wife & 4 children (page 32) as "Mrs. Emily
 J. Hamilton"
Mrs. J.C. Young (page 32) as "Mrs. C.H. Young"
James Tenno (Tenso?) (page 32) as "James Fenno"
Dr. F.W. Hatch (page 32) as "from Wisconsin"
A.O. Garrett and son (page 32) as "a doctor from Illinois"
S. Anderson (page 32) as "Sam J. Anderson"
Abraham Emanuel (page 32) as "A.H. Emmanuel"
D.A. Arnold (page 32) as "Daniel A. Arnold"
John H. Grover (page 32) as "J.H. Grove" (Reader should
 note reference to "James L. Groves (Groven), above.)
E. Leach (page 32) as "E. Leach Jr."
Mrs. J.R. Crandall and daughter (page 32) as "Mrs. H.J.
 Crandall"
Mrs.___ King, 3 children and servant (page 32) as "Mrs.
 Anna S. King"
Mrs. Henry Gratlel (Gratiel?, Gratlei?) (page 32) as
 "Mrs. Henry Gratlol" (Reader should note reference on
 foregoing page of "Notes" that "B. Gratrol" was also
 a passenger on the "Pacific").
J.S. Joselyn (page 33) as "J.S. Josselyn".
A.M. Humphreys (page 32) as "A.N. Humphreys".

A. Baker and wife (page 32) as "Asa G. Baker".

E. Smith (page 32) as "Eldrick Smith Jr.

Mrs. ___ Garrett and daughter (page 32) Daughter further
identified as "Miss M.S. Garrett".

Miss Emily Gobbins, Rebecca Gobbins, Mrs. Martha F.
Gobbins (page 32) as "Miss Emily Gibbons, Miss Rebecca
Gibbons, Mrs. Martha P. Gibbons". (Author is of opin-
ion that this was the wife and daughters of Henry
Gibbons, a famous early California doctor).

D.A. Coburn (page 33) as "D.A. Colburn and wife, Mrs.
Sarah Colburn".

P. Reefer and H. Reefer (page 33) as Peter Keefer and
H. Keefer".

T. Gallagher (page 33) as "Thomas Gallagher".

Page 35 - (Ship/Carolina, from Panama; "Antonio Caramryer"):- The
surname of this passenger bears an unusual spelling. A
degree of suspicion arises that the surname should be
"Antonio Caramayer".

Page 35 - (Ship/Carolina, from Panama; "R. Barker"):- Note listing
for passenger immediately following foregoing name. The
original source reflected next passenger as "O. Parker".
As family groups were generally carried in sequence in
the original sources, judgment dictates that "R. Parker"
and "O. Barker" should be regarded as alternatives.

Pages 35-36 - (Ship/Carolina, from Panama; "___ Cogswell, C.M. Cogswell, R.P. Cogswell, O. Cogswell, Samuel Cogswell"):-
Note "L.J. Coggswell"(page 36) with two "g's" in surname.

Page 36 - (Ship/Carolina, from Panama; "A. Mastereon"):-Foregoing
passenger name is listed as found in original source.
Author speculates "A. Masterson" as alternative listing
on grounds of possible error in source material.

Page 36 - (Ship/Carolina, from Panama; "D. Brunton" and "J. Bunton"):
- Foregoing passenger names listed as found in original
source. Author opinion- error in original source.

Page 36 - (Ship/Carolina, from Panama; "R. Smericker" and "Mr.
___ Dericker"):- Both foregoing passenger names listed
as found in original source. Both names are carried in
sequence. Author opinion-possible error in original
source data.

Page 36 - (Ship/ Carolina, from Panama; "M.M. Pheters" and "___
Preters"):- Both foregoing passenger names listed as
found in original source. Author opinion- error in
original source.

Page 36 - (Ship/Columbia, from Astoria, Oregon Territory):- The
"Columbia" also brought intelligence that citizens of the
Oregon Territory were in a great quandary with respect to
the "locus in quo" of their seat of government.

Page 40 - (Ship/Tennessee, from Panama; "B.A. Mosler"):- Forementioned passenger name difficult to decipher. Possible
listing could be "B.A. Mosier". Author selected "Mosler"
based on entry for passenger "M. Mosler", same vessel,
page 41

Page 43 – (Ship/Columbus, from Panama):– Two passengers died from dysentery during the passage of the "Columbus". Their names were not revealed in the source data.

Page 43 – (Ship/Columbus, from Panama; "G. Caliorda"):– Note also "A. Caliorda" (page 44) and "G. Calliordo" (page 44).

Page 44 – (Ship/Columbus, from Panama; "A. Stugis"):– Note also "G. Sturges", same vessel, page 45.

Page 46 – (Ship/Unidine, from Panama; "Z. Tabor"):– Foregoing passenger name listed as found in original source. Note "H. Taber", same vessel, same page.

Page 46 – (Ship/Unidine, from Panama; "W.F. Lomell"):– Difficult to decipher surname of forementioned passenger. Possible listing could be "W.F. Lowell".

Page 48 – (Ship/New England; from Mazatlan, Mexico):– On the night of December 30, 1851, while anchored off the North Beach area of San Francisco, and just a few days after its arrival in port, the "New England" dragged its anchor in a violent storm. A number of her passengers were still on board as the vessel drifted across to Angel Island. The force of the gale drove her ashore and she soon filled with water. Her passengers were taken off by boats.

Page 50 – (Ship/Columbia, from Portland, Oregon Territory; "Col. Redick McKee"):– Colonel McKee was the U.S. Indian Commissioner on his way to San Francisco. He had succeeded in making a peace treaty with the Indian tribes inhabiting the area near the Scott and Shasta Rivers and the creeks and valleys in the vicinity. The lower part of Scott Valley was taken up by the Commissioner as a reservation for the Indians and also for a military post.

Page 54 – (Added Ship Arrivals):– The following vessels arrived in San Francisco on January 16, 1852:

SHIP: COL. FREMONT
TYPE Brig   FROM: San Pedro, California
ARRIVED: January 16, 1852   CAPTAIN: Nason
PASSAGE: 9 days from San Pedro, California.
CARGO: Produce (unspecified type).

Passengers

W.F. Burr	C.J. Murray	J. Fisk
W. Hall	A. Olney	J. Marquerel
M. Carby		

– – – – – –

SHIP: TRIUMPH
TYPE: Brig   FROM: Realejo, Nicaragua
ARRIVED: January 16, 1852   CAPTAIN: Rogers
PASSAGE: 40 days from Realejo, Nicaragua. The following passengers died during the passage:

January 2, 1852:– Herman M. Tobin, seaman, believed to be from Maine.

January 13, 1852:– Henry Holland, of Panama Fever, a passenger, believed to be from New York.

CARGO: 30 bbls of provisions (not identified).

Passengers

W. Henry	J. Davis	G.D. French
Mrs.___ Henry	Mrs.___ Davis	R. Evans
Henry Howland and	C.B. Haskill	J. McCarty
lady*	M.T. Yellett	

    (*) Henry Howland listed as "Henry Holland" in the passage
       notes. A secondary source also carries "Howland" as
       "Holland".

- - - - - -

SHIP: SEA BIRD
TYPE: Steamer   FROM: San Diego, California
ARRIVED: January 16, 1852   CAPTAIN: Robert Haley
PASSAGE: 3 days from San Diego, California, via intermediate ports.
         Captain Robert Haley reported that the steamer "Ohio" was
         Monterey, California harbor awaiting the arrival of
         machinery from San Francisco to repair her engine.
CARGO: Not listed.

Passengers

Dr.___ Wozencroft*	Lt. T.H. Stevens	J.W. Robinson
Mr.___ Goggin	Hon. J.J. Warner**	C.P. Ellenwood
J.N. Nider	J. Cortada	J.D. Shelde /sic/
Capt. J.D. Nason	Ignacio del Valli#	Manuel Gasfrias
Mrs.___ Lee	Don Antonio Maria de	G. Nideever
Dr. J.B. Shaw	la Guerra+	Dr.___ Ord
S. Osio	T.J. McGuire	J.H. Swain
Miss___ McKenny	J.M. Hurst	John Scott
Mr.___ McKenny	A. McDonnell	Capt.___ Haig
Mr.___ Leonard	Mr.___ Stormer	Mr.___ Butte
Mr.___ Sibley	Mr.___ Helmon	Mr.___ Arnold
E. Rice	J.T. Overstreet	Henry Smith
Don Andreas Pico	A. Yeoman	M.C. Palmer
S. Howe	J.C. Ketchum	H.C. Palmer

    (*) Identified in secondary contemporary source as "Dr.___
       Wozencraft, Indian Commissioner."
    (**) Identified in secondary source as a Senator from San
       Diego, California.
    (#) Listed in secondary source as "Ignacio de Valle" and
       identified as an Assemblyman from Los Angeles, California.
    (+) Identified as the newly elected Senator from the district
       of Santa Barbara, California in a secondary source.

- - - - - - -

Page 57 - (Ship/Marietta, from Valparaiso, Chile; "Julio
        Chapapo"):- Forementioned passenger name carried as
        "Julio Chaparro" in another contemporary source.
Page 57 - (Ship/Marietta, from Valparaiso, Chile; "Capt.___
        Jeuranaovich"):- A secondary contemporary source lists
        the captain of the "Marietta" as "Captain Don N. Guirano-
        vich". In addition, the secondary source lists the foll-
        owing passengers as also being aboard the vessel:- Jose

Rafael Arenas, Manuel Antonio Puito, Juan de Ds. Gonzalez,
Cruz Garcia, Francisco Martinez, Francisco Rojas and
Lorenzo Boza.

Page 60 - (Ship/Panama, from Panama; "Horace Ballou, wife and 3
children"):- Foregoing entry as found in original source.

Page 60 - (Ship/Panama, from Panama; "Mrs. C.A. Deau"):- Foregoing
passenger name as found in original source. Surname was
difficult to decipher. Entry could be "Mrs. C.A. Dean".

Page 62 - (Ship/Panama, from Panama; "A.H. Washbvn"):- Foregoing
passenger name as found in original source. Author
opinion- obvious error in original data. Reader should
consider alternatives of "A.H. Washburn" or "A.H. Washbun".

Page 63 - (Ship/Golden Gate, from New York; "Capt.___Freeman):- One
contemporary source states that the master of "Golden Gate"
(during this voyage) was "Capt.___Truman".

Page 64 - (Ship/Pacific, from San Juan del Sur, Nicaragua; "Mrs.
Alexina Fisher Baker" and "Mr. Lewis Baker"):- Forementioned two passengers were members of the theatrical pro-
fession and were well known in the Atlantic States. Mrs.
Baker, under hermaiden name of Alexina Fisher, appeared on
Broadway (in New York) and in the Chestnut Theatre in
Philadelphia, Pennsylvania. Mr. Baker had been given high
praise for his more than ordinary merit by the press of
the same two cities. The author has added their names to
the foot of the passenger list of the "Pacific" based on
a reliable contemporary source which noted they arrived on
the vessel. The basic research source for the passenger
list did not reflect (per se) the Baker's by their stage
name identification. Readers will note the entry "J.L.
Baker and wife" (page 64) which denotes the only "Baker"
entry in the original source. Historians can speculate
whether or not this listing represented the acting team.

Page 65 - (Ship/Pacific, from San Juan del Sur, Nicaragua; "N.A.
Pettygrou"):- Note spelling of surname. "N.A. Petty-
grew" would represent the conventional spelling.

Page 66 - (Ship/Pacific, from San Juan del Sur, Nicaragua; "J. Peel
and svt, J. Peel Jr. Mary A. Peel and Mary Peele"):- Note
additional "e" on listing for "Mary Peele".

Page 66 - (Ship/Pacific, from San Juan del Sur, Nicaragua; "R. Craton" and "J. Crayton"):- Forementioned passenger names
are listed as found in original source. Author opinion-
obvious error.

Page 66 - (Ship/Pacific, from San Juan del Sur, Nicaragua; "G.
Pearks" and "F. Pea?ks"):- One letter of surname could
not be deciphered in entry on "F. Pea?ks". As passenger
"G. Pearks" appears on same vessel, reader could regard
"F. Pearks" as the possible surname.

Page 66 - (Ship/Pacific, from San Juan del Sur, Nicaragua; "H.B.
Platt and wife"):- Identified in another contemporary
source as "Henry B. Platt, Manager of the original New
Orleans Serenaders". Platt, his wife and the group came
to San Francisco aboard the "Pacific" and gave their first

concert at San Francisco's Adelphi Theatre. The company
was as famous in the Southern Atlantic States as Christy's
Minstrels were in New York. Theatrical posters identified members of the group as G. Swaine Buckley (bone and
banjo player), J.H. Collins (ballad singer), Master F.
Buckley (violinist), R. Bishop Buckley (tambourinist),
A.H. Barry (basso) and J.H. Mullen (dancer). The passenger list of the "Pacific" (see page 66) carried the company members as F. Buckley, R. Buckley, O. Buckley, J.
Mullins, A.H. Berry and ____ Collins.

In March, 1852, the New Orleans Serenaders went to
Marysville, California and staged a performance in a
church, at which the moral sensibilities of a portion of
the community were shocked. Platt disposed of his con-
tract with the Serenaders at Mokelumne Hill, California
on May 25, 1852. The troupe was thereafter known as
"Buckley's New Orleans Serenaders" and it functioned
under the management of Mr. E.N. Hill.

Page 67 - (Ship/Republic, from Panama; "Rev. S. Reynolds"):- The
contemporary account of the passage states that "Rev.
S. Reynolds" officiated at the burial service of James
O'Neal. Note that the passenger list of this vessel
carries "Rev. J. Reynolds".

Page 67 - (Ship/Republic, from Panama; "Charles Maurice","Maurice
Martin", "Maurice Sanders"):- Foregoing passenger names
listed as found in original source.

Page 68 - (Ship/Republic, from Panama; "Hiram Russel" and "G.
Russell"):- Note use of single "l" and double "l" in the
surnames.

Page 68 - (Ship/Republic, from Panama; "W.D. Kierse" and "A.I.
Peirse"):- Author experienced difficulty in deciphering
"W.D. Kierse" in the original source. Readers may specu-
late on the alternative of "W.D. Peirse".

Page 68 - (Ship/Republic, from Panama; "J. O'Neil"):- Foregoing name
listed as found in original source. Note death of passenger "James O'Neal" in "PASSAGE" (page 67).

Page 69 - (Ship/Republic, from Panama; "O. Hanscomb"):- Note listing
for passenger "H.D. Hanscome", same vessel, page 67.

Page 69 - (Ship/Republic, from Panama; "J. Lafkin" and "Mrs.____
Lufkin"):- Forementioned passenger names listed as found
in original source.

Page 69 - (Ship/Republic, from Panama; "N. Halt"):- Author of
opinion that there was an error in original source.
Readers should "N. Hall" as the alternative entry.

Page 69 - (Ship/Republic, from Panama; "B. Galliard", "P. Galliardet"):- Forementioned names listed as found in source.

Page 69 - (Ship/Republic, from Panama; "M. Nagle"):- Forementioned
passenger name listed as found in source. Note entry
"Mrs.____ Naglee and 2 children", page 67. Author opinion-
error in original source.

Page 73 - (Ship/Oregon, from Panama; "T. Tollman" and "J.L. Tillman"):- Forementioned passenger names listed as found in

original source.

Page 73 - (Ship/Oregon, from Panama; "H. Manser", "G.B. Mauser", "Mrs.___Manser and boy"):- All foregoing names listed as found in source.

Page 73 - (Ship/Oregon, from Panama; "N. Gay" and "Robert Gray"):- Foregoing passenger names listed as found in source. Reader should consider "N. Gray" as alternative.

Page 73 - (Ship/Oregon, from Panama; "P. Dismond"):- Foregoing passenger name difficult to decipher. Note "H. Diamond", same vessel, page 75.

Page 74 - (Ship/Oregon, from Panama; "E. Staffords" and "T.F. Haffords"):- The listing for "T.F. Haffords" appears to be an apparent error in original source. Reader should regard "T.F. Staffords" as possible alternative.

Page 74 - (Ship/Oregon, from Panama; "W.H. Silsby"):- Full name of this passenger was "William Henry Silsby". Foregoing passenger was the son of "H. Silsby" (full name-"Henry Silsby"), listed on page 73. (From information in author's possession)

Page 75 - (Ship/Oregon, from Panama; "A.H. Lilly", "A. Libby", "M. Libby"):- Passenger names listed as found in source. Reader should consider alternatives of "A.H. Libby", "A. Lilly" and "M. Lilly".

Page 75 - (Ship/Oregon, from Panama; "Joseph Cornelius", "William Cornelious" and "M. Cornelious"):- Passenger names listed as found in original source.

Page 75 - (Ship/Oregon, from Panama; "W.O. Brien"):- Questionable surname. Consider "W. O'Brien" as alternative listing.

Page 77 - (Ship/Flying Fish, from Boston, Mass.):- Additional cargo carried by this vessel was an assortment of fruit trees, packed in hermetically sealed tin cases. The shipment consisted of apple trees, pear trees, strawberry plants, raspberry bushes and plum trees. The San Francisco outlet for the fruit trees was the firm of Thompson & DuPrat. The "Flying Fish" also carried 13 academy, church, factory and ship bells in assorted sizes weighing from 50 to 1800 pounds per bell. The bells were from the Boston firm of Hooper & Company.

A secondary source varied, somewhat, in listing the passengers of this vessel. R.F. Ellis was carried as "R.F. Ellis, lady and 2 children"; Mrs. Alborne Allen appeared as "Mrs. A.B. Allen"; Mr. G.W. Webster as "G.W. Webster Jr."; Mr.___Bond" as "J.G. Bond" and Miss Josephine Morrow was listed as "Miss E. Morrow". The author speculates that "Miss E. Morrow" was, in fact, an additional passenger. The secondary source also listed "J.L. Grover, lady and 2 children" as additional passengers.

On March 11, 1852, not quite a month after the arrival of the "Flying Fish", the first of a series of lithograph engravings of California clipper ships was published in San Francisco. The "Flying Fish" was the initial lithograph subject. The drawing was executed by Mr. J. Prender-gast (sic), an artist well known in California. The litho-graph work was executed by Quirot & Company.

Page 78 - (Ship/Sea Bird, from San Diego, California):- One con-temporary source states that General___Bean was aboard this vessel when it arrived in San Francisco.

Page 79 - (Added Ship Arrival):- The following vessel arrived in San Francisco on February 16, 1852:

SHIP: BUENA DEA
TYPE: Schooner   FROM:Trinidad, California
ARRIVED: February 16, 1852   CAPTAIN: Tichenor /sic/
PASSAGE: 3 days from Trinidad, California. This vessel brings in-telligence that the steamer "Sea Gull" had wrecked at Humboldt Bay, California on January 26, 1852. The "Sea Gull" was one of the coastal vessels that plied between San Francisco and the Oregon Territory. The wrecked steam-er had started for the Oregon Territory and had crossed the bar at Trinidad, California when the steam chest burst. Captain___Tichenor (sic), master of the "Sea Gull", ran her ashore, where she became a total loss. Passengers and crew got ashore safely. Tichenor then ac-quired the schooner "Buena Dea" (of 17 tons) and sailed it to San Francisco.
CARGO: In ballast.

Passengers

Mr.___Aspinwall	Mr. J. Moore	Mr. W. Stevens
Mr.___Rogers	Mr.___Shepard /sic/	Mr.___Stanton
Mr.___Callahan	Mr.___Terrey (or Terray)	Mr.___Neuhammer (?)

and 8 unidentified Chinamen

- - - - - -

Page 81 - (Ship/Constitution, from Honolulu, Sandwich Islands; "Capt.___McLane"):- A secondary source identified this passenger as "Captain Allen McLane, one of the Directors of the Sandwich Island Steam Company".

Page 87 - (Ship/Independence, from San Juan del Sur, Nicaragua; "N.O. Goddell"):- Foregoing passenger name listed as found in source. Note passenger entry on page 86 for "Mrs. S.P. Goodell and 2 children". "N.O. Goodell" might be considered as an alternative surname.

Page 83 - (Ship/Home, from Sydney, N.S.W.):- One contemporary source states the following additional passengers were on board; "Miss___Jackson" and "Miss___Hicks". In addi-tion, the secondary source carried M. Hill and wife as "Mr. & Mrs. Michael Hill"; J. Vennison and wife were listed as "Mr. & Mrs. James Dennistown"; G.J. Hayes, lady and child appeared as "Mr. & Mrs. James Hayes and child" and Mrs.___Cooke and 4 children were reflected as "Mrs. A. Cook and 4 children".

Page 87 - (Ship/Independence, from San Juan del Sur, Nicaragua;

"Mrs. H.P. Breyfoggle" and "S. Breyfogle"):- Forementioned passenger names listed as found in original source.

Page 81 - (Ship/Constitution, from Honolulu, Sandwich Islands):- In December, 1851, an association was formed in San Francisco under the name "North Pacific Steam Navigation Company". The object of this association was to introduce steam in navigating between the various Sandwich Islands (Hawaiian Islands). In anticipation of this, the association's leaders had obtained from the Hawaiian government the exclusive right to employ steam in that channel for the period of five years. The "Constitution" was chartered for two months and sent down to the Islands, under the management of William Glen. The aim was to determine the nature and extent of the field open for the exclusive operation of the association. Glen arrived at a period of depression, unequalled in the commerical history of the Islands. He established the fact that the prospects of the association had no parallel on the Pacific Coast compared to the amount of the capital employed. Glen returned to San Francisco and proposed re-organizing the association and issuing stock. He foresaw the future establishment of a number of coffee and sugar plantations and the consequent introduction of a large number of Chinese coolies. These enterprises, Glen concluded, would result in a profitable inter-island steam route. In March, 1852, under the name "Sandwich Island Steam Company", stock was opened for subscription.

The passage notes of the "Constitution" (page 81) state the vessel departed from San Francisco for Honolulu on January 1, 1852. This is based on primary source material. However, the passage notes of the "Tarquina" (page 51), indicates that the "Constitution" was at sea and bound for Honolulu on December 27, 1851.

Page 81 - (Ship/Brant, from Hongkong, China):- Contemporary item notes that when the "Brant" tied up at the California Street Wharf, in San Francisco, "about three hundred long-tailed Celestials" were unloading their "traps". Some of the Chinese settled in San Francisco and others departed for the gold fields. The item closed, noting, "when engaged in earnest conversation they (the Chinese) make a noise to which the cackling of a flock of geese is nowhere".

Page 88 - (Ship/California, from Panama):- When this vessel stopped at San Diego, California it dropped off a detachment of 250 U.S. troop recruits from New York. Officers debarking with the troops at San Diego were Major___Patten, Lieutenants___Bond and ___Curtis (2nd Infantry) and Assistant Surgeon___Milhau. The recruits were assigned to Company I, 1st Artillery (in the San Diego area) and the balance to the companies of the 2nd Infantry in the same area. Major Patten and Lieutenant Bond later took the "Sea Bird" to San Francisco (see page 116).

Page 88 - (Ship/California, from Panama; "Mr. & Mrs.___ Hamilton and
3 children", "Mr.___ Chapman" and "Miss Caroline Chapman")
:- One contemporary source identified Mr.___ Chapman as
"Mr. W.B. Chapman". Miss Caroline Chapman, Mr. W.B. Chapman and Mr. & Mrs. Hamilton were late of Burton's Theatre
in New York City. They were engaged to appear at San
Francisco's Jenny Lind Theatre by Mr. T. Maguire. W.B.
Chapman and Mrs.___ Hamilton opened on March 16, 1852 in
the comedy "Heir at Law", Chapman in the role of Dr. Pan-
gloss and Mrs. Hamilton as Lady Duberly.

Page 90 - (Ship/Golden Gate, from Panama; "L. Berekzenski"):- Foregoing passenger listed in two other contemporary sources
as "Colonel___ Berenzcy" and "Colonel Ladislaus Berzenc-
zei, a Hungarian gentleman". One of the sources notes
that Berekzenski occupied a prominent position during the
Hungarian war and afterward was a companion of Kossuth
(Lajos Kossuth) during his confinement in Asia Minor.
Berekzenski was also a leader of the refugees who came to
America on the steamer "Mississippi". San Francisco was
a mid-stop for Berekzenski as he was on his way to Canton,
China, where he would proceed into the interior in search
of the origin of the Magyar nation. He was also going to
study certain tribes in China that spoke a language similar to the Hungarian dialect. When Berekzenski arrived
in San Francisco he carried favorable letters from Secretary Daniel Webster, the Hon. Thomas Corwin, Secretary of
the U.S. Treasury and other distinguished Americans.

Page 90 - (Ship/Golden Gate, from Panama; "R.H. Vance and 2 boys"):-
Forementioned passenger listing as found in source. Note
passenger "A.Hance", same vessel, page 93.

Page 91 - (Ship/Golden Gate, from Panama; "P. Kelley"):- Forementioned passenger listing as found in source. Note name
of passenger immediately following P. Kelley, namely,
"D. Kelly".

Page 93 - (Ship/Golden Gate, from Panama; "J.M. Vandenhoff"):- Forementioned passenger name listed as found in source. Note
passenger, same vessel, page 92, bearing name of "E. Van
Heff". This latter passenger name could not be accurate-
ly deciphered due to legibility of source material. The
author arrived at possible alternative surnames of "Van
Haff" or "Van Hoff". Consideration could be given to
"E. Vandenhoff" as the surname.

Page 93 - (Ship/Golden Gate, from Panama; "J. Efner"):- Foregoing
passenger name listed as found in source. Note two passengers, same vessel, page 90, bearing names of "J. Efder (?)" and "H. Efder (?)".

Page 94 - (Ship/Golden Gate, from Panama; "F. Solomon", "___ White",
and "___ Donaldson"):- A contemporary report notes these
three passengers were members of the "Ethiopian Serenaders". The complete group, comprised of other members,
opened at San Francisco's Jenny Lind Theatre. The company,
under the management of Messrs. Rainer & Donaldson, was

also known as "Rainer & Donaldson's Serenaders". They had
given concerts in England and America for eight years. The
complete cast included Mr. F. Solomon (violin), Mr. M.W.
White (first tenor), Mr. T. Brower (second tenor), Mr.
W.B. Donald (tenor), Mr. J.C. Rainer (basso) and Mr. E.B.
Donaldson (no position listed).

Page 95 - (Ship/Sea Bird, from San Diego, California; in reference
to the British brig "Tryphene"):- Still another contemporary source refers to this vessel as the "Tryphenia".
The "Judson", a whaling brig, Captain___Sherman commanding, put into San Francisco on March 6, 1852, 23 days from
St. Bartholomew's Bay, with sea elephant oil. Upon arriving, Captain Sherman stated that the British brig "Tryphenia" (sic), 45 days from Panama, for San Francisco, put
into St. Mark's Bay during the latter part of January,
1852. The vessel was short of water, food and wood. The
"Tryphenia" had 121 passengers on board and 5 passengers
had died during the passage. Two of the "Tryphenia's"
passengers, Mr. A.M. Ensign and Mr. L.B. Bogart, had trans-
ferred to the "Judson" in order to secure passage to San
Francisco.

Page 96 - (Ship/Sea Bird, from San Diego, California; "R.D. Cutts"):-
Foregoing passenger identified as "Richard D. Cutts,
Assistant in charge of the U.S. Coast Survey". Identifi-
cation was made by a contemporary source which noted that
Cutts and his party (members not identified) were return-
ing from Monterey, California. The group had just com-
pleted the triangulation and survey of the Monterey harbor.
The map that Cutts had compiled was sent by the next
steamer leaving San Francisco to Professor___Bache, the
Superintendent of U.S. Coast Survey, in Washington, D.C.

Page 97 - (Ship/Alphonse N. Cezard, from Nantes, France):- One
contemporary source lists this vessel as sailing from
Havre, France. There was some concern over the arrival of
the "Alphonse N. Cezard" in San Francisco. The character
of immigration pouring into the city was of deep and in-
tense interest to the local citizens. The moral worth of
foreign arrivals commanded more attention than a passing
thought. It was feared by many San Franciscans that many
of the "Cezard's" passengers were convicts who were shipp-
ed to rid their native country of their presence. The
editor of the French Department of one of San Francisco's
daily journals, the "Evening Picayune", defended the newcomers. He observed that among the "Cezard's" passengers were skilled mechanics and learned professors-all
sorely needed in California. The defense stand was duly
accepted and it was determined that the French arrivals
deserved a "friendly and cordial reception". One "hold-
out" newspaper still chipped away at the French immigrants
by trumpeting they "attract no little attention, from the
similarity of their dress and personal appearance, and
the large number that are generally together".

Page 97 - (Ship/Alphonse N. Cezard, from Nantes, France; "A.S. Oufresnoy, A. Dufresnoy"):- Both foregoing passenger names
listed as found in source. Reader should regard "A.S.Du-
fresnoy" as alternative surname listing. Author of opinion that "Oufresnoy" was source error.

Page 98 - (Ship/Comet, from Panama; "J. Furgeson"):- Foregoing
passenger name listed as found in source. Note"H.J.
Ferguson", same vessel, same page.

Page 98 - (Ship/Lexington, from New York; "Lt. W. Radford"):- One
contemporary source lists "Lt. W. Redford" as the master
of the "Lexington". It adds, in addition, that the vessel
was off San Francisco for 14 days in a heavy gale, being
driven 150 miles to the leeward, then experiencing light
winds and calms.

Page 100 - (Ship/Luna de Paiti-/Luna de Paita, from Paita, Peru;
"400 bbls sweet potatoes"):- A separate item notes that
the sweet potatoes brought by this vessel were produced
at Paita. These potatoes excelled in soundness and size
any sweet potatoe yet imported. The Sandwich Islands
productions"were totally unlike it, the Paita potatoe
being much superior".

Page 101 - (Ship/Huntress, from Valparaiso, Chile):- Shortly after
their arrival in San Francisco the "170 Chilenos" congregated on Telegraph Hill. This was the first large emigration that had arrived from Chile for some months, the
recent revolution in that country having disturbed the
usual order of affairs. A week after their arrival one
of the Chilenos claimed he discovered gold on Telegraph
Hill. The "find" was shortlived for a contemporary
account noted "the gold had undoubtedly been lost by some
person, there being several accounts published of gold
being found on that hill".

Page 101 - (Ship/William Watson, from Hongkong, China; "Captain
___ Ritchie"):- Identified in one source as "Captain
David Ritchie". Ritchie died on board the "William Watson"
in San Francisco harbor on April 24, 1852. Death was due
to congestion of the lungs. There is some question as to
the correctness of the surname for the obituary listing
refers to this individual as "Capt David Pritchie". The
"congestion of the lungs" was caused by injuries he received from two men who assaulted him on April 15, 1852.
Captain Ritchie (Pritchie) was a native of Scotland.

Page 103 - (Ship/Monumental City, from Panama; "H.B. Bodwell" and
"G. Bordwell"):- Foregoing passenger names listed as
found in source. Author opinion- obvious error. Alternative listings "H.B. Bordwell" and "G. Bodwell".

Page 103 - (Ship/Monumental City, from Panama; "J.M. Picktel" and
"C.H. Pecktel"):- Foregoing passenger names listed as
found in source. Author opinion- obvious error. Alternative listings "J.M. Pecktel" and "C.H. Picktel".

Page 103 - (Ship/Monumental City, from Panama; "H. Marlow" and
"F.A. Barlow"):- Foregoing passenger names listed as found

in source.

Page 105 — (Ship/New Orleans, from Panama; "J.J.Westlake & lady"):-
Note also listing for "J.J. Westlake", same vessel, page
107. Both entries appeared in source.

Page 106 — (Ship/New Orleans, from Panama; "Mrs. P. Cosgrove" and
"P. Cosgrove). Note listing for two passengers carried
as "P. Cosgrove and lady", same vessel, page 106. Note
"Mr.___Cosgrove and lady", same vessel, page 107. All
listings are noted as found in research source.

Page 105 — (Ship New Orleans, from Panama; "Mrs.___Desplat"):- Note
entry "Madame___Desplat", same vessel, page 106. Both
entries listed as found in source.

Page 106 — (Ship/New Orleans, from Panama; "Jesse Carroll"):- Note
entry "G. Carrell", same vessel, page 107

Page 108 — (Ship/Cabargo, from Panama; "H.B. Chapin"):- Foregoing
passenger name appears twice in passenger list. Author
unable to determine if entries represent two individuals.

Page 108 — (Ship/Cabargo, from Panama; "J. Hallegan" and "Mary
Halligan"):- Note different surnames. Author opinion-
source error. Consider alternatives of "J. Halligan"
and "Mary Hallegan".

Page 110 — (Ship/Northern Light, from Boston, Massachusetts):- The
"Northern Light" was 49 days from Boston to Cape Horn,
39 days from Cape Horn to the Line, 18 days from the Line
to San Francisco. She experienced strong NW gales for
23 days after passing Cape Horn. Her greatest daytime
run was 260 miles. On December 23, 1851, in lat. 23S,
the vessel ran into a white squall which carried away the
jibboom, flying jibboom and fore top gallant mast. She
also sprung her fore topsail yard.

Page 111 — (Ship/Tennessee, from Panama; reference to the wreck of
the "North America"):- Survivors of the wrecked "North
America" made their way to San Francisco aboard a number
of vessels. Some of the passengers went to San Francisco
aboard the "Northern Light", boarding it at Acapulco,
Mexico. The arrival of the "Northern Light" is recorded
in Volume I, SAN FRANCISCO SHIP PASSENGER LISTS. The
arrival date of the "Northern Light" is listed in the
foregoing volume as "May 25, 1852", an incorrect date.
The date, substantiated by research, should read "May
20, 1852" (see Correction Page, Volume III, SAN FRANCIS-
CO SHIP PASSENGER LISTS).

On May 13, 1852, some of the passengers of the ill-
fated "North America" held a meeting on board the "Northern Light" for the purpose of extending thanks to the
city of Acapulco for aid received. The identity of those
attending the meeting was never fully recorded. A few
names were preserved but some of these are in conflict
with the "Northern Light" passenger listed contained in
Volume I. Where there arises a difference in given or
surname listings the author has entered the appropriate
remark. The following named passengers attended the

May 13th meeting on board the "North America":

J.C. Murdock(#)
Mr. W. Kilborn, of Napa, California (#)
Dr.___ Buden
___Sandford

Thomas Hunt, of New York City
T.H. Pierce
___Densmore(#)
___Cross(#)

(#) The primary source used in compiling Volume I, SAN FRANCISCO SHIP PASSENGER LISTS carried these individuals as "W. Kilburn, lady and 3 children"(page 122, Vol. I); "James C. Murdock" (page 123, Vol. I); "G.G. Dinsmore"(page 123, Vol.I) and two entries for passengers named "Cross" (page 122, Vol. I).

When the "Northern Light" put into San Francisco on May 20, 1852 it was actually carrying passengers from two distressed vessels. First, the passengers of the wrecked "North America" and secondly, the barque "Isabel". The "Isabel" had set out from Panama with her destination port being San Francisco. On March 3, 1852 the "Isabel" was forced to put into Acapulco, due to, as one passenger put it,"the short-sightedness or rascality of the owners and captain". In Acapulco, the "Isabel's" passengers were cast upon their own resources. Through the kindness of a relief committee they were able to secure passage on the "Northern Light".

Research has not completely solved the separate identity of the two sets of distressed passengers on board the "Northern Light". As in the case of the "North America", only a handful of ex-Isabel passengers can be identified--even then, two contemporary research sources differ on the spelling of passenger names. Following is a list of passengers aboard the "Northern Light" who originally bought passage on the barque "Isabel":

E. Woolson(+)
A. Wood (+)
A. Broadwell

George Bramall
L.D. Latimer (+)

(+) The primary source used in compiling Volume I, SAN FRANCISCO SHIP PASSENGER LISTS carried these individuals as "E. Woolsen"(page 124, Vol. I); "A.R. Woods and child" (page 124, Vol. I) and "L. Lattimer"(page 124, Vol. I).

Page 112 - (Ship/Tennessee, from Panama; "Madame___ Biscaccianti"):- Identified in a contemporary source as "Madame Eliza Biscaccianti", a famous singer of the period. Her husband and musical director, George Loder, came to San Francisco prior to Madame Biscaccianti to arrange her concerts. Loder, well known in his own right, arrived on the steamer "Golden Gate"in February, 1852. Besides giving concerts in San Francisco they toured a number of the principal towns in California. Madame Biscaccianti opened at the American Theatre in San Francisco on

March 22, 1852. Her itinerary after her California tour
called for an appearance at the Grand Opera in Paris,
France.

Page 112 - (Ship/Tennessee, from Panama; "Madame___Celeste"):- Fore-
going passenger was a celebrated danseuse who came to San
Francisco for an engagement at the Jenny Lind Theatre.
John Dunn, known to theater-goers for his role as "Rascal
Jack", was,according to another contemporary source,
supposed to be a passenger on the "Tennessee". Mr.
Dunn is not reflected in the passenger list because of
the absence of authoritative documentation.

Page 112 - (Ship/Tennessee, from Panama; "R. Elliott"):- Note two
listings on this name.

Page 112 - (Ship/Tennessee, from Panama; "Mrs.___Brooks"):- Note
listing for another "Mrs.___Brooks", same vessel, page
113.

Page 113 - (Ship/Tennessee, from Panama; "C. Burden", "E. Burden",
"J. Borden"):- Forementioned passenger names listed as
in source. Alternatives of "C. Borden", "E. Borden" and
"J. Burden" should be considered.

Page 114 - (Ship/Tennessee, from Panama; "O. Force"):- Foregoing
passenger name listed as found in source. In the passage
notes of this vessel, page 112, there will be found a
reference to the death of "O.O. Force". Author unable to
locate data which would indicate the two names represent
one individual.

Page 114 - (Ship/Tennessee, from Panama; "H. Sanderson" and "W.
Standerson"):- Foregoing passenger names listed as in
source.

Page 115 - (Ship/Tennessee, from Panama; "P. Hayden"):- Foregoing
passenger name listed as found in source. Note "J. Hadden", next passenger, same vessel, same page.

Page 115 - (Ship/Tennessee, from Panama; "Elizr Bell"):- Foregoing
passenger name listed as found in source. Author speculates the given name might be "Eliza" or incorrect
abbreviation for "Elizabeth".

Page 116 - (Ship/Tennessee, from Panama; "S.B. Knig", "J.S. Lovell",
"G. Lovett", "J.W. Nicollt", "P. Pierson" and "J.G.
Pearson"):- All foregoing passenger names listed as
in source. Author opinion- reader should consider
"S.B.Knig" as "S.B. King"; "J.W. Nicollt" as "J.W.
Nicollet" and the similar surnames,"Lovell/Lovett" and
"Pierson/Pearson", as obvious spelling errors.

Page 117 - (Ship/Columbia, from Portland, Oregon Territry; "Capt.
W.L. Dall", "Dr.___Gerry", "Lloyd Brooks" and "H.
Burns"):- This was the first trip to Oregon and back to
San Francisco by Captain W.L. Dall in the steamer
"Columbia". A number of the passengers expressed their
appreciation for his able seamanship. They noted the
captain had fixed his course so that the vessel, contrary
to custom, ran close to shore affording his passengers an
opportunity to see places which had become interesting

from the various attempts at settlements, viz:- Humboldt, California; Trinidad, California and Port Orford, Oregon Territory.

One contemporary source listed "Dr.___ Gerry" as "S.R. Geny, M.D."; "Lloyd Brooks" (page 118) as "Lloyd Brooke" and "H. Burns" (page 118) as "E.H. Burns".

Page 118 - (Ship/Noble, from Honolulu, Sandwich Islands; "Capt.___ Robinson"):- One contemporary source states that the "Noble" was a Baltimore clipper brig and the master for this voyage was "Captain___ Robertson".

Page 120 - (Ship/Prince Charlie, from London, England):- Another contemporary source lists "Mr.___ Rushby" as "J. Rushby"; "Mr.___ Smith" as "Sidney W. Smith"; "Mr.___ Newman" as "Henry Newman"; "Mr.___ Calden" as "Charles E. Calder"; "Mrs.___ Valverdie and family" as "Mrs. Eliza Valverde and family"; "Mr.___ Fleming" as "John Fleming" and "Mrs.___ Tennent and family" as "Dorinda Tennant, John Tennant, William Tennant and Mary Tennant".

The secondary source also added the following passengers to the "Prince Charlie":

John Hughsdon	James Mansell
Thomas Arthur	J.G. Crane

Page 120 - (Ship/Versailles, from Boston, Mass.; "Capt. Knowles"):- Capt.___ Knowles, the master of the "Versailles", died in San Francisco on April 2, 1852. His obituary carried his full name as "Thomas Knowles".

In comparing the Versailles" passenger list with a secondary contemporary source the author noted these counter listings:- "Mrs. M.S. Phillips and child" was entered as "Mrs.___ Phelps and child"; "Mrs. R.A. Grant and family" as "Mrs. N.B. Grant and 3 children" and "Mr. A. Walker and family" as "Mr. A. Walker, lady and two children".

Page 122 - (Ship/Henbury, from Hongkong, China; "236 unidentified Chinamen"):- In commenting on the arrival of the Chinese a local newspaper stated "Such a large accession is very desirable if they are but as industrious, honest and peaceable as their brethren generally, who are already established here".

Page 123 - (Added Ship Arrival):- The following vessel arrived in San Francisco on March 26, 1852:

SHIP: BERTRAM (also known as "JOHN BERTRAM)

TYPE: Clipper   FROM: Boston, Massachusetts
ARRIVED: March 26, 1852   CAPTAIN: Lendholm /sic/
PASSAGE: 105 days from Boston, Massachusetts.
CARGO: 3 pianos, drugs, 9 wagons, 1 bureau, 20 bbls butter, wheels, axels, books, 24 horserobes, cranberries, 25 pigs, 100 cases tobacco, 84 plough castings, 6 threshers, 6 separators, 72 boxes oysters, 34 boxes buckwheat and assorted goods.

Passengers

Mr. H. Eckley	Mr. J. Maer	Mr. J.H. Rosenberg

(Continued next page)

Mr. H. Kunser	James M. Schwab	Mr. M. Pintz
Mrs. Anna D. Titcomb	Phillip Wachler	Thomas Symmes /sic/
Miss Anna J. Titcomb	George Andrews	John Q. Pratt
Mrs. Elizabeth D. Kimball		William H. Cogswell
Miss Mary L. Poore	John Hooper	George S. Duren
Miss Mary P. Poore	Miss Ellen J. Poore	Edwin Merrill

- - - - - -

Page 123 - (Ship/Pacific, from San Juan del Sur, Nicaragua; "J. Hathorn"):- Foregoing passenger name listed as found in source material. Note listing for passenger "R.W. Hasthorne", same vessel, page 124. Apparent error in source.

Page 124 - (Ship/Pacific, from San Juan del Sur, Nicaragua; "A.A. Relpatrick"):- Foregoing passenger name listed as found in source material. Author believes surname entry should have been "A.A. Kilpatrick".

Page 124 - (Ship/Pacific, from San Juan del Sur, Nicaragua; "Mrs. L.E. Shutleff"and"Mrs. E. Shutleff"):- Foregoing passenger names listed as found in source material. Attention is directed to page 126, same vessel, wherein the source listed two additional different spellings, "L.E. Shitleff" and "E. Shurtleff". Research by author reveals correct surname is "Shurtleff" and entries should be "Mrs. E. Shurtleff", "L.E. Shurtleff", "Mrs. L.E. Shurtleff" and "E. Shurtleff".

Page 126 - (Ship/Orleans, from El Realejo, Nicaragua; "George Hobsan"):- Foregoing passenger name listed as found in source material.

Page 127 - (Ship/Orleans, from El Realejo, Nicaragua; "Tarlton Turner"):- Foregoing passenger name listed as found in source material. Reader might consider "Carlton Turner" as alternative spelling.

Page 128 - (Ship/Columbia, from Oregon Territory; "H.H. Tickner"):- Foregoing passenger name listed as found in source material. Author believes name might be "H.H. Tichnor" or "H.H. Tichenor".

Page 130 - (Ship/Panama, from Panama; "Miss Emma M. Horstman"):- Foregoing passenger name listed as found in source data. A secondary source used to obtain data on the marriage of this party reflected the name as "Miss Emma M. Horstmann".

Page 131 - (Ship/Panama, from Panama; "J. Dimon"):- Foregoing passenger name difficult to decipher in original source. Author interprets as "J. Dimon". Note listing for "J.J. Dimon and lady", same vessel, page 130.

Page 131 - (Ship/Panama, from Panama; "L. Baryie"):- Foregoing passenger name listed as found in source material. Note "P. Barrie", same vessel, same page. Reader should consider "L. Barrie" and "P. Baryie" as alternatives.

Page 131 - (Ship/ Panama,from Panama; "L. Simons"):- Foregoing passenger name listed as found in source data. Note "G.D.

Simmons", same vessel, same page.

Page 132 - (Ship/Panama, from Panama; "J. Linepheh"):- Foregoing passenger name listed as found in source material. Note listing for passenger "J. Limpech", same vessel, page 133.

Page 132 - (Ship/Panama, from Panama; "F. Keney"):- Foregoing passenger name listed as found in source material. Author believes surname might be "Kenney". Note entry for "J. Kenney", same vessel, page 131.

Page 132 - (Ship/Panama, from Panama; "A. Pohler"):- Foregoing passenger name listed as found in source material. Note entry "J. Kuhler", same vessel, same page. Author of opinion that correct surname entry for both passengers might be "A. Kohler" and J. Kohler".

Page 133 - (Ship/Panama, from Panama; "G. Nerman"):- Author of opinion that this passenger entry should be "G. Norman". Note passenger "W. Norman, same vessel, same page.

Page 133 - (Ship/Panama, from Panama; "J. Bardor"):- Foregoing passenger name listed as found in source material. Note passenger, "W. Brandor", same vessel, same page.

Page 133 - (Ship/Panama, from Panama; "J.T. Olercland"):- Foregoing passenger name listed as found in source material. Reader might consider "J.T. Clereland" as alternative spelling, based on passenger entry following subject listing.

Page 134 - (Ship/Fremont (Colonel Fremont), from Panama; "A.J. Durfy"):- Foregoing passenger name listed as found in source material.

Page 134 - (Ship/Fremont (Colonel Fremont), from Panama; "J.W. Tritipo"):- Foregoing passenger name listed as found in source material. Note "S. Tritips", same vessel, page 135. Reader should consider alternatives of "S. Tritipo" and "J.W. Tritips".

Page 134 - (Ship/Fremont (Colonel Fremont), from Panama; "T. O'Dul") :- Foregoing passenger name listed as found in source material. Reader might consider "T. O'Doul" as an alternative.

Page 135 - (Ship/ Fremont (Colonel Fremont), from Panama; "C. Kister"):- Foregoing passenger name listed as found in source. Note listing for "P. Koster", same vessel, same page, and "H. Koster", same vessel, page 134. Reader might consider "C. Koster" as alternative for "C. Kister".

Page 135 - (Ship/Fremont (Colonel Fremont), from Panama; "J.F. Daly"):- Foregoing passenger name listed as found in source. Note also entry for "D. Daley", same vessel, same page.

Page 136 - (Ship/Agate, from Tahiti; "Mr. E.P. Adams"):- A secondary source identifies Mr. Adams as "Mr. Edward P. Adams". Secondary source also notes that the Agate's 28 day passage time from Tahiti to San Francisco was near record time. The Agate, on her previous passage down, made the trip in 19 days and 14 hours, a record from San Francisco to Tahiti.

Page 136 – (Ship/Vincennes, from Astoria, Oregon Territory; "Edward
J. Rutter"):– One April 30, 1852, Edward J. Rutter was
accidentally drowned while attempting to board the "Vice-
nnes" in San Francisco harbor. His body was found on
May 23, 1852 on the beach near the "Old Fort"(sic). Rutter was from Baltimore, Maryland.

Page 138 – (Ship/Oregon, from Panama;"S.S.Pierse"):– Foregoing passenger name listed as found in basic source. Note passenger entry for "Mrs.___ Pierce", same vessel, same page.
Note also entry for "A.G. Pierce", same vessel, page 139
Reader should consider "S.S. Pierce" as alternative.

Page 138 – (Ship/Oregon, from Panama; "William Cashner"):– Foregoing passenger name listed as found in source material.
Note passenger entry for "D. Castner", same vessel, same
page. Reader should consider alternatives of "William
Castner" and "D. Cashner".

Page 139 – (Ship/Oregon, from Panama; "Water King"):– Forementioned passenger name listed as found in source material.
Author believes name should read "Walter King".

Page 139 – (Ship/Oregon, from Panama; "R. Dyuglass"):– Foregoing
passenger name listed as found in source material.
Author believes "R. Dyuglass" should read "R. Douglass".

Page 140 – (Ship/Oregon, from Panama; "G. Martyne"):– Foregoing
passenger name listed as found in source material. Note
also passenger entry for "John Mertyn", same vessel, on
page 139.

Page 140 – (Ship/Oregon, from Panama; "M. Dougherty"):– Foregoing
passenger name listed as found in source material. Note
also passenger entry for "D. Dorrity", same vessel, on
page 138.

Page 142 – (Ship/Ohio, from San Diego, California; "M. Corne us"):–
Foregoing passenger name listed as found in source data.
Note listings on page 141, same vessel, for "M. Cornel-
ius", "M. Cornelius Jr." and "S. Cornelius".

Page 143 – (Ship/Independence, from San Juan del Sur, Nicaragua):–
The "Independence" carried some of the passengers of the
wrecked steamer "North America" (see page 145). The survivors had boarded the "Independence" at Acapulco, Mexico.

Page 144 – (Ship/Independence, from San Juan del Sur, Nicaragua;
"C.C.P. Severance"):– Foregoing passenger name listed
as found in source material. Due to fact there was some
space separation between the first and second initials
the possibility arises that this entry represented, in
fact, two passengers. In which case the listings would
read "C. Severance" and "C.P. Severance".

Page 145 – (Ship/Independence, from San Juan del Sur, Nicaragua;
"James Carbury"):– Forementioned passenger name listed
as found in source material. See passage notes of the
"Independence" (page 143) relative to the death of "James
Carburg". The death notice was obtained from a secondary
source with the surname listed as "Carburg".

Page 145 - (Ship/Sea Bird, from San Diego, California):- Upon arriving in San Francisco the "Sea Bird" was laid up for a short time to undergo repairs. As an interim replacement the fast sailing schooner "Lydia" took her place on the coastal run.

Page 146 - (Added Ship Arrival):- The "Backus" arrived in San Francisco on April 11, 1852. Even though this vessel did not carry passengers its arrival is of historical interest. The "Backus", a barque, under command of Captain ____ Sevige, came to San Francisco from the Russian settlement at Sitka, Alaska. The passage from Sitka took 16 days and the barque carried the first importation of ice from Sitka to San Francisco. The ice, consigned to the Pacific Ice Company, was heralded as a "luxury in San Francisco". The company's wagons commenced delivering the ice to San Francisco residents and firms on April 18, 1852. Some eight hundred pounds of fresh halibut was an additional part of the cargo carried by the "Backus".

Page 146 - (Ship/Invincible, from New York; "Wilmarth Waller", Miss ____ Eardley" and "Henry Tuthill"):- The foregoing three passengers were not listed in the basic research source used to compile the passenger list of the "Invincible". Other reliable contemporary research sources definitely indicate that Waller, Eardley and Tuthill were on board the vessel when it arrived in San Francisco. Waller was a young American actor highly praised by the New York press. In 1849 he paid a visit to England where he made a decided hit. Tuthill was a well known comedian of the period. One source identified the comedian as "Harry Tuthill". Miss Eardley was late of Madame Vestris' Lyceum Theatre, of London, England. Tuthill made his first San Francisco appearance at the Jenny Lind Theatre on April 21, 1852. Waller opened at the Jenny Lind on April 25, 1852 in "Hamlet".

Page 147 - (Ship/Northerner, from Panama; "Capt.____Randall"):- Captain Randall, the master of the "Northerner" is identified in a secondary source as "Captain Henry Randall". Randall retired from the command of the vessel when it arrived in San Francisco on April 14, 1852. He was presented with a gold chain by the following officers of the "Northerner" on his retirement:

W.F. Lapidge	W.M. Kilduff
J. McNulty	J.R. Mayer
W.B. Perry	J. Van Doren (or Vandoren?)

Page 147 - (Ship/Northerner, from Panama; "Miss Julia M.H. Hall"):- The notice of marriage of Miss Hall reflected her middle initials as "M.H.", whereas, she appears in the passenger list bearing the name-"Miss E. Hall".

Page 148 - (Ship/Northerner, from Panama; "W. Timpson"):- Foregoing passenger name listed as found in source material. Author believes passenger name might have been "W. Simpson".

Page 148 - (Ship/Northerner, from Panama; "J.R. Fennell"):- Foregoing passenger name listed as found in source material. Note passenger "F.M. Fennill", same vessel, page 149. Reader should consider"J.R.Fennill" and "F.M. Fennell" as alternatives.

Page 149 - (Ship/Northerner, from Panama; "J. Hurges" and"Mrs.____ Hurges"):- Forementioned passengers listed as found in source material. Author questions surname listings. Consider "J. Hughes" and "Mrs.____Hughes" as possible alternatives.

Page 149 - (Ship/Northerner, from Panama; "Mrs.____ Eagan" and "Miss ____ Eagan"):- The day after the arrival of the "Northerner" in San Francisco,a "Lost and Found" notice was inserted in one of the local newspapers. Subject notice related that "Mrs. Margaret Egan" (sic) had lost her black leather trunk (with red hoops and brass nails) on board the vessel. Mrs. Egan posted a $10.00 reward for its return. The newspaper notice differs from the passenger list surname spelling. Reader should consider alternatives of "Mrs.____Egan", "Mrs. Margaret Eagan" and "Miss ____ Egan".

Page 150 - (Ship/Northerner, from Panama; "J. Myres"):- Foregoing passenger name listed as found in source material. Note passenger "O. Myers", same vessel, page 149, and passenger "William Myers", same vessel, page 152. Author is of opinion that "J. Myres" was mis-spelt in original text and entry should have been "J. Myers".

Page 150 - (Ship/Northerner, from Panama; "J. Humphreys"):- Forementioned passenger name listed as found in source data. Note passenger "A. Humphries", same vessel, page 151.

Page 150 - (Ship/Northerner, from Panama; "____ Hamilton, colored"):- Forementioned passenger name listed as found in source data. Author believes cited surname may, instead, be the "given" name of this passenger. In which case the entry would be "Hamilton ____".

Page 150 - (Ship/Northerner, from Panama; "J.M. Hanford"):- Foregoing passenger name listed as found in source material. Note also entry "L. Handford, wife and child", same vessel, page 152.

Page 151 - (Ship/Northerner, from Panama; "S. H?rtapples"):- Second letter of surname not decipherable. Reader might consider alternatives of "Hartapples", "Hertapples", "Hirtapples", "Hortapples" and "Hurtapples".

Page 152 - (Ship/Williamantic, from Astoria, Oregon Territory):- A secondary contemporary source refers to this vessel as the "Williamtic".

Page 153 - (Ship/Isthmus, from Panama; "L.W. Fee" and "N.H.Lee"):- Both foregoing passenger names listed as found in source. Reader should consider alternatives of "L.W. Lee" and "N.H. Fee". Author suspects correct surname in both cases should be "Lee".

Page 153 - (Ship/Isthmus, from Panama; "J. Faber" and "J.C. Tabor"):-

Both foregoing passenger names listed as found in source.

Page 155 - (Ship/Hurricane, from New York; "Capt.___Verry"):- One
contemporary source lists the master of the "Hurricane"
as "Captain S. Very Jr.".

Page 156 - (Ship/Wyandott, from Hawaii, Sandwich Islands, "Captain
___West"):- One contemporary source refers to this
vessel as the "Wyandot" with the master being "Captain
W.A. West".

Page 157 - (Ship/Emma Packer, from Huanie, Society Islands; "150
oranges" and "Capt.___Buckley"):- This vessel listed
in another contemporary source as the "Emma". Same
source notes that Captain W.L. Terril was the commander
during the voyage. There is some supporting evidence
that the cargo consisted of "150,000 oranges" rather than
"150 oranges".

Page 158 - (Ship/Eclipse, from New York; "1 reaping machine" and
"assorted goods"):- On April 30, 1852 a demonstration of
the reaping machine was held in San Francisco. The device was referred to as "a new machine for cutting and
gathering hay, worked by horses, and it is perhaps the
first that has been brought to the country (California)".
The machine, a "McCormick Patent Reaping Machine", was a
two-horse power device equipped with an extra knife and
separator with extra links, wheel and band. It was
placed on sale in San Francisco by Goodwin & Company.
   Part of the "assorted goods" in the hold of the
"Eclipse" was a large boiler assigned to Captain John T.
Wright. The boiler was intended to be placed aboard the
steamer "West Point"--hopefully making her one of the
swiftest boats navigating the Sacramento River.

Page 158 - (Ship/Eclipse, from New York; "Capt.___Robertson", "Mrs.
___Cummings and 3 children", "___Hussey and lady",
"Mrs.___Collins and 4 children", "Dr.___Turnbull", "Dr.
___Crane", "Dr.___Thorne", "___Birdsall", "___Morris",
"___Tallman", "___Fisher" and "___Jolly"):- Another
contemporary source differs in its accounting of the
passengers of the "Eclipse". The secondary source lists
the passengers as:

Capt.___Robinson and lady	Mrs.___Cummings
	Miss___Cummings
Mr.___Collins*	Miss___Cummings
Miss___Collins	Master___Cummings
Master___Collins	Mrs.___Husey and child
Master___Collins	Mr.___Monias (?)
Master___Collins	(Moniss?)
Z. Burtzill	Dr. J. Turnbull
S.E. Crane	Dr. N. Thorne
C.N. Tallman	J.N. Fisher
J.H. Jolly	

   (*) Note the secondary source reflects this party
       as "Mr.", not "Mrs.".

Page 159 - (Ship/Challenge, from Hongkong, China; "553 Chinese emi-

grants"):- A curious event took place on the day after
the "Challenge" arrived in San Francisco with its 553
Chinese emigrants. The Governor of California, John Big-
ler, initiated a special message to the California Senate
and Assembly advocating the adoption of measures to check
the tide of Asiatic immigration and to prevent the expor-
tation by them of the precious metal (gold) which they
removed from the California soil.
   (Early records indicate that the first Chinese emigrants to arrive in California came on the brig
"Eagle", from Hongkong, in the month of February,
1848--two men and one woman. Only four Chinese
arrived in the succeeding twelve months.)

Page 159 - (Ship/Benjamin Howard, from Boston, Massachusetts; "Miss
Sophia Moulton"," "H.J. Johnson and lady", "Miss___John-
son", "Miss___Newhall", "E. Delaroy and lady", "J. Mc-
Insp and lady", "F. Nutter", "G. Harley" and "J.Harley"):-
On April 26, 1852 a notice appeared in a local San Francisco newspaper that "John H. Kimball" married "Sophia T.
Moulton" on board the "Benjamin Howard". Miss Moulton
was listed as being from York, Maine.
   Another contemporary source differs in its accounting
of the passengers on board the "Benjamin Howard". The
secondary source lists the passengers as:

Henry L. Johnson	Edmund Delory
Miss Harriet L. Johnson	Mrs. Anna Delory
Miss Maria G. Johnson	Joseph Delory
John McInnes	Frank Nutter
Mrs. C. McInnes	George Herley
Mrs. I. McInnes	William Newhall
Miss Sophia Moneton	Mrs. P. Newhall

Page 161 - (Ship/Ceres, from Panama; "W. Thersher" and "R. Thresher"):- Foregoing passenger names listed as found in
source data. Note different surnames. Reader should
consider alternatives of "W. Thresher" and "R. Thersher".

Page 164 -(Ship/Active, from San Pedro, California; "J. Kidder" and
"J. Kidd"):- Foregoing passenger names listed as found
in source data. Note also listing for passenger "G.
Kidder", page 156.

Page 162 - (Ship/Active, from San Pedro, California; "Lt.___Am-
men", "Lt.___Blunt", "___Jackson", "Mr.___Green",
"Mr.___Gallaer" and "T. Sanger"):- The "Active" detach-
ed herself from an important surveying service for the
purpose of bringing to San Francisco the intelligence of
the distress of the steamer "California". The disabled
"California", under the command of Captain R.L. Whiting,
had departed from Panama on April 8, 1852 with its destination as San Francisco. The"California"broke down and
made for San Pedro, California. Aboard the"California"
were Commodore___Sloat and other officers of the California Dock and Navy Yard Commission. Sloat and the other
members of the Commission disembarked from the disabled

steamer and immediately boarded the "Active" in order to
proceed to San Francisco. The rapid transfer between
vessels by the Commission members was made due to the
fact they had to conclude their labors of deciding on a
location of a Navy Yard before the adjournment of Congress.

One contemporary source differs in spelling the names
of some of the Commission members who traveled aboard the
"Active". Spelling variations are cited with the basic
research source spelling noted in the first column and
the secondary contemporary source spelling noted in the
opposite column:

Basic Source	Secondary Source
Lt.___Ammen	Lt. D.F. Amnen, U.S.N.
Lt.___Blunt	Lt. S.F. Blunt, U.S.N.
___Jackson	A.C. Jackson, Midshipman, U.S.N.
Mr.___Green	Colonel C.N. Green, Deputy Collector of San Francisco
Mr.___Gallaer	Mr. W.W. Gallagher, Collector of Benicia, California
T. Sanger	W.P. Sanger Esq., Engineer to the California Dock & Navy Yard Comm.

A month after the "Active" was engaged in its mercy
role the vessel went into drydock for repairs. At that
time it was revealed that the "Active" had previously
borne the name "Gold Hunter".

Page 163 - (Ship/California, from Panama, in distress at San Pedro,
California):- Prior to arriving in San Pedro, California
the following deaths took place on board the "California":

    April 14, 1852 - Elita I.S. Hall, of quinsy, aged
        4 years, daughter of William C. and Emeline
        Hall, of Chelsea, Massachusetts.
    April 18, 1852 - Robert Crozier, of dysentery, of
        Queens Cty, New Brunswick, aged 35 years.

The following passenger boarded the "California" at
Panama but died in San Pedro, California:

    April 29, 1852 - H.B. Arnold, of dysentery, aged 46
        years, of Providence, Rhode Island.

Page 164 - (Ship/California, from Panama, in distress at San Pedro,
California; "J.C. Make"):- Foregoing passenger name listed as found in source. Note passenger "J.B. Mackie",
same vessel, page 165.

Page 165 - (Ship/California, from Panama, in distress at San Pedro,
California; "A.S. Schuyle"):- Foregoing passenger name
listed as found in source material. Author believes this
entry should read "A.S. Schuyler". Note "G.S. Schuyler",
same vessel, page 163.

Page 166 - (Ship/Winfield Scott, from New York):- A contemporary source states that the "Winfield Scott" carried one of the largest assortments of diamonds ever received in California. They were imported by J.W. Tucker and placed on sale in San Francisco the day after the vessel arrived.

Page 168 - (Ship/Winfield Scott, from New York; "Mrs.___Bordur" and "D.S. Buduor"):- Foregoing passenger names listed as found in source material. Author regards both entries as obvious errors. Reader should consider "Mrs.___Buduor" and "D.S. Bordur" as alternatives.

Page 168 - (Ship/Winfield Scott, from New York; "John Bagan" and "M.Obagan"):- Foregoing passenger names listed as found in source material. Author regards both entries as obvious errors. Reader should consider alternatives of "John Obagan","John O'Bagan", "M.O. Bagan" and "M. O'Bagan".

Page 168 - (Ship/Winfield Scott, from New York; "Mrs.___Garrow" and "G.W. Gomarrow"):- Foregoing passenger names listed as found in source material. Author regards both entries as possible errors. Consider "Mrs.___Gomarrow" and "G.W. Garrow" as alternatives.

Page 169 - (Ship/Winfield Scott, from New York; "R.Lilly"):- Foregoing passenger name listed as found in source. Note also listing for passenger "R. Lilley", same vessel, same page.

Page 169 - (Ship/Winfield Scott, from New York; "B. Bowell"):- Foregoing passenger name listed as found in source data. Author considers this entry as possible error. Passenger name might have been "B. Dowell". Note passengers listed as "Thomas Dowell" and "Mrs.___Dowell", same vessel, same page, and death mention of "Mary Dowell", same vessel, page 166.

Page 173 - (Ship/Blonde, from Panama; "Dennis Racer"):- Foregoing passenger also listed as "D. Racer", same vessel, page 174.

Page 173 - (Ship/Blonde, from Panama; "Francis Pargman"):- Foregoing passenger also listed as "F. Pargman", same vessel, page 175.

Page 173 - (Ship/Blonde, from Panama; "Charles Dazotell"):- Foregoing passenger name listed as found in report of death. The passenger list of the "Blonde" reflects this party as "C. Dozotel".

Page 173 - (Ship/Blonde, from Panama; "J.B. Sugee"):- Listed in two other contemporary sources as "J.B. Suyce" and "J.B. Sryce".

Page 173 - (Ship/Blonde, from Panama; "R. McGinigans"):- Listed in a secondary source as "R. McGiningan".

Page 173 - (Ship/Courser, from Boston, Massachusetts; "S. Hooper", "L.L. Thorndike", "Mrs. W. Cole and 2 children" and "W. Amory"):- One contemporary source lists the passengers of the "Courser" as follows:

W.S. Hooper   Mrs.___Cole(Captain's wife)

(Continued next page)

William Amory Jr.   Master F.A. Cole
Samuel L. Thorndike   Master Lemuel Cole

Page 174 - (Ship/Blonde, from Panama; "John Chapen"):- Foregoing
          passenger name listed as found in source. Note also "J.
          Chapin", same vessel, same page.

Page 174 - (Ship/Blonde, from Panama; "R. McGinningan"):- Fore-
          going passenger name listed as found in source. Note
          also listing for "R. McGinigans", same vessel, page 173.

Page 174 - (Ship/Blonde, from Panama; "H. Haggadon", "G. Russell"
          and O.J. Mitchell"):- Foregoing passenger names listed
          as found in source. The obituary notices (see page 173)
          carry these individuals as "Henry Hagadon", "Gurley
          Russell" and "Orlando J. Mitchell".

Page 174 - (Ship/Blonde, from Panama; "___ Beach", "J. Bantz", "D.
          Barrkan", "A. Saw", "J. Saw", "G.C. Dockunn", "A.C.
          Holloday", "J.D. Hoff", "James Boaker", "A. Semmett"
          "W. Nicewonger"):- Foregoing passenger names are listed
          as found in the primary research source. A secondary
          contemporary source lists these passengers, respectively,
          as: "S.G. Beach", J. Barrtz", "D. Bankan", "A. Law", "J.
          Law", "G.C. Dockman", "A.C. Hollody", "J.D. Huff", "J.
          Booker", "A. Lemmett" and "W. Nicewoyer".

Page 175 - (Ship/Blonde, from Panama; "J.H. Houston"):- Foregoing
          passenger name listed as "James H. Houston" in obituary
          notice, page 173.

Page 175 - (Ship/Blonde, from Panama; "Thomas Clerk"):- Foregoing
          passenger name listed as found in source. A number of
          errors appeared in the passenger list of the "Blonde".
          Author of opinion that this passenger entry should have
          been "Thomas Clark".

Page 175 - (Ship/Blonde, from Panama; "J.C. Tibetts"):- Foregong
          passenger name listed as found in source. Note also
          "R. Tiblett" , same vessel, page 174. Consider alter-
          natives of "J.C. Tiblett" and "R. Tibetts". Author of
          opinion that error existed in source data.

Page 175 - (Ship/Blone, from Panama; "J.T. Palmes"):- Foregoing
          passenger name listed as found in source. Author of
          firm opinion that entry should read "J.T. Palmer".

Page 175 - (Ship/New Orleans, from Panama):- This vessel brought to
          San Francisco the U.S. Government contractor of the Cus-
          tom House which was to be built in the city. The contrac-
          tor was identified in a secondary source as "Mr.___
          Adams" (no given name listed). Parties bearing surname
          of Adams will be found on page 176 (___ Adams, lady, 3
          children and servant), page 177 (J.T. Adams), page 177
          (W. Adams), page 177 (G. Adams) and page 178 (Henry
          Adams and J.L. Adams).

Page 176 - (Ship/New Orleans, from Panama; "J.J. Laring"):- Fore-
          going passenger name listed as found in source. Author
          of belief that entry should have read "J.J. Loring".
          Note "J.H. Loring", same vessel, page 179, and "N. Lor-
          ing", same vessel, page 176.

Page 176 - (Ship/New Orleans, from Panama; "Mrs.___Oorham"):- Foregoing passenger name listed as found in source. Author
of opinion that entry was in error and should have been
"Mrs.___Gorham". Note "Squire Gorham" a passenger on
same vessel, page 178.

Page 176 - (Ship/New Orleans, from Panama; "Mrs. J.W. Raymond, 3
children and servant"):- Note mention of Nathaniel
Kendrick Raymond and I.W. Raymond in passage notes, page
175.

Page 176 - (Ship/New Orleans, from Panama; "S. Ewings" "W. Ewings",
and "S. Ewing"):- Foregoing passenger names listed as
found in source. Reader should regard "S. Ewing" and
"W. Ewing" as alternative.

Page 177 - (Ship/New Orleans, from Panama; "A.M. Nichols" and "T.
Nichol"):- Both passenger names listed as in source.
Consider alternatives of "A.M. Nichol" and "T. Nichols".

Page 177 - (Ship/New Orleans, from Panama; "Charles Caney" and "J.
Canen"):- Both passenger names listed as in source.
Author regards these as questionable entries and reader
should consider alternatives of "Charles Canen" and "J.
Caney".

Page 177 - (Ship/New Orleans, from Panama; "T.A. Gardener", "B.F.
Gardner"):- Foregoing passenger names listed as found in
source. Note also "Henry Gardner" (page 178) and "G.
Gardiner" (page 178).

Page 178 - (Ship/New Orleans, from Panama; "J.A. Huddock" and "S.
Haddook"):- In addition to the alternative surnames listed on page 178 the reader should consider "J.A. Haddock"
and "S. Haddock".

Page 178 - (Ship/New Orleans, from Panama; "E. Harmon"):- Foregoing passenger name listed as found in source. Note
listings for "George Harman", "A.H. Harman" and "M. Harman", same vessel, same page. Reader should consider
alternatives of "E. Harman", "George Harmon", "A.H. Harmon" and "M. Harmon".

Page 179 - (Ship/New Orleans, from Panama; "J.B. Bayley"):- Foregoing passenger name listed as in source. Note listing
for passenger "R.W. Bailey", same vessel, same page.
Consider "J.B. Bailey" and "R.W. Bayley" as alternate
entries.

Page 180 - (Ship/Clarita, from Acapulco, Mexico; "G. Ryes", "D.
Ryes" and "C. Resey"):- According to the passage notes
of the steamer "Fremont" (also known as the "Colonel
Fremont")(see page 134, Volume III), the "Clarita"
carried a number of passengers from the wrecked "North
America". The author is unable to determine which passengers on board the "Clarita" were from the "North America".
        The "Ryes" and "Resey" surnames are listed as found in
source material. Author suspects they may have been
incorrectly spelt.

Page 180 - (Ship/John M. Mayo (or J.M. Mayo), from New York:- This vessel also referred to as the "John Mayo".

Page 182 - (Added Ship Arrival):- The following vessel is believed to entered San Francisco harbor on or about May 7, 1852:

SHIP: FRANCES AND LOUISE
TYPE: Unknown   FROM: Unknown*
ARRIVED: May 7, 1852 (?)   CAPTAIN: Unknown
CARGO: 75,000 feet of lumber, 4000 bushels of potatoes, 500 sacks of wheat and feed, 200 sheep.

Passengers

J.W. Caron, lady and 4 children
(*) Probably from the Oregon Territory.

Page 183 - (Ship/Grecian, from the Oregon Territory; "140,000 feet of lumber"):- A contemporary research source revealed that by the month of May, 1852 the problem of bringing in lumber to San Francisco from distant sources was nearing an end. The southern hills and valleys along the coast of California were but sparsely timbered. The great Sacramento and San Joaquin Valleys produced trees only on the banks of the rivers, and the woods upon the foothills barely sufficed to shade the miner at his work. These sections of the State were the first explored and known. Hence, the opinion became general that California was compelled to look to the Oregon Territory for lumber. But as the Californians pushed into the far north of the State they found enough timber to supply the whole Pacific Coast. During the early summer of 1852 reports filtered into San Francisco of immense and thick growths of timber in Mendocino, Trinity and Klamath Counties.

Page 184 - (Added Ship Arrival):- The author has been unable to verify the arrival of the vessel "Benard" in San Francisco. This vessel supposedly arrived in the city during May, 1852, after having set out from Boston, Massachusetts. The "Benard" carried two passengers as listed below:

SHIP: BENARD
TYPE: Unknown   FROM: Boston, Massachusetts
ARRIVED: May, 1852 (?)   CAPTAIN: Unknown
PASSAGE: Unknown   CARGO: Unknown

Passengers

Mr. George M. Appleton   Mr. Luther Hinckley

Page 185 - (Ship/Tennessee, from Panama; "J. Van Valkenburg, death of"):- Forementioned passenger name listed as found in source. Note passenger listing for "S. Van Volkenburgh", same vessel, page 187. Consider alternatives of " J. Van Volkenburgh" and "S. Van Valkenburg".

Page 185 - (Ship/Tennessee, from Panama; added passenger):- According to one contemporary source Jonathan Peabody was also a passenger on the "Tennessee". Peabody died at Monterey,

California on May 17, 1852, of Panama Fever. He was 28
years of age.

Page 185 - (Ship/Tennessee, from Panama; relative to deaths aboard
the"Monumental City"):- One contemporary source reports
the following additional deaths took place on board the
"Monumental City" during her passage between the ports of
San Juan del Sur, Nicaragua and Acapulco, Mexico:

  April 23, 1852 - Mr. Norton Weston, of dysentery, of
    Massachusetts.
  April 26, 1852 - Mr.___Allen, of dysentery, of
    Connecticut.
  April 27, 1852 - Rev. T.W. Caldwell, of dysentery,
    of Providence, Rhode Island.
  April 28, 1852 - Mr.___Marshall, of dysentery, of
    Massachusetts.

Page 185 - (Ship/Tennessee, from Panama; "D.A. Fostea"):- Foregoing
passenger name listed as found in source. Correct entry
is believed to be "D.A. Foster". Note "G. Foster", same
vessel, same page.

Page 186 - (Ship/Tennessee, from Panama; "J. Madasa"):- Foregoing
passenger name listed as found in source. Note also
passengers "J. Medasa" and "W. Madusa", same vessel, same
page.

Page 186 - (Ship/Tennessee, from Panama; "Rev. P.G. Buchananan and
lady"):- Foregoing passengers listed as found in source.
Reader should consider alternative entry of "Rev. P.G.
Buchanan and lady".

Page 186 - (Ship/Tennessee, from Panama; "Valentine Almy" and
"Charles Almy"):- Both foregoing passenger names listed
as found in source. Note listing for passenger "Mrs. C.
Alpy", page 188, same vessel. Note listing for passenger
"A.M. Allbe", same vessel, page 189. Author regards
these four passenger listings as possible errors in the
original source material.

Page 187 - (Ship/Tennessee, from Panama; "F. Nill"):- Foregoing
passenger name listed as found in source. Note passengers, same vessel, "F. Nall"(page 187) and "N. Nall"
(page 189).

Page 188 - (Ship/Tennessee, from Panama; "E. Ingersol" and "A. Ingersol"):- Both foregoing passenger names listed as found
in source. Note passenger, same vessel, "A.H. Ingersoll"
on page 189.

Page 191 - (Ship/Pacific, from San Juan del Sur, Nicaragua; "George
Diety"):- Foregoing passenger name listed as in source.
Note "Thomas W. Duty", same vessel, same page.

Page 191 - (Ship/Pacific, from San Juan del Sur, Nicaragua; "T.
Dean"):- Foregoing passenger name listed as found in
source. Note entry "James S. Deans and lady", same
vessel, same page.

Page 191 - (Ship/Pacific, from San Juan del Sur, Nicaragua; "Mrs.
___Woff, 5 children and infant"):- Foregoing entry
listed as found in source. Author believes that surname

entry might be "Mrs.____Wolff, 5 children and infant".
Note "L. Wolff", same vessel, page 193.

Page 191 - (Ship/Pacific, from San Juan del Sur, Nicaragua; "Miss
____Disbrough"):- Difficult to decipher this name in
source material. It appeared that "Miss____Dishrough"
could be alternative spelling. However, note entry on
page 192, same vessel, for passenger "D. Disbrough".
Latter entry was distinguishable.

Page 191 - (Ship/Pacific, from San Juan del Sur, Nicaragua; "R.W.
Van Sychles"):- Difficult to decipher foregoing passen-
ger name in source material. Note entry for passenger
"W.B. Van Sykles", same vessel, page 192.

Page 192 - (Ship/Pacific, from San Juan del Sur, Nicaragua; "Mrs.
T. Phair and infants", "H. Phair", "T. Phar and sons"):-
Foregoing passenger names listed as found in source.
Note absence of "i" in entry "T. Phar and sons".

Page 192 - (Ship/Pacific, from San Juan del Sur, Nicaragua; "S.S.
Dovoner and servant"):- Foregoing entry listed as found
in source. Note entry for passenger "John Donver", same
vessel, page 193.

Page 193 - (Ship/Pacific, from San Juan del Sur, Nicaragua; "B.
Crooker"):- Foregoing passenger name listed as found in
source. Note passenger entry for "G.D. Crocker", same
vessel same page.

Page 193 - (Ship/Pacific, from San Juan del Sur, Nicaragua; "J.J.
Way"):- Foregoing passenger name listed as found in
source. Note name of next passenger in column, same page,
"L.S. Gay".

Page 195 - (Ship/Guadalope Premere(also listed as the "Guadalope"),
from Acapulco, Mexico; "Thomas Laka"):- The passengers
on board the "Guadalope Premere" were from the disabled
steamer "North America", having boarded the vessel at
Acapulco, Mexico. One contemporary source notes that
some sixty additional passengers from the "North America"
had sailed from Acapulco on the schooner "Thomas".
The entry for passenger "Thomas Laka" is listed as
found in source. Author suspects the entry should read
"Thomas Lake".

Page 197 - (Possible Ship Arrival):- On May 24, 1852 the vessel
"McKim" was reported as laid up at Monterey,California
undergoing repairs. It sailed from Panama on November
28, 1852 (destination not reported in source). The
following deaths were listed in the "McKim" log book:
Died at Sea:
December 6, 1851 - Robert Gemmel, of Canada
December 7, 1851 - William Cotts, of England
December 7, 1851 - Amasa Rowell, of Michigan
December 10,1851 - Niel McQuarry, of Ireland (Neil?)
December 11,1851 - John Clapp Jr.,of Massachusetts
December 11,1851 - William Oakstrong, of New York, a
seaman
December 11,1851 - John Sayers, of Germany

December 15,1851 – Benjamin Herrick, of Maine
December 17,1851 – Joseph Bolen, of Georgia
December 24,1851 – Lovan Conaway (sic), of Maine
December 27,1851 – William W. Johnson, of Georgia
January 2, 1852 – John M. Dodge, of Massachusetts
Died in California:
February 10, 1852 – John Cart, of Indiana
March 1, 1852 – J.J. Simons, of Georgia
March 14, 1852 – George Sandford, of New York
April 2, 1852 – John W. Moore, of Baltimore, Md.
May 3, 1852 – A. Bisson, of Canada, seaman
May 13, 1852 – Michael Conway (sic), of Philadel-
phia, Pennsylvania, a steward.

Page 199 – (Ship/Brutus, from Panama; "P.C. Aplin"):- Foregoing
passenger name listed as found in source. Note "P.C.
Appling" and "R.A. Appling", same vessel, same page.
Also note "E.R. Appling", same vessel, page 200.

Page 201 – (Ship/Independence, from San Juan del Sur, Nicaragua;
"Miss H. Ferris):- Foregoing passenger name listed as
found in source. Note "J. Farris", same vessel, page
202.

Page 201 – (Ship/Independence, from San Juan del Sur, Nicaragua;
"C. Grimskey" and "Mrs.___ Grumsky"):- Foregoing passenger names listed as found in source. Reader should consider "C. Grumsky" and "Mrs.___ Grimskey" as alternatives.

Page 201 – (Ship/Independence, from San Juan del Sur, Nicaragua;
additional passengers):- The author has located a secondary source which reveals that a number of additional passengers were aboard the "Independence" during this voyage.
The secondary source was in the form of a "card notice"
and it supplied some background on a troubled passage.

Upon arriving in San Francisco a number of the passengers of the "Independence" voiced complaints relative to
the treatment they had received on board the vessel. As
a group they signed a "card" indicating their displeasure
and affixing their names.

The disgruntled passengers noted they had departed from
New York on April 20, 1852 aboard the "Daniel Webster".
After arriving at Greytown, Nicaragua eight days were
spent in crossing the Isthmus (beforehand they had been
advised the crossing would only take 36 hours). Shortly
after reaching San Juan del Sur, Nicaragua they were put
on board the "Independence". Hopes for some degree of
comfort were only mocked. The "card" stated that "the
insolence of officers and insolent uncouthness of subor-
dinates were a much nearer approach to the gutter school
of breeding". The sick were uncared and unprovided for,
unless they paid a fee of $10.00 to the ship's physician.
Even the relatives of those who died during the passage
were treated "as if they had no more feeling than the mis-
named captain who commanded the steamer". The accomodations were "pig-styes", in which filth and cockroaches

occupied much the larger space.

Passengers signing the "card notice" are listed below. A number of names do not appear on the passenger list of the "Independence" appearing on pages 201-203, this volume. The passengers not appearing on the aforementioned pages are regarded as "additional" passengers during this voyage and they are indicated in the list by the symbol "#".

If the reader compares the below "card notice" list with the passenger list (pages 201-203) it will be noted that a number of variations appear in given names and surnames. Diverse spellings are referenced by numerical citations and appropriate remarks appear at the close of the list.

Passenger names affixed to the "Independence Card Notice:

#William W. Stow	#T.S. Murfey (1)
#U.C. Palmer	H. Murfey
Smith Baldwin (2)	E. Booth
William Baldwin	#W.N. Dunn (3)
#P.C. Reid (4)	Sidney Mosher (5)
C. Kingsbury	D. Star(sic) (6)
Charles Atkinson (7)	#David Walley
James B. Campbell (8)	Jonathan Seymour (9)
William Beach (10)	J.L. Polhemus (11)
W.H. McClung (12)	William B. French (13)
#Enoch W. Brainerd (14)	#Benjamin Ludd(sic)(15)
William H. Fleming (16)	#John A. Jones
D.V. Dingman Jr. (17)	Cornelius B. Mills (18)
#Perry L. Matteson	#William C. Dow
William Smeaton (19)	#Henry Brickwald (20)
#E.P. Lindsey (21)	#W. Miller
#William M. Cain	#C.J. Lansing
#S.B.Matlock	E.B. Cahoon
Henry Kimball (22)	William Smith
#John Wanser (23)	W.L. Kilbourn
#Josiah Koller (sic)	Edwin Smith (24)
#George Dewing	#F.L. Smith
Joseph Dayton (25)	#Ira A. Marina (26)
#H.L. Bissett (27)	Samuel E. McCormick (28)
#John F. Heilman (29)	#John F. Jones
#Robert McCracken	#D.M. Webster
#Jeromus Rapelye (?)	Joseph R. McCloud (31)
(Rapelve?)(30)	Lewis Dawson (32)
#J.J. Bennett	#Israel Heald Jr.(33)
#Thomas Loyd(sic) (34)	#Samuel Moore (35)
#J.H. Cunningham	#D.D. McFarlane
George Kincaid (36)	#Marston Hazleton
#William Walter	B. Fales
#J.D. Dickinson (37)	A.C. Beckwith
C.H. Rumrill	#M.Y. Maynard

(Continued next page)

#R.T. Holmes
H.E. Johnson
Charles Ford (38)
#T.W. Sigourney (39)
#George G. Powell
#George A. Nutter
#Rufus K. Slosson
Thomas Bigley (42)
#C.A. McCloud
#Caleb Holliday
#Henry K. White
#William L. Ramsdell
#John Davies
#N.T. Smith
#Timothy Heald (49)
#Winchester Spalding (sic)
#Mrs. Mary J. Ray (51)
Mrs. A.C. Waterman (53)
Mrs. L.H. Crowell (55)
Judson Judd (57)
#H.P. DeGraaf (59)
#Mary P. Fales (61)
#Mrs. Sarah A. Northrop(62)
George G. Ellis (63)
G. Beach
S.W. Woolsey (65)
#Mrs. S.E. Dewing
#Mrs. H.C. Tappan (68)
#A. Cram (70)
Nathaniel Hoyt (72)
#James Keon (sic)

#W. Deming
#N. Deming
#John Swigert
#B.C. Nickels(sic) (40)
M.T. Joice
#W. Davis
J.A. McFarlin (41)
#Samuel Levy (43)
M.S. Lincoln (44)
#Lawrence Beaghan (45)
David Dennison (46)
Burnet Cook (47)
John A. Hiller(sic) (48)
#Horace Hillyer (sic)
#A. Doench
John W. Cherry (50)
Mrs. C.P. Green (52)
Zenas Crowell (54)
Newton Judd (56)
Jared B. Walker (58)
E.R. Waterman (60)
Mr. C.J. Dutton
#E.N. Taylor
Albert Sleeper (64)
#M.H. Lamberson
J.B. Green (66)
#Mrs. Anna N. Baggs (67)
Hiram Garrett (69)
William Palui (71)
Reuben Howes and
    lady (73)

(1) Note "S.S. Mursey (Murfey?)", page 202.
(2) Reflected as "S. Baldwin", page 201.
(3) Note also "M. Dunn", page 202
(4) Note also "P. Reed", page 202.
(5) Listed as "S. Mosher", page 202. Note "T. Mosh-
    ier", page 202. Author of opinion that "T.
    Moshier" should be listed as "T. Mosher".
(6) Listed as "D. Starr", page 202.
(7) Listed as "C. Atkinson", page 202.
(8) Listed as "J. Campbell", page 201.
(9) Listed as "J.L. Seymour", page 203.
(10) Listed as "W.L. Beach", page 203.
(11) Listed as "John L. Polhemus", page 201
(12) Listed as "William H. McClung", page 202.
(13) Listed as "W.B. French & lady", page 201.
(14) Note "A.W. Brainard", page 201.
(15) Note "B. Ladd", page 202. This may have been
     spelling error in contemporary source. Atten-
     tion is directed to "Newton Judd"(56) and
     "Judson Judd"(57).
(16) Listed as "W.H. Fleming", page 202.

(17) Listed as "D.B. Dingman Jr", page 203.

(18) Listed as "C.B. Miles", page 202.

(19) Listed as "W. Sneaton", page 202.

(20) Note "H. Brinkwedd", page 202 - believed to be same passenger.

(21) Note "O.P. Lindsley", page 201 - believed to be same passenger. Also note "S.A. Lindsley", page 201.

(22) Listed as "H. Kimball", page 202.

(23) Note "J. Wanger", page 202 - believed to be same passenger.

(24) Listed as "E. Smith", page 202.

(25) Listed as "J. Dayton", page 202.

(26) Note "J.A. Marriner", page 203 - believed to be same passenger.

(27) Note "H.L. Bissell", page 202 - believed to be same passenger.

(28) Note"E.S. McCormick", page 202 - believed to be same passenger.

(29) Note "John Hillman", page 202 - believed to be same passenger.

(30) Note "J. Rapaljo", page 202 - believed to be same passenger.

(31) Listed as "J.R. McCloud", page 202.

(32) Listed as "L. Dawson", page 201.

(33) Listed as "Hild" surname on page 202 (see entry "T. Hild" and "A. Hild"). Entry "A. Hild" on page 202 is believed to be "Israel Heald Jr" on the card notice source. Also see footnote entry for "Timothy Heald"(#49).

(34) This passenger believed to be "Thomas Lloyd", see "T. Lloyd", page 203.

(35) Listed as "S. Moore", page 202.

(36) Listed as "G. Kincaid", page 202.

(37) Note "J.L. Dickinson", page 202.

(38) Listed as "C. Ford", page 201

(39) Note "J.W. Sigourney", page 201 - believed to be same passenger.

(40) Note "B. Nichols", page 202 - believed to be same passenger.

(41) Listed as "J.A. McFarland", page 203

(42) Listed as "T. Bigley", page 202.

(43) Note "Mrs.___ Levi, child & svt", page 201.

(44) Listed as "M. Lincoln", page 202.

(45) Note "L. Beajan", page 202 - believed to be same passenger.

(46) Note "D. Dennisan (Dennison?)", page 202 - believed to be same passenger.

(47) Listed as "B. Cook", page 203.

(48) Listed as "J.A. Hiller", page 201.

(49) Listed as "T. Hild", page 202. See also footnote #33.

(50) Listed as "J.W. Cherry", page 202.
(51) Note "B.J. Ray", page 201. Note "R. & J. Ray", page 202.
(52) Note "J.B. Green & lady", page 201.
(53) Note "E.R. Waterman & lady", page 201.
(54) Listed as "Z. Crowell & lady", page 201.
(55) See footnote #54, above.
(56) Listed as "N. Judd", page 202.
(57) Listed as "J. Judd", page 202.
(58) Listed as "J.B. Walker", page 202.
(59) Note "H.P. DePoff & svt", page 201.
(60) Listed as "E.R. Waterman & lady", page 201.
(61) Note "Mrs. N. Fales", page 201.
(62) Note "Mrs. S.A. Moulthrop", page 201 - believed to be same passenger.
(63) Listed as "G.G. Ellis", page 202.
(64) Listed as "A. Sleeper", page 202.
(65) This passenger listed on page 201. Note entry for passenger "R. Woolley", page 203. Both surnames listed as found in source.
(66) Listed as "J.B. Green & lady", page 201.
(67) Listed as "Mrs. A.M. Baggs", page 201.
(68) Listed as "Mrs.____Tappen, 2 children & svt", page 201. Note also "J. Tappen", page 203.
(69) Listed as "H. Garrett", page 201.
(70) Note "A. Crane", page 201. Possible this is same passenger.
(71) Note "W.A.L. Paulp", page 202 - believed to be same passenger.
(72) Listed as "N. Hoyt", page 202.
&3) Listed as "R. Howes & lady", page 201.

Page 203 - (Ship/Panama, from Panama; "Capt. R.H. Pearson"):- This ship master listed in a number of contemporary sources as "Captain R.H. Pierson".

Page 204 - (Ship/Panama, from Panama; "S. Atchisen"):- Foregoing passenger name listed as found in source. Note entry for "Mrs.____Atchison", same vessel, same page.

Page 205 - (Ship/Panama, from Panama; "L.C. Waldo" and "J. Walbro"):- Foregoing passenger names listed as found in source.

Page 206 - (Ship/Panama, from Panama; "J. Guess"):- Foregoing passenger name listed as found in source. Note entries for passengers "J. Gue" and "Z. Guest" on page 206. Author of opinion that error exists in original source material. Reader should consider alternatives of "J. Guest", "Z. Guess" and "Z. Gue".

Page 206 - (Ship/Panama, from Panama; "Mrs.____Shephard" and "J. Shepherd"):-Both foregoing names listed as found in source. Consider alternatives of "Mrs.____Shepherd" and "J. Shephard".

Page 207 - (Added Ship Arrival):- The vessel "Isabella" arrived in San Francisco on May 28, 1852, from San Juan del Sur, Nicaragua, via Lahaina, Sandwich Islands. The author

speculates that one of the passengers on board the
"Isabella" was "Charles Bunker". If other passengers
were on board this vessel their names remain a mystery.
Coinciding with the arrival of the "Isabella" was the
report of the arrival of Charles Bunker in San Francisco.
Bunker was the U.S. Consul at Lahaina, Sandwich Islands.
He was scheduled to return to his post during the first
or second week of June, 1852. Bunker may have booked
passage aboard the "Baltimore" (page 209) when he came to
San Francisco but it is probable that he departed from
Lahaina on the "Isabella". The "Baltimore" departed from
Waimea, Sandwich Islands. The passenger list of the "Balt-
imore" contains a listing for "C. Baulker and daughter".
There is the possibility that both contemporary sources
misspelled the surname of the consul.

Page 208 - (Ship/Hoogly-also known as Hoogley, from Boston, Massachusetts; "Rev. Benjamin Brierly", "J. McLand", "D. Mc-
Land","M.B. Frost(of Groton, Conn.)", "Benjamin McKendry
and lady", "G. Gardner(of Boston, Mass.)" and "D.W.
Pinkham (of Maine)"):- One source lists the "Hoogly" as
arriving in San Francisco on May 28, 1852. The secondary source adds"J.B. Raven, of Lynn, Massachusetts" as
an additional passenger. Variations exist between the
two research sources in spelling the names of certain
passengers. Secondary source carried "Rev. Benjamin
Brierly" as "Rev. B. Brierly, lady and four children";
"J. McLand" and "D. McLand" appear as "J. McLaud" and
"D. McLaud"; "M.B. Frost" listed as "W.Frost"; "Benjamin
McKendry and lady"are reflected as "Benjamin McKindry
and lady" and "G. Gardner" is noted as "G. Gurdner".

Page 210 - (Ship/J.C. Legrand, from San Juan del Sur, Nicaragua;
"J. Igram"):- Forementioned passenger listed as found
in source.

Page 211 - (Ship/Exact, from Puget Sound, Washington Territory;
"Capt.___Folger"):- On arriving in San Francisco the
master of the "Exact", Captain ___ Folger, reported that
there was great excitement in the Oregon Territory due
to the gold rush at Queen Charlotte's Island. Folger
stated he had recently taken the "Exact" to the island
and had visited nearly every one of the island's harbors
without accident. He represented the gold as lying among
the hills and reaching down to the shore. Folger planned
to unload his vessel in San Francisco and return to the
island with gold seekers. The island, at this time, was
claimed by the Hudson Bay Company.

Page 212 - (Added Ship Arrival):- The ship "Rowena" is believed to
have arrived in San Francisco on June 7, 1852. The craft
sailed from Panama carrying 250 passengers and some 200
tons of coal. The full list of passengers is not avail-
able. A number of deaths took place during the passage
and they are listed as follows:

Isaac Foster, of Bloomingdale, New York

Thomas Tate, of New York State
J. Show, of Madrid, New York
William Murphy, of Madrid, New York
Thomas Stevens, of New York State
W. Wilson, of Montgomery, New York
A. Williams, of Georgia
B. Filbert, of Vermont
Mr. Smith, Of New York, New York (no given name)
Mr. Woodward, of New York, New York (no given name)

Page 212 - (Ship/Laura Bevan, from Monterey, California):- The steamer "McKim" was laid up at Monterey, California.* See "Index" for deaths of passengers on this vessel.

Page 214 - (Ship/Winfield Scott, from Panama; "David Letz", "Andrew Letz", "Lawton Letz" and "Henry Letz"):- Foregoing passenger names listed as found in source. Note "D. Getz and lady", same vessel, page 215.

Page 214 - (Ship/Winfield Scott, from Panama; "Miss___Ayers"):- Foregoing passenger name listed as found in source. Note "A. Ayres", "O.H. Ayres" and "J. Ayres", same vessel, page 215. Also note "R. Ayers", "A. Ayers" and "S. Ayers" on board same vessel, page 217. Author believes errors exist in source material. Reader might consider alternatives of "Miss___Ayres", "A. Ayers", "O.H. Ayers", "J.A. Ayers", "R. Ayres", "A. Ayers" and "S. Ayers".

Page 215 - (Ship/Winfield Scott, from Panama; "Robert Duke, lady and servant"):- Four days after the "Winfield Scott" arrived in San Francisco two notices appeared in one of the local newspapers. The notices were in the form of "Information Wanted" advertisements and it is probable they were inserted by Robert Duke. One notice requested information about Richard Henry Duke who had left New York on March 5, 1852, by the Nicaragua route. Any party who left San Juan del Sur, Nicaragua during this time was to communicate with his brother, Robert Duke, at the Oriental Hotel in San Francisco. The second notice was inserted by "Robert C. Duke", of No. 16, Oriental Hotel, San Francisco. The latter item requested information on Richard Henry Duke, of Kilkenny, Ireland.

Page 216 - (Ship/Winfield Scott, from Panama; "F.W. Feild"):- Foregoing passenger name listed as found in source. Consider alternative of "F.W. Field". Note entry for passenger "J. Field", same vessel, same page.

Page 216 - (Ship/Winfield Scott, from Panama; "J. Haster", "William Hasser" and "W. Kaster"):- Foregoing passenger names listed as found in source. Author of opinion that errors exist in source material. Consider alternatives of "William Haster", "W. Haster","J. Hasser", "W. Hasser", "J. Kaster" and "William Kaster".

Page 216 - (Ship/Winfield Scott, from Panama; "E.T. Ettington" and "A. Etting"):- Foregoing passenger names listed as found in source. Author of opinion that error exists in

(*)The "McKim" still at Monterey on June 12,1852. Captain and entire crew had deserted the vessel.

source material. Consider Alternatives of "E.T. Etting" and "A. Ettington".

Page 216 - (Ship Winfield Scott, from Panama; "W. Sanyard" and "J. Maynard"):- Foregoing passenger names listed as found in source.

Page 217 - (Ship/Winfield Scott, from Panama; "W. Freind"):- Foregoing passenger name listed as found in source. Author of opinion that source material is in error and entry for passenger should read "W. Friend". Note passengers "A. Friend"(page 215) and "T. Friend"(page 216), same vessel.

Page 217 - (Ship/Northerner, from Panama; "Levi Scoffield"):- Foregoing passenger name listed as found in source. Note listings for passengers, same vessel, "Mrs.___Scofield" (page 218) and "L.N. Scofield" (page 220).

Page 217 - (Ship/Northerner, from Panama):- This vessel brought word from San Diego, California of the death of Captain (Brev. Lieutenant Colonel)___Craig, 3rd Infantry, U.S. Army. Craig set out from San Diego on June 1, 1852 for the Gila River, on his way to New Mexico. He was in command of a small escort of troops accompanying the Boundary Commission in its move towards the Colorado River. On the fourth day of travel, midway across the desert, Craig encountered four or five men in the dress of U.S. soldiers. The men identified themselves as deserters from Major___Heintzelman's command at Camp Yuma. Craig identified himself as an officer of the U.S. Army and endeavored to persuade them to return to duty. The deserters responded by firing at Craig and two sergeants who were in his company. Craig and one of the sergeants (Sgt.___Bales, 1st Artillery, U.S. Army) fell and the other sergeant escaped, bringing word of the incident to the main marching column. Craig was buried at a camp where wells had lately been dug, at Alamo Muncho (sic, Alamo Mocho?).

Page 218 - (Ship/Northerner, from Panama; "James de la Montayne"):- Foregoing passenger name listed as found in source.

Page 218 - (Ship/Northerner, from Panama; "J. Tonella" and "L. Tonnella"):- Foregoing passenger names listed as found in source. Reader should consider "J. Tonnella" and "L. Tonella" as alternatives.

Page 219 - (Ship/Northerner, from Panama; "Miss___Conway"):- Three days after the arrival of the "Northerner" an "Information Wanted" notice appeared in one of the San Francisco newspapers, which read:

> "Wanted- Information of Jerry Hartnett or Thomas Conway, late of Channel Rock, Ireland, by his sister, Catharine Conway, who arrived by the "Northerner", on the 16th Inst. Apply immediately to John Griffin, Tin Shop, Stockton Street, near Green, San Francisco."

Page 220 - (Ship Northerner, from Panama; "R. Burham"):- Foregoing passenger name listed as found in source. Author specu-

lates passenger entry may be in error. Note presence on
on same vessel of passengers "Mr. and Mrs.___Burnham and
two children"(page 219). Consider "R. Burnham" as alternative.

Page 220 - (Ship/Northerner, from Panama; "C. Betta"):- Foregoing
passenger name listed as found in source. Note "V.
Beffa", "J. Beffa" and "A. Beffa", same vessel, page 219.
Also note "A. Beffa", same vessel, page 220.

Page 220 - (Ship/Northerner, from Panama; "J. Broas"):- Foregoing
passenger name listed as found in source. Note same
name, same vessel, page 221.

Page 220 - (Ship/Northerner, from Panama; "B. Bantesta"):- Foregoing
passenger name listed as found in source. Note "A. Ban-
testor", same vessel, page 221.

Page 221 - (Ship/Northerner, from Panama; "J. Graffe"):- Foregoing
passenger name listed as found in source. Note "P.
Graff", same vessel, same page. Reader should consider
alternatives of "P. Graffe" and "J. Graff".

Page 221 - (Ship/Northerner, from Panama; "M. Hustin" and "J.H.
Houston"):- Foregoing passenger names listed as found in
source. Consider alternatives of "M. Houston" and "J.H.
Hustin".

ADDENDA NOTES

Pages 20-21 - (Ship/North America, from San Juan del Sur, Nicaragua; "Mr. Joseph Proctor and wife"):- Contemporary
source identifies Mrs. Joseph Proctor as "Mrs. Elizabeth
Proctor".

Page 112 - (Ship/Tennessee, from Panama; "Madame___Celeste"):-
Madame___Celeste was an entertainer and a theatrical
poster of the period bills the lady as "Miss Mattie
Celeste".

Page 146 - (Ship/Invincible, from New York; "Wilmarth Waller"):-
Some contemporary sources refer to this passenger as
"Mr. D. Wilmarth Waller".

Page 146 - (Ship/Invincible, from New York; "Captain___Johnson"):-
Dimensions of the "Invincible" were:- 245 feet extreme
length; breadth of beam, 42 feet, 10 inches; depth of
hold, 25 feet, 6 inches; tonnage register, 1768. Main
cabin accomodations for 10 passengers. The vessel was
built by W.H. Webb, of New York and it was owned by
J.W. Phillips, Esq. One source lists the master of the
craft as "Captain Henry W. Johnson".

ADDENDA TO
SAN FRANCISCO SHIP PASSENGER LISTS, VOLUME I

The following material represents addenda facts pertinent to "SAN FRANCISCO SHIP PASSENGER LISTS, VOLUME I". The data comprises essential information which could not be substantiated at the time the first volume was published. Below listings are indexed in this volume (Volume III) and will be reflected in the Master Index Volume (Volume XVI).

Vol. I, page 48 - (Ship/Courrier de Inde,from Havre, France):- One contemporary source states that 96 additional passengers were aboard this vessel, 42 of the passengers being females. The passengers on board the "Courrier de Inde" were part of the 5000 French citizens that had drawn prizes in the "Lottery of the Golden Ingots". Between 600-700 prize-winners had arrived prior to the appearance of the "Courrier de Inde" and some 4000 remained to take passage to California.

Vol. I, page 58 - (Ship/Frances Helen, from San Juan del Sur, Nicaragua; "Captain___Leeds"):- One source carries this vessel as "of Philadelphia, Pennsylvania, mastered by Captain Mark H. Leads". This secondary source adds the following passengers to the "Frances Helen":

James F. Johnson	William Powell
G.W. Hill	W. L. Lytle
Jackson Barwise	D. Lytle

The secondary source varies in listing three passengers as noted below:

L.L. Bradbury*	W.E. Harris+
D.B. Carver#	

(*)Listed as "L. Bradbury"in Vol.I
(+)Listed as "Mr.___Harris" in Vol. I
(#)Listed as "Mr.___Carver" in Vol. I

Vol. I, page 59 - (Ship/Fremont, from Oregon Territory, arrival of May 23, 1852):- A secondary contemporary source differs in spelling some of the passenger names as follows:- "Capt.___Coussins" is listed as "R.W. Cussans"; "C.M. Carter" carried as "Charles Carter"; "J.F. Bybee" appears as "James F. Biby"; "Mr.___Northrup" reflected as "N. Northrup" and "H. Toomey" is booked as "Henry Toomey". According to the secondary source there were two more passengers on board the "Fremont"-namely, "George H. Atkinson" and "Justus Dunn".

Vol. I, page 111 - (Ship/Mechanic's Own, from New York, N.Y.):- Listed in Volume I as arriving in San Francisco on "May 20, 1852". One source states it arrived on "May 21,1852".

Vol. I, page 113 - (Ship/Monumental City, from San Juan del Sur, Nicaragua):- The following passengers died during the passage:

> April 26,1852 - Isaac Brown, of dysentery, from Atkinson, Maine
>
> April 28,1852 - J.W. Brown, of fever, from Foster, Rhode Island (listed on page 115, Vol.I).
>
> April 29,1852 - Mr.___Cook, of dysentery, from Maine.
>
> April 29,1852 - Oliver Denton, of dysentery, aged 20 years, from New York.
>
> April 30,1852 - Thomas Rich, of fever, aged 25 years, from Delaware County, New York (listed as "T. Rich", page 114, Vol. I).
>
> April 30,1852 - Isaac Peckham, of fever, from New York.
>
> April 30,1852 - Thomas Mund, of fever, from Amboy, New Jersey.
>
> May 12, 1852 - Alexander Rose, of dysentery, aged 27 years, from Lowell, Massachusetts (listed as "A. Rose", page 114, Vol.I).
>
> May 15, 1852 - Mrs. Hannah Burt, of consumption, from Worcester, Massachusetts.
>
> May 17, 1852 - Nathaniel Leetch, of diarrhea, aged 45 years, from Vermont.

Vol. I, page 158 - (Ship/Sir Charles Napier, from Panama-"deaths during passage"):- A secondary source furnished additional details relative to the deaths taking place during the passage of the "Sir Charles Napier". Where variations occur between the two source lists they are so depicted. <u>Deaths on Board the "Sir Charles Napier"</u>:

> March 9, 1852 - A. Buckelin, of Grafton County, aged 38 years (no State listed).
>
> March 17, 1852 - T. Buckelin, of Grafton County, aged 20 years (no State listed). (Source used in compiling Volume I carried "T. Buckelin" as "S. Buckelin")
>
> April 2, 1852 - M. Williams, of Grafton County, aged 29 years (no State listed).
>
> March 9, 1852 - T. Banks of Murray County, aged 45 years (no State listed).
>
> March 1, 1852 - M. Rodgers, of Cherokee County, aged 22 years (no State listed).
>
> March 6, 1852 - M. Burns, of Jackson County, aged 21 years (no State listed).
>
> March 3, 1852 - T. Harris, of Jackson County, aged 34 years (no State listed) (Source used in compiling Volume I carried "T. Harris" as "G. Harris")
>
> March 7, 1852 - Z. Grimble, Gordon County, aged 34 years (no State listed). (Source used in compiling Volume I carried

"Z. Grimble" as "___ Grindle")

March 16, 1852 - John Sears, Gordon County, aged 22
 years (no State listed).

March 28, 1852 - J.W. Qumlin, Cass County, aged 20
 years (no State listed).
 (Source used in compiling Volume I carried
 "J.W. Qumlin" as "J. Tumlin")

April 3, 1852 - W.J. Croane, Gordon County, aged 19
 years (no State listed).
 (Source used in compiling Volume I carried
 "W.J. Croane" as "W.S. Croane")

March 8, 1852 - ___ Adley (a black boy), Burke County,
 aged 23 years (no State listed).

March 4, 1852 - J. Vincent, Cass County, aged 30 years
 (no State listed).

March 7, 1852 - W.A. Dawson, Gordon County, aged 30
 years (no State listed).

March 5, 1852 - A.D. Loveless, Cass County, aged 22
 years (no State listed).
 (Source used in compiling Volume I carried
 "A.D. Loveless" as "A.W. Loveless")

February 24, 1852 - J.M. Kincaid, Burke County, aged
 22 years (no State listed).

March 2, 1852 - James Hamblin, Murray County, Georgia,
 aged 33 years.

March 2, 1852 - Jesse Walton, McDowell County, aged
 46 years (no State listed).
 (Note listing in Volume I, page 158 for "G.
 Walker")

March 2, 1852 - James Finley, McDowell County, aged 20
 years (no State listed).

March 3, 1852 - Z. Baker, Lumpkin County, aged 35 years
 (no State listed).

March 11, 1852 - Boly Wickett, Gordon County, aged 23
 years (no State listed).

March 10, 1852 - ___ Osborne (a black boy), Burke
 County, aged 18 years (no State listed).

March 5, 1852 - A. Conley, McDowell County, aged 21
 years (no State listed).

March 5, 1852 - G. Carson, Lumpkin County, aged 26
 years (no State listed).

March 30, 1852 - A.K. Birt, Lumpkin County, aged 23
 years (no State listed).

March 25, 1852 - William Birt, Lumpkin County, aged 20
 years (no State listed).

March 16, 1852 - J.P. Conley, McDowell County, aged 20
 years (no State listed).

March 19, 1852 - T. Robertson, Gordon County, aged 25
 years (no State listed).

March 13, 1852 - James O'Neill, Jersey City, aged 35
 years (no State listed).
 (Source used in compiling Volume I carried

"James O'Nei11" as "James O'Nei1")

March 5, 1852 - W. Rodgers, of Pennslyvania, aged 40
years.

April 8, 1852 - _____ Alec (or Alec____), a black boy, of
McDowell County, aged 27 years (no State
listed).

April 13, 1852 - E. Dickenson, of New York, aged 21
years.

April 15, 1852 - E. Rouse, of Lumpkin County, aged 24
years (no State listed).

April 13,1852 - A. Reid, of Cass County, aged 25 years
(no State listed).

March 3, 1852 - James King, of Boston, Massachusetts,
aged 30 years.
(Source used in compiling Volume I carried
"James King" as "James Ring")

March 2, 1852 - James McGuire, of New Orleans, La.,
aged 45 years.

Vol. I, page 172 - (Ship/Wisconsin, from New York):- One contemporary source listed six of the eight passengers of the "Wisconsin" somewhat differently. Where variations occur
between the two passenger lists they are so depicted.

Henry Suydam*   W.H. Bagley#
George W. Morley**   Charles S. Eddy
Thomas S. Andrews and
      lady***
(*) Listed as "H. Suydam" in Volume I
(**) Listed as "G.W. Moreley" in Volume I
(***) Listed as "Capt. T.S. Andrews & lady" in
Volume I
(#) Listed as "W.S. Bagley" in Volume I
(+) Listed as "C.S. Eddy" in Volume I

- - - - - - -

CORRECTIONS TO
SAN FRANCISCO SHIP PASSENGER LISTS, VOLUME I

The following corrections in "San Francisco Ship Passenger
Lists, Volume I" are to be made:

Vol. I, page 122 - (Ship/Northern Light, from Acapulco, Mexico):-
Arrival date listed in Volume I as "ARRIVED: May 25,
1852" should read "ARRIVED: May 20, 1852".

Vol. I, page 155 - (Ship/Sea Bird, from San Diego, California):-
Passenger listed as "J.R. Thompson" should read "J.P.
Thompson".

Vol. I, page 222 - (LAY, Charles H.):- Appears in Surname Index as
"LAY, Charles H., 88" should read "LAY, Charles H., 8"

CORRECTIONS TO
SAN FRANCISCO SHIP PASSENGER LISTS, VOLUME II

The following corrections in "San Francisco Ship Passenger Lists, Volume II" are to be made:

Vol. II, page 344 - (TICHNOR, H.H.(Mr) & lady):- Appears in Surname Index as "Tichnor, H.H.(Mr) & lady, 230" should read "Ticknor, H.H.(Mr) & lady, 230".

Vol. II, page 376 - (Ship/Ceuador):- Appears in Subjective and Geographical Index as "Ship/Ceuador,25,28" should read "Ship/Ecuador,25,28".

SURNAME INDEX

(x)-Denotes more than one entry for name on cited page.
See "Key To Abbreviations and Symbols" for the
definition of symbols, abbreviations and figures.
Index for passengers with unidentified given and
surnames (missing letters) will be found at the
conclusion of this index.

274

278

Bouicher, (Don)Juan, 51
Boukise, J.,29
Boulden, P.,102
Boullett,____(Mrs) and boy,137
Bourdeau, S.V.,97
Bourguignon, R.,97
Bourn, F.A.,102
Bourne,____(Capt), 181
____(Mrs),38
J.(Mr),38
Bournouvelle,__(Mr), 47
Bouton, T.,180
Boux, J.,97
Bovey, M.C.,199
Bow, E.,31
Thomas,61
Bowden,____(Capt),157
J.,16
N.,125
Bowel, J.B.,111
Bowell, B.,169,249
Bowen (see also Bowon)
____(Capt),19,80
____(Mrs),112
F.,39
J.,113
John,87
Bower, A.,113
Benjamin F.,102
E.,10,139
G.,70
H.F.,103
Bowers, Francis,18
J.,220
J.B.,35
J.T. & lady,30
M.J.,68
P.,145
R.,15
T.S.,28
Bowie, A.,179
G.W.,34
Bowles, C.,192
D.,192
G.W.,132
Bowls, J.,30
Bowman,Charles, 106

Bowman (Cont'd)
D.,169
F.M.,189
H.,42
J.,24,151
J.C.,130
J.H.,185
J.K.,138
John,106
Z.,153
Bowmaster, J.,106
Bowne,____(Mr & Mrs) & child,73
O.,38
Bowon (see also Bowen)
J. & lady,205
Bowrig, J.W.,28
Bowstead,____(Miss), 167
Bowyer, H.L.,93
Boyce, G.,218
James,91
T.,29,218
Boyd, A.,162
D.,65
J.,91
M.,64
N.G.,198
S.,94,108
Thomas,50
W.,wife and five chldrn,36
Boydan, E.,112
Boyden,____,lady & 3 childrn,159
A.,75
Boye, G.(Mr),128
Boyellter, C.R.,13
Boyer, A.,62
Benjamin,36
Boyington, G.,64
Boyle, Arthur,26
E.,138
J.,138
L.,46
M.,103
P.,61
R.,46
Boylen, James,102
Boyles, H.,113
Boynes, John,35

Boynes (Cont'd)
S.,35
Boynton, A.,192
H.,75
J.W.,73
Boysen,____(Capt), 172
Boza, Lorenzo, 223
Bozec,____(Capt),97
Brabende, A.,206
Brace, D.,151
Brache, Jacob, 106
Bracia, Roman, 96
Brackenenridge,R.H., 92
Brackets, A.,67
Brackett, Daniel,86
E.,170
J.W.,65
Mary H.(Mrs),110
S.,107
Bradbury,____(Mr),29
B.B.,75
D.,113
L.,264
L.L.,264
Braden, M.,203
S.A.,108
Bradford, D.M.,108
J.,28
W.,112
Brading,____(Mr),215
J.R.,103
Bradley (see also Bradly)
____,135
____(Capt),7
A.,167
C.W.,179
F.,25
G.,112
J.,10,199
J.P.,204
J.W.,78
Bradly (see Bradley --no entry for Bradly this volume)
Bradshaw, G.,10
J.A.,141
W.D.,121
Brady (next page)

Chase (Cont'd)
  J.,132
  J.A.,134
  J.L.,39
  James,87
  L.G.,112
  O.,169
  R.,22
Chastano, J.M.,155
Chatellin, J.,169
Chatfield, H.F.,86
Chattendon, J.A.,177
Chattle, H.,75
Chaumont, J.B.,97
Chauncey, Francis,28
  Job (Jr.),63
  M.B.,33
Cheavey, D.J.,174
Cheeney, E.,4
  J.,74
  Thomas,220
Cheesebro (see also
    Chesebro)
  A.,24
Cheevers, W.H.,4
Chenaist, D.,97
Chenery, H.,104
  N.,178
Cheney, Cyrus,77
  E.G.,155
  G.A.,132
Chenu, C.,97
  J.,97
Cheparr, A.,98
Cherry, C.,92
  C.M. & lady,201
  J.,41
  J.W.,202,259
  John W.,257
  Margaret,207
  Maria,207
  William M.,56
Chesebro (see also
    Cheesebro)
  Charles,28
  D.A.,40
  R.D.,40
Chesley,____(Mrs),38
  T.,17
Chesrand, E.,103
Chester, B.,9
  G.F.,221

Chester (Cont'd)
  J.,112
Chetwood, Jese,99
  John,99
Chevalier, A.P.,199
Choar, E.,193
Choate, G.,143
Chomley, A.,200
Chornping, G.V.,109
Choparr, A.,98
Chick, E.(Mrs),63
  Mary(Miss),63
  R.,63
  W.A.,63
Chichester, L.,39
Chickering, O.,220
Child, Henry,204
  O.M.,4
  P.,211
  R.B.(Capt),48
Childers,____(Mrs),
    221
  G.W.,104
  J.,104
Childs, C.H.,128
  D.,73
  J.C.,149
  M.,184
  O.W.,55
  P.G.,60
China, J.,121
China/Royalty of:
  Hien-Fung (Emperor)
    49
Ching, Wang(Mr),82
Chinn, H.J.,135
Chipchase, N.,139
Chipman, N.,21
  S.S.,38
Chisholm,____,46
  A.,15
  E.,139
  Thomas,178
Christian,____(Mrs),
    112
  A.,210
Christie,____,145
  C.,93
  J.,92
  W.,93
Christman (see Crist-
    man,this volume)

Christophe, C.,140
Christopher,B.P.,
    69
Chubb, A.B.,94
Chuhuck, C.F.,61
Chumbolles, T.,161
Chunk, E.,165
Chupal, S.,116
Church,____(Mrs) &
    daughter,204
  A.,72
  C.,114
  E.,72(x),161
  F.,91
  H.,140
  J.,15,53,167
  J.L.,35
  J.S.,204
  T.G.,26
  W.W.,71
Churchill,____(Dr),
    lady & svt,105
  C.,87
  F.,26
  S.M.,17
Chusen, L.,180
Chussman, H.,128
Chute, John, 50
  M.A.,50
Cilley, J.,40
Citteridge, F.,165
Claflin, E.,220
Clapp, C.S.,198
  I.,124
  J.,73,114
  J. & lady,95
  John Jr.,254
  S.,114
  W.,133
Clare,____(Mrs),218
  Francis,219
  Fras (sic),219
Clarivele,____(Mrs)
    & dau.,204
Clark,____,35,36
  ____ & lady,166
  ____(Capt),81,122
  ____(Miss),88,166
  ____(Mrs),85,166
  ____(Mrs) and
    child,38,201
  (see next page)

Clark (Cont'd)
    ____(Mrs) and
      son,137
    A.,206
    A.L.,33
    A.R.,23,165
    B.F.,26
    B.W.,167
    Benjamin,28
    C.,68,220
    C.C.,143
    C.H.,214,222
    D.,91,124
    E.,33
    E.M.,193
    E.R.,38
    E. St.Clair,99
    E.W.,65
    H.,133,179
    H.S.(Capt),111
    J.,16,63,102,114,
      124,131,178,
      206
    J. & lady,191
    J.A.,6,177
    J.B.,33
    J.M.,128
    J.R.,73
    J.V.O.,28
    J.W.,174
    John,28
    L.,56
    L.B.,56
    M.,146
    Martin,87
    O.A.,143
    O.C.,74
    P.,5
    R.,69,200
    R.C.,6,90
    R.E.,144
    S.(Mrs) & two
      chldrn,7
    S.S.,178
    Smyth,47
    T.,7,187
    T.M.,125
    Thomas,124,250
    W.,7,39,68,92
    W.H. & wife,66
    W.Y.,138
    William,38

Clarke (see also
    Clark)
    ____(Miss),112
    Caroline(Mrs),79
    E.F.,134
    F.A.,7
    G.D.,7
    H.D.,158
    J.,107
    J.(Miss),105
    J.J.,133
    P.G.,107
    R.,199
    T.,196
Clarkson, S.,114
Clary, R.(Capt),163
Claudeat, J.,97
Claudest, J.,97
Claughney,____(Mrs),
    203
Clauson (see also
    Clawson and
    Clousen)
    P.,29
Clavers,____(Miss),112
Clavie, J.,98
Clawbot,____(Mr),136
Clawson (see also
    Clauson and
    Clousen)
    John,70
Claxton, E.,210
    G.,210
    J.W.,210
Clay, F.E.,216
    W.J.M.(Rev),186
Clayanore, F.,139
Clayton, B.,93
    J.C.,91
    N.(Miss),67
Cleach, G.B.M.,13
Clear,____,103
Cleariane, P.S.,96
Cleary (see also
    Clery)
    J.,95
Cleaveland, A.,71
Cleaver, L.H.,69
Cleenens,____(Miss),
    112
Clemans, W.,2
Clemens(next column)

Clemens, William S.
    & lady,196
Clement, J.,175
    J.H.,75(x)
    P.,77
Clements, H.F.,13
    H.W.G.,146
    John,86,105
    W.C.,95
    William,176
Clereland, J.T.,242
    M.P.,133
Clerentin, A.,97
Cleret, C.,177
    J.,177
Clerk, T.,215
    Thomas,175,250
Clerken, Phillip,65
Clery (see also
    Cleary)
    M.,153
Cleveland, A., 41
    Daniel,178 (as
      Clevland)
    J.T.,133
    M.P.,133
Clevis, A.,17
    S.,17
Clifford, A.B.,43
    J.G.,10
Clifton,____(Mr),39
    S.L.,124
Cline, W.,148
    W.E.,188
Clinet,____(Mr) and
    lady,213
Clinton, A.,132
    E.,203
    J.,203
    W.,109
Clissold, E.M.,223
Clock, John R.,186
Clogston, J.D.,126
Cloque, J.,151
Close, H.,87,171
    J.,68
    J.B.,170
    J.W.,56
Clotz, R.,170
Cloud, J.,192
Clough, D.,40
    J.,141

300

Cummings (Cont'd)
 P.,197
 R.,132
 W.,121
Cummins (see also
 Cummings)
 ____(Miss),160
 D.,170
 H.,121
 T.,135
Cuney, R.,206
Cunfield, D.,125
Cunneff, E.H.,96
Cunnell, M.,152
Cunningham (see also
 Coningham)
 A.,75
 B.,55
 F.,187
 G.(Mr)46
 H.,43,98
 J.,107,168,215
 J.A.,175
 J.H.,256
 John,151
 T.,164
 W.,122,132,168
 W.J.,178
Cupps, J.,108
Curm, M.,122
Curnass, B.F.,65
Curran, B.,153
 E.,69
Currie (see also
 Curry)
 C.,169
 J.,lady and
  child,134
 James,10
Currier, L.,187
 W.,91
Currnel, J.,142
Curry (see also
 Currie)
 Charles,107
 John,79
 M.,107
 Q.,22
 W.,29
Curtagne, T.,207
Curtin. M.,174
Curtis(next column)

Curtis,____,70
 ____(Capt),118
 ____(Lt),233
 ____(Mr),184,213
 A.T. & lady,83
 C.E.,154
 D.,189
 H.,188
 J.,199
 N.,124
 R.,135
 S.R.,93
 S.W.,93
 W.,4,114
 W.B.,6
 William,195
Curtiss, Martin,218
Cusade, J.D.,127
 Thomas,127
Cushing, A.,74
 G.S.,73
 J.,74,124
 M.L.,133
 W.B.,189
Cushman, Charles H.,
  157
 G.,94
 R.,90
 S.(Capt),70
Cussans, R.W.,264
Custan, H.W.,83
Custer (see also
 Kuster)
 -no Custer this
 volume-
Custon, A.,30
Cutell, W.,212
Cuthbert, William(Capt),
  48
Cuthbertson, N.,140
Cutler, E.,114
Cutlew, T.,15
Cutter, B.S.,15
 C.F.,177
 E.,172
 H.,17
 J.S.,22
 L.,79
 L.C.,193
 L.H.,90
Cutting, C.B.,202
 D.,202

Cutts, J.,109
 P.,109
 R.D.,96,235
 Richard D.,235
Cuyler, E.,141
 M.B.(Mrs),87
 R.,174
Cypalana,____(Col.),
  90
Cypher, John,60
 S.,60

-D-

Dabas, M.,205
Dacon, M.,75
Dacutt, F.,43
Dacy, C.,221
 T.,220
Dade, J.C.,31
 S.,31
Daffycy,____,205
Dagget (see also
 Daggett and
 Daggott)
 ____(Capt),158
Daggett (see also
 Dagget and
 Daggott)
 A.,201
 F.,177
 J.H.,93
 M.,167
 O.(Capt),69
 W.F.,193
 William,202
Daggott (see also
 Dagget and
 Daggett)
 D.T.,124
Daghert, D.,178
Daguahan, P.,61
Dailey (see also
 Daily, Daley and
 Daly)
 P.,61
 S.,27
Daily (see also
 Dailey, Daley
 and Daly)
 J.,92
 T.,109
Dain, W.M.,22

Dixon (Cont'd)
  O.S.,40
  W.S.,86
Dlaly, P. and lady,
  171
Dmith, J.F.(sic),
  165
Doaer, M.D.,96
Doak, J.,103
  J.K.,103
Doane, D.,175
  H.,27
  J.,61
  J.G.,138
  W.E.,175
Dobbins,____(Capt),73
Dobinson, H.,59
Dochman, D.S.(Capt),34
Dockery, J.,107
Dockman, G.C.,250
Dockunn, G.C.,174,250
Dodd, J.,10,172
  L.,210
Dodge,____,68
  A.,23,151
  B.,65
  D.,224
  F.,177
  H.L. & wife,124
  J.,179
  J.C.,9
  J.S.,8
  John M.,255
  L.W.,125
  Noah,126
  S.,84
  T.,169
  W.H.,65
Dodlear, L. and
  lady,140
Dodson, B.F.,94
  R.,167
Doe, A.A.,169
  N.,61
  T.,133
Doench, A.,257
Doerick, A.,201
Doherty (none this
  volume, see
  Dorety, Doroty,
  Dorrity and
  Dougherty)

Dohling, G.,73
Doily, B.,36
Dolan, S.,139
Doland,____(Mrs),105
Dolby, A.(Miss),180
  J.(Mrs),180
Dolds,____(Mr),155
Dole, J.S.,lady,
  infant & svt,
  143
Dollarhide,____(Mr),81
Dolliver, O.G.,22
Dolons, T.,197
Dolpheim, G.C.,189
Dolsen, A.E.(Mrs),60
Dolwell, J.,43
Domecq, J.,98
Dominga, A.,40
Donaghu, T.,217
Donahoe (see also
  Donaghu,Donahue,
  Donnohoe, Donn-
  ough and Donohue)
  M.,174,
  S.,164
Donahue (no entry
  this volume,
  see Donahoe)
Donald, W.B.(Mr),235
Donalds, J.,9
Donaldson (see also
  Donnelson)
  ____,56,94,234
  ____(Mrs),138
  A.,135,176,179
  E.B.(Mr),235
  J.,94,102
  S.,189
  W.B.,107
  William,219
Donerly,____(Mrs),214
Dongyear, E.,105
Donigan, L.,190
Donlan, T.,189
Donley, W.,131
Donlyn, T.,184
Donnelan, J.,57
Donnell, Pat,135
  W.E.,86
  W.O.,57
  William O.,44
Donnelly, J.,95

Donnelly (Cont'd)
  L.,107
Donnelson (see also
  Donaldson)
  John,45
Donney, John,29
Donnivan, D.,145
Donnohoe (see also
  Donaghu,
  Donahoe,
  Donahue,
  Donnough and
  Donohue)
  D.,61
Donnough (see remark
  under Donnohoe
  in addition to
  following)
  ____(Mrs),59
Donnovan (see also
  Donovan)
  J.,23
Donoa,____(Mrs),134
Donohue (see also
  Donaghu,
  Donahoe,
  Donahue,
  Donnohoe,
  Donnough and
  following)
  F.,134
  J.,215
  P.,61
Donos,____(Mrs),134
Donovan (see also
  Donnovan)
  ____(Miss),12
  ____(Mr) and
  lady,102
  ____(Mrs),148
  A.,13
  D.,141
  J.,149
  John,66
  M.,206
  Mary,149
Donver, John,193,254
Donzelle, A.,42
Dooley, J.,44
Doolittle, E.,117
  J.,39
  O.W.,173

Earnest (Cont'd)
  W.,206
Eas, Hans,151
Easan, W.G. & svt,12
Easley, J.B.,150
Easling, H.,179
Easman, L.D.,75
East, G.,25
Eastbro, J.,98
Eastbrook, Jane(Mrs),
  110
Easterly, J.M.,87
Eastman, C.B.,210
  John,66
  M.,114
  S.,131
  T.M.,64
Easton, A.S.,186
Eastwood, W.,21
Eatan (see also
  Eaton)
  J.B.,127
  Samuel,127
  William,127
  William(Jr),127
Eaton (see also
  Eatan)
  ___(Mr),81
  ___(Mrs) and
  child,152
  A.,45,199
  B.F.,67
  E.,150
  H.,27
  H.A.,126
  J.,34
  J.A.(Mr & Mrs),25
  J.B.,127
  J.S.,141
  John,150
  Lyman,65
  O.C.,210
  S.,179
  S.(Mrs),176
  Samuel,127
  William,127
  William(Jr),127
Ebbetts, A.N.,73
  E.A.,73
Eberheart, T.V.,117
Ebinger,___,15
Echub, N.,29

Eckart, Ignatius,86
Eckhart, J.,148
  P.,170
Eckles, B.,87
Eckley, H.(Mr),240
Eddis, R.,151
Eddy (see also
  Ede)
  ___,43
  ___(Mr),197
  A.L.,215
  C.S.,267
  Charles S.,267
  E.W.,128
  G.E.,132
  L.,124
Ede (see also Eddy)
  Joseph,16
Eden, D.M.,203,204
Eder,M. & lady,203,
  204
Edes,___(Mr),25
Edetrall, J.,30
Edgar, J.,133
  Jerome,56
  S.,102
  T.,105
Edgerly, S.,124
Edgill, L.,102
Edington,___(Capt),31
  J.,171
Edmar, R.,108
Edmond, B.(Jr),62
  C.,64
Edmonds, E.,144
Edmundson, William,86
Edsall, J.R.,201
Edson, S.,142
  W.B.,93
Edward, J.,184
  T.,210
Edwards,___(Mrs),5
  ___(Mrs) and svt,
  186
  A.,151
  A.C.,132
  A.D.,198
  A.J.,174
  C.,35,206
  C.E.,50
  C.H.,13
  D.,175

Edwards (Cont'd)
  D.W.,23
  E.E.,33
  G.,16,188
  G.R.,41
  H.P.,126
  J.,9,33,69
  J. & lady,167
  J.P.,121
  R.,43
  T.,175
  W.,75,203
Efder, H.,90,234
  J.,90,234
Efner, H.,90
  J.,90,93,234
Egan,___(Miss),245
  ___(Mrs),245
  A.,41
  J.,57
  Margaret(Mrs),245
Egbert, B.E.,131
  J.M.,165
  W.G.,165
Eggin, B.,168
Eggleston, G.W.,56
Egles, W.,114
Ehinger,___,15
Ehle, Henry (Jr),144
Ehler, F.,167
Ehlinge, M.,193
Ehrhard, Maria,18
Eider, S.,14
Eigenbradt, D.,27
Eivenstone,___ and
  lady,17
Eizar,___(Mr),48
Elandson, J.,187
Elder, J.,42
  N.,217
  W.,86
Eldred,___(Mrs) and
  child,218
Eldridge,___(Capt),
  137
  J.O.,87
  J.T.(Mr),121
  W.S.,89
Elend, E.K. and wife
  32,225
Elevenstone (see
  Elvenstone)
Eley,___(Mr),5

Foertera, C.,97
Foerters, C.,97
Fogarty, J.,168
Fogerty,____(Mrs),145
Fogg, A.H.,66
  Henry,219
  J.B.,93
  J.L.,30
  P.S.,114
Foleat, J.,171
Folest, J.,171
Foley, E.,164
  J. & lady,134
  L.,15,169
  M.,135
  R.A.,114
  T. and wife,125
  Thomas,29
  W.,15
  W.D.,186
Folger,____(Capt),211,
  260
  ____(Mr),7
  William D.,223
Folinsbee,____(Mr),73
Folks, R.W.,169
  W.,181
Follett, H.B.,33
Folley, T.,219
Folsom, J.,64
Fonley, J.(Jr.),113
Fontaine, A.,97
Fontalrosa, A.,160
Fontellsilla, L.,128
Foode, A.,29
Foot, C.,204
Foote, C.O.,139
Fopus, S.C.(Mrs),7
Forbe,____,133
Forbes (see also
  Forbs)
  ____,133
  ____(Capt),156
  ____(Mr),70
  ____(Mrs) & child,
  126
  D.,39
  G.,135
  J.,149
  O.,149
  W.F.,60
  William,126

Forbos, O.,149
Forbs (see also
  Forbes)
  W.,16
Forbush, C.,220
Forbx (sic)
  ____,133
Force, J.H.,157
  O.,114
  O.,239
  O.O.,112,239
  W.H.(Mr),85
Ford, C.,201,258
  Charles,257
  D.N.,199
  E.M.,39
  F.R.,17
  F.S.,65
  J.,150
  J.B.,75
  J.G.,139
  J.S.,68
  P.,130
  Robert,94
  S.,61
  S.H.,130
  W.,150,164,171(x)
  W.B.,68
  W.T.,139
Fordham, J.H.,217
Fordice, J.M.,34
Foreman,____(Mrs)
  & child,43
  C.,43
  D.,43
  William,43
Forest (see also
  Forrest)
  S.,6
Forga,____(Capt),221
Forister (see also
  Forrester)
  W.B.,136
Forizey, R.,205
Forke, L.,46
Forks, L.,46
Forlie, D.,164
Forrest (see also
  Forest)
  Dulany A.,79
Forrester (see also
  Forister)-no

Forrester (Cont'd)
  -no Forrester this
  volume-
Forsham, M.,165
Forshay, W.,141
Forsyth, J.,107
Fort, J.B.,9
Forthacker, J.,22
Fortune, W.,205
Forysth, A.,33
Fosdick, O.F.(Capt),
  85
Foss,____(Mr) and
  lady,72
  A.S.,138
  C.,91
  E.,60
  J.B.,9,15
  L.C.,61
Fossett, G.,39
Fostas,____(Mr),47
Fostea, D.A.,185,
  253
Foster,____(Miss),
  181(x)
  ____(Mr),56
  ____(Mr) & son,
  181
  ____(Mrs),125,134
  ____(Mrs) & child
  176
  A.,33
  A.F.,179
  A.J.,199
  C.,79,152
  C.M.,193
  D.A.,253
  E.B.,22
  Ezra,168
  F.,125
  F.(Mrs),12
  F.A.,192
  G.,185,253
  G.D.,215
  H.,218
  H.G.,118
  H.H.,219
  Isaac,260
  J.,43,125,132,
  152,170
  John,55
  John (Esq.),143

McKie (see also
    McKee)
    A.,206
McKim, P.,164
McKindry, Benjamin &
    lady,260
McKinley,____(Mrs),129
    H.,135
McKinney, T.,33
McKinnon, D.,219
    J.,141
McKinsey, James,219
McKinstry,___(Maj.),116
    J.(Maj.),59
McKintley, R.,69
McKittley, R.,69
McKittrell, S.,210
McKittrick, J.,210
McKnight,____(Mrs) and
    child,137
    G.L.,169
    J.,135,140,221
    W. & boy,138
McKnighton, H.,99
McLain (see also
    McLane)
    ____,167
    C.,167
McLand, D.,208,260
    F.,208
    J.,208,260
    M.E.(Mrs),208
McLane (see also
    McLain)
    ____(Capt),81,232
    Allen(Capt),232
    P.,219
    R.,16
McLaud, D.,260
    J.,260
McLaughlin (see also
    McLoughlin)
    ____(Mrs),113
    C.,95
    E.,169
    Ellen(Miss),143
    H.,177
    J.,91,177
    P.,29
    R.,115
    R.W.,17
McLean(next col.)

McLean, A.,219
    A.(Miss),134
    C.(Miss),134
    D.,10
    E.,153,155
    G.,199
    H.A.,199,200
    H.W.,200
    John,168
    L.,134
    N.,106
    P.,135
    P. & lady,105
    T.,203
McLellan (see alo
    McLellen)
    D.R.,140
    Rufus(General),100
    T.S.,33
McLellen, W.T.,68
McLenore, Y.L.,106
McLeod, C.,34
    J.K.,205
    R.,187
McLlean, A.(Miss),134
McLoughlin (see also
    McLaughlin)
    C.,36
    W.A.,22
McLure, A.T.,92
McMahon, James(Capt),
    196
    M.,180
McManamee, R.,140
McMann, J. & lady,210
McManus, F.,28
    John,174
    P.,65
    T.,204
McMaraton, John,103
McMartin, A.,115
    J.,15
McMaster, A.P.,66
    J.,206
    L.,66
    M.,62
McMellan, D.,21
McMentor,___ and
    wife,216
McMickle, D.,15
    P.,15
McMillan, R.,149

McMillen (see also
    McMillan)
    W.R.,198
McMullen, J.,178,
    192
    John,168
    M.J.(Miss),86
    N.,167
    Thomas,177
McMullin, J.,17
McMunamee, R.,140
McMurphy, A.,107
McMurray,____,lady,
    & child,94
    G.,188
    S.,154
    T.,69
McMuston,____(Miss),
    66
McNair,____(Mrs),140
    T.,139
McNamara, M.,187
McNamer, Lim,29
McNaught, R.,167
McNaughton,___(Dr),
    185
    Alex(Dr),38
    J.,43
McNay, H.W.,218
McNeal, C.,108
McNear, J.,206
    R.H.,213
McNeas, J.,106
McNeely, T.,188
McNeery, J.J.,131
McNeil (see also
    McNiel)
    C.,140
    J.,83
    J.S.,171
    John,75
    N.,187
McNellis, J.,95
McNiel (see also
    McNeil)
    J.,115
    M.,44
    S.,115
McNight, W.,216
McNighton, J.,154
    S.,154
McNulty (next page)

Smyer, E.F.,106
Smyth (see also
   Smith)
  A.,163
  H.,163
Snastiga, M.,109
  R.R.,109
Snavely,___(Mr),12
Sneaton, W.,202,258
Snedecour, A.,98
Sneesly, H.,44
Snell, C.,170
  W.H.,65
Snelling, J.P.,105
  W.W.(Mr),111
Snider (see also
   Schneider,
   Schnider,Scneider
   and Snyder)
  J.H.,200
Snipkins,___(Mr),wife
   & son,1
Snow,___,94
  ___(Mrs),89
  A.,114,150
  J.,22
  L.,131
  L.D.,22
  Lucien,77
  Martha,205
  W.,180
  W.S.,177
Snowden, H.C.
  R.,177
  W. & child,193
Snyder (see also
   Schneider
   Schnider,Scneider
   and Snider)
  ___(Mr & Mrs),27
  D.,188
  E.,210
  Ezra,145
  G.H.,199,200
  H.,189
  J.,167
  J.W.,140
  N.,179
  N.W.,134
  Peter,139
  S.,114
  S.L.,96

Snyder (Cont'd)
  W.,167
Sock, J.,189
Solaire, G.,44
Solar,___(Mr),47
Solarie, L.,206
Solomon, F.,94,234
  F.(Mr.),235
Soltere,___(Mr),47
Somely, J.B.,171
  J.E.,171
Somenly,___,216
Somers,___(Miss),86
  A.J.,69
  J.,68
  J.(Mrs)60
  J.S.,214
Somerville, G.,114
Sond, S.,186
Soniden, W.H.,203
Sonkie, J.C.,148
Sontag,___(Mr),lady,
   family & svt,172
Soraery, W.G.,65
Sorel, J.F.,98
Sorewood, G.,151
Sorge, H.,167
Sosies,___(Mr),12
Sota, S.,109
Soule,___(Capt),101
  H.G.,163
  H.O.,163
  J.M.,74
  P.,131
  P.H.,22
  R.G.,163
Soules, M.,93
Souling, F.,36
South,___,168
Southam, Jesse(Mr),
  101
Souther, J.F.,165
Southers,___(Mr),55
Southerstone, R.,15
Southey, Richard,30
Southmage, A.,22
Southward, John,35
Southwick, I.,39
  S.A.,125
Southworth, P.T.,62
Soutter,___(Capt),173
Sowles(next column)

Sowles,___(Mrs) &
   child,204
  L.F.,141
Spacke, J.J.,116
Spaco, S.,142
Spahn, E.,186
Spaker, A.,90
Spalding (see also
   Spaulding)
  E.,87
  J.,74
  John,74
  R.W.,66
  Winchester,257
Spang, Peter,102
Spaniard, J.,170
Spann, H.,37
Spanner, J. & svt,
  86
Sparegrove, W.,16
Spark,___(Mr & Mrs),
  4
  W.,lady & four
   chldrn,4
Sparks,___(Three
   Misses),3,4
  ___(Mr & Mrs),3,
   4
  Q.J.,128
  R.,19
Sparrow, Isaac,77
Spaulding (see also
   Spalding)
  A.B.,142
  A.M.,133
  C.,206
  S.,62
Spear,___,186
  A.,132
  F.H.,131
  H.,132
  J.,66,131(x),148
  J.W.,163
  M.,166
Spearin, E.S.,27
Spears, F.M.,150
Speckles,___(Mrs)
  & 2 chldrn,222
Speel, H.,19
Spehn, E.,186
Spence, D. & lady,
  129

Susoki, G.,206
Sutcliff, James,177
Suters, J.B.,105
Sutherland,___(Judge),
 184
 G.D.,153
Sutler, J.H.,24
Sutro (see also
 Satro)
 A.,140
Sutter, J.,106
Sutton,___(Mrs),187
 ___(Mrs) & three
 chldrn,113
 Charles,163
 G.W.,60
 J.,204
 J.J.,164,205
 W.,163
Suvey, D.G.,79
Suyce, J.B.,249
Suydam, H.,267
 Henry,267
Swab (see Schwab)
 -no Swab this
 volume-
Swaggerty, L.,135
Swain (see also
 Swaine)
 E.,172
 J.F.,178
 J.H.,70,228
 J.M.,192
 R.R.,204
 S.,194
 T.T.,96
 W.M.,24
Swaine (see also
 Swain)
 John,207
Swan (see also
 Swane)
 ___(Miss),83
 D.W.,51
 G.K.,125
 G.V.,87
 J.S.,59
 L. & lady,157
 N.,216
Swane (see also
 Swan)
 ___(Mrs),12

Swaney, J.A.(Rev.),
 lady & two
 infants,186
Swanker, H.,187
Swanzey, J.N.,108
Swart, J.A.,174
Swartswaller, C.,6
Swartwout, H.,128
Swartz (see also
 Schwartz and
 Schwarz)
 ___(Mrs),108
 B.,175
 C.,9
Swasey, C.,98
 D.,98
Swatch, C.,170
Swaynay, G.A.,210
Swearinger, A.S.,218
Sweat (see also
 Swett,Switt)
 A.,218
Sweed, William,178
Sweeney (see also
 Sweeny)
 ___(Mrs) & three
 chldrn,152
 G.,218
 J.,63
 J.M.,175
 John,220
Sweeny (see also
 Sweeney)
 F.,16
Sweet (see also
 Sweed)
 ___(Mr & Mrs),8
 C.,67
 E.,63,70
 J.,217
 James,145
 O.,47
 R.,126
 R.M.,133
 S.,17
 T.,13
 William,178
Sweetland, C.G.,62
 E.,151
 M.,150
Sweetzer, J.E.,117
 S.,128

Swenker, H.,187
Swett (see also
 Sweat, Switt)
 M.,167
Swetts,___(Miss),32
Swift,___(Mrs),113
 A.,179
 A.P.(Mrs) and
 4 chldrn,130
 C.,73
 C.A.,179
 D.W.,218
 E.E.,150
 H.A.,64
 J.C.,190
 J.W.,6
 John,16
 M.,74
 R.,193
 Z.,130
Swigert, John,257
Swin, W.R.,163
Swindles, J. and
 sister,6
Swindley, W.F.,179
Swine (see also
 Swin)
 ___(Capt),18
Swinington,George H.,
 193
Swininton (sic)
 George H.,193
Swins,___(Capt),18
Switt (see also
 Sweat,Swett)
 ___,23
Switzer, M.,50
Sykes, J.B.,15
 J.M.,62
 P.,149
Sylabor, John,144
Sylom, Manuel,50
Sylver, Andrew,50
Sylvester,___(Miss),
 64
 A.,153
 F.,43
 H.,22
 J.,175
 John,69
 N.,187
 S.,22

Wininger, W. & lady, 216
Winkleman, J.,117
Winkler, J.J.,6
Winley, A.,204
Winn, M.L.,lady and 2 chldrn,215
Winne, E.G.,148
Winnett,___(Capt),196
Winni,___(Mr) & lady, 145
Winreich,___,195
Winser, A.,164
  L.,164
Winsloo, M.,41
  T.,40
Winslow (see also Winsloo)
  E.,29,65
  H.,41
  L.P.,8
  R.,169
  S.T.F.,192
Winson, Z,41
Winsor, George,189
Winston, W.A.,116
Winter, J.,221
  J.C.,56
  O.,37
Winterbottom, S.H.,192
Winters, M. & svt,154
Winthrop, N.,40
  T.,40
Wire, W.,196
Wiren,___(Mr),24
Wirts, G.W.(Mrs) and child,86
Wise, A.,216
  J.,179
Wissman, F.C.,192
Wistch, J.,142
Wiswell, B.,177
Witham, M.H.,9
Withan,___,44
Witherby (see also Wetherby)
  ___(Judge),34
  M.,61
Withey, N.,68
Witt, M.,103
Wittenbrock, H.,221
Witton, B.,140

Witzler, M.C.,33
Wively, J.,178
Wmite, W.R.(sic),203
Woff,___(Mrs),five chldrn & infant, 191,253
Wofford, N.,41
Wogenstart, T.,117
Wolcott, E.,10
  E.R.,195
  J.,115
Woldow, Gustave and lady,48
Wolf (see also Woolf, Wolfe,Wolff,Woolfe)
  ___(Capt),209
  ___(Mr) & lady, 215
  ___(Mrs),64
  C.A.,16
  G.W.,128
  H.,151
  J.,152
  P.A.,151
Wolfe (see also Woolf, Wolff,Wolf,Woolfe)
  E.,62
  J.,62
  J.E.,186
  P.B.,9
  W.,61(x)
Wolfenburger, P.,176
  W.W.,176
Wolff(see also Woolf, Wolfe,Wolf,Woolfe)
  ___(Mrs),five chldrn & infant, 254
  L.,193,254
  M.L.,119
Wolfskill, W.,116
Wolland, R.(Mr),63
Wolmering, J.,60
Womerly, Sarah and 2 chldrn,103
Wonnamaker, G.,74
Wontrode, G.,148
Wood,___,203
  ___(Mr),81
  ___(Mrs),38
  A.,23(x),43,143,150, 154,192,238

Wood (Cont'd)
  B.,38
  C.D.,62
  Charles,123
  D.,24,154
  E.M.,41
  G.A.,205
  H.,65,144
  J.,2,57,144,216
  J.C.,69
  J.H.,216
  J.L.,205
  J.M.,154
  J.W.,132,154
  James,87,195
  L.,65,154,188
  N.F.,220
  R.,66,94
  R.P.(Mr),122
  S.,154
  W.,205
  W.(Jr),62
  W.D.,60
  W.E.,167
Woodbridge,___(Mr), 38
  ___(Mrs) and 3 chldrn,38
  S.,38
Woodburn,___(Capt), 71
Woodbury, B.,17
  C.,6
  J.,65
Wooden, P.R.,68
  W.C.,68
Woodey (see also Woody)
  O.A.,90
Woodford, E.,13
  H.,86
Woodhouse, P.,195
Wooding, F.,115
Woodlaw, J.,205
Woodman, C.,64
  G.A.,34
  G.M.,133
  J.L.,8
  R.P.,12,13
Woodring, E.,172
Woodrow,James,205
Woodruff, A.C.,187

UNIDENTIFIED PASSENGER LISTINGS

The following entries pertain to passenger listings in which the given name, or surname, could not be deciphered in the original source material.

A question mark (?) represents a missing letter. The first block of names, (Surnames Absent),reflects passengers with given initials or given names identifiable-but with entire surname lacking identification. Entries in this section are listed with the given names first, in alphabetical order.

The second block of names, (Incomplete Surname), reflects those passengers with character segments of their surname missing. The entries in this block are listed in alphabetical order, surname first. Page numbers follow each entry.

Surnames Absent

H.G._____,117
Hamilton,_____
  (colored),150
  -Hamilton is
  possibly the
  surname-
Henry_____
  (colored),151
J.W._____,152
John_____,115
Patrick_____
  (colored),150
Stephen_____
  (colored),150
William R._____,135

Incomplete Surname

_____son, C.,95
_____son, W.,95
_____mons, C.,17
??etter, G. and family,
  96
?arder, James,190
?eyer, W. & wife,26
Ād_____, J.,41
Argo?a, D.,96
Back?in, A.S.,91
Bi?gs,_____,187
Bo?ke, L.,70
Bo??frod, J.E.,97
Carm?n?, H.A.,154
Carr?il,___(Mrs),187
Co?larde, D.,97
Co?tman, A.C.,9

Co?er, J.D.,145
Con?dit, W.,91
Cypa?ana,___(Col.)
  and svt,90
Draefo?, W.,187
Dupli?,____(Mrs),90
Ea?ling, H.,179
Eve?dding, J.,186
Fal?s, C.,108
Fre?het, M.,46
Froi?sart, L.,6
G?isley, R. and boy,
  78
Gilles?e?, B.,98
Gow?n, James,96
H?rtapples, S.,151,
  245
Hant?man, H.,59
Hel?burn, G.,115
Ho?t, C.,180
J?nchont, C.,97
John____,S.J.,74
Jourdan, ?.P.,97
K?einsworth, J.,91
Kīs?am,____(Dr),2
L??kfield, B.F.,87
L??que?nec, P.,97
Le??dileur, A.,98
Lebo?gne, E.,98
Louw??, J.,35
Lu?et, E.,97
M??reton, N.,33,225
M?dden, John,186
M?scarro, Martina,102

Mc_____,E.B.,65
N?vitt,____(Mrs) &
  daughter,186
P?i?o?, N.,97
P?il, J.,98
Pa?view, P.A.,218
Pe?kley, A.,151
Pea?ks, F.,66,229
Penn?, J.,69
Pra?ley, C.,148
R?hn, H.,187
R?nny, C.,189
R?rt, John,102
Ra???eze, J.,86
Rem?inger, V.,98
S?ott, L.,141
Sīm????, F.,15
Spe??y, C.,187
Sp?eene, W.,189
To?ry, D.,13
U??l, James,95
U?ter, William,190
Ve?morel,___(Mr),92
Vo?n?, J.G.,97
W?ese, W.,41
W?r??n, B.O.,186
Wa?ten,____,36
Wi?khouse, W.,177
Wo?e, J.E.,186
Z?dtmah, H.,lady,
  2 chldren and
  svt,186

ADDITIONAL SAN FRANCISCO SHIP ARRIVALS
Period of
November 7,1851 to June 17,1852

The passenger lists contained in Volume III incorporates the period of November 7,1851 to June 17,1852. SAN FRANCISCO SHIP PASSENGER LISTS, VOLUME I has additional ship arrivals for the same period. The passenger lists reflected in Volume I were not duplicated in Volume III.

The following list represents ship arrivals which will be found in Volume I dealing with the period of November 7,1851 to June 17, 1852. Below vessels have been included in the "Subjective and Geographical Index" of Volume III.

Vessel Name	Arrival Date	Vol. I,Page
Amphitrite	Feb.1,1852	4
Andreas	Jan.2,1852	6
Aurora	Jan.14,1852	9
Clara	May 17,1852	28
Clarendon	May 20,1852	29
Clarissa Andrews	May 22,1852	29
Clarita	Jan.2,1852	31
Colorado	Jan.15,1852	31
Columbia	Jan.13,1852	32
Comet	Jan.13,1852	32
Constitution	May 22,1852	42
Courrier De Inde	June 2,1852	48
Curlew	May 16,1852	48
Diana	Jan.16,1852	49
Doctrina & Amicitia	Jan.16,1852	50
Dracut	May 20,1852	50
Dudley	May 21,1852	50
Eagle	June 9,1852	51
Edward L. Frost	May 15,1852	52
Emma Preston	May 22,1852	55
Exchange	June 8,1852	56
Falmouth	June 4,1852	56
Flying Fish	Jan.14,1852	57
Frances Helen	June 2,1852	58
Fremont	May 23,1852	59
Fremont	June 9,1852	59
George Emory	Jan.19,1852	60
Gold Hunter	Jan.2,1852	62
Golden Gate	Jan.9,1852	67
Golden Gate	May 21,1852	73
Golden Rule	Jan.1,1852	83
Goliah	Jan.2,1852	83
Helen A. Miller	Jan.15,1852	85
Independence	Jan.8,1852	87
Iowa	June 9,1852	89

Vessel Name	Arrival Date	Vol. I,Page
Isthmus	Jan.14,1852	94
J.B. Lunt	Jan.18,1852	96
John Wade	Jan.14,1852	99
Jupiter	May 22,1852	100
L.M. Yale	Jan.10,1852	103
Laura Bevan	Jan.10,1852	104
Lysa	Jan. 2,1852	105
Margaret	May 15,1852	106
Maria	May 20,1852	107
Maria	June 2,1852	108
Mechanic's Own	May 20,1852(?)-see page 264,Vol.III re May 21,1852-	111
Monumental City	May 17,1852	113
Nahumkeag	May 15,1852	116
Nassau	May 23,1852	117
North America	Jan.18,1852	120
Northern Light	Jan.14,1852(?)	122
Northern Light	May 25,1852-see page 267,Vol.III correcting to May 20,1852	122
Northerner	Jan.1,1852	125
Ohio	June 7,1852	129
Oriental	May 15,1852	138
Paragon	May 16,1852	146
Roanoke	May 17,1852	150
Sea Bird	Jan.4,1852	155
Seaman's Bride	May 20,1852	157
Sir Charles Napier	May 21,1852	158
Speed	June 7,1852	161
Susan Sturgess	May 22,1852	162
Tepic	June 2,1852	163
Thomas	May 15,1852	167
Vandalia	June 9,1852	169
Versailles	Jan.14,1852	169
Wisconsin	May 22,1852	172
Witchcraft	May 16,1852	172
Wyandot	Jan. 2,1852	172

Addenda

| Salem | Jan.16,1852 | 151 |

SAN FRANCISCO SHIP ARRIVALS
Overlap Periods, Volume I and II

The passenger lists contained in SAN FRANCISCO SHIP PASSENGER
LISTS, VOLUME II catalogued arrivals during the period of April 6,
1850 to November 4, 1851. VOLUME I contains additional ship passenger lists for the forementioned period. Lists printed in Volume I
were not duplicated in Volume II.

As an aid to the researcher, the below table depicts the ship
arrivals recorded in Volume I which occur during April 6, 1850 to
November 4, 1851, the overlap period of Volume II. Below vessels
have been included in the "Subjective and Geographical Index" of
Volume III.

Vessel Name	Arrival Date	Vol.I Page
Adeline	July 25, 1850	1
Adirondack	Aug.1, 1850	2
Agincourt	July 30, 1850	2
Alexandrine	July 30, 1850	2
Alpha	Aug.3, 1850	3
America(German)	July 25, 1850	3
America	July 30, 1850	4
Anemona	August 6, 1850	6
Ann Parry	Nov.5, 1850	7
Anson	July 30, 1850	7
Antelope	July 29, 1850	7
Antelope	Jan.9, 1851	8
Aurelie	March 29, 1851	9
Avon	Jan.2, 1851	10
Balmoral	Dec.31, 1850	10
Borneo	Aug.3, 1850	10
Bredalbane	May 6, 1851	11
Broad Axe	Aug.3, 1850	11
Cacholet	July 1, 1850	13
California	June 23, 1850	17
Camilla	July 24, 1850	20
Carolina	May 7, 1850	21
Carolina	July 1, 1850	23
Carolina	July 23, 1850	24
Carolina	Aug.7, 1850	24
Carthagena	July 30, 1850	25
Catharine	Aug.3, 1850	25
Ceres	July 28, 1850	25
Charles J. Dow	Jan.2, 1851	26
Chaseley	Jan.5, 1851	26
Chenango	Aug.7, 1850	26
Cheasapeake(sic)	Mar.30, 1851	27
Chesapeake (sic)	Aug.7, 1850	27
Chester	Mar.31, 1851	27
Circassian	Aug.4, 1850	28

Vessel Name	Arrival Date	Vol.I Page
Columbia	March 30,1851	33
Columbus	June 6,1850	34
Columbus	May 23,1851	37
Columbus	Aug.6,1850	40
Constitution	April 4,1851	41
Crescent City	Aug.4,1850	48
Diadem	May 23,1851	49
Dispatch	July 30,1850	49
Donna Carmolita	Jan.5,1851	50
Edwin Johnson	Jan.6,1851	52
Eclipse	July 28,1850	52
Eliza	Jan.5,1851	53
Eliza Taylor	Aug.3,1850	53
Eliza Warwick	July 25,1850	53
Emily	July 31,1850	54
Emily Francis	Aug.4,1850	54
Erato	Jan.2,1851	55
Euroda	Jan.21,1851	55
F.A. Everett	Jan.4,1851	56
Fanny	Aug.5,1850	57
Flavius	Aug.4,1850	57
Gold Hunter	April 29,1850	61
Gold Hunter	Jan.10,1851	62
Gustave	July 28,1850	84
Hallowell	July 28,1850	85
Harvard	Aug.5,1850	85
Henry Kelsey	July 28,1850	86
Hercules	Aug.3,1850	87
Isthmus	May 4,1850	89
Isthmus	July 12,1850	92
J.A. Jesuran	July 31,1850	96
Jackin	April 3,1851	97
John Calvin	Aug.4,1850	98
John Davis	June 9,1850	98
John Fish	Aug.3,1850	99
John Kendall	Aug.6,1850	99
Kensington	July 24,1850	100
Kezia	April 3,1851	100
Kingston	Aug.14,1850	102
Laura Bevan	Aug.4,1850	104
Lawson (or Lawsons)	Aug.3,1850	104
Lowell	Aug.5,1850	105
Marianna	May 23,1851	108
Mary	Jan.18,1851	108
Mary Ellen	July 30,1850	109
Mary Melville	Jan.9,1851	109
Mary Mitchell	Jan.7,8, or 9,1851	109
Mary Phoebe	Mar.30,1851	110
Mary A. Jones	July 28,1850	110
Mary Ann Folliott	Aug.4,1850	110
Mary M. Wood	Jan.8,1851	111

Vessel Name	Arrival Date	Vol.I Page
Montalembert	Jan.20,1851	112
Montezuma	Jan.6,1851	112
Mousan	Aug.5,1850	116
New World	July 11,1850	117
Ocean	Aug.4,1850	128
Ocean Hero	Jan.8,1851	129
Oella	April 3,1851	129
Oregon	May 20,1850	130
Oregon	July 20,1850	133
Oregon	Jan.20,1851	135
Oregon	April 3,1851	136
Oriental	July 31,1850	138
Ortolean	Aug.6,1850	139
Palmyra	Dec.30,1850	141
Panama	April 22,1850	142
Panama	July 6,1850	144
Phoenix	Aug.5,1850	147
Polka	Aug.6,1850	147
Potomac	April 4,1851	147
Powhatan	July 29,1850	147
Prince	April 5,1851	148
Providence	July 29,1850	148
R.C. Winthrop	April 3,1851	149
Ralph Thompson	Aug.,1850	149
Roe	Aug.4,1850	150
Royal Sovereign	Jan.6,1851	150
Sarah McFarland	Jan.13,1850	152
Sarah Sands	June 5,1850	152
Saratoga	July 30,1850	155
Sea Gull	Jan.17,1851	156
Sea Witch	July 24,1850	157
Susan G. Owens	July 24,1850	162
Tarquin	Aug.5,1850	162
Tennessee	April 14,1850	163
Toe	? ,1850	167
Unidine	April 3,1851	169
Vesta	Jan.21,1851	170
William Melville	July 28,1850	170
Will-O-The-Wisp	Aug.3,1850	171
Winthrop	July 30,1850	171
Wisconsin	June 24,1850	171
York	Jan.6,1851	173

Addenda

| Fabius | Aug.6,1850 | 56 |

SUBJECTIVE AND GEOGRAPHICAL INDEX

The symbol "x" following a page number denotes
more than one entry for data on cited page.